D1248444

Critical Essays on

MARY WOLLSTONECRAFT SHELLEY

CRITICAL ESSAYS
ON
BRITISH LITERATURE

Zack Bowen, General Editor
University of Miami

Critical Essays on
MARY WOLLSTONECRAFT
SHELLEY

edited by

MARY LOWE-EVANS

G. K. Hall & Co.

New York

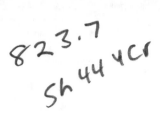

823.7
Sh44 YCr

G. K. Hall & Co.
1633 Broadway
New York, NY 10019

Library of Congress Cataloging-in-Publication Data

Critical essays on Mary Wollstonecraft Shelley / edited by Mary Lowe-Evans
   p.   cm. — (Critical essays on British literature)
   Includes bibliographical references and index.
   ISBN 0-7838-0057-6 (alk. paper)
   1. Shelley, Mary Wollstonecraft, 1797–1851—Criticism and interpretation.   2. Women and literature—England—History—19th century.   I. Lowe-Evans, Mary.   II. Series.
   PR5398.C75   1998
823'.7—dc21   97-40297
                                                          CIP

This paper meets the requirements of ANSI/NISO Z3948-1992 Permanence of Paper.

10 9 8 7 6 5 4 3

Printed in the United States of America

To Ron and also Timmy, Hannah, and Molly

Contents

General Editor's Note

♦

The Critical Essays on British Literature series provides a variety of approaches to both classical and contemporary writers of Britain and Ireland. The formats of the volumes in the series vary with the thematic designs of individual editors, and with the amount and nature of existing reviews and criticism, augmented, where appropriate, by original essays by recognized authorities. It is hoped that each volume will be unique in developing a new overall perspective on its particular subject.

In her introduction Mary Lowe-Evans reads Mary Shelley's work as representative of the author's own private obsessions and distress at various cultural debates of nineteenth-century England and Europe. Lowe-Evans offers a biographical publication history and a critical selection that treats all of Shelley's work, even as it places *Frankenstein* in special focus, including its personal psychology, its imitators, and the variety of impact it made on nineteenth- and twentieth-century fiction and film. Her selection of essays includes three written especially for this volume.

ZACK BOWEN
University of Miami

Publisher's Note

◆

Producing a volume that contains both newly commissioned and reprinted material presents the publisher with the challenge of balancing the desire to achieve stylistic consistency with the need to preserve the integrity of works first published elsewhere. In the Critical Essays series, essays commissioned especially for a particular volume are edited to be consistent with G. K. Hall's house style; reprinted essays appear in the style in which they were first published, with only typographical errors corrected. Consequently, shifts in style from one essay to another are the result of our efforts to be faithful to each text as it was originally published.

Introduction

MARY LOWE-EVANS

Having recently celebrated the 200th anniversary of Mary Shelley's birth in 1797, it is appropriate to observe both that her novel *Frankenstein or The Modern Prometheus* has remained in print since its original publication in 1818 and that virtually every year since 1910, when the first *Frankenstein* film appeared, yet another version has been released somewhere in the world. In this introduction I assert that *Frankenstein*'s staying power has to do with Mary Shelley's sensitivity to her own rather awkward position in society and her ability to elaborate on the most compelling trends in her culture. In organizing the essays for this collection I have grouped together those that represent Mary Shelley as a "sensitive register" of her milieu and those that reveal her as a "prodigious generator" of cultural myths, ethical conundrums, and haunting metaphors. The discussion that follows is arranged along the same lines. Since there are several readily available critical histories and chronologies of Mary Shelley's work,[1] I will not repeat those accounts but rather consider the less empirical features of her achievement—her instincts for registering and generating meaning from the cultural conversation—especially those strategies addressed in the essays collected here.

Because it is often the *only* work by which Mary Shelley is known, *Frankenstein* is, perforce, the key to understanding her accomplishments. The novel is many things—a semi-Gothic horror tale, a work of science fiction, the tragedy of an obsessed young man or of his Creature or both—but above and beyond these formal categories, the novel is a complex sign of a very young woman's genuine distress about the direction that various cultural debates were taking in nineteenth-century England and Europe. Of necessity, since no author can entirely disassociate authorship from personal preoccupations, *Frankenstein* is also a sign of Mary Shelley's private obsessions. What gives her work its power are the ways she has articulated the personal with the political.

In describing *Frankenstein* as a sign of Mary Shelley's distress, I use the term much the same way that I imagine Edna St. Vincent Millay used it nearly a century after Shelley's novel appeared. If one considers the opening line of Millay's sonnet "I, being born a woman and distressed," as a stand-alone title, the nonrestrictive phrase emphasizing "woman" becomes an interrupter implying that to be born a woman is to be born distressed.[2] Thus, the line forms a wonderfully effective pluri-signifier for Millay's experience as a woman and a poet in 1923. If one were to slash through the word "woman" and write above it the word "Creature," the sense in which Mary Shelley prefigures Millay's experience through her monster may become clear. Of course the analogy is not exact, for the Creature embodies not only Mary Shelley's personal stressful experiences associated with gender and authorship but also her wish to rise above gender, class, and even profession-determined limitations, as well as her despair about ever being able to do so. Years after writing *Frankenstein* Mary would have Katherine Gordon, a character modeled after herself in her novel *Perkin Warbeck,* admit, "I am doomed to a divided existence, and I submit."[3]

In Millay's sonnet the word "distressed" reinforces the contradictions established by the punctuation and grammar of the opening line. Incorporating the notions of anxiety and suffering, "distressed" also connotes a forcing apart, being pulled in two directions at once, *di*-stressed. The word also might be taken to mean twice stressed, doubly pressured, as it were. From yet another angle, there is the suggestion of not being stressed or taken seriously at all, as in *dis*-stressed, trivialized; or dis-*tressed,* shorn of power as Samson was shorn of his tresses by Delilah.[4] The multiple meanings of the opening line of Millay's sonnet transfer quite readily to Mary Shelley's life and work especially as expressed in *Frankenstein,* which in its original form was a complex response to womanly angst, the female authorship of which was unstressed. Years after *Frankenstein*'s publication, Shelley's friend, author and editor Caroline Norton, would ask, "Does it not provoke you . . . how 'in vain' the gift of genius is for a woman? How far from binding her more closely to the admiration and love of her fellow-creatures it does in effect create that gulf across which no one passes?"[5]

At the personal level Mary Shelley had been distressed quite early by her mother's death from puerperal infection 10 days after Mary's birth. She would come to know her infamous mother, the pioneer feminist Mary Wollstonecraft, via her mother's letters and works, including *A Vindication of the Rights of Woman,* and also through the limited though flattering lens of her father's remembrances. Available portraits of Mary Wollstonecraft display her beauty, and love letters express her passion. Her published works reveal an intelligent being asking to be respected on a par with men because of her reasoning powers. For Mary Shelley, her father's second wife Jane Clairmont made a pathetically poor substitute for this absent, fascinating maternal icon. Mary "lost" her mother again and again, repeatedly killing off perfect mothers in her fiction while occasionally, as with Justine's mother in *Frankenstein,* depicting a mother who actively disliked one of her daughters (as Mary believed Jane Clairmont had done).

Mary Shelley's father was William Godwin, author of *An Enquiry Concerning Political Justice* (1793), a polemic for egalitarianism, and several novels that promoted his philosophical views. Sympathetic with the original goals of the French Revolution—liberty, fraternity, equality—Godwin and

Wollstonecraft had been members of the radical "English Jacobins" during the 1780s and '90s; but by the time Mary was born, following the reign of terror in France, her parents had modified their views considerably. Godwin remained, however, an eccentric, controversial figure who encouraged his daughter's independence of thought on one hand yet deplored her elopement at age 16 with Percy Shelley, a married man, on the other. During the years she spent with her father, stepmother, and their extended family (including stepsister Claire, who would vex Mary throughout her life) Mary developed an abiding, jealous love for her father. He nurtured Mary's lively intellect by making his extensive and eclectic library available to her and by including her in the many literary and political discussions held in their home. Among her early memories is the sight of Samuel Taylor Coleridge animatedly reciting his own "Rime of the Ancient Mariner," still one of the most effective treatments of the overreaching individual's sin against the community. Mary Shelley would recall Coleridge's haunting words and use them to reinforce the same theme in *Frankenstein.*

Like the recurring image of the absent idealized mother, Mary's love for her father and the resentment she harbored over his rejection of her (after she married Percy Shelley) repeatedly find their way into her fiction in stylized form. Victor Frankenstein's Creature and the title character of *Matilda* (also spelled *Mathilda*) are just two of many examples of motherless "children" in Shelley's works who experience extremes of love and revulsion for the unstable fathers who reject them. As Sandra Gilbert points out in the essay reprinted in this collection, Shelley's complex relationship with her parents—their emotional and intellectual hold on her—becomes connected to her authorship and her resistant attitude toward conventional gender roles. This complicated family romance accounts in part for the oppressive guilt and obsessive urge to confess that pervade many of her works. Family ties also help explain the strengths of her female characters. The originality and intelligence of Euthanasia, the young heroine of *Valperga,* for example, are attributed to her father's training, while Safie, the liberator of the De Lacey family in *Frankenstein,* owes her courage and convictions to a mother created in the image of Mary Wollstonecraft.

While acknowledging the need, recognized by such critics as Muriel Spark, Sandra Gilbert, and Anne Mellor, to liberate Mary Shelley from the shadow of Percy Shelley (another form of Mary's *dis*-stress), one must also own the importance of the Percy-Mary liaison both to Mary's growth as a writer and to her expanding scientific, political, sexual, and philosophic sensibilities. Mary was first attracted to Percy Shelley under her father's roof when she was barely 15 years old. Percy's unabashed admiration for her beloved father's political agenda only reinforced the natural attraction she felt for this volatile, exciting young man. That he had a wife worried Mary no more in the early days of her adolescent infatuation than it would most young girls in the throes of a first crush. The memory of Harriet Shelley's suicide would surface later in Mary's fiction and letters, however; for her attraction to Percy, while remaining strong, developed into a discerning, resistant dialogue spelled out during the decades of her writing career. Through a variety of compelling though imperfect characters, from *Frankenstein*'s Victor (a name Percy had assigned himself as a youth) to the idealistic though naive Adrian of *The Last Man* to the "victim of the . . . feeling inspired by the reaction of the French Revolution"[6] described in Mary Shelley's "Preface to the Poetical Works of Percy Bysshe Shelley," her idol, mentor, lover, husband, collaborator, friend, and sometimes antagonist influenced nearly every aspect of Mary's life and works. Besides his own impressive personality, Percy Shelley brought Lord Byron and a host of more or less talented literati into Mary's life. After his drowning in a storm on the Gulf of Spezia in 1822 until Mary's death in 1851, Percy Shelly remained both inspiration and albatross as Mary struggled to edit and publish his poems and secure the inheritance of their son Percy Florence Shelley from her father-in-law, the impervious Sir Timothy Shelley.

Ellen Herson Wittman's essay "Mary Shelley's Daemon," published for the first time in this volume, addresses one of the more subtle examples of Percy Shelley's collaboration with Mary, one that resulted in a monster who embodies a frustrated ideal of platonic love. Mary also shared Percy's interest in the virtue of sympathy, a variant of love. Frequently in her works and letters one encounters characters seeking others with whom they can sympathize:

> I desire the company of a man who could sympathize with me; whose eyes would reply to mine.
>
> (Robert Walton to Margaret Saville)[7]

> Come, give me your hand, one look of joyous sympathy and we will go [to our deaths] together.
>
> (Matilda to Woodville)[8]

> Passionate desire of sympathy, and ardent pursuit for a wished-for object still characterized me.
>
> (Lionel Verney, *The Last Man*)[9]

> I to whom sympathy—companionship—the interchange of thought is more necessary than the air I breathe.
>
> (Mary Shelley to Maria Gisborne, June 11, 1835)[10]

The conception of sympathy that interested Percy and Mary Shelley derived from the eighteenth-century doctrine promulgated by Adam Smith and Auguste Comte among others. It exceeds current definitions of friendship and was implicated in the cultural debates about "the moral sense" that began with the Earl of Shaftesbury in 1699 and continued throughout the nineteenth century. George Eliot's novels, for example, invariably feature characters who have broken bonds of sympathy with the community and must somehow pay the price. At issue in the dialogue about sympathy and the moral sense was whether moral judgment is founded on reason or sentiment, self-interest or altruism. Mary Shelley's works—including her letters and journals—reveal a more cynical and yet sensitive view of the subject than do Percy Shelley's; sympathy for her seems always to be weighted. We find her Perkin Warbeck admitting that "we make ourselves the central point of the universe."[11] As she matured, Mary Shelley would develop the belief that such egocentrism could be overcome only by a concerted and unrelenting act of will, but that fidelity to another was necessary to the individual's emotional growth and well-being.

Mary Shelley implies in her fiction, however, the impossibility of a complete sympathetic union between men and women in a world in which egalitarian principles often do not apply consistently across genders; a world in which women are increasingly pressured (in part by the philosophies of the same Auguste Comte who advocated sympathy as a unifying force) to keep to their places apart from men. Domestic feminism—a philosophy that assigned separate spheres of influence for the sexes—would become for Mary Shelley in the years following her husband's death one of the most difficult of all cultural "doctrines" to resist, yet one of the most ideologically abhorrent. Domestic feminism represented a paradoxical trap that held women responsible for the moral well-being of a society over which only men could rule.

The untenableness of the separate sphere philosophy is encapsulated in Robert Walton's ingenuous words to his sister: "You have been tutored and *refined* by books and *retirement from the world,* and you are therefore somewhat fastidious; but this only renders you the more fit to appreciate the extraordinary merits of [Victor Frankenstein]" (232, emphasis added). In this passage, which was added for the 1831 edition of *Frankenstein,* Mary Shelley seems to take her cue from a growing number of domestic feminist propagandists like Catherine Beecher, renowned *woman* educator (and sister of Harriet Beecher Stowe), who urged,

> in the domestic and social circle . . . let every woman become so cultivated and refined in intellect that her taste and judgement will be respected; so benevolent in feeling and action; that her motives will be reverenced; so unassuming and unambitious, that collision and competition will be banished . . . then, the fathers, the husbands, and the sons, will find an influence thrown around them to which they will yield . . . willingly. . . . But the moment the woman begins to feel the promptings of ambition or the thirst for power, her aegis of defence is gone.[12]

When Walton praises his sister's refinement and retirement from the world, he speaks Catherine Beecher's language. He also replicates the contradictions, the *di*-stress inherent in Beecher's argument. For if, as he says, Margaret is refined *from* the world (implying the public, political, and scientific world of men), how can she be fit to appreciate a man like Victor Frankenstein, a "divine wanderer" (24) who has purposefully taken his place in an all-male world?

Mary Shelley's approach-avoidance conflict about domestic feminism as well as her emphasis on sympathy are also evident in the character of Elizabeth Lavenza as reconstituted for the 1831 *Frankenstein:*

> The saintly soul of Elizabeth shone like a shrine-dedicated lamp in our peaceful home. Her sympathy was ours; her smile, her soft voice, the sweet glance of her celestial eyes, were ever there to bless and animate us. She was the living spirit of love to soften and attract: I might have become sullen in my study, rough through the ardour of my nature but that she was there to subdue me to a semblance of her gentleness. (237)

This apparently unequivocal celebration of Elizabeth, however, is undercut by Victor's behavior. In effect he excludes her from his world of scientific experimentation and then returns to her domestic sphere just long enough to put her in mortal danger. Elizabeth ultimately dies in the "unassuming and unambitious" cause of domestic feminism. The essays of Stephen Behrendt, Chris Baldick, and myself in this collection further discuss the problem of women's compromised position in the nineteenth century and Mary Shelley's continuing distress about the subject.

Mary Shelley's interest in controversies other than domestic feminism is illustrated in "Roger Dodsworth, the Reanimated Englishman," an essay that also nicely illustrates her largely unrecognized talent for humorous writing. Written in 1826 not long after "the discovery and reanimation" of a certain Roger Dodsworth had been reported in six British newspapers,[13] the essay takes its place in an ongoing discussion about reanimation, extended dormancy, and the possible reactions of one who returns after years of absence to a continually "advancing" civilization:[14] "Will he be an advocate for perfectibility or deterioration? He must admire our manufacturers, the progress of science, the diffusion of knowledge, and the fresh spirit of enterprise characteristic of our countrymen."[15]

In *The Last Man,* published in the year of the Roger Dodsworth hoax, Mary Shelley represents the failure of sympathy, domestic feminism, and virtually all optimistic philosophies about human perfectability. The "progress," "knowledge," and "enterprise" that Dodsworth "must admire" are entirely undercut. Muriel Spark finds that Shelley's theme in *The Last Man* "was the objectified result of personal distress of mind"[16] resulting from the situation in which she found herself after Percy Shelley's death. Byron's death in May 1824, failing friendships, impending poverty, and a strained relationship with Sir Timothy Shelley that threatened the future financial well-being of her son

Percy Florence Shelley contributed to her malaise during this period. Surely the novel reveals her saturation with and loathing for indiscriminate and irreversible death—perhaps the verso of her interest in reanimation—but, as Spark observes, the novel also demonstrates Mary Shelley's "immersion in broader cultural concerns":

> The conception of *The Last Man* is eminently a product of the early nineteenth century. . . . As factory gates nightly emitted their begrimed victims like smoke from their chimney stacks; as every whistle-stop on the new railroad engendered its Mechanic's Institute; so mankind lost confidence in its natural faculties. Science lined up with industry to form a force as vast and irrational as Mary's Plague; and all premises seemed to point to a last man.[17]

Thus, just as the threat of nuclear holocaust in the 1950s spawned the films *Dr. Strangelove* and *On the Beach* (as well as a renewed interest in *Frankenstein* films), the cultural contaminants in Mary Shelley's England contributed to the conception of *The Last Man*.

In *Perkin Warbeck* Mary Shelley again articulates the personal with the political. Mary had decided to try her hand at historical fiction in this rendering of young Warbeck, who had claimed to be Richard Plantagenet, one of the two princes in the Tower and heir to the throne who had escaped execution by order of Richard III. But the second half of the novel, according to Emily Sunstein, reveals Mary's attempt to "work through the emotional and philosophical ramifications" of her part in the death of Harriet Shelley.[18] In the character of Katherine, whose consciousness, like Mary Shelley's own, is divided between a past of impulsive loyalty to a controversial princely man and a future of submission to the "laws" of respectable behavior for women, Mary Shelley seems to come to terms with her position in society: "Mary Shelley, however, was not the passive, one-dimensional Katherine who had never had ambitions. She submitted based on a sense of reality belatedly acquired, her drive for the preservation of herself and her son, and the mature branching of her rooted [liberal] philosophy."[19]

During the years between *Perkin Warbeck* (1829) and her death in 1851 Shelley remained engaged in the political and scientific debates of her time. In 1830, for example, she became friends with Roderick Murchison, notable in the budding science of geology; *The Athenaeum* ranked her the most distinguished contemporary Englishwoman of letters; and she completed revisions for the 1831 edition of *Frankenstein* (still the version most widely published) that reflected her ambivalence about the refining and defining of women's roles. Cries for the reform of Parliament during this time resulted in the fall of the Tories and the introduction by the Whigs of a sweeping reform bill supported by mass demonstrations. When the reform bill carried in 1832 Mary Shelley wrote to her friend Fanny Wright, "Will not our children live to see a new birth for the world! . . . the people *will* be redressed—will the Aristocrats sacrifice enough to tranquilize them [?]—if not we must be revolutionized."[20]

The reform victories had vindicated many of Percy Shelley's political opinions, thus creating a favorable atmosphere for publication of his works that Mary encouraged and facilitated. Also, another *affaire de coeur* kept her interested in the political scene of the 1830s; she became enamored of Aubrey Beauclerk, who, as her husband had been, was heir to a considerable fortune and a political radical. Mary followed and supported Beauclerk's successful campaign for a seat in Parliament as an independent radical in November of 1832 on a platform of "wider suffrage, army retrenchment, a graduated property tax, Irish relief from Anglican tithes, abolition of slavery, aid to the poor, and an end to primogeniture."[21] Although their love affair ended with Beauclerk's marriage to a woman more socially acceptable to his family, Mary Shelley's commitment to his politics remained steadfast.

It was also during this period that Shelley signed a contract to write three volumes of *Lives of the Most Eminent Literary and Scientific Men of Italy, Spain, and Portugal* over a five-year period for Dr. Dionysius Lardner's *Cabinet Cyclopedia.* This project kept her involved with the details of literary and scientific history-making in Italy, France, Spain, and Portugal even as she continued work at home on her "modern" novel, *Lodore,* and desperately attempted to keep her father employed during the ups and downs of the Whig party. *Lodore* became more successful than any of her novels since *Frankenstein* and probably led to the invitation from publisher Charles Ollier to write another.

Falkner, which Shelley claimed "wrote itself,"[22] was her last novel. She composed it while also working on the memoir of her recently deceased father and, like her short story "The Parvenue," written in the same period, the novel is almost painfully autobiographical. It features an orphaned protagonist (another Elizabeth), a child rejected by his father, a parent's refusal to provide financial aid, an elopement, and an unhappy wife who drowns herself in an attempt to escape the overtures of her lover. At the end of the novel Elizabeth wins both father and lover, but before *Falkner* was completed, Shelley herself had experienced a minor breakdown, possibly due to the personal pain her narrative revived. *The Athenaeum* reviewer deemed *Falkner* "among the best of Mary Shelley's romances in the Godwinian mode."[23] Nonetheless, Shelley decided to write exclusively nonfiction and short stories in the future.

As Victoria ascended the throne in 1837 Shelley, too, was figuratively and critically entering—or being propelled into—the Victorian Age. In 1836 the *Metropolitan Literary Journal* described her as "amazingly feminine, beautifully spoken, and natural, for the author of *Frankenstein,*" and she was to tell the American statesman Charles Sumner that "the greatest happiness of a woman . . . is to be the wife or mother of a distinguished man."[24] Accordingly, she began in 1838 what she considered to be her sacred duty, the publication of Percy Shelley's complete works, while at the same time refusing Edward Trelawny's request that she write a pamphlet on women's rights for the Philosophic Radicals. Her response to Trelawny's charge that she had deserted liberalism clearly reveals her distress: "I feel the counter arguments too strongly . . . on some topics (especially with regard to my own sex). I am far from making up my mind."[25]

The process of collecting and editing Percy Shelley's poetry exacted a great toll on Mary Shelley's emotional and physical health. The result, however, was the establishment of Percy Shelley as an institution, one of England's greatest poets. Her insistence on placing the poems within the circumstances of their production began a trend in criticism. In her notes she emphasized Percy's political views as well as his poetic views and attitudes toward love, many of which she continued to share throughout her life in spite of the seductions of domestic feminism. Unfortunately, she underrated her own contributions to his intellectual life; nonetheless, the completed publication of his works brought her great satisfaction and short-lived peace of mind.

The equanimity she experienced during this period was disturbed briefly by the now widowed Aubrey Beauclerk's return to the scene. He admitted to having loved her in spite of his marriage of convenience and indicated that, after a period of grieving, he would make Mary his wife. While on a tour of the continent with her son, however, Mary learned of Beauclerk's remarriage. Only the news that Sir Timothy Shelley had finally agreed to provide her son, on his 21st birthday, with a substantial income somewhat relieved her ravaged spirit. Very much the opposite of Victor Frankenstein, she eventually dedicated herself to nurturing a circle of friends who could contribute to her son's social well-being. She was dismayed to learn, however, that the increasingly moralistic and unforgiving Victorian society would make it difficult for a "tainted" woman like herself to assure her son a place in society even if he was the son of a poet who was internationally celebrated due to her efforts.

Between 1837 and 1848 Mary Shelley fought off ill health, depression, a variety of extortioners, the continuing snubs of the social elite, and critics of her handling of Percy Shelley's works. She survived these attacks by traveling with her son and completing her last lengthy work, *Rambles in Germany and Italy*. In March of 1848 she introduced her son to Mrs. Jane Gibson St. John, the young widow of an aristocrat and illegitimate daughter of a banker. Jane St. John married Percy Florence Shelley in June just in time to become Mary Shelley's caregiver; from the autumn of 1848 until her death on February 1, 1851, Mary Shelley became increasingly debilitated by a brain tumor.

In their tribute to Mary Shelley published in the *Leader* following her death, George Lewes and Thornton Hunt called *Frankenstein* "one of those books that become the parent of whole generations of romances."[26] Yet they could not have foreseen the amazing extent of *Frankenstein*'s generative power. In 1984 Donald Glut's *The Frankenstein Catalog* listed 2,666 variants, editions, and critiques.[27] But Glut's catalog is already woefully out-of-date since every year another hybrid is spawned. The latest serious variant, *Extreme Measures,* is a film released in 1996, featuring Gene Hackman as a scientist who experiments on live bodies that he steals from the ranks of the homeless in the cause of the future good of spinal damage victims.

Mary Shelley herself seems to have been delighted with the first of the dramatic versions of her masterpiece. "Lo and behold! I am famous," she wrote Leigh Hunt in 1819 about the unprecedentedly successful drama *Presumption.* Like all of its successors, this dramatization shamelessly reshaped her novel. But the audience shrieked their horror and approval as the toga-clad monster, blue-bodied, green-faced, and black-lipped, smashed down the laboratory door and leaped onto center stage to Frankenstein's cry of "It's alive!"[28]

Explanations for *Frankenstein*'s reproductive power are almost as varied as its progeny, but they are effectively covered in the essays included in this collection. More puzzling than *Frankenstein*'s generative energy is the period of eclipse that Mary Shelley experienced for nearly 100 years.[29] By 1950, although *Frankenstein* (first published in 1818) had never gone out of print and increasingly eccentric dramatic versions of it were produced almost annually, Mary Shelley was relatively unknown to students of literature. Even the publication in 1951 of Muriel Spark's *Child of Light: A Reassessment of Mary Shelley* did little to revive interest in "Shelley's Mary."[30] Spark's tribute, published during the centenary anniversary year of Mary Shelley's death, enjoyed only modest circulation in the United Kingdom and was never published in the United States. But in the 1960s and 1970s, with the rise to academic respectability of science fiction and the feminist drive to recuperate women writers whose reputations were in decline, interest in Mary Shelley began to grow. The more recent recognition of popular culture as a legitimate area for scholarly analysis has also helped enhance *Frankenstein*'s and Shelley's reputation. Scholars and casual readers alike have been interested and fascinated to learn that Mary, Percy Shelley's teenaged lover, produced the mythic story of Victor Frankenstein, the young scientist who reanimates a monstrous corpse that becomes his nemesis. From the novel, and its seemingly endless film variants, attention then turned to the circumstances of the novel's production[31] and the conditions of Mary Shelley's life.

Having previously been viewed as the dimmest in a firmament of Romantic stars that included her parents as well as her eventual husband and his friend Lord Byron, Mary Shelley has recently come to be appreciated not only as a "child of light," but as a bringer of light, a modern female Prometheus, on the one hand, and a Pandora, the reproach of Prometheus, on the other. For Mary Shelley seems to have acquired an uncanny prescience, literally a "pre-science," that equipped her to predict monstrosities conceived in scientific laboratories, behind governmental walls, and around family hearths that would hound their creators to the ground. While the major focus of critical interest in Shelley remains the novel *Frankenstein,* the range of interest has expanded to include her entire, quite extensive oeuvre from journals and letters to her scholarly biographical essays on the "eminent literary and scientific men" of Europe to critical reviews and short stories and her eulogistic "Preface to the Poetical Works of Percy Bysshe Shelley."

This collection of essays attempts to reflect the progress, range, weight, and controversies of Mary Shelley criticism from the period of her rediscovery to the present. Nine of the essays are devoted primarily to discussions of Shelley's sensitivity to her immediate cultural milieu as evidenced in her writings. The remaining four focus on Shelley's generative power and the ways in which her work has been transformed. Of the 13 essays, 10 have been previously published; all contribute provocative and innovative readings of Mary Shelley's life, works, and influence.

George Levine and U. C. Knoepflmacher brought together in 1979 some of the most insightful *Frankenstein* criticisms of the 1960s and 1970s celebrating the staying power of Mary Shelley's novel in their collection *The Endurance of Frankenstein*. Levine's introduction to that collection, reprinted here in modified form, still provides one of the very best initiations into the world of the novel, its author, and its critics. Levine attributes the novel's power to its metaphoric representation of "our own cultural crises [characterized by] a consumer technology, neurotically obsessed with 'getting in touch' with its authentic self and frightened at what it is discovering." Levine notes the novel's literary heritage—its debts to *Faust, Prometheus,* and *Paradise Lost*—but also recognizes as perhaps more important to its longevity the modernity, immediacy, and secularity it projects. Elaborating on the "distinctness of the Frankenstein metaphor" Levine admiringly cites James Rieger, editor of the 1818 edition of *Frankenstein,* whose findings about the extent of Percy Shelley's involvement in the production of the novel have recently been questioned, especially by feminist critics. Thus, this opening essay introduces both the givens and the debates of Mary Shelley studies. Levine, too, begins a tradition of criticism wherein *Frankenstein* and Shelley herself are viewed as literary half-breeds, drawing both from Romantic and Victorian ideologies. Most helpfully for students, Levine devotes much of his essay to an outline of seven "major implications of the Frankenstein metaphor in contemporary consciousness . . . as they have their sources in the novel proper." These analogies, which subsequently provide rich ground for every variety of critical exploration, include birth and creation; the overreacher (Faust, Prometheus, Satan); rebellion and moral isolation; the unjust society; the defects of domesticity; the double; and technology, entropy, and the monstrous.

Sandra Gilbert's essay, which first appeared in *Feminist Studies* and was later reprinted in the landmark feminist collection *The Madwoman in the Attic,*[32] has engendered much interest concerning the degree to which Mary Shelley's personal, specifically female, bogeys find their way into *Frankenstein*'s characters. Joining the ranks of critics who read *Frankenstein* as a response to

Paradise Lost, Gilbert treats Shelley's novel as a clarification of Milton's epic, which ironically conceals "fantasies of equality that occasionally erupt in monstrous images of rage." Gilbert asks that we consider how femaleness and literariness were related to one another in Shelley's consciousness as we consider her fictional responses to Milton's misogynistic representations of creation. Finding Eve, that is, versions of Mary Shelley herself, in all of *Frankenstein's* characters, Gilbert interprets the novel as Shelley's psychodramatic protest against not simply Milton's misogyny, but the cultural conspiracy that continues to reproduce it.

Like Sandra Gilbert, Anne K. Mellor revises earlier readings of *Frankenstein* by providing a feminist perspective on Mary Shelley's works. At the same time Mellor clearly establishes Shelley's right to be hailed as the creator of science fiction. For Mellor, a work of science fiction is grounded in scientific research, predicts future scientific accomplishments, and critiques those accomplishments (or the perceptions that led to them) from an ethical, humane point of view. *Frankenstein* may be the first to meet all of these criteria. As Mellor shows, Shelley was not only thoroughly familiar with the most influential scientific research of her day, but, anticipating the consequences of that research, she created in *Frankenstein* a warning about the obsessive drive to conquer and control natural forces.

An attentive reader, daughter of an ardent feminist, and intimate of science afficionado Percy Shelley, Mary Shelley was among the earliest writers of either sex to understand and depict in her fiction the problems involved with scientific theories and projects that represent a virile, male *science* that conquers and subdues a fertile but passive or reluctant female *nature.* Mellor points out, however, that Shelley was no simplistic naysayer when it came to the subject of science. She distinguished between the "good" science of an Erasmus Darwin whose painstaking recording of plant evolution led to a better understanding of the interdependence of *all* nature, and the "bad" science of chemists like Humphrey Davy who sought ways to conquer and control nature. Most obviously, perhaps, Shelley invokes in *Frankenstein* the work of Luigi Galvani, whose nephew—using his uncle's techniques in 1803—applied galvanic electricity to the body of Thomas Forster, a recently hanged murderer. The response was immediate and dramatic: "The jaw began to quiver . . . the left eye actually opened . . . as to give an appearance of reanimation" (quoted in Mellor). Mellor aptly suggests that this "galvanized" corpse was a precursor of Mary Shelley's Creature. She would likely have heard of the Galvani experiments from the trio with whom she and her stepsister Claire exchanged stories during the summer of 1816 when *Frankenstein* was conceived. Percy Shelley, Byron, and Byron's physician, William Polidori, were all fascinated by the potential of science to create life. Finally, in her review of Mary Shelley's "Critique of Science," Mellor draws our attention to the direction that scientific research continues to take toward manipulating and controlling human life forces by such processes as gene splicing and extrauterine fertilization. Like Victor Frankenstein, however, modern science seems ill-equipped to handle the moral and ethical consequences of unnaturally conferring life.

In "Mary Shelley's Daemon," Ellen Herson Wittmann modifies the critical attitude (which Stephen Behrendt addresses in this collection) that Shelley, like other Romantic women writers, in some sense fell victim to a masculinist literary industrial complex of writers, critics, and publishers. In particular, Wittmann rejects the notion that Mary Shelley was diminished or oppressed by Percy Shelley and his humanist ideology. Focusing on Mary Shelley's use of the word "daemon" to describe Victor Frankenstein's creature, especially in the final third of the novel, Wittmann proposes both that Mary and Percy collaborated on the use and implications of that term and that Mary considerably influenced Percy's poetic career even prior to his death. Wittmann surmises that Mary Shelley's understanding of the word, given her use of the Latinate spelling, would have derived from its pre-Christian meaning, incorporating such notions as genius, soul, spirit, fortune, divine power, deity, friendship, and erotic love.

The word "daemon" appears prominently in Plato's *Symposium,* a work that, Wittmann notes, Percy Shelley translated in 1818, having previously read it only in translation, purportedly to give Mary some idea of the "manners and feelings of the Athenians." Wittmann also notes Mary Shelley's prior encounter with Greek—her independent study in 1814 of that almost exclusively learned "male" language—suggesting that Mary may have been striving to "hold her own in an area where Percy had as yet little advantage."

Wittmann asserts that Mary's handling of the relationship between virtue and erotic love (which is not clearly distinguished from friendship) inspired Percy not only to reconsider the *Symposium* but also to celebrate (in *Prometheus Unbound*) love's power to effect good. In his translation of the *Symposium,* Percy Shelley retains the term "daemon" as he recounts the words of Diotima to Socrates on the nature of love, which she classifies "A Great daemon . . . and everything daemoniacal holds an intermediate place between what is divine and what is mortal." Wittmann's argument is strengthened by Mary Shelley's choice of the name Diotima for the narrator's mentor in "The Fields of Fancy," the first draft of what was to become *Matilda.*

Wittmann compares the position of Mary Shelley's Creature with that of Diotima—especially with regard to the Creature's experience of mixed pain and pleasure as he observes the loving gestures of the De Lacey family. It is the intermediacy, the mixedness, the suspension of opposites implied both in the word "daemon" and in the Creature himself that Wittmann sees as the distinguishing quality of Mary's and Percy's collaboration and their ideology. In some respects Wittman's argument parallels that of William Veeder's in *Mary Shelley and Frankenstein: The Fate of Androgyny.*[33] Wittman, like Veeder, contends that Mary Shelley meant to promote an androgynous philosophy of love in *Frankenstein.* She concludes: "*Frankenstein* demonstrates how—through the distortion of *erōs* into an evil demon, the displacement of *erōs* onto unattainable objects . . . , and the division of *erōs* into good and bad, selfless and selfish, spiritual and appetitive forms of love—virtue is degraded into vice.

As I have attempted to demonstrate, Shelley's complex responses to the rather chaotic world of learning, love, poverty, extravagance, uncontrolled births, and untimely deaths in which she grew up did not end with the publication of *Frankenstein* in 1818. On November 19, 1819, she completed the final version of *Matilda* and subsequently sent it off to her father for his approval and aid in getting it published. Finding the story "disgusting and detestable," William Godwin failed to promote it. Terence Harpold's essay interprets the phenomenon of *Matilda*—its composition and circulation—as Shelley's attempt to understand, revise, and finally neutralize some of the tormenting ghosts of her personal past.

Like *Frankenstein,* Harpold argues, *Matilda* refigures Mary Shelley's family dramatis personae. In *Matilda,* however, the primal scene represented in *Frankenstein*'s "workshop of filthy creation" is reconstituted as a seduction between father and daughter. The story expresses Mary's need to identify with her dead mother (the object of her father's desire), to exorcize her guilty feelings about her mother's death and her own succession to her mother's place, and to overcome her mother's (imagined) haunting, primitive power. Harpold proposes that Mary's sending the manuscript to Godwin by way of Maria Gisborne, one of his former love interests and Mary's caregiver after her mother's death, indicates Mary's desire to engage her father in the incest fantasy while recognizing the "authority of his desire." Certainly Harpold's psychoanalytical interpretation accounts for the story's strange intensity and pervasive, exaggerated atmosphere of guilt and unfulfilled desire.

Perhaps the best evidence of Mary Shelley's sensitivity to familial, social, and professional stimuli is found in documents that directly speak her mind where are recorded the needs, emotions, sympathies, frustrations, and philosophies that in her fiction are more calculated and therefore more suspect. What are the occasions that prompt her to use her own voice? How does she couch a persuasive phrase or shape a difficult thought? More importantly for students of literature, how can knowledge gleaned from journals, letters, and such enlighten us about Shelley's (or any author's) more formal works and the literary milieu that helped produce them?

Betty T. Bennett addresses just such questions in "Finding Mary Shelley in Her Letters." Bennett's article is more than a critical essay. It is a marvelous lesson in literary sleuthing. She demonstrates how the physical properties of the letters (postmarks, watermarks) together with the subjects addressed, sentence structure, changes in handwriting and tone of voice, and use of eccentric punctuation all provide evidence that allows us "to revise Mary Shelley's image from . . . a passive, conventional Victorian lady into a multidimensional, complex Romanticist." Bennett notes that it is in our interest as students of the Romantics (and of women writers generally, I would add) to investigate the letters of one who was in frequent communication with the leading figures of her era. The compendium of that communication reveals at various times a determined, exasperated, optimistic, ill, accomplished author, homemaker, and mother. Shelley's letters speak to us of a tireless researcher and deliberate, professional editor. Her later letters show a circling back of memory to her early days as a revolutionary young member of the Shelley-Byron menage; but they also reveal an unabated interest in reformist politics. Bennett assures us that Mary Shelley never posed in her letters and that, therefore, the letters should inspire significant critical revisions of her life and works.

Elaborating on a theme previously established by Mary Poovey, among others,[34] Stephen Behrendt examines *Frankenstein* from the perspective of the lessons it teaches about the "hazards of authorship," especially for the Romantic woman author. Coming to us second or thirdhand, the action of *Frankenstein* is always kept offstage, a strategy that, for Behrendt, renders the violence of the novel "powerfully imminent." Further, *Frankenstein*'s epistolary frame associates it especially with women's writing while, at the same time, women characters in the novel are denied the opportunity to speak for themselves (except in letters). *Frankenstein,* then, is a "construct of words" rather than a "direct representation of actions." Behrendt finds in this complex relationship of words, inaction, and imminent violence an analogue to the "dilemma of the woman writer at the beginning of the nineteenth century." That dilemma resulted from cultural pressures on women to adopt masculinist literary conventions, thereby often misrepresenting or silencing their female characters. Alternatively, women writers who challenged the reigning conventions of appropriate masculine and feminine use of language were subject to self-disgust, self-hatred, and hostility from the literary establishment. *Frankenstein,* Behrendt argues, "at once trespasses on [such] 'forbidden' territory and at the same time comments on the nature and consequences of that incursion." Shelley's Creature is placed in a situation like that of overreaching Romantic women. Possessing "feminine" sensibilities, he is nonetheless spurned by his creator/father as well as by the society he seeks to enter precisely because of his unfeminine ugliness and aggressive behavior. Behrendt expands his observations about Mary Shelley's and her Creature's compromised positions to her female contemporaries, writers like Caroline Norton.

William D. Brewer discusses another aspect of Mary Shelley's novella *Matilda,* that of Matilda's failure to speak the name of the sin that causes her suffering. He finds in this work a theme that recurs in virtually all of Shelley's fictions: "the predicament of a suffering human being torn between the impulse to communicate and the urge to retreat into isolation and death." Here again I might point out the sensitivity Mary Shelley displays; by engaging this issue—to speak out on or retreat from taboo subjects—she insists on keeping a major dilemma of the Victorian woman in the minds of the reading public. Brewer also examines Mary Shelley's short story "The Mourner" and her novel *Valperga* in some detail. In these and other works Shelley seems to return almost obsessively to questions concerning the power or impotence of words. On balance, Brewer finds that Shelley—anticipating psychoanalytic theory—does recognize "the human need to put suffering into words." But she assigns only short-term relief to such therapy and, in the case of extreme trauma, seems to advocate writing rather than speaking out about one's pain. In nearly all cases, Brewer notes, the *refusal* to communicate leads to depression and death.

Victoria Middleton identifies the theme of writing as therapy also in Mary Shelley's *The Last Man,* where "the self-reflexive action of writing nullifies the pain of consciousness" for Lionel Verney, the title character. Middleton's major thesis, however, is one that has been challenged in recent years, as both Betty T. Bennett's and Emily Sunstein's essays indicate. Simply stated, Middleton argues that after Percy Shelley's death—and in large part because of his death—Mary Shelley became increasingly conservative in her life, works, and politics. In this first novel of Mary Shelley's after the death of Percy Shelley (and of Lord Byron, as well) Middleton notes that Lionel Verney's transformation from a Romantic to a Victorian narrator parallels Mary Shelley's purported conversion: Verney transforms from "a (Romantic) sublime egotist, proudly superior to society if tragically alienated from it, into a (Victorian) scribe for whom writing becomes life-preserving Carlylean *work.*"

Whether one finds Middleton's well-argued thesis convincing in light of recent revelations from Mary Shelley's letters and journals, the relentless pessimism of this apocalyptic novel is undeniable. The theme of a devastating plague that degrades the population and devalues everything except mere life is in some ways more compelling than Victor Frankenstein's overwrought creation. And certainly, Shelley's obsession with death is understandable considering the number of apparently senseless deaths that had plagued her life during the period just before she wrote *The Last Man.*

The three main characters of the novel are rather obviously versions of Percy Shelley, Byron, and Mary herself. That she represents herself as the male narrator Lionel Verney may be explained in a number of ways. Perhaps she is developing the androgynous vision that William Veeder finds throughout her works, or perhaps she is distancing her present self from a past that included the living Percy Shelley and Lord Byron.

In any case, as Muriel Spark points out, this novel not only revisits the events—writ metaphorically—that led to Mary Shelley's isolation after Percy's death, but also reveals her as "Godwin's daughter as Shelley's wife and as a student of Platonic literature."[35] In other words, like *Frankenstein* and *Matilda, The Last Man* reveals a sensitivity to influences in her milieu that compels her to "figure them out" in fictional patterns. In this novel Mary Shelley puts Godwin's *Political Justice* in contention with Shelleyan metaphysics, ultimately concluding that all moral and political concepts lose their meaning in the face of implacable, universal death. Whether this apparent succumbing to nihilism can be interpreted as Mary Shelley's own retreat from the radical philosophies of her youth remains a vexed question. The representation of her as a withdrawn, somber widow lacking intellectual vitality, however, is certainly not borne out in her letters and journals; nor is the record of her publications after *The Last Man* that of a woman in retreat.

The next essay in this collection moves from the texts of *Frankenstein* and its progenitors into the pages of its progeny. In his critical study *In Frankenstein's Shadow* Chris Baldick reveals the enormous influence of Mary Shelley's mythic work on writers who followed her. The essay reprinted here provides what might be termed a Marxist/colonialist interpretation of *Frankenstein's* suggestive power over the works of Joseph Conrad and D. H. Lawrence. In "Monsters of Empire: Conrad and Lawrence," Baldick finds that *Heart of Darkness* bears "a number of uncanny resemblances to the design of *Frankenstein*," including its self-conscious exclusion of women from the enterprises of men. Furthermore, Conrad's protagonist Kurtz, like Victor Frankenstein and even Walton, falls squarely into George Levine's "overreacher" category; but it is imperialism itself that assumes the implacable monstrous qualities of Frankenstein's Creature in Conrad's works. *Nostromo* and *Heart of Darkness* especially depict blatant "Frankensteinian transgression"; for Baldick, however, Conrad's understanding of how such "disinterested professions" as the maritime service became complicit with the gargantuan appetites of imperialism was limited and flawed compared to that of D. H. Lawrence.

Baldick discovers in Lawrence an abiding, culturally induced mistrust of polar exploration that directly opposes the enthusiasms of *Frankenstein's* narrator Robert Walton. Lawrence sees quests like Walton's not as Romantic ventures but as urges toward conquest. In *Women in Love,* Baldick argues, Lawrence seems to employ a "vocabulary of geographical symbols derived from the Shelley-Byron circle's Alpine obsessions" to attack modern imperialism. Further, Baldick notes, Lawrence specifically associates the intense imposition of the individual will on nature with Frankensteinian overreaching and represents America as a monstrous reflection, an uncontrollable offspring, of European ambition.

My own essay, "Sweetheart of Darkness: Kurtz's Intended as Progeny of Frankenstein's Bride," elaborates on themes established by Behrendt and Baldick. I argue that the separate spheres represented as so inimical to male-female equality and communication in *Frankenstein* become thoroughly uncivilizing in *Heart of Darkness*. When Conrad's Marlow lies to Kurtz's Intended about Kurtz's last words, he replaces her name with the famous expletive, "The horror, the horror." The equation of the Intended, living in her protected domestic sphere thousands of miles from Kurtz's Africa, with raw horror indicates the complete breakdown of civilization. The Intended's ignorance and the lie Marlow tells to protect it represent a whole century of keeping women both in and out of the business of empire building. The potential ramifications of such gender segregation were all incorporated in *Frankenstein,* as Conrad seems to have observed, but by the time he wrote *Heart of Darkness,* the potential had become reality.

The most conclusive evidence of Mary Shelley's generative power as an author is surely found in the endless series of *Frankenstein* films that began with the Thomas A. Edison Company's 1910 production. Since then it has become increasingly clear that cinema and the Creature were made for each other. Mary Shelley's insistence on his hideous looks, gigantic size, and physical prowess made the monster just the kind of visual, kinetic attraction that early filmmakers needed to display their newly developing camera techniques. There is a certain irony in the fact that the first film creature was played by Charles Ogle, whose very name invites us to stare rudely at his form.

As film has become a more sophisticated multidimensional medium, threatening even to supersede the novel as a legitimate form of "literature," the story of Victor Frankenstein and his Creature has retained its attractions for producers and audiences. Filmmakers have increasingly perceived and attempted to present not just the physicality of the monster, but the novel's more subtle and complex social, psychological, ethical, and gender-related themes. Whatever the level of sophistication, however, only those films that exploit the Creature's potential both for sensationalism and sympathy seem to attain the status of classic, for the Creature remains the quintessentially cinematic feature of Mary Shelley's tale. The iconic status of Boris Karloff's version of the Creature (Universal Studios, 1931) testifies to its staying power. As much as to Karloff's performance, credit for the Creature's strange attractiveness should perhaps go to Jack Pierce, who designed the makeup and repeated it for the numerous horror films produced by Universal Studios in the 1930s. The sale of Universal Studios' 1931 *Frankenstein* to television in 1957 "led directly to the new horror film cycle of the late 1950s."[36] Thus, the popular culture revival of Shelley's "hideous progeny" coincides with and reinforces the scholarly interest that began increasing at the same time.

As Tracy Cox points out in her essay "*Frankenstein* and Its Cinematic Translations," newly published for this collection, Karloff's Creature, though unable to speak, reflects the nuances of Shelley's original. Even contemporary reviewers for the *Motion Picture Herald* found that "because of his restraint his intelligent simplicity of gesture, carriage, voice and makeup, Karloff has truly created a Frankenstein monster."[37] Cox examines three films, the Edison (1910), the Universal (1931), and the more recent Kenneth Branaugh (1994) productions of *Frankenstein,* not to provide a one-to-one comparison of novel and film but rather to demonstrate how the films succeed or fail in the particular area that should be the most cinematically effective, that is, the representation of the Creature. These three films also bear comparison with one another because they purport to take themselves seriously and exhibit their own philosophical complexities that in the long run may return us to the novel, where we may once again test its suggestive powers. It is appropriate to include here this essay on *Frankenstein* films since, as Harriet Margolis contends, it has become virtually impossible to discuss Frankenstein's novel without "confronting the Hollywood versions of Mary Shelley's vision."[38]

Just as her fiction continues to inspire variants and hybrids, so does Mary Shelley's life story stimulate endless retellings. Emily W. Sunstein recounts the history of those retellings in the closing chapter of her 1989 biography *Mary Shelley: Romance and Reality,* reprinted as the final essay in this collection. Sunstein traces the roller-coaster pattern of Shelley's reputation from idealization to defamation, the "distress" of her postmortem critical history if you will. The final effect of Sunstein's account, however, is to reinforce the sense of Shelley's power to capture the imagination.

Like Betty T. Bennett's article, Sunstein's also teaches something about her own craft—in this case constructing a biography—and its relationship to literary studies. Understanding the biases, grudges, and favoritisms incorporated in the numerous versions of Mary Shelley's life in turn helps us to understand the critical controversies surrounding her fiction. Most obviously, the low critical regard that Shelley suffered for decades readily explains previous lack of interest in *Frankenstein*'s origins; but Sunstein's history of Mary Shelley biographies also chronicles ideological trends, especially with regard to culturally sanctioned roles and opportunities for women. Thus, Mary Shelley becomes a martyr sacrificing herself at the altar of Percy Shelley's fame in one era and a virago hindering his poetic progress in another. She is touted at various times as both liberal and conservative, household angel and domestic sloven, poorly educated and too learned for her own good. Sunstein's own treatment of Mary Shelley is the kind of balanced, sensitive, but powerful representation that reveals the lifelong distress that continues, even after her death, to give Mary Shelley and her work mythic proportions.

Notes

1. For both a chronology and a critical history, see Mary Lowe-Evans, *Frankenstein: Mary Shelley's Wedding Guest* (New York: Twayne, 1993). The St. Martin's Press Critical Casebook edition of *Frankenstein,* ed. Joanna Smith (New York: St. Martin's Press, 1992), also provides an extensive critical history. *The Mary Shelley Reader,* ed. Betty T. Bennett and Charles E. Robinson (Oxford: Oxford University Press, 1990), also provides a chronology.

2. "I, being born a woman and distressed," from the sonnet sequence *The Harp Weaver,* is included in Edna St. Vincent Millay, *Collected Sonnets of Edna St. Vincent Millay,* ed. Norma Millay (New York: Harper & Row, 1988), 41.

3. Mary Shelley, *The Fortunes of Perkin Warbeck, A Romance.* (London: Henry Coburn & Richard Bentley, 1830), 3: 351.

4. The unsigned entry for *Frankenstein* in *Masterplots,* a source widely used by undergraduates, epitomizes the subordination or *dis*-stress of Mary Shelley, which appropriately incenses feminist critics: "[*Frankenstein* is] a wholly incredible story told with little skill. . . . [Nonetheless] Mary Shelley would be remembered if she had written nothing, for she was the wife of Percy Bysshe Shelley under romantic and scandalous circumstances" ("Frankenstein," in

Masterplots: English Fiction Series, ed. Frank N. Magill [New York: Salem Press, 1964]), 235.

5.   Quoted in Emily Sunstein, *Mary Shelley: Romance and Reality* (Baltimore: Johns Hopkins University Press, 1989), 322. When Caroline Norton's husband sensationally divorced her in 1836, naming Whig Prime Minister Lord Melbourne as correspondent (Melbourne was acquitted), Norton lost custody and visitation rights over her children and was replaced as the editor of *Keepsake.* Mary Shelley lent her emotional and social support in the face of Norton's ostracism by many of her respectable literary "friends" (Sunstein, *Mary Shelley,* 333).

6.   Quoted in *The Mary Shelley Reader,* ed. Betty T. Bennet and Charles E. Robinson (Oxford: Oxford University Press, 1990), 378.

7.   Mary Shelley, *Frankenstein or the Modern Prometheus: The 1818 Text,* ed. James Rieger (Chicago: University of Chicago Press, 1982), 13. Subsequent references to this text are made parenthetically within the text.

8.   *Mary Shelley Reader,* 236.

9.   Mary Shelley, *The Last Man* (London: Henry Colburn, 1826), 1: 33.

10.   *The Letters of Mary Wollstonecraft Shelley,* ed. Betty T. Bennett, (Baltimore: Johns Hopkins University Press, 1980–1988), 2: 245.

11.   *Perkin Warbeck,* 2: 299.

12.   Quoted in Susan Groag Bell and Karen M. Offen, eds., *Women, the Family and Freedom: The Debate in Documents, Vol. 1, 1750–1880* (Stanford, Calif.: Stanford University Press, 1983), 182.

13.   *Mary Shelley Reader,* 274 n.

14.   Perhaps the most popular of such imaginative reawakenings is found in Washington Irving's *The Legend of Sleepy Hollow.* Mary Shelley's playful attraction to Irving makes the coincidence of their subject matter intriguing.

15.   *Mary Shelley Reader,* 279.

16.   Muriel Spark, *Mary Shelley* (New York: E. P. Dutton, 1987), 180.

17.   Spark, *Mary Shelley,* 198.

18.   Sunstein, *Mary Shelley,* 299.

19.   Sunstein, *Mary Shelley,* 300.

20.   Sunstein, *Mary Shelley,* 310.

21.   Sunstein, *Mary Shelley,* 319.

22.   Sunstein, *Mary Shelley,* 330.

23.   Sunstein, *Mary Shelley,* 336.

24.   Sunstein, *Mary Shelley,* 228, 240.

25.   Quoted in Sunstein, *Mary Shelley,* 384.

26.   Quoted in Sunstein, *Mary Shelley,* 388.

27.   Donald J. Glut, *The Frankenstein Catalog,* (Jefferson: McFarland & Company, 1984).

28.   Sunstein, *Mary Shelley,* 342–43.

29.   Jane Dunn's biography of Mary Shelley refers to her as "Moon in eclipse"; *Moon in Eclipse: A Life of Mary Shelley* (London: Weidenfeld & Nicholson, 1978).

30.   Margaret Leighton uses "Shelley's Mary" as the title of her 1973 biography *Shelley's Mary: A Life of Mary Wollstonecraft Shelley* (New York: Farrar, Strauss & Giroux, 1973).

31.   Two films from the 1980s focus on the period of time at the Villa Diodati immediately preceding Mary Shelley's waking dream, the inspiration for *Frankenstein:* Ken Russell's *Gothic,* 1987; and Ivan Passer's *Haunted Summer,* 1988.

32.   See Sandra M. Gilbert and Susan Gubar, *The Madwoman in the Attic: The Woman Writer and the Nineteenth-Century Literary Imagination* (New Haven, Conn.: Yale University Press, 1979), 213–47.

33.   William Veeder, *Mary Shelley and Frankenstein: The Fate of Androgyny* (Chicago: University of Chicago Press, 1986).

34.   See Mary Poovey, *The Proper Lady and the Woman Writer: Ideology as Style in the Works*

of Mary Wollstonecraft, Mary Shelley and Jane Austin (Chicago: University of Chicago Press, 1986), 243–61.

35. Spark, *Mary Shelley,* 184.

36. Richard Bojarski and Kenneth Beals, *The Films of Boris Karloff* (Seacaucus, N.J.: The Citadel Press), 61, 62.

37. Bojarski and Beals, *Films of Boris Karloff,* 63.

38. Harriet E. Margolis, "Lost Baggage: Or, The Hollywood Sidetrack," in *Approaches to Teaching Shelley's Frankenstein* (New York: MLA, 1990), 160.

MARY SHELLEY,
A "SENSITIVE REGISTER"

◆

The Ambiguous Heritage of *Frankenstein*

George Levine

It's a commonplace now, that everybody talks about *Frankenstein,* but nobody reads it. That depends on what is meant by "nobody." It is possible, of course, that "Frankenstein" became an entry in every serious recent dictionary by way of the variations—dramas, films, television versions—through which Mary Shelley's monster and his creator most obviously survive. But while *Frankenstein* is a phenomenon of popular culture, it is so because it has tapped into the center of Western feeling and imagination: we can hear echoes of it, not only in Gothic fiction, science fiction, and fantasies of all sorts, but in far more "respectable" works, written before the glut of popular cinematic distortions. *Frankenstein* has become a metaphor for our own cultural crises, and survives even yet in high literary culture whose professors may have seen Boris Karloff stumbling through the fog, hands outstretched, at least once too often. . . .

If we return to the text for a check on Boris Karloff, or recently, Mel Brooks, or for some further light on Percy Shelley, invariably we find that the book is larger and richer than any of its progeny and too complex to serve as mere background. Even in our dictionaries, "Frankenstein" has become a vital metaphor, peculiarly appropriate to a culture dominated by a consumer technology, neurotically obsessed with "getting in touch" with its authentic self and frightened at what it is discovering: "a work, or agency that proves troublesomely uncontrollable, esp. to its creator."[1] Latent in the metaphor are some of the fundamental dualisms, the social, moral, political and metaphysical crises of Western history since the French Revolution. It may well appear that the metaphorical implications are far more serious than the novel that gave birth to them, but that novel has qualities that allow it to exfoliate as creatively and endlessly as any important myth; if it threatens to lapse into banality and bathos, it yet lives through unforgettable dreamlike images. . . .

Frankenstein echoes the old stories of Faust and Prometheus, exploring the limits of ambition and rebelliousness and their moral implications; but it is also the tale of a *"modern Prometheus,"* and as such it is a secular myth, with

From *Endurance of Frankenstein: Essays on Mary Shelley's Novel,* ed. George Levine and U. C. Knoepflmacher (Berkeley: University of California Press, 1979), 3–30. Reprinted with permission by the University of California Press. Copyright © 1979 The Regents of the University of California.

no metaphysical machinery, no gods: the creation is from mortal bodies with the assistance of electricity, not spirit; and the deaths are not pursued beyond the grave. The dream vision out of which the work grows—Mary Shelley's vision embodied in that "dreary night in November"—is echoed by Victor Frankenstein's dream vision within the novel proper, of worms and shrouds, not of angels or of devils. The dreams emerge from the complex experiences that placed the young Mary Shelley, both personally and intellectually, at a point of crisis in our modern culture, where idealism, faith in human perfectibility, and revolutionary energy were counterbalanced by the moral egotism of her radical father, the potential infidelity of her ideal husband, the cynical diabolism of Byron, the felt reality of her own pregnancy, and a great deal more. . . .

The distinctiveness of the Frankenstein metaphor, its peculiar appropriateness to the developing cultures of nineteenth- and twentieth-century England and America, can be usefully clarified by remarking briefly on Percy Shelley's relation to the novel. In the introduction to his excellent edition of the text, James Rieger has shown that Percy watched closely over the development of Mary's manuscript in all of its stages, and received "carte blanche" from her to revise it as he would.[2] More than editor, Percy was, in Rieger's view, "a minor collaborator" (p. xliv). Yet, despite his involvement in many details of the writing, despite the persistence of Shelleyan images and parallels between Victor's and Percy Shelley's education,[3] the central imagination is certainly Mary's alone. Under Percy's eyes, perhaps without his fully knowing it (perhaps without fully knowing it herself), Mary created a narrative that put her husband himself to the test—that juxtaposed an ideal vision against the banalities and corruption of ordinary physical and social life in ways that, as I have described them elsewhere,[4] anticipated the preoccupations of the Victorian novel, and through it, of the culture itself. Shortly after *Frankenstein,* Percy Shelley was to create his own Prometheus, a figure who triumphs by renouncing revenge for a visionary love and generative passivity. . . .

But *Frankenstein,* of course, denies love its triumph. Men and monster are anything but rulers over guilt and pain: Walton's narrative ends in the frustration of his enterprise; Victor's ends in a death caused by his creature or, more precisely, by his own vengeful pursuit of it; the Monster, with no relation consummated except through murder, goes off to self-immolation. Early on, Frankenstein tells Walton that "a human being in perfection ought always to preserve a calm and peaceful mind, and never to allow passion or a transitory desire to disturb his tranquility" (p. 51). But the novel refuses to allow human beings to remain "in perfection." Percy Shelley's "loftiest star" may resemble Walton's or Victor's aspirations, yet the novel itself is located, with the weight of earthly gravity, in the material world. The weight is a continuing comment on Victor's ambition, as the obscene flesh of the charnel house is the imaged irony of Victor's attempt to create life out of matter. To attempt to transcend time, chance, death, and mutability by means of matter—the materials of time—is literally chimerical.

Yet the novel offers us no other means. The passivity and acquiescence of Percy Shelley's Prometheus, by which he triumphs over Jupiter, has its analogue in Victor Frankenstein's unwilled obsession with creating life. Victor falls into a "trance," so driven by his creative energy that even what is loathsome becomes possible to him. In his "work-shop of filthy creation" he loses "all soul or sensation" (and the equation of the two is itself interesting). But it is almost a parody of the loss of self in the Christian ideal, or the Shelleyan one. And the trance of the laboratory is echoed in the various trances by which Victor lapses out of action and overt responsibility throughout the narrative. Such trances are obviously not Promethean triumphs of the spirit, but physical, material, time-bound effects of the very passion that man "in perfection" ought not allow to disturb him. *Frankenstein* rejects the conception of man's spirit unanchored in flesh. In contrast to Percy Shelley's exploration and celebration of at least the dream of the power of spirit to fold "over the world its healing wings," Mary Shelley's novel can be seen as an exploration of the powerlessness of love to control the passions that are hidden deep in our being, that are sure to find physical expression, and, finally, that are unimaginable without pain or guilt.

Ironically, then, *Frankenstein*'s mysterious power derives from a thoroughly earthy, practical, and unideal vision of human nature and possibility. Its modernity lies in its transformation of fantasy and traditional Christian and pagan myths into unremitting secularity, into the myth of mankind as it must work within the limits of the visible, physical world. The novel echoes, for example, with the language and the narrative of *Paradise Lost,* but it is *Paradise Lost* without angels, or devils, or God. When the Monster invokes the analogy between himself and Adam or Satan, we are obviously invited to think of Frankenstein as God. Yet, we know that the Monster is a double of Victor himself, and that as he acts out his satanic impulses he is acting out another aspect of Victor's creation of him. God, however, cannot be a rebel; nor can he be Adam or Satan's "double." He cannot be complicit in his creature's weaknesses, cannot be destroyed by what he creates. The whole narrative of *Frankenstein* is, indeed, acted out in the absence of God. The grand gestures of *Frankenstein* may suggest a world of fantasy that has acquired a profound escapist appeal in modern culture, but they take place in a framework that necessarily makes an ironic commentary on them, even while our sympathies are drawn to dreams of the more than human the narrative will not allow.

This characteristic tension between an impinging, conditional, and time-bound world and a dream of something freer and better makes the central subject matter and form of the nineteenth-century novel and, ironically, of nineteenth-century science as well. The old myths enter nineteenth-century fiction, but they do so in the mode of realism (which Northrop Frye, in another context, has described as an "ironic mode"[5]). Thus, though it would be absurd to claim Mary Shelley as a direct "influence" on the dominant literary and scientific forms of the century, we can see that in her secularization of the creation myth she invented a metaphor that was irresistible to the culture as a whole. . . . In writers as central and various as Feuerbach, Comte, Darwin, Marx, Frazer, and Freud we can find Victor Frankenstein's activity: the attempt to discover in matter what we had previously attributed to spirit, the bestowing *on* matter (or history, or society, or nature) the values once given to God. . . .

The pervasiveness of the Frankenstein metaphor in modern consciousness testifies to the richness and variousness of its implications. The dictionary definition focuses only on the uncontrollable nature of the thing created; but the image of the created Monster, emerging from the isolated workshop of the obsessed but otherwise gentle scientist, unfolds into more possibilities than I can describe. . . . [Nonetheless,] at the risk of arbitrary exclusions and of belaboring what may seem obvious, I want to outline some of the major implications of the Frankenstein metaphor in contemporary consciousness, and as they have their sources in the novel proper.

1. *Birth and Creation.* In *Frankenstein* we are confronted immediately by the displacement of God and woman from the acts of conception and birth. Where Victor imagines himself embarked on the creation of a new race that would bless him, he behaves, even before his creation proves a monster, as though he is engaged in unnatural, shameful activity. Neither of the two attitudes is entirely undercut by the narrative, even though the dream of the new race is, of course, exploded. The image of Frankenstein in his laboratory is not only of an unnatural act, but also one of an heroic dream, and the novel's insistence, even through Walton and the Monster, on Victor's heroic nature, implies that the creation without God, without woman, need not be taken as an unequivocal evil.

The displacement of woman obviously reflects a fear of birth and Mary Shelley's own ambivalence about childbearing . . . ; the Monster's presence on the wedding night becomes a permanent image of the horror of sexuality as opposed to the ideal and nonsexual love of the cousins, Victor and Elizabeth. The image of the Monster lurking ominously in the background, with Elizabeth sprawled on the bed, is one of the dominant icons of the film versions. Obviously, the image is profoundly phallic and profoundly violent, an unacceptable alternative to and consequence of the act of conception in the laboratory. Indeed, in the novel itself (as I shall point out later) the two scenes precisely echo each other. In both cases, there is an association that runs as constant ground-motif through the novel.

Sexuality and birth, imagination and creation are, in this heavily material world, reverse images of death and destruction. Frankenstein and his creature come to represent, in part, an alternative to the violence of sexuality, on the one hand, and to the sheer spirituality of divine creation, on the other. Victor and his Monster hover between, leaning away from the flesh alive (ironically, only to dabble in dead flesh), imitating the divine rather than the human sexual act.

2. *The Overreacher.* The aspiration to divine creative activity (akin to Romantic notions of the poet) places Victor Frankenstein in the tradition of Faustian overreachers. Frankenstein the creator is also Frankenstein the modern Prometheus, full of the great Romantic dream—concretized for a moment in the French Revolution—of a rebirth of mankind. True, Victor is seeking a kind of immortality, but, . . . Mary Shelley works the Faust tradition in an unusual (and, I might again add, secularizing) way by having Victor seek immortality not directly for himself but in the creation of offspring. If we detect the stirrings of selfishness in Victor's desire to have a whole species that would bless him, the text still insists on the profundity of his moral character and the conscious morality of all of his choices save the fatal one. Indeed (by a strategy that other novelists would have to adopt[6]), Frankenstein is removed from direct personal responsibility even for his own ambitions: for the most part he is described as passively consumed by energies larger than himself or as quite literally unconscious and ill when his being conscious might have changed the course of the narrative.

The theme of the overreacher is largely complicated by the evidence that Victor's worst sin is not the creation of the Monster but his refusal to take responsibility for it. It is as though God had withdrawn from his creation. Characteristically, in the secularizing myth, Mary Shelley has imagined the responsibilities of God shifted to mankind. The burden is too great to allow us an easy moral placing of Victor. The theme of the overreacher in this context brings us to the kind of impasse that *Frankenstein* itself reaches in the mutual destruction of creator and created. That is, we see that the ambition is heroic and admirable, yet deadly because humans are incapable of fulfilling their dreams in material reality, or, paradoxically, of bearing the responsibility for them should they succeed.

When Victor refuses to tell Walton the secrets of infusing dead matter with life, we find the fullest justification of the popular anti-intellectual interpretation of the Faustian theme. Early, Victor warns Walton: "Learn from me, if not by my precepts, at least by my example, how dangerous is the acquirement of knowledge, and how much happier that man is who believes his native town to be the world, than he who aspires to become greater than his nature will allow" (p. 48). Victor puts himself forth as a living parable of the dangers of overreaching, yet by the end he refuses to deny the validity of his undertaking and cries, "Yet another may succeed." The novel will not resolve the issue.

3. *Rebellion and Moral Isolation.* Obviously, these aspects of the myth are related to "overreaching." Yet it is important to note that they apply not only to Victor but to the Monster as well, whose ambition is really limited to the longing for domestic affection. Victor himself is not quite imagined as a rebel, except perhaps in his pursuit of alchemical knowledge after his father ridicules him for reading Paracelsus. In any case, unlike the Monster, he does not consciously rebel against authority. Yet, "animated by an almost supernatural enthusiasm," Victor takes up an intellectual pursuit (whence did the "principle of life proceed") that places him outside the traditional Christian world, and that ought to make him, like Adam eating the apple, a rebel against God. The context, however, is quietly un-Christian. Victor speaks in a scientific or at least naturalistic language that assumes a natural material answer to what was once a religious and metaphysical question. "One of the phenomena which had peculiarly attracted my attention was the structure of the human frame, and, indeed, any animal endued with life" (p. 46). And though he concedes that "some miracle might have produced" the discovery, "the stages of the discovery were distinct and probable" (p. 47). Such passages, in their insistence on the merely human credibility of the extraordinary narrative, are characteristic; and although we can recognize here that Victor has stepped over the limits of safe human behavior, and that his success will be blighted, the rhetoric of scientific probability is never seriously undercut in the book.

The moral isolation into which Victor sinks is, in effect, chosen for him by his obsession. Like Raskolnikov plotting murder, like Dimmesdale guilty of adultery, Victor lives with a secret that we understand, without explanation, must be kept from public knowledge. Here the residue of metaphysical shame works its effects, but social and psychological explanations offer themselves immediately. In any case, the activity separates Victor from normal life as fully as a direct act of murder would. He works in a solitary chamber, or cell, "at the top of the house" (p. 50). After analyzing "all the minutiae of causation," he wonders why "among so many men of genius, who had directed their inquiries towards the same science, . . . I alone should be reserved to discover so astonishing a secret" (p. 47). This humble pride echoes the tone of the peaceful Frankenstein household in Geneva; but its association with Victor's obsession with "filthy" work makes even the humility of the scientific quest an act of rebellion against the enclosed harmony of that household.

The Monster's isolation derives not so much from his actions as from his hideousness. Where Victor moves from domestic bliss to the garret, the Monster leaves the garret to seek that bliss. Victor's revolutionary action causes his isolation; the Monster's isolation causes his revolutionary action. "Believe me, Frankenstein," he says, "I was benevolent; my soul glowed with love and humanity; but am I not alone, miserably alone?" (p. 95). Unless Victor creates a companion for him, he warns, he will not again be "virtuous"; "I will glut the maw of death until it be satiated with the blood of your remaining friends" (p. 94).

Despite the apparent moral simplicity of most modern versions of *Frankenstein,* the Frankenstein metaphor implies great ambiguity about where the burden of good and evil rests. Both Victor and the Monster imply resistance to the established order. Lee Sterrenburg points out how the iconography of the monster is clearly connected with Bonaparte and political revolution. In early Romantic literature, of course, rebellion is more likely to be a virtue than a sin, and the Monster makes a strong case against social injustice. Even Walton, though warned by Victor, is instinctively convinced of the justice of the Monster's arguments.

The constantly shifting moral perspective of the narrative results from the fact that each of its major figures—Walton, Victor, the Monster—is at once victimizer and victim; and this tradition is even continued in modern movie versions. In novel and films, any singularity is punished by the community, either by forcing isolation or by literal imprisonment. The three major figures and Felix De Lacey variously challenge the established order and acquire dignity by virtue of the challenge and of the punishment that ensues. Thus the novel, which might be taken as a parable of the necessity of limits in an entirely secular world, may also be taken as a parable of the necessity for revolutionary reprisal (at whatever cost) because of the social and political limits that frustrate the noblest elements of the human spirit.

4. *The Unjust Society.* After the execution of the innocent Justine, Elizabeth Lavenza, the vessel of domestic purity, tells Victor that "men appear to me as monsters thirsting for each other's blood" (p. 88). Even if she retracts immediately ("Yet I am certainly unjust"), the notion that the world of men is itself "monstrous" is a constant motif of the novel. Even in the most conventional of the modern Frankenstein films, the motif emerges when, in the obligatory misty night, the villagers turn out as a maddened lynch mob and transform Frankenstein and the Monster into victims of an overwhelming attack on the castle. In almost every film, the townspeople are almost comically banal, the burgomeisters and gendarmerie officious and totally without sensibility. Absurd though these figures may be (Cedric Hardwicke's wooden arm is transformed in *Dr. Strangelove* and *Young Frankenstein* into appropriately grotesque and comic parodies), they

echo the essentially shallow ambitions and dreams of security that fill the background of the novel.

There the motif is handled subtly enough to make the monstrous problematic. Elizabeth's sense that "men are monsters" recurs in the monster's ingenious hectoring of Victor in a fine Godwinian rational discourse. Moreover, the De Lacey story is a continuing narrative of injustice, on all sides. And in his last speech to Walton, the Monster makes clear once more that his own monstrousness is not really different from that of the world that condemns him. Of Victor, he says:

> For whilst I destroyed his hopes, I did not satisfy my own desires. They were for ever ardent and craving; still I desired love and fellowship, and I was still spurned. Was there no injustice in this? Am I to be thought the only criminal, when all human kind sinned against me? Why do you not hate Felix, who drove his friend from his door with contumely? Why do you not execrate the rustic who sought to destroy the saviour of his child? Nay, these are virtuous and immaculate beings. I, the miserable and the abandoned, am an abortion to be spurned at, and kicked, and trampled on. Even now my blood boils at the recollection of this injustice. (p. 219)

The novel has taught us to distrust the evenhandedness of the law that Victor's father praises before Justine is executed; we understand with the Monster that greed is a commonplace of social activity. Not even the family unit—Frankenstein's and the Monster's ideal—escapes the contamination that almost makes rebellion necessary and that makes Victor's escape to his laboratory from Geneva seem psychologically and socially explicable.

5. *The Defects of Domesticity.* The theme of the overreacher and the rebel—the Promethean theme—is the other side of the theme of ideal domesticity. Percy Shelley, in the preface he wrote—in the guise of Mary—for the 1818 edition, insisted that *Frankenstein*'s chief concern is "the exhibition of the amiableness of domestic affection, and the excellence of universal virtue" (p. 7). Although this assertion is more than a devious defense of a possibly offensive story, it is only part of the truth. . . . Mary Shelley treats "domestic affection" in such a way as to make it possible to read *Frankenstein* as an attack on the very traditions of bourgeois society it purports to be celebrating. Certainly, as we have seen, "the amiableness of domestic affection" does nothing to satisfy Victor Frankenstein's ambitions, or to prevent the monstrous creation; nor, in the tale of the Monster's wanderings, does it extend to anything outside itself to allow for the domestication of the Monster's loving

energies. "Domestic affection" is, in a way, defined by its exclusion of energy and by its resistance to the larger community.

The Monster instinctively believes in the rhetoric of domesticity and the need for community; it is psychologically and dramatically appropriate that he should exhaust himself in the total destruction of ostensibly ideal domesticity when he discovers that he is excluded from it, and that the ideal is false.

The dream of moving beyond the ideal prison of domesticity and the warning that such dreaming is deadly are among the staple patterns of nineteenth-century realistic fiction. Realism tends to remove the spirit, the ideal vision, the angel, from the Miltonic worldscape to the bourgeois household. The final reduction of the religious to the secular is perhaps most evident in the way the home is imagined as a temple. In the idealized Elizabeth Lavenza, in Frankenstein's self-sacrificing mother, in selfless Justine, we have foreshadowings of the Victorian angel in the house. None of the angels survive: the monstrous (which turns out to be at least partly sexual, the creation of human energy exerted on matter) intrudes on the angelic world. The threat of such intrusion is central to the meaning of the Frankenstein metaphor, and brings us to the edge of the conception of civilization and its discontents. Even domestic affection is imprisoning, a weight on individual freedom, and it may be only less disastrous than the energy required to break free. Either way one turns, to a defective society or a rampant individualism, there is no peace without the sort of frustrated compromise Walton makes and that the Victorian novel will insist on.

6. *The Double.* Almost every critic of *Frankenstein* has noted that Victor and his Monster are doubles.[7] The doubleness even enters some of the popular versions and is un-self-consciously accepted by everyone who casually calls the Monster "Frankenstein." The motif of the *Doppelgänger* was certainly in Mary's mind during the writing, as it was part of the Gothic tradition in which she wrote; moreover, it is one with which she would have been intimately connected through Shelley himself, as in "Alastor" and "Epipsychidion." . . . The narrative requires us to see that the doubling extends beyond the two major narrators: Walton is obviously another aspect of Frankenstein, and Clerval yet another; Elizabeth can be paired with Victor's mother, with Justine, and with the unfinished "bride" of the Monster. . . . (In the film *The Bride of Frankenstein* . . . Elsa Lanchester plays both Mary Shelley and the monstrous bride; and in the recent Warhol *Frankenstein,* Victor's wife is also, and accurately, his sister.) Such doublings and triplings, with reverberations in and out of the novel in Mary Shelley's own life and in modern psychological theory, suggest again the instability and ambivalence of the book's "meanings."

They point centrally to the way "Frankenstein" as a modern metaphor implies a conception of the divided self, the creator and his work at odds. The civilized man or woman contains within the self a monstrous, destructive, and self-destructive energy. The angel in the house entails a demon outside it, the Monster leering through the window at the horrified Victor and the murdered Elizabeth. Here, in particular, we can watch the specially secularized versions of traditional mythology. The devil and the angel of the morality play are replaced by a modern pre-Freudian psychology that removes the moral issue from the metaphysical context—the traditional concepts of good and evil—and places it entirely within the self. Morality is, as it were, replaced by schizophrenia. Frankenstein's longing for domesticity is echoed in the Monster's (and in Walton's expression of loneliness in the opening pages); Frankenstein's obsession with science is echoed in the monster's obsession with destruction. The two characters haunt and hunt each other through the novel, each evoking from us sympathy for their sufferings, revulsion from their cruelties.

The echoes force themselves on us with a persistence and intensity that override the mere narrative and even enter into popular versions that are not intrinsically concerned with doubling. The book creates a psychomachia, an internal war that has its own authenticity despite the grotesqueness of the external action. If the characters seem shallow as novelistic figures within the conventions of realism we have come to assume are natural to nineteenth-century fiction, it is partly because they are imagined from the start as incomplete. . . . They can be seen, indeed, as fragments of a mind in conflict with itself, extremes unreconciled, striving to make themselves whole. Ambition and passivity, hate and love, the need to procreate and the need to destroy are seen, in *Frankenstein,* as symbiotic: the destruction of one is, through various narrative strategies, the destruction of the other.

7. *Technology, Entropy, and the Monstrous.* Perhaps the most obvious and continuing application of the word "Frankenstein" in modern society is to technological advances. This is altogether appropriate to Mary Shelley's original conception of the novel since Victor's discovery of the secret of life is fundamentally scientific; and he talks of his "animation" of the Monster's body as a mere trick of technology. Modern science fiction and modern industry are full of such "animated" beings, the products of computer technology; with the discovery of DNA, biologists even seem on the verge of simulating the natural process of creation of life. But both of these developments are part of the same imagination as Mary Shelley gives us with her Monster: that life is not "spirit" but matter imbued with energy, itself another form of matter.

Martin Tropp has noted that "when Mary Shelley gave her intended 'ghost story' a scientific context, she linked the Gothic concept of the double with technology."[8] Her fears of the creation of life by mere mechanisms, Tropp notes, resulted from her awareness that "technology can never be more than a magnified image of the self" (p. 55). And when that self is engaged in a psychomachia, the result can only be large-scale disaster. In a psychic world of the divided self, in a social world in which domesticity and ambition are seen as incompatible poles, the self expressed in technology can only be what our original dictionary definition tells us, "troublesomely uncontrollable, esp. to its creator," i.e., monstrous. The nightmare quality of the novel depends on this projection of the self into an objectively existing, independent reality over which one necessarily loses control as it acts out one's own monstrous passions. Here all the battery of Freudian equipment comes neatly or, perhaps, explosively into play. All the elements of moral isolation, the grubbing in filthy flesh, the obsessed and inhuman energies that went into the creation of the Monster, can be seen acting themselves out in the destruction they really imply—in the incestuous destructiveness of Victor's ostensibly ideal relation to Elizabeth, in the fraternal hostility buried in his love for poor William, in the hatred of his mother implied in his failure to save Justine (who has adopted Mrs. Frankenstein's very way of life). Such implications are explored in a great deal of criticism of the novel. But the point here is that technology becomes the means by which these buried aspects of the self are enacted. The "work or agency" does not rebel against the creator but actually accomplishes what the creator wants. It is only in his "mental consciousness" as D. H. Lawrence would have called it, that the creator does not know what he wants. The uncontrolled technological creation is particularly frightening and obsessively attractive to modern consciousness because it forces a confrontation with our buried selves. It promises to reveal to us our deepest and most powerful desires, and to enact them. The Monster demands our sympathetic engagement while our social consciousness must be an act of will—almost like Walton's when he finds himself irresistibly attracted by the Monster's talk—reject him.

The duality of our relationship to creator and creature is an echo of our relationship to the technology that we worship even as we recognize that it is close to destroying us. Another way to express the duality, in technological terms, is through the idea of entropy. Victor's overreaching is an attempt to create *new* life. He fails to recognize the necessary secular-scientific myth of entropy: that in any closed system, the new energy generated will be less than the energy expended in its creation, and that ultimately the system will run down. It took a great deal of death to make the new life; the making of the Monster is at the expense of all of Victor's immediate world—brother, father, bride, friend. The world of mere matter is both finite and corrupted. Without the incalculable presence of divine spirit, creation can only entail destruction larger than itself. It is, ultimately, this nightmare image that the Monster represents to our culture.

These seven elements of the Frankenstein metaphor are, of course, arbitrarily chosen; each of them has further implications that remain alive for us in the idea of Frankenstein and that have sources in the novel itself. The creator-monster dualism, for example, is also the traditional dualism of mind and body, another form of schizophrenia. The novel has achieved its special place in modern consciousness through its extraordinary resistance to simple resolutions and its almost inexhaustible possibilities of significance.

The echoes of the form and implications of the novel are pervasive through the following century. . . . Unlike many of its Gothic predecessors, for example, *Frankenstein* has a tight structure, a pervasively self-contained set of relevancies. The nightmarish and anarchic energies of its subjects are restrained formally and within a language inherited from a rationalist literary tradition; and the restraint can itself be seen as evidence of the authenticity of the experience. Northrop Frye, for example, identifies the special quality of genuine romance as just such formal tightness as we find in the Chinese-box-like structure of the narratives, and in the echoes and parallels that bind them together. Walton, imagining himself a scientific explorer who will do wonders for mankind, is, of course, a potential Frankenstein. The whole story is told through his letters to his sister, and Frankenstein's narrative to him is both a series of moral connections and a potentially redeeming example. Frankenstein's relation to Walton is similar to the relation of the Monster to Frankenstein himself. . . .

The nightmare into which Victor lapses after he has brought the Monster to life, though full of conventional images, has a resonance that echoes through the book. In that dream Elizabeth is transformed into "the corpse of my dead mother": a "shroud enveloped her form, and I saw the grave-worms crawling in the folds of the flannel." The nightmare vision is followed by the waking vision that conflates remarkably with Elizabeth, Victor's mother, and the Monster. The Monster appears "by the dim and yellow light of the moon," the same light that will later fall on the Monster when Victor sees him after the murder of Elizabeth: "He held up the curtain of the bed; and his eyes, if eyes they may be called, were fixed on me. His jaws opened, and he muttered some inarticulate sound, while a grin wrinkled his cheeks." His "yellow" skin "scarcely covered the work of muscles and arteries beneath" (pp. 52–53). However close to absurdity, such grisly moments are part of the still living metaphor of Frankenstein.

In fact, the Gothic trappings are essential to the book's power. *Franken-stein* is, as I have suggested in describing it as a psychomachia, a psychological novel, but certainly not in the sense that would mean anything to readers of George Eliot or Henry James. Psychological analysis in fiction tends to depend on the assumption that the workings of the human mind, if mysterious seem-ing, are nevertheless comprehensible within the terms of our language. And criticism, attempting to "understand" characters, tends to seek explanations that make the irrational rational. This is the peculiar strength of George Eliot, who did more to develop psychological analysis in English fiction than any English nineteenth-century writer. But the "psychology" of *Frankenstein* is essentially a psychology without explanation. To be sure, the book is full of the appearance of explanation, but its apparent absurdity is precisely its strength. The elaborate formal rhetoric actually tends to disguise the absence of expla-nation. In traditional psychological terms, the explanations for all the crucial events in the novel (except, ironically, the Monster's decision to make evil his good) are totally inadequate. Yet, in the long run, they are entirely credible. It is not possible, for example, to understand why Victor goes to the "filthy" lengths he does in handling corpses to create his Monster; or to explain, first, why he immediately assumes that the Monster is guilty of William's murder; second, why Justine confesses; and third, why, being so sure of her innocence, Victor does not defend her. And why does he fail to credit the Monster's threat to be with him on his wedding night? Obviously, no single set of explanations will do; yet nobody, I think, would have the action work out otherwise. . . . The inadequacy of Mary Shelley's explanatory language is almost precisely the point—rational discourse cannot fully account for the experience, which comes to us with the authenticity of irrational dreams. . . .

Wherever we attempt to find an image of human aspiration in a techno-logical and scientific world, wherever we attempt to find an image for the failure of that aspiration, the metaphor of Frankenstein comes immediately to hand. . . . *Frankenstein* is the perfect myth of the secular, carrying within it all the ambivalences of the life we lead here, of civilization and its discontents, of the mind and the body, of the self and society. It is, indeed, the myth of real-ism. To find another myth, . . . we must look elsewhere if we can.

Notes

1.   This definition is from *Webster's Third New International Dictionary* (1971). *The Ameri-can Heritage Dictionary* (1969) defines it similarly: "Any agency or creation that slips from the control of and ultimately destroys its creator."

2.   James Rieger, ed., *Frankenstein; or, The Modern Prometheus* (the 1818 text) (Indi-anapolis, 1974). All quotations from *Frankenstein* will be from this edition; references will be incorporated into the text.

3.   Joan Baum, of York College, CUNY, has pointed out to me several very interesting parallels between Victor Frankenstein's scientific training and Percy Shelley's.

4.   "Frankenstein and the Tradition of Realism," *Novel* VII, no. 1 (1973): 517–29.

5.   Northrop Frye, *Anatomy of Criticism* (Princeton, 1957), p. 134 and *passim*.

6.   The figure of the passive hero in Scott's novels is described carefully in Alexander Welsh, *The Hero of the Waverly Novels* (New York, 1968). This figure recurs with extraordinary persistence in Victorian fiction, most obviously in Dickens (cf. Oliver Twist himself), and all the way from Dobbin to Daniel Deronda.

7.   See, for example, Masao Miyoshi, *The Divided Self* (New York, 1969), and Robert Kiely, *The Romantic Novel in England* (Cambridge, Mass., 1972), esp. pp. 170–73.

8.   Martin Tropp, *Mary Shelley's Monster* (Boston, 1976), p. 52.

Horror's Twin: Mary Shelley's Monstrous Eve

SANDRA GILBERT

I probed Retrieveless things
My Duplicate—to borrow—
A Haggard Comfort springs

From the belief that Somewhere—
From within the Clutch of Thought—
There dwells one other Creature
Of Heavenly Love—forgot—

I plucked at our Partition
As One should pry the Walls—
Between Himself—and Horror's Twin
Within Opposing Cells—
—Emily Dickinson

Many critics have noticed that *Frankenstein* (1818) is one of the key Romantic "readings" of *Paradise Lost*.[1] Significantly, however, as a woman's reading it is most especially the story of hell: hell as a dark parody of heaven, hell's creations as monstrous imitations of heaven's creations, and hellish femaleness as a grotesque parody of heavenly maleness. But of course the divagations of the parody merely return to and reinforce the fearful reality of the original. For by parodying *Paradise Lost* in what may have begun as a secret, barely conscious attempt to subvert Milton, Shelley ended up telling, too, the central story of *Paradise Lost,* the tale of "what misery th' inabstinence of Eve / Shall bring on men."

Mary Shelley herself claims to have been continually asked "how I . . . came to think of and to dilate upon so very hideous an idea" as that of *Frankenstein,* but it is really not surprising that she should have formulated her anxieties about femaleness in such highly literary terms. For of course the nineteen-year-old girl who wrote *Frankenstein* was no ordinary nineteen-year-old but

This article is reprinted in part from FEMINIST STUDIES, Volume 4, number 2 (Summer 1978): 48–73, by permission of the publisher, FEMINIST STUDIES, Inc., c/o Women's Studies Program. University of Maryland, College Park, MD 20742.

one of England's most notable literary heiresses. Indeed, as "the daughter of two persons of distinguished literary celebrity," and the wife of a third, Mary Wollstonecraft Godwin Shelley was the daughter and later the wife of some of Milton's keenest critics, so that Harold Bloom's useful conceit about the family romance of English literature is simply an accurate description of the reality of her life.[2]

In acknowledgment of this web of literary/familial relationships, critics have traditionally studied *Frankenstein* as an interesting example of Romantic myth-making, a work ancillary to such established Promethean masterpieces as Shelley's *Prometheus Unbound* and Byron's *Manfred.* ("Like almost everything else about [Mary's] life," one such critic remarks, *Frankenstein* "is an instance of genius observed and admired but not shared."[3]) Recently, however, a number of writers have noticed the connection between Mary Shelley's "waking dream" of monster-manufacture and her own experience of awakening sexuality, in particular the "horror story of Maternity" which accompanied her precipitous entrance into what Ellen Moers calls "teen-age motherhood."[4] Clearly they are articulating an increasingly uneasy sense that, despite its male protagonist and its underpinning of "masculine" philosophy, *Frankenstein* is somehow a "woman's book," if only because its author was caught up in such a maelstrom of sexuality at the time she wrote the novel.

In making their case for the work as female fantasy, though, critics like Moers have tended to evade the problems posed by what we must define as *Frankenstein*'s literariness. Yet, despite the weaknesses in those traditional readings of the novel that overlook its intensely sexual materials, it is still undeniably true that Mary Shelley's "ghost story," growing from a Keatsian (or Coleridgean) waking dream, is a Romantic novel about—among other things—Romanticism, as well as a book about books and perhaps, too, about the writers of books. Any theorist of the novel's femaleness and of its significance as, in Moer's phrase, a "birth myth" must therefore confront this self-conscious literariness. For as was only natural in "the daughter of two persons of distinguished literary celebrity," Mary Shelley explained her sexuality to herself in the context of her reading and its powerfully felt implications.

For this orphaned literary heiress, highly charged connections between femaleness and literariness must have been established early, and established specifically in relation to the controversial figure of her dead mother. As we shall see, Mary Wollstonecraft Godwin read her mother's writings over and over again as she was growing up. Perhaps more important, she undoubtedly read most of the reviews of her mother's *Posthumous Works,* reviews in which Mary Wollstonecraft was attacked as a "philosophical wanton" and a monster, while her *Vindication of the Rights of Woman* (1792) was called "A scripture, archly fram'd for propagating w[hore]s."[5] But in any case, to the "philosophical wanton's" daughter, all reading about (or of) her mother's work must have been painful, given her knowledge that that passionate feminist writer had died in giving life to *her,* to bestow upon Wollstonecraft's death from complications of childbirth the melodramatic cast it probably had for the girl herself. That Mary Shelley was conscious, moreover, of a strangely intimate relationship between her feelings toward her dead mother, her romance with a living poet, and her own sense of vocation as a reader and writer is made perfectly clear by her habit of "taking her books to Mary Wollstonecraft's grave in St. Pancras' Churchyard, there," as Muriel Spark puts it, "to pursue her studies in an atmosphere of communion with a mind greater than the second Mrs. Godwin's {and} to meet Shelley in secret."[6]

Her mother's grave: the setting seems an unusually grim, even ghoulish locale for reading, writing, or lovemaking. Yet, to a girl with Mary Shelley's background, literary activities, like sexual ones, must have been primarily extensions of the elaborate, gothic psychodrama of her family history. If her famous diary is largely a compendium of her reading lists and Shelley's that fact does not, therefore, suggest unusual reticence on her part. Rather, it emphasizes the point that for Mary, even more than for most writers, reading a book was often an emotional as well as an intellectual event of considerable magnitude. Especially because she never knew her mother, and because her father seemed so definitively to reject her after her youthful elopement, her principal mode of self-definition—certainly in the early years of her life with Shelley, when she was writing *Frankenstein*—was through reading, and to a lesser extent through writing.

Endlessly studying her mother's works and her father's, Mary Shelley may be said to have "read" her family and to have been related to her reading, for books appear to have functioned as her surrogate parents, pages and words standing in for flesh and blood. That much of her reading was undertaken in Shelley's company, moreover, may also help explain some of this obsessiveness, for Mary's literary inheritance was obviously involved in her very literary romance and marriage. In the years just before she wrote *Frankenstein,* for instance, and those when she was engaged in composing the novel (1816–17), she studied her parents' writings, alone or together with Shelley, like a scholarly detective seeking clues to the significance of some cryptic text.[7]

To be sure, this investigation of the mysteries of literary genealogy was done in a larger context. In these same years, Mary Shelley recorded innumerable readings of contemporary gothic novels, as well as a program of study in English, French, and German literature that would do credit to a modern graduate student. But especially, in 1815, 1816, and 1817, she read the works of Milton: *Paradise Lost* (twice), *Paradise Regained, Comus, Areopagetica, Lycidas.* And what makes the extent of this reading particularly impressive is the fact that in these years, her seventeenth to her twenty-first, Mary Shelley was almost continuously pregnant, "confined," or nursing. At the same time, it is precisely the coincidence of all these disparate activities—her family studies, her initiation into adult sexuality, and her literary self-education—that makes her vision of *Paradise Lost* so significant. For her developing sense of herself as a literary creature and/or creator seems to have been inseparable from her emerging self-definition as daughter, mistress, wife, and mother. Thus she cast her birth myth—her myth of origins—in precisely those cosmogenic terms to which her parents, her husband, and indeed her whole literary culture continually alluded: the terms of *Paradise Lost,* which (as she indicates even on the title page of her novel), she saw as preceding, parallel-ing, and commenting upon the Greek cosmogeny of the Prometheus play her husband had just translated. It is as a female fantasy of sex and reading, then, a gothic psychodrama reflecting Mary Shelley's own sense of what we might call bibliogenesis, that *Frankenstein* is a version of the misogynistic story implicit in *Paradise Lost.*

It would be a mistake to underestimate the significance of *Frankenstein*'s title page, with its allusive subtitle ("The Modern Prometheus") and carefully pointed Miltonic epigraph ("Did I request thee, Maker, from my clay / To mould me man? Did I solicit thee / From darkness to promote me?"). But our first really serious clue to the highly literary nature of this history of a creature born outside history is its author's use of an unusually *evidentiary* technique for conveying the stories of her monster and his maker. Like a literary jigsaw puzzle, a collection of apparently random documents from whose juxtaposi-tion the scholar-detective must infer a meaning, *Frankenstein* consists of three "concentric circles" of narration (Walton's letters, Victor Frankenstein's recital to Walton, and the monster's speech to Frankenstein), within which are embedded pockets of digression containing other miniature narratives (Frankenstein's story, Elizabeth Lavenza's and Justine's stories, Felix's and Agatha's story, Safie's story), etc.[8] As we have noted, reading and assembling documentary evidence, examining it, analyzing it and researching it com-prised for Shelley a crucial if voyeuristic method of exploring origins, explain-ing identity, understanding sexuality. Even more obviously, it was a way of researching and analyzing an emotionally unintelligible text, like *Paradise Lost.* In a sense, then, even before *Paradise Lost* as a central item on the mon-ster's reading list becomes a literal event in *Frankenstein,* the novel's literary structure prepares us to confront Milton's patriarchal epic, both as a sort of research problem and as the framework for a complex system of allusions.

The book's dramatic situations are equally resonant. Like Mary Shelley, who was a puzzled but studious Miltonist, this novel's key characters—Wal-ton, Frankenstein, and the monster—are obsessed with problem-solving. "I shall satiate my ardent curiosity with the sight of a part of the world never before revisited," exclaims the young explorer, Walton, as he embarks like a child "on an expedition of discovery up his native river" (2, letter 1). "While my companions contemplated . . . the magnificent appearance of things," declares Frankenstein, the scientist of sexual ontology, "I delighted in investigating their causes" (22, chap. 2). "Who was I? What was I? Whence did I come?" (113–15, chap. 15) the monster reports wondering, describing endless speculations cast in Miltonic terms. All three, like Shelley herself, appear to be trying to understand their presence in a fallen world, and trying at the same time to define the nature of the lost paradise that must have existed before the fall. But unlike Adam, all three characters seem to have fallen not merely from Eden but from the earth, fallen directly into hell, like Sin, Satan, and—by implication—Eve. Thus their questionings are in some sense female, for they belong in that line of literary women's questionings of the fall into gender which goes back at least to Anne Finch's plaintive "How are we fal'n?" and forward to Sylvia Plath's horrified "I have fallen very far!"[9]

From the first, however, *Frankenstein* answers such neo-Miltonic questions mainly through explicit or implicit allusions to Milton, retelling the story of the fall not so much to protest against it as to clarify its meaning. The parallels between those two Promethean overreachers Walton and Frankenstein, for instance, have always been clear to readers. But that both characters can, therefore, be described (the way Walton describes Frankenstein) as "fallen angels" is not as frequently remarked. Yet Frankenstein himself is perceptive enough to ask Walton "Do you share my madness?" at just the moment when the young explorer remarks Satanically that "One man's life or death were but a small price to pay . . . for the dominion I [wish to] acquire" (13, letter 4). Plainly one fallen angel can recognize another. Alienated from his crew and chronically friendless, Walton tells his sister that he longs for a friend "on the wide ocean," and what he discovers in Victor Frankenstein is the fellowship of hell.

In fact, like the many other secondary narratives Mary Shelley offers in her novel, Walton's story is itself an alternative version of the myth of origins presented in *Paradise Lost*. Writing his ambitious letters home from St. Petersburgh [*sic*], Archangel, and points north, Walton moves like Satan away from the sanctity and sanity represented by his sister, his crew, and the allegorical names of the places he leaves. Like Satan, too, he seems at least in part to be exploring the frozen frontiers of hell in order to attempt a return to heaven, for the "country of eternal light" he envisions at the Pole (1, letter 1) has much in common with Milton's celestial "Fountain of Light" (*PL* 3. 375).[10] Again, like Satan's (and Eve's) aspirations, his ambition has violated a patriarchal decree: his father's "dying injunction" had forbidden him "to embark on a seafaring life." Moreover, even the icy hell where Walton encounters Frankenstein and the monster is Miltonic, for all three of these diabolical wanderers must learn, like the fallen angels of *Paradise Lost*, that "Beyond this flood a frozen Continent / Lies dark and wild . . . / Thither by harpy-footed Furies hal'd, / At certain revolutions all the damn's / Are brought . . . From Beds of raging Fire to starve in Ice" (*PL* 2. 587–600).

Finally, another of Walton's revelations illuminates not only the likeness of his ambitions to Satan's but also the similarity of his anxieties to those of his female author. Speaking of his childhood, he reminds his sister that, because poetry had "lifted [my soul] to heaven," he had become a poet and "for one year lived in a paradise of my own creation." Then he adds ominously that "You are well-acquainted with my failure and how heavily I bore the disappointment" (2–3, letter 1). But of course, as she confesses in her introduction to *Frankenstein*, Mary Shelley, too, had spent her childhood in "waking dreams" of literature; later, both she and her poet-husband hoped she would prove herself "worthy of [her] parentage and enroll [herself] on the page of fame" (xii). In a sense, then, given the Miltonic context in which Walton's story of poetic failure is set, it seems possible that one of the anxious fantasies his narrative helps Mary Shelley covertly examine is the fearful tale of a female fall from a lost paradise of art, speech, and autonomy into a hell of sexuality, silence, and filthy materiality, "A Universe of death, which God by curse / Created evil, for evil only good, / Where all life dies, death lives, and Nature breeds, / Perverse, all monstrous, all prodigious things" (*PL* 2. 622–25).

Walton and his new friend Victor Frankenstein have considerably more in common than a Byronic (or Monk Lewis-ish) Satanism. For one thing, both are orphans, as Frankenstein's monster is and as it turns out all the major and almost all the minor characters in *Frankenstein* are, from Caroline Beaufort and Elizabeth Lavenza to Justine, Felix, Agatha, and Safie. Victor Frankenstein has not always been an orphan, though, and Shelley devotes much space to an account of his family history. Family histories, in fact, especially those of orphans, appear to fascinate her, and wherever she can include one in the narrative she does so with an obsessiveness suggesting that through the disastrous tale of the child who becomes "an orphan and a beggar" she is once more recounting the story of the fall, the expulsion from paradise, and the confrontation of hell. For Milton's Adam and Eve, after all, began as motherless orphans reared (like Shelley herself) by a stern but kindly father-god, and ended as beggars rejected by God (as she was by *God*win when she eloped). Thus Caroline Beaufort's father dies leaving her "an orphan and a beggar," and Elizabeth Lavenza also becomes "an orphan and a beggar"—the phrase is repeated (18, 20, chap.1)—with the disappearance of her father into an Austrian dungeon. And though both girls are rescued by Alphonse Frankenstein, Victor's father, the early alienation from the patriarchal chain-of-being signalled by their orphanhood prefigures the hellish fate in store for them and their family. Later, motherless Safie and fatherless Justine enact similarly ominous anxiety fantasies about the fall of woman into orphanhood and beggary.

Beyond their orphanhood, however, a universal sense of guilt links such diverse figures as Justine, Felix, and Elizabeth, just as it will eventually link Victor, Walton, and the monster. Justine, for instance, irrationally confesses to the murder of little William, though she knows perfectly well she is innocent. Even more irrationally, Elizabeth is reported by Alphonse Frankenstein to have exclaimed "Oh, God! I have murdered my darling child!" after her first sight of the corpse of little William (57, chap. 7). Victor, too, long before he knows that the monster is actually his brother's killer, decides that his "creature" has killed William and that therefore he, the creator, is the "true murderer": "the mere presence of the idea," he notes, is "an irresistible proof of the fact" (60, chap. 7). Complicity in the murder of the child William is, it seems, another crucial component of the Original Sin shared by prominent members of the Frankenstein family.

At the same time, the likenesses among all these characters—the common alienation, the shared guilt, the orphanhood and beggary—imply relationships of redundance between them like the solipsistic relationships among artfully placed mirrors. What reinforces our sense of this hellish solipsism is the barely disguised incest at the heart of a number of the marriages and romances the novel describes. Most notably, Victor Frankenstein is slated to marry his "more than sister" Elizabeth Lavenza, whom he confesses to having always considered "a possession of my own" (21, chap. 1). But the mysterious Mrs. Saville, to whom Walton's letters are addressed, is apparently in some sense *his* more than sister, just as Caroline Beaufort was clearly a "more than" wife, in fact a daughter, to her father's friend Alphonse Frankenstein. Even relationless Justine appears to have a metaphorically incestuous relationship with the Frankensteins, since as their servant she becomes their possession and more than sister, while the female monster Victor half-constructs in Scotland will be a more than sister as well as a mate to the monster, since both have the same parent/creator.

Certainly at least some of this incest-obsession in *Frankenstein* is, as Ellen Moers remarks, the "standard" sensational matter of Romantic novel.[11] Some of it, too, even without the conventions of the gothic thriller, would be a natural subject for an impressionable young woman who had just spent several months in the company of the famously incestuous author of *Manfred*.[12] Nevertheless, the streak of incest that darkens *Frankenstein* probably owes as much to the book's Miltonic framework as it does to Mary Shelley's own life and times. In the Edenic cosiness of their childhood, for instance, Victor and Elizabeth are incestuous as Adam and Eve are, literally incestuous because they have the same creator, and figuratively so because Elizabeth is Victor's pretty plaything, the image of an angelic soul or "epipsyche" created from his own soul just as Eve is created from Adam's rib. Similarly, the incestuous relationships of Satan and Sin, and by implication of Satan and Eve, are mirrored in the incest fantasies of *Frankenstein,* including the disguised but intensely sexual waking dream in which Victor Frankenstein in effect couples with his monster by applying "the instruments of life" to its body and inducing a shudder of response (42, chap. 5). For Milton, and therefore for Mary Shelley, who was trying to understand Milton, incest was an inescapable metaphor for the solipsistic fever of self-awareness that Matthew Arnold was later to call "the dialogue of the mind with itself."[13]

If Victor can be likened to both Adam and Satan, however, who or what is he *really*? Here we are obliged to confront both the moral ambiguity and the symbolic slipperiness which are at the heart of all the characterizations in *Frankenstein.* In fact, it is probably these continual and complex reallocations of meaning, among characters whose histories echo and re-echo each other, that have been so bewildering to critics. Like figures in a dream, all the people in *Frankenstein* have different bodies and somehow, horribly, the same face, or worse—the same two faces. For this reason, as Muriel Spark notes, even the book's subtitle "The Modern Prometheus" is ambiguous, "for although at first Frankenstein is himself the Prometheus, the vital fire-endowing protagonist, the Monster, as soon as he is created, takes on [a different aspect of] the role."[14] Moreover, if we postulate that Mary Shelley is more concerned with Milton than she is with Aeschylus, the intertwining of meanings grows even more confusing, as the monster himself several times points out to Frankenstein, noting "I ought to be thy Adam, but I am rather the fallen angel," (84, chap. 10), then adding elsewhere that "God, in pity, made man beautiful . . . after His own image; but my form is a filthy type of yours. . . . Satan had his companions . . . but I am solitary and abhorred" (115, chap. 15). In other words, not only do Frankenstein and his monster both in one way or another enact the story of Prometheus, each is at one time or another like God (Victor as creator, the monster as his creator's "Master"), like Adam (Victor as innocent child, the monster as primordial "creature"), and like Satan (Victor as tormented overreacher, the monster as vengeful fiend).

What is the reason for this continual duplication and reduplication of roles? Most obviously, perhaps, the dreamlike shifting of fantasy figures from part to part, costume to costume, tells us that we are in fact dealing with the psychodrama or waking dream that Shelley herself suspected she had written. Beyond this, however, we would argue that the fluidity of the narrative's symbolic scheme reinforces in another way the crucial significance of the Miltonic skeleton around which Mary Shelley's hideous progeny took shape. For it becomes increasingly clear as one reads *Frankenstein* with *Paradise Lost* in mind that because the novel's author is such an inveterate student of literature, families, and sexuality, and because she is using her novel as a tool to help her make sense of her reading, *Frankenstein* is ultimately a mock *Paradise Lost* in which both Victor and his monster, together with a number of secondary characters, play all the neo-biblical parts over and over again—all except, it seems at first, the part of Eve. Not just the striking omission of any obvious Eve-figure from this "woman's book" about Milton, but also the barely concealed sexual components of the story as well as our earlier analysis of Milton's bogey should tell us, however, that for Mary Shelley the part of Eve *is* all the parts.

On the surface, Victor seems at first more Adamic than Satanic or Eve-like. His Edenic childhood is an interlude of prelapsarian innocence in which, like

Adam, he is sheltered by his benevolent father as a sensitive plant might be "sheltered by the gardener, from every rougher wind" (19–20, chap. 1). When cherubic Elizabeth Lavenza joins the family, she seems as "heaven-sent" as Milton's Eve, as much Victor's "possession" as Adam's rib is Adam's. Moreover, though he is evidently forbidden almost nothing ("My parents [were not] tyrants . . . but the agents and creators of many delights"), Victor hints to Walton that his deific father, like Adam's and Walton's, did on one occasion arbitrarily forbid him to pursue his interest in arcane knowledge. Indeed, like Eve and Satan, Victor blames his own fall at least in part on his father's apparent arbitrariness. "If . . . my father had taken the pains to explain to me that the principles of Agrippa had been entirely exploded. . . . It is even possible that the train of my ideas would never have received the fatal impulse that led to my ruin" (24–25, chap. 2). And soon after asserting this he even associates an incident in which a tree is struck by Jovian thunder bolts with his feelings about his forbidden studies.

As his researches into the "secrets of nature" become more feverish, however, and as his ambition "to explore unknown powers" grows more intense, Victor begins to metamorphose from Adam to Satan, becoming "as Gods" in his capacity of "bestowing animation upon lifeless matter," laboring like a guilty artist to complete his false creation. Finally, in his conversations with Walton he echoes Milton's fallen angel, and Marlowe's, in his frequently reit-erated confession that "I bore a hell within me which nothing could extin-guish" (72, chap. 8). Indeed, as the "true murderer" of innocence, here cast in the form of the child William, Victor perceives himself as a diabolical creator whose mind has involuntarily "let loose" a monstrous and "filthy demon" in much the same way that Milton's Satan's swelled head produced Sin, the dis-gusting monster he "let loose" upon the world. Watching a "noble war in the sky" that seems almost like an intentional reminder that we are participating in a critical rearrangement of most of the elements of *Paradise Lost,* he explains that "I considered the being whom I had cast among mankind . . . nearly in the light of my own vampire, my own spirit let loose from the grave and forced to destroy all that was dear to me" (61, chap. 7).

Even while it is the final sign and seal of Victor's transformation from Adam to Satan, however, it is perhaps the Sin-ful murder of the child William that is our first overt clue to the real nature of the bewilderingly disguised set of identity shifts and parallels Mary Shelley incorporated into *Frankenstein.* For as we saw earlier, not just Victor and the monster but also Elizabeth and Justine insist upon responsibility for the monster's misdeed. Feeling "as if I had been guilty of a crime" (41, chap. 4) even before one had been committed, Victor responds to the news of William's death with the same self-accusations that torment the two orphans. And, significantly, for all three—as well as for the monster and little William himself—one focal point of both crime and guilt is an image of that other beautiful orphan, Caroline Beaufort Frankenstein. Passing from hand to hand, pocket to pocket, the smiling miniature of Victor's "angel mother" seems a token of some secret fellowship in sin, as does Victor's post-creation nightmare of transforming a lovely, living Elizabeth, with a single magical kiss, into "the corpse of my dead mother" enveloped in a shroud made more horrible by "grave-worms crawling in the folds of the flannel" (42, chap. 5). Though it has been disguised, buried, or miniaturized, femaleness—the gender definition of mothers and daughters, orphans and beggars, monsters and false creators—is at the heart of this apparently masculine book.

Because this is so, it eventually becomes clear that though Victor Frankenstein enacts the roles of Adam and Satan like a child trying on costumes, his single most self-defining act transforms him definitively into Eve. For as both Ellen Moers and Marc Rubenstein have pointed out, after much study of the "cause of generation and life," after locking himself away from ordinary society in the tradition of such agonized mothers as Wollstonecraft's Maria, Eliot's Hetty Sorel, and Hardy's Tess, Victor Frankenstein has a baby.[15] His "pregnancy" and childbirth are obviously manifested by the existence of the paradoxically huge being who emerges from his "workshop of filthy creation," but even the descriptive language of his creation myth is suggestive: "incredible labours," "emaciated with confinement," "a passing trance," "oppressed by a slow fever," "nervous to a painful degree," "exercise and amusement would . . . drive away incipient disease," "the instruments of life" (39–41, chap. 4), etc. And, like Eve's fall into guilty knowledge and painful maternity, Victor's entrance into what Blake would call the realm of "generation" is marked by a recognition of the necessary interdependence of those complementary opposites, sex and death: "To examine the causes of life, we must first have recourse to death," he observes (36, chap. 4), and in his isolated workshop of filthy creation—filthy because obscenely sexual[16]—he collects and arranges materials furnished by "the dissecting room and the slaughterhouse." Pursuing "nature to her hiding places" as Eve does in eating the apple, he learns that "the tremendous secrets of the human frame" are the interlocked secrets of sex and death, although, again like Eve, in his first mad pursuit of knowledge he knows not "eating death." But that his actual orgasmic animation of his monster-child takes place "on a dreary night in November," month of All Souls, short days, and the year's last slide toward death, merely reinforces the Miltonic and Blakean nature of his act of generation.

Even while Victor Frankenstein's self-defining procreation dramatically transforms him into an Eve-figure, however, our recognition of its implications reflects backward upon our sense of Victor-as-Satan and our earlier vision of Victor-as-Adam. Victor-as-Satan, we now realize, was never really the masculine, Byronic Satan of the first book of *Paradise Lost,* but always, instead, the curiously female, outcast Satan who gave birth to Sin. In his Eve-like pride ("I was surprised . . . . that I alone should be reserved to discover so astonishing a secret" [37, chap.4]) this Victor-Satan becomes "dizzy" with his creative powers, so that his monstrous pregnancy, bookishly and solipsistically conceived, reenacts as a terrible bibliogenesis the moment when, in Milton's version, Satan "dizzy swum / In darkness, while [his] head flames thick and fast / Threw forth, till on the left side op'ning wide" and Sin, Death's mother-to-be, appeared like "a Sign / Portentous" (*PL* 2: 753–61). Because he has conceived—or, rather, misconceived—his monstrous offspring by brooding upon the *wrong* books, moreover, this Victor-Satan is paradigmatic, like the falsely creative fallen angel, of the female artist, whose anxiety about her own aesthetic activity is expressed, for instance, in Mary Shelley's deferential introductory phrase about her "hideous progeny," with its plain implication that in her alienated attic workshop of filthy creation she has given birth to a deformed book, a literary abortion or miscarriage. "How [did] I, then a young girl, [come] to think of and to *dilate* upon so very hideous an idea?" is a key (if disingenuous) question she records. But we should not overlook her word play upon *dilate,* just as we should not ignore the anxious pun on the word *author* that is so deeply embedded in *Frankenstein.*

If the adult, Satanic Victor is Eve-like both in his procreation and his anxious creation, even the young, prelapsarian, and Adamic Victor is—to risk a pun—*curiously* female, that is, Eve-like. Innocent and guided by silken threads like a Blakeian lamb in a Godwinian garden, he is consumed by "a fervent longing to penetrate the secrets of nature," a longing which—expressed in his explorations of "vaults and charnelhouses," his guilty observations of "the unhallowed damps of the grave," and his passion to understand "the structure of the human frame"—recalls the criminal female curiosity that led Psyche to lose love by gazing upon its secret face, Eve to insist upon consuming the "intellectual food," and Prometheus's sister-in-law Pandora to open the forbidden box of fleshly ills. But if Victor-Adam is also Victor-Eve, what is the real significance of the episode in which, away at school and cut off from his family, he locks himself into his workshop of filthy creation and gives birth by intellectual parturition to a giant monster? Isn't it precisely at this point in the novel that he discovers he is not Adam but Eve, not Satan but Sin, not male but female? If so, it seems likely that what this crucial section of *Frankenstein* really enacts is the story of Eve's discovery not that she must fall but that, having been created female, she *is* fallen, femaleness and fallenness being essentially synonymous. For what Victor Frankenstein most importantly learns, we must remember, is that he is the "author" of the monster—for him alone is "reserved . . . so astonishing a secret"—and thus it is he who is "the true murderer," he who unleashes Sin and Death upon the world, he who dreams the primal kiss that incestuously kills both "sister" and "mother." Doomed and filthy, is he not, then, Eve instead of Adam? In fact, may not the story of the fall be, for women, the story of the discovery that one is not innocent and Adam (as one had supposed) but Eve, and fallen? Perhaps this is what Freud's cruel but metaphorically accurate concept of penis-envy really means: the girl-child's surprised discovery that she is female, hence fallen, inadequate. Certainly the almost grotesquely anxious self-analysis implicit in Victor Frankenstein's (and Mary Shelley's) multiform relationships to Eve, Adam, God, and Satan suggest as much.

The discovery that one is fallen is in a sense a discovery that one is a monster, a murderer, a being gnawed by "the never-dying worm" (72, chap. 8) and therefore capable of any horror, including but not limited to sex, death, and filthy literary creation. More, the discovery that one is fallen—self-divided, murderous, material—is the discovery that one has released a "vampire" upon the world, "forced to destroy all that [is] dear" (61, chap. 7). For this reason—because *Frankenstein* is a story of woman's fall told by, as it were, an apparently docile daughter to a censorious "father"—the monster's narrative is embedded at the heart of the novel like the secret of the fall itself. Indeed, just as Frankenstein's workshop, with its maddening, riddling answers to cosmic questions is a hidden but commanding attic womb/room where the young artist-scientist murders to dissect and to recreate, so the murderous monster's single, carefully guarded narrative commands and controls Mary Shelley's novel. Delivered at the top of Mont Blanc—like the North Pole one of the Shelley family's metaphors for the indifferently powerful source of creation and destruction—it is the story of deformed Geraldine in "Christabel," the story of the dead-alive crew in "The Ancient Mariner," the story of Eve in *Paradise Lost,* and of her degraded double Sin—all secondary or female characters to whom male authors have imperiously denied any chance of self-explanation.[17] At the same time the monster's narrative is a philosophical meditation on what it means to be born without a "soul" or a history, as well as an exploration of what it feels like to be a "filthy mass that move[s] and talk[s]," a thing, an other, a creature of the second sex. In fact, though it tends to be ignored by critics (and film-makers), whose emphasis has always fallen upon Frankenstein himself as the archetypal mad scientist, the drastic shift in point of view that the nameless monster's monologue represents probably constitutes *Frankenstein*'s most striking technical *tour de force,* just as the monster's bitter self-revelations are Mary Shelley's most impressive and original achievement.[18]

Like Victor Frankenstein, his author and superficially better self, the monster enacts in turn the roles of Adam and Satan, and even eventually hints at a sort of digression into the role of God. Like Adam, he recalls a time of primordial innocence, his days and nights in "the forest near Ingolstadt," where he ate berries, learned about heat and cold, and perceived "the boundaries of the radiant roof of light which canopied me" (88, chap. 11). Almost too quickly, however, he metamorphoses into an outcast and Satanic figure, hiding in a shepherd's hut which seems to him "as exquisite . . . a retreat as Pandemonium . . . after . . . the lake of fire" (90, chap. 11). Later, when he secretly sets up housekeeping behind the De Laceys' pigpen, his wistful observations of the loving though exiled family and their pastoral abode ("Happy, happy earth! Fit habitation for gods . . ." [100, chap. 12]) recall

Satan's mingled jealousy and admiration of that "happy rural seat of various view" where Adam and Eve are emparadised by God and Milton (*PL* 4. 247). Eventually, burning the cottage and murdering William in demonic rage, he seems to become entirely Satanic: "I, like the arch-fiend, bore a hell within me" (121, chap. 16); "Inflamed by pain, I vowed eternal hatred . . . to all mankind" (126, chap. 16). At the same time, in his assertion of power over his "author," his mental conception of another creature (a female monster), and his implicit dream of founding a new, vegetarian race somewhere in "the vast wilds of South America" (131, chap. 17), he temporarily enacts the part of a God, a creator, a master, albeit a failed one.

As the monster himself points out, however, each of these Miltonic roles is a Procrustean bed into which he simply cannot fit. Where, for instance, Victor Frankenstein's childhood really was Edenic, the monster's anxious infancy is isolated and ignorant, rather than insulated or innocent, so that his groping arrival at self-consciousness—"I was a poor, helpless, miserable wretch; I knew and could distinguish nothing; but feeling pain invade me on all sides, I sat down and wept" (87–88, chap. 11)—is a fiercely subversive parody of Adam's exuberant "all things smil'd, / With fragrance and with joy my heart o'erflowed. / Myself I then perus'd, and Limb by Limb / Survey'd, and sometimes went, and sometimes ran / With supple joints, as lively vigor led" (*PL* 8. 265–69). Similarly, the monster's attempts at speech ("Sometimes I wished to express my sensations in my own mode, but the uncouth and inarticulate sounds which broke from me frightened me into silence again" [88, chap. 11]) parody and subvert Adam's ("To speak I tri'd, and forthwith spake, / My Tongue obey'd and readily could name / Whate'er I saw" [*PL* 8. 271–72]). And of course the monster's anxiety and confusion ("What was I? The question again recurred to be answered only with groans" [106, chap. 13]) are a dark version of Adam's wondering bliss ("who I was, or where, or from what cause, / [I] Knew not . . . [But I] feel that I am happier than I know" [*PL* 8. 270–71, 282]).

Similarly, though his uncontrollable rage, his alienation, even his enormous size and superhuman physical strength bring him closer to Satan than he was to Adam, the monster puzzles over discrepancies between his situation and the fallen angel's. Though he is, for example, "in bulk as huge / As whom the Fables name of monstrous size, / *Titanian,* or *Earth-born,* that warr'd on *Jove,*" and though, indeed, he is fated to war like Prometheus on Jovean Frankenstein, this demon/monster has fallen from no heaven, exercised no power of choice, and been endowed with no companions in evil. "I found myself similar yet at the same time strangely unlike to the beings concerning whom I read and to whose conversation I was a listener," he tells Frankenstein, describing his schooldays in the De Lacey pigpen (113, chap. 15). And, interestingly, his remark might well have been made by Mary Shelley herself, that "devout but nearly silent listener" (xiv) to masculine conversations who, like her hideous progeny, "continually studied and exercised [her] mind upon" such "histories" as *Paradise Lost,* Plutarch's *Lives,* and *The Sorrows of Werter* [*sic*] "whilst [her] friends were employed in their ordinary occupations" (112, chap. 15).

In fact, it is his intellectual similarity to his authoress (rather than his "author") which first suggests that Victor Frankenstein's male monster may really be a female in disguise. Certainly the books which educate him— *Werter,* Plutarch's *Lives,* and *Paradise Lost*—are not only books Mary had herself read in 1815, the year before she wrote *Frankenstein,* but they also typify just the literary categories she thought it necessary to study: the contemporary novel of sensibility, the serious history of Western civilization, and the highly cultivated epic poem. As specific works, moreover, each must have seemed to her to embody lessons a female author (or monster) must learn about a male-dominated society. Werter's story, says the monster—and he seems to be speaking for Mary Shelley—taught him about "gentle and domestic manners," and about "lofty sentiments . . . which had for their object something out of self." It functioned, in other words, as a sort of Romantic conduct book. In addition, it served as an introduction to the virtues of the proto-Byronic "Man of Feeling," for, admiring Werter and never mentioning Lotte, the monster explains to Victor that "I thought Werter himself a more divine being than I had ever . . . imagined," adding, in a line whose female irony about male self-dramatization must surely have been intentional, "I wept [his extinction] without precisely understanding it" (113, chap. 15).

If *Werter* introduces the monster to female modes of domesticity and self-abnegation, as well as to the unattainable glamour of male heroism, Plutarch's *Lives* teaches him all the masculine intricacies of that history which his anomalous birth has denied him. Mary Shelley, excluding herself from the household of the second Mrs. Godwin and studying family as well as literary history on her mother's grave, must, again, have found in her own experience an appropriate model for the plight of a monster who, as James Rieger notes, is especially characterized by "his unique knowledge of what it is like to be born free of history."[19] In terms of the disguised story the novel tells, however, this monster is not unique at all, but representative, as Shelley may have suspected she herself was. For, as Jane Austen has Catherine Morland suggest in *Northanger Abbey,* what is woman but man without a history, at least without the sort of history related in Plutarch's *Lives?* "History, real solemn history, I cannot be interested in," Catherine declares ". . . the men all so good for nothing, and hardly any women at all—it is very tiresome" (*NA* 1, chap. 14).

But of course the third and most crucial book referred to in the miniature *Bildungsroman* of the monster's narrative is *Paradise Lost,* an epic myth of origins which is of major importance to him, as it is to Mary Shelley, precisely because, unlike Plutarch, it does provide him with what appears to be a personal history. And again, even the need for such a history draws Shelley's monster closer not only to the realistically ignorant female defined by Jane Austen but also to the archetypal female defined by John Milton. For, like the monster, like Catherine Morland, and like Mary Shelley herself, Eve is characterized by her "unique knowledge of what it is like to be born free of history," even though as the "Mother of Mankind" she is fated to "make" history. It is to Adam, after all, that God and His angels grant explanatory visions of past and future. At such moments of high historical colloquy Eve tends to excuse herself with "lowliness Majestic" (before the fall) or (after the fall) she is magically put to sleep, calmed like a frightened animal "with gentle Dreams . . . and all her spirits compos'd / To meek submission" (*PL* 12. 595–96).

Nevertheless, one of the most notable facts about the monster's ceaselessly anxious study of *Paradise Lost* is his failure even to mention Eve. As an insistently male monster, on the surface of his palimpsestic narrative he appears to be absorbed in Milton's epic only because, as Percy Shelley wrote in the preface to *Frankenstein* that he drafted for his wife, *Paradise Lost* "most especially" conveys "the truth of the elementary principles of human nature," and conveys that truth in the dynamic tensions developed among its male characters, Adam, Satan, and God (xvii). Yet not only the monster's uniquely ahistorical birth, his literary anxieties, and the sense his readings (like Mary's) foster that he must have been parented, if at all, by *books*; not only all these facts and traits but also his shuddering sense of deformity, his nauseating size, his namelessness, and his orphaned, motherless isolation link him with Eve and with Eve's double, Sin. Indeed, at several points in his impassioned analysis of Milton's story he seems almost on the verge of saying so, as he examines the disjunctions among Adam, Satan, and himself:

> Like Adam, I was apparently united by no link to any other being in existence; but his state was far different from mine in every other respect. He had come forth from the hands of God a perfect creature, happy and prosperous, guided by the especial care of his Creator; he was allowed to converse with and acquire knowledge from beings of a superior nature, but I was wretched, helpless, and alone. Many times I considered Satan as the fitter emblem of my condition, for often, like him, when I viewed the bliss of my protectors, the bitter gall of envy rose within me. . . . Accursed creator! Why did you form a monster so hideous that even *you* turned from me in disgust? God, in pity, made man beautiful and alluring, after his own image; but my form is a filthy type of yours, more horrid even from the very resemblance. Satan had his companions, fellow devils, to admire and encourage him, but I am solitary and abhorred. [114–15, chap. 15]

It is Eve, after all, who languishes helpless and alone, while Adam converses with superior beings, and it is Eve in whom the Satanically bitter gall of envy rises, causing her to eat the apple in the hope of adding "what wants / In Female Sex." It is Eve, moreover, to whom deathly isolation is threatened should Adam reject her, an isolation more terrible even than Satan's alienation from heaven. And finally it is Eve whose body, like her mind, is said by Milton to resemble "less / His Image who made both, and less [to express] / The character of that Dominion giv'n / O'er other Creatures . . ." (PL 8. 543–46). In fact, to a sexually anxious reader, Eve's body might, like Sin's, seem "horrid even from [its] very resemblance" to her husband's, a "filthy" or obscene version of the human form divine.[20]

As we argued earlier, women have seen themselves (because they have been seen) as monstrous, vile, degraded creatures, second-comers, and emblems of filthy materiality, even though they have also been traditionally defined as superior spiritual beings, angels, better halves. "Woman [is] a temple built over a sewer," said the Church father Tertullian, and Milton seems to see Eve as both temple and sewer, echoing that patristic misogyny.[21] Mary Shelley's conscious or unconscious awareness of the monster woman implicit in the angel woman is perhaps clearest in the revisionary scene where her monster, as if taking his cue from Eve in *Paradise Lost* book 4, first catches sight of his own image: "I had admired the perfect forms of my cottagers . . . but how was I terrified when I viewed myself in a transparent pool. At first I started back, unable to believe that it was indeed I who was reflected in the mirror; and when I became fully convinced that I was in reality the monster that I am, I was filled with the bitterest sensations of despondence and mortification" (98–99, chap. 12). In one sense, this is a corrective to Milton's blindness about Eve. Having been created second, inferior, a mere rib, how could she possibly, this passage implies, have seemed anything but monstrous to herself? In another sense, however, the scene supplements Milton's description of Eve's introduction to herself, for ironically, though her reflection in "the clear / Smooth Lake" is as beautiful as the monster's is ugly, the self-absorption that Eve's confessed passion for her own image signals is plainly meant by Milton to seem morally ugly, a hint of her potential for spiritual deformity: "There I had fixt / Mine eyes till now, and pin'd with vain desire, / Had not a voice thus warn'd me, What thou seest, / What there thou seest fair Creature is thyself . . ." (PL 4. 465–68).

The figurative monstrosity of female narcissism is a subtle deformity, however, in comparison with the literal monstrosity many women are taught to see as characteristic of their own bodies. Adrienne Rich's twentieth-century description of "a woman in the shape of a monster / A monster in the shape of a woman" is merely the latest in a long line of monstrous female self-definitions that includes the fearful images in Djuna Barne's *Book of Repulsive Women,* Denise Levertov's "a white sweating bull of a poet told us / our cunts are ugly" and Sylvia Plath's "old yellow" self of the poem "In Plaster."[22] Animal and misshapen, these emblems of self-loathing must have descended at least in part from the distended body of Mary Shelley's darkly parodic Eve/Sin/Monster, whose enormity betokens not only the enormity of Victor Frankenstein's crime and Satan's bulk but also the distentions or deformities of pregnancy and the Swiftian sexual nausea expressed in Lemuel Gulliver's horrified description of a Brobdignagian breast, a passage Mary Shelley no doubt studied along with the rest of *Gulliver's Travels* when she read the book in 1816, shortly before beginning *Frankenstein*.[23]

At the same time, just as surely as Eve's moral deformity is symbolized by the monster's physical malformation, the monster's physical ugliness represents his social illegitimacy, his bastardy, his namelessness. Bitchy and dastardly as Shakespeare's Edmund, whose association with filthy femaleness is established not only by his devotion to the material/maternal goddess Nature but also by his interlocking affairs with those filthy females Goneril and Regan, Mary Shelley's monster has also been "got" in a "dark and vicious place." Indeed, in his vile illegitimacy he seems to incarnate that bestial "unnameable" place. And significantly, he is himself as nameless as a woman is in patriarchal society, as nameless as unmarried, illegitimately pregnant Mary Wollstonecraft Godwin may have felt herself to be at the time she wrote *Frankenstein*.

"This nameless mode of naming the unnameable is rather good," Mary commented when she learned that it was the custom at early dramatizations of *Frankenstein* to place a blank line next to the name of the actor who played the part of the monster.[24] But her pleased surprise was disingenuous, for the problem of names and their connection with social legitimacy had been forced into her consciousness all her life. As the sister of illegitimate and therefore nameless Fanny Imlay, for instance, she knew what bastardy meant, and she knew it too as the mother of a premature and illegitimate baby girl who died at the age of two weeks without ever having been given a name. Of course, when Fanny dramatically excised her name from her suicide note Mary learned more about the significance even of insignificant names. And as the stepsister of Mary Jane Clairmont, who defined herself as the "creature" of Lord Byron and changed her name for a while with astonishing frequency (from Mary Jane to Jane to Clara to Claire), Mary knew about the importance of names too. Perhaps most of all, though, Mary's sense of the fearful significance of legitimate and illegitimate names must have been formed by her awareness that her own name, Mary Wollstonecraft Godwin, was absolutely identical with the name of the mother who had died in giving birth to *her*. Since this was so, she may have speculated, perhaps her own monstrosity, her murderous illegitimacy, consisted in her being—like Victor Frankenstein's creation—a reanimation of the dead, a sort of galvanized corpse ironically arisen from what should have been "the cradle of life."

This implicit fantasy of the reanimation of the dead in the monstrous and nameless body of the living returns us, however, to the matter of the monster's Satanic, Sin-ful and Eve-like moral deformity. For of course the crimes that the monster commits once he has accepted the world's definition of him as little more than a namelessly "filthy mass" all reinforce his connection with Milton's unholy trinity of Sin, Eve/Satan, and Death. The child of two authors (Victor Frankenstein and Mary Shelley) whose mothers have been stolen away by death, this motherless monster is after all made from dead bodies, from loathsome parts found around cemeteries, so that it seems only "natural" for him to continue the Blakeian cycle of despair his birth began, by bringing further death into the world. And of course he brings death, in the central actions of the novel: death to the childish innocence of little William (whose name is that of Mary Shelley's father, her half-brother, and her son, so that one can hardly decide to which male relative she may have been alluding); death to the faith and truth of allegorically named Justine; death to the legitimate artistry of the Shelleyan poet Clerval; and death to the ladylike selflessness of angelic Elizabeth. Is he acting, in his vile way, for Mary Shelley, whose elegant femininity seemed, in view of her books, so incongruous to the poet Beddoes and to literary Lord Dillon? "She has no business to be a woman by her books," noted Beddoes. And "your writing and your manners are not in accordance," Dillon told Mary herself. "I should have thought of you—if I had only read you—that you were a sort of . . . Sybil, outpouringly enthusiastic . . . but you are cool, quiet and feminine to the last degree. . . . Explain this to me."[25]

Could Mary's coolness have been made possible by the heat of her monster's rage, the strain of her decorous silence eased by the demonic abandon of her nameless monster's ritual fire dance around the cottage of his rejecting "Protectors"? Does Mary's cadaverous creature want to bring more death into the world because he has failed—like those other awful females, Eve and Sin—to win the compassion of that blind and curiously Miltonic old man, the Godlike musical patriarch De Lacey? Significantly, he is clinging to the blind man's knees, begging for recognition and help—"Do not you desert me in the hour of trial!"—when Felix, the son of the house, appears like the felicitous hero he is, and, says the monster, "with supernatural force [he] tore me from his father . . . in a transport of fury, he dashed me to the ground and struck me violently with a stick . . . my heart sank within me as with bitter sickness" (119, chap. 15). Despite everything we have been told about the monster's physical vileness, Felix's rage seems excessive in terms of the novel's overt story. But as an action in the covert plot—the tale of the blind rejection of women by misogynistic/Miltonic patriarchy—it is inevitable and appropriate. Even more psychologically appropriate is the fact that having been so definitively rejected by a world of fathers, the monster takes his revenge, first by murdering William, a male child who invokes his father's name ("My papa is a syndic—he is M. Frankenstein—he will punish you") and then by beginning a doomed search for a maternal, female principle in the harsh society that has created him.

In this connection, it begins to be plain that Eve's—and the monster's—motherlessness must have had extraordinary cultural and personal significance for Mary Shelley. "We think back through our mothers if we are women," wrote Virginia Woolf in *A Room of One's Own*.[26] But of course one of the most dramatic emblems of Eve's alienation from the masculine garden in which she finds herself is her motherlessness. Because she is made in the image of a man who is himself made in the image of a male creator, her unprecedented femininity seems merely a defective masculinity, a deformity like the monster's inhuman body.[27] In fact, as we saw, the only maternal model in *Paradise Lost* is the terrifying figure of Sin. (That Eve's punishment for *her* sin is the doom of agonized maternity—the doom of painfully becoming no longer herself but "Mother of Human Race"—appears therefore to seal the grim parallel.) But all these powerful symbols would be bound to take on personal weight and darkness for Shelley, whose only real "mother" was a tombstone—or a shelf of books—and who, like all orphans, must have feared that she had been deliberately deserted by her dead parent, or that, if she was a monster, then her hidden, underground mother must have been one too.

For all these reasons, then, the monster's attitude toward the possibility (or impossibility) of finding a mother is unusually conflicted and complex. At first, horrified by what he knows of the only "mother" he has ever had—Victor Frankenstein—he regards his parentage with loathing. Characteristically, he learns the specific details of his "conception" and "birth" (as Mary Shelley may have learned of hers) through reading, for Victor has kept a journal which records "that series of disgusting circumstances" leading "to the production of [the monster's] . . . loathsome person."[28] Later, however, the ill-fated miniature of Caroline Beaufort Frankenstein, Victor's "angel mother," momentarily "attract[s]" him. In fact, he claims it is because he is "forever deprived of the delights that such beautiful creatures could bestow" that he resolves to implicate Justine in the murder of William. His reproachful explanation is curious, though ("The crime had its source in her; be hers the punishment"), as is the sinister rape fantasy he enacts by the side of the sleeping orphan ("Awake, fairest, thy lover is near—he who would give his life but to obtain one look of affection from thine eyes" [127–28, chap. 16]). Clearly feelings of rage, terror, and sexual nausea, as well as idealizing sentiments, accrete for Mary and the monster around the maternal female image, a fact which explains the later climactic wedding-night murder of apparently innocent Elizabeth. In this fierce, Miltonic world, *Frankenstein* says, the angel woman and the monster woman alike must die, if they are not dead already. And what is to be feared above all else is the reanimation of the dead, specifically of the maternal dead. Perhaps that is why a significant pun is embedded in the crucial birth scene ("It was on a dreary night of November") that, according to Mary Shelley, rose "unbidden" from her imagination. Looking at the "demoniacal corpse to which I had so miserably given life," Victor remarks that "A *mummy* again endued with animation could not be so hideous as that wretch" (43, chap. 5). For a similarly horrific (and equally punning) statement of sexual nausea, one would have to go back to Donne's "Loves

Alchymie" with its urgent, misogynistic imperative: "Hope not for minde in women; at their best / Sweetnesse and wit, they are but / *Mummy* possest."

Interestingly, the literary group at Villa Diodati received a packet of books containing, among other poems, Samuel Taylor Coleridge's recently published "Christabel," shortly before Mary had her monster-dream and began her ghost story. More influential than "Loves Alchymie"—a poem Mary may or may not have read—"Christabel"'s vision of femaleness must have been embodied for the author of *Frankenstein* not only in the witch Geraldine's withered side and consequent self-loathing ("Ah! What a stricken look was hers!") but also in her anxiety about the ghost of Christabel's dead mother ("Off, wandering mother! Peak and pine!") and in Christabel's "Woe is me / She died the hour that I was born." But even without Donne's puns or Coleridge's Romanticized male definition of deathly maternity, Mary Shelley would have absorbed a keen sense of the agony of female sexuality, and specifically of the perils of motherhood, not just from *Paradise Lost* and from her own mother's fearfully exemplary fate but also from Wollstonecraft's almost prophetically anxious writings.

Maria, or the Wrongs of Woman (1797), which Mary read in 1814 (and possibly in 1815) is about, among other "wrongs," Maria's search for her lost child, her fears that "she" (for the fantasied child is a daughter) may have been murdered by her unscrupulous father, and her attempts to reconcile herself to the child's death. In a suicide scene that Wollstonecraft drafted shortly before her own death, as her daughter must have known, Maria swallows laudanum: "her soul was calm . . . nothing remained but an eager longing . . . to fly . . . from this hell of disappointment. Still her eyes closed not. . . . Her murdered child again appeared to her . . . [But] 'Surely it is better to die with me, than to enter on life without a mother's care!'"[29] Plainly, *Frankenstein's* pained ambivalence toward mothers and mummies is in some sense a response to *Maria's* agonized reaching—from beyond the grave, it may have seemed—toward a daughter. "Off, wandering mother! Peak and pine!" It is no wonder if Coleridge's poem gave Mary Wollstonecraft Godwin Shelley bad dreams, no wonder if she saw Milton's "Mother of Human Race" as a sorrowful monster.

Though *Frankenstein* itself began with a Coleridgean and Miltonic nightmare of filthy creation that reached its nadir in the monster's revelation of filthy femaleness, Mary Shelley, like Victor Frankenstein himself, evidently needed to distance such monstrous secrets. Sinful, motherless Eve and sinnedagainst, daughterless Maria, both paradigms of woman's helpless alienation in a male society, briefly emerge from the sea of male heroes and villains in which they have almost been lost, but the ice soon closes over their heads again, just as it closes around those two insane figure-skaters, Victor Frankenstein and his hideous offspring. Moving outward from the central "birth myth" to the icy perimeter on which the novel began, we find ourselves caught up once more in Walton's naive polar journey, where Frankenstein and his monster reappear as two embattled grotesques, distant and archetypal figures solipstically drifting away from each other on separate icebergs. In Walton's scheme of things, they look again like God and Adam, Satanically conceived. But now, with our more nearly complete understanding of the bewildered and bewildering perspective Mary Shelley adopted as "Milton's daughter," we see that they were Eve and Eve all along.

Nevertheless, though Shelley did manage to still the monster's suffering and Frankenstein's and her own by transporting all three from the fires of filthy creation back to the ice and silence of the Pole, she was never entirely to abandon the sublimated rage her monster-self enacted, and never to abandon, either, the metaphysical ambitions *Frankenstein* incarnated. In *The Last Man* she introduced, as Spark points out, "a new, inhuman protagonist," PLAGUE (the name is almost always spelled entirely in capitals), who is characterized as female and who sees to it that "disaster is no longer the property of the individual but of the entire human race."[30] And of course PLAGUE's story is the one that Mary claims to have found in the Sibyl's cave, a tale of a literally female monster that was merely foreshadowed by the more subdued narrative of "The Modern Prometheus."

Interestingly, PLAGUE's story ends with a vision of last things, a vision of judgment and of paradise nihilistically restored that balances *Frankenstein*'s vision of first things. With all of humanity wiped out by the monster PLAGUE, just as the entire Frankenstein family was destroyed by Victor's monster, Lionel Verney, the narrator, goes to Rome, that cradle of patriarchal civilization whose ruins had seemed so majestically emblematic to both Byron and Shelley. But where Mary's husband had written of the great city in a kind of ecstasy, his widow has her disinherited "last man" wander lawlessly about empty Rome until finally he resolves, finding "parts of a manuscript . . . scattered about," that "I also will write a book . . . [but] for whom to read?—to whom dedicated? And then with silly flourish (what so capricious and childish as despair?) I wrote,

DEDICATION
TO THE ILLUSTRIOUS DEAD
SHADOWS, ARISE, AND READ YOUR FALL!
BEHOLD THE HISTORY OF THE LAST MAN.[31]

His hostile, ironic, literary gesture illuminates not only his own career but his author's. For the annihilation of history may well be the final revenge of the monster who has been denied a true place in history: the moral is one that Mary Shelley's first hideous progeny, like Milton's Eve, seems to have understood from the beginning.

Notes

Epigraph: Emily Dickinson, *The Poems of Emily Dickinson,* ed. Thomas Johnson, 3 vols. (Cambridge, Mass.: Harvard University Press, Belknap Press, 1955), p. 532.

1.   See, for instance, Harold Bloom, "Afterword," *Frankenstein* (New York and Toronto: New American Library, 1965), p. 214.

2.   Author's introduction to *Frankenstein* (1817; Toronto, New York, London: Bantam Pathfinder Edition, 1967), p. xi. Hereafter page references to this edition will follow quotations, and we will also include chapter references for those using other editions. For a basic discussion of the "family romance" of literature, see Harold Bloom, *The Anxiety of Influence* (New York: Oxford University Press, 1973).

3.   Robert Kiely, *The Romantic Novel in England* (Cambridge, Mass.: Harvard University Press, 1972), p. 161.

4.   Ellen Moers, *Literary Women,* (New York: Doubleday, 1976), pp. 95–97.

5.   See Ralph Wardle, *Mary Wollstonecraft* (Lincoln, Neb.: University of Nebraska Press, 1951), p. 322, for more detailed discussion of these attacks on Wollstonecraft.

6.   Muriel Spark, *Child of Light* (Hodleigh, Essex: Tower Bridge Publications, 1951), p. 21.

7.   See *Mary Shelley's Journal,* ed. Frederick L. Jones (Norman, Okla.: University of Oklahoma Press, 1947), esp. pp. 32–33, 47–49, 71–73, and 88–90, for the reading lists themselves. Besides reading Wollstonecraft's *Maria,* her *Vindication of the Rights of Woman,* and three or four other books, together with Godwin's *Political Justice* and his *Caleb Williams,* Mary Shelley also read parodies and criticisms of her parents' works in these years, including a book she calls *Anti-Jacobin Poetry,* which may well have included that periodical's vicious attack on Wollstonecraft. To read, for her, was not just to read her family, but to read *about* her family.

8.   Marc A. Rubenstein suggests that throughout the novel "the act of observation, passive in one sense, becomes covertly and symbolically active in another: the observed scene becomes an enclosing, even womb-like container in which a story is variously developed, preserved, and passed on. Storytelling becomes a vicarious pregnancy." "'My Accursed Origin': The Search for the Mother in *Frankenstein,*" *Studies in Romanticism* 15, no. 2 (Spring 1976): 173.

9.   See Anne Finch, "The Introduction," in *The Poems of Anne Countess of Winchilsea,* ed. Myra Reynolds (Chicago: University of Chicago Press, 1903), pp. 4–6, and Sylvia Plath, "The Moon and the Yew Tree," in *Ariel* (New York: Harper & Row, 1966), p. 41.

10.   Speaking of the hyperborean metaphor in *Frankenstein,* Rubenstein argues that Walton (and Mary Shelley) seek "the fantasied mother locked within the ice . . . the maternal Paradise beyond the frozen north," and asks us to consider the pun implicit in the later meeting of Frankenstein and his monster on the *mer* (or *Mère*) *de Glace* at Chamonix (Rubenstein "'My Accursed Origin,'" pp. 175–76).

11.   See Moers, *Literary Women,* pp. 99.

12.   In that summer of 1816 Byron had in fact just fled England in an attempt to escape the repercussions of his scandalous affair with his half-sister Augusta Leigh, the real-life "Astarte."

13.   Matthew Arnold, "Preface" to *Poems* (London: Longman, Brown, Green & Longmans, 1853).

14.   Spark, *Child of Light,* p. 134.

15.   See Moers, *Literary Women,* "Female Gothic"; also Rubenstein, "'My Accursed Origin,'" pp. 165–66.

16.   The *OED* gives "obscenity" and "moral defilement" among its definitions of "filth."

17.   The monster's narrative also strikingly echoes Jemima's narrative in Mary Wollstonecraft's posthumously published novel, *Maria, or The Wrongs of Woman.* See *Maria* (1798; rpt. New York: Norton, 1975), pp. 52–69.

18.   Harold Bloom does note that "the monster is . . . Mary Shelley's finest invention, and his narrative . . . forms the highest achievement of the novel." ("Afterword" to *Frankenstein*, p. 219.)

19.   James Rieger, "Introduction" to *Frankenstein, (the 1818 Text)* (Indianapolis: Bobbs-Merrill, 1974), p. xxx.

20.   In Western culture the notion that femaleness is a deformity or obscenity can be traced back at least as far as Aristotle, who asserted that "we should look upon the female state as being as it were a deformity, though one which occurs in the ordinary course of nature." (*The Generation of Animals*, trans. A. L. Peck [London: Heinemann, 1943], p. 461.) For a brief but illuminating discussion of his theories see Katharine M. Rogers, *The Troublesome Helpmate*.

21.   See Simone de Beauvoir, *The Second Sex* (New York: Knopf, 1953), p. 156.

22.   Adrienne Rich, "Planetarium," in *Poems: Selected and New* (New York: Norton, 1974), pp. 146–48; Djuna Barnes, *The Book of Repulsive Women* (1915; rpt. Berkeley, Calif., 1976); Denise Levertov, "Hypocrite Women," *O Taste & See* (New York: New Directions, 1965); Sylvia Plath, "In Plaster," *Crossing the Water* (New York: Harper & Row, 1971), p. 16.

23.   See *Mary Shelley's Journal*, p. 73.

24.   Elizabeth Nitchie, *Mary Shelley* (New Brunswick, N.J.: Rutgers University Press, 1953), p. 219.

25.   See Spark, *Child of Light*, pp. 192–93.

26.   Virginia Woolf, *A Room of One's Own* (New York: Harcourt Brace, 1929), p. 79.

27.   In "The Deluge at Norderney," Isak Dinesen tells the story of Calypso, niece of Count Seraphina Von Platen, a philosopher who "disliked and mistrusted everything female" and whose "idea of paradise was . . . a long row of lovely young boys . . . singing his poems to his music." "Annihilated" by her uncle's misogyny, Calypso plans to chop off her own breasts with a "sharp hatchet." See *Seven Gothic Tales* (New York: Modern Library, 1934), pp. 43–51.

28.   Marc Rubenstein speculates that as a girl Shelley may actually have read (and been affected by) the correspondence that passed between her parents around the time that she was conceived.

29.   Mary Wollstonecraft, *Maria; or The Wrongs of Woman* (New York: Norton, 1975), p. 152.

30.   Spark, *Child of Light*, p. 205.

31.   Mary Shelley, *The Last Man* (Lincoln: University of Nebraska Press, 1965), p. 339.

A Feminist Critique of Science

Anne K. Mellor

From a feminist perspective, the most significant dimension of the relationship between literature and science is the degree to which both enterprises are grounded on the use of metaphor and image. The explanatory models of science, like the plots of literary works, depend on linguistic structures which are shaped by metaphor and metonymy. When Francis Bacon announced, "I am come in very truth leading to you Nature with all her children to bind her to your service and make her your slave,"[1] he identified the pursuit of modern science with the practice of sexual politics: the aggressive, virile male scientist legitimately captures and enslaves a fertile but passive female nature. Mary Shelley was one of the first to comprehend and illustrate the dangers inherent in the use of such gendered metaphors in the seventeenth-century scientific revolution.

Mary Shelley grounded her fiction of the scientist who creates a monster he cannot control upon an extensive understanding of the most recent scientific developments of her day. She thereby initiated a new literary genre, what we now call science fiction. More important, she used this knowledge both to analyze and to criticize the more dangerous implications of the scientific method and its practical results. Implicitly, she contrasted what she considered to be "good" science—the detailed and reverent description of the workings of nature—to what she considered "bad" science, the hubristic manipulation of the elemental forces of nature to serve man's private ends. In *Frankenstein, or the Modern Prometheus,* she illustrated the potential evils of scientific hubris and at the same time challenged the cultural biases inherent in any conception of science and the scientific method that rested on a gendered definition of nature as female. To appreciate the full significance of Mary Shelley's feminist critique of modern science, we must look first at the particular scientific research upon which her novel is based.

The works of three of the most famous scientists of the late eighteenth and early nineteenth century—Humphry Davy, Erasmus Darwin, and Luigi

From Anne K. Mellor, *Mary Shelley: Her Life, Her Fiction, Her Monsters* (New York: Routledge, Chapman and Hall, Inc., 1988), 89–114. Reprinted with permission.

Galvani—together with the teachings of two of their ardent disciples, Adam Walker and Percy Shelley, were crucial to Mary Shelley's understanding of science and the scientific enterprise. While no scientist herself (her description of Victor Frankenstein's laboratory is both vague and naive; apparently Victor does all his experiments in a small attic room by the light of a single candle), Mary Shelley nonetheless had a sound grasp of the concepts and implications of some of the most important scientific work of her day. In her novel, she distinguishes between that scientific research which attempts to describe accurately the functionings of the physical universe and that which attempts to *control* or *change* the universe through human intervention. Implicitly she celebrates the former, which she associates most closely with the work of Erasmus Darwin, while she calls attention to the dangers inherent in the latter, found in the work of Davy and Galvani.

Victor Frankenstein chooses to work within the newly established field of chemical physiology. He must thus become familiar with recent experiments in the disparate fields of biology, chemistry, mechanics, physics, and medicine. The need to span the entire range of science is stressed by Victor's chemistry professor, M. Waldman, who observes that "a man would make but a very sorry chemist, if he attended to that department of human knowledge alone" and therefore advises Victor "to apply to every branch of natural philosophy, including mathematics" (43).

After his misguided and self-taught education in the theories of the medieval and renaissance alchemists, Cornelius Agrippa, Paracelsus, and Albertus Magnus, Victor Frankenstein at the age of fifteen was suddenly forced to acknowledge the ignorance of these pseudo-scientists when, during a storm in the Jura, lightning struck a nearby tree:

> As I stood at the door, on a sudden I beheld a stream of fire issue from an old and beautiful oak, which stood about twenty yards from our house; and so soon as the dazzling light vanished, the oak had disappeared, and nothing remained but a blasted stump. When we visited it the next morning, we found the tree shattered in a singular manner. It was not splintered by the shock, but entirely reduced to thin ribbands of wood. I never beheld any thing so utterly destroyed.
>
> The catastrophe of this tree excited my extreme astonishment; and I eagerly inquired of my father the nature and origin of thunder and lightning. He replied, "Electricity;" describing at the same time the various effects of that power. He constructed a small electrical machine, and exhibited a few experiments; he made also a kite, with a wire and string, which drew down that fluid from the clouds.
>
> This last stroke completed the overthrow of Cornelius Agrippa, Albertus Magnus, and Paracelsus, who had so long reigned the lords of my imagination. (35)

In the first edition of *Frankenstein,* Victor is introduced to the recent discoveries of Benjamin Franklin by his father, but in her later edition, Mary

Shelley remembered that she had described the Frankenstein family as not interested in science.[2] In 1831, she therefore attributed Victor Franken-stein's initiation into legitimate science to an unnamed "man of great research in natural philosophy" who happened to join them and who then "entered on the explanation of a theory which he had formed on the sub-ject of electricity and galvanism" which Victor found at once "new and astonishing" (238–39).

At the University of Ingolstadt, Victor enrolls in courses in chemistry and natural philosophy, inspired by the charismatic M. Waldman. Both Vic-tor's and Professor Waldman's concept of the nature and utility of chemistry is based upon Humphry Davy's famous introductory lecture to a course in chemistry given at the newly founded Royal Institution on January 21, 1802.[3] Immediately published as *A Discourse, Introductory to a Course of Lectures on Chemistry* in 1802, this pamphlet is probably the work that Mary Shelley read on Monday, October 28, 1816, just before working on her story of Frankenstein. Her Journal entry for that day notes: "Read the Introduction to Sir H. Davy's 'Chemistry'; write."[4] Waldman's enthusiasm for and descrip-tion of the benefits to be derived from the study of chemistry seem to be based on Davy's remarks, as does Victor Frankenstein's belief that chemistry might discover the secret of life itself.

Davy probably also supplied Mary Shelley's description of the first parts of Professor Waldman's introductory lecture on chemistry—the opening "recapitulation of the history of chemistry and the various improvements made by different men of learning," followed by "a cursory view of the pre-sent state of the sciences," an explanation of several key terms and a few preparatory experiments—which comes not so much from Davy's *Discourse* as from Davy's later textbook, *Elements of Chemical Philosophy* (London: 1812), which Percy Shelley ordered from Thomas Hookham on July 29, 1812.[5] This may be the book listed in Mary's *Journal* on October 29, 30, November 2 and 4, 1816, when Mary notes that she "read Davy's 'Chemistry' with Shelley" and then alone. A glance at the table of contents of this book would have given Mary Shelley the outline she attributes to Waldman: a brief history, fol-lowed by a discussion of several specific elements and compounds, with descriptions of experiments performed. The contents probably also provided her with the description of the lectures on natural philosophy that Victor Frankenstein attended in Geneva while still living at home:

> Some accident prevented my attending these lectures until the course was nearly finished. The lecture being therefore one of the last was entirely incomprehensi-ble to me. The professor discoursed with the greatest fluency of potassium and boron, of sulphates and oxyds, terms to which I could affix no idea. (36)

Davy's *Discourse,* written to attract and keep a large audience, provided Mary Shelley with both the content and the rhetoric of Waldman's final panegyric on modern chemistry, the panegyric that directly inspired Victor Frankenstein's subsequent research. Waldman concludes

> the ancient teachers of this science . . . promised impossibilities, and performed nothing. The modern masters promise very little; they know that metals cannot be transmuted, and that the elixir of life is a chimera. But these philosophers, whose hands seem only made to dabble in dirt, and their eyes to pour over the microscope or crucible, have indeed performed miracles. They penetrate into the recesses of nature, and shew how she works in her hiding places. They ascend into the heavens; they have discovered how the blood circulates, and the nature of the air we breathe. They have acquired new and almost unlimited powers; they can command the thunders of heaven, mimic the earthquake, and even mock the invisible world with its own shadows. (42)

Davy, in his celebration of the powers of chemistry, asserted that "the phenomena of combustion, of the solution of different substances in water, of the agencies of fire; the production of rain, hail, and snow, and the conversion of dead matter into living matter by vegetable organs, all belong to chemistry."[6] Arguing that chemistry is the basis of many other sciences, including mechanics, natural history, minerology, astronomy, medicine, physiology, pharmacy, botany, and zoology, Davy insists

> how dependent, in fact, upon chemical processes are the nourishment and growth of organized beings; their various alterations of form, their constant production of new substances; and, finally, their death and decomposition, in which nature seems to take unto herself those elements and constituent principles which, for a while, she had lent to a superior agent as the organs and instruments of the spirit of life! (8)

After detailing the necessity of chemical knowledge to all the operations of common life, including agriculture, metal-working, bleaching, dyeing, leather-tanning, and glass and porcelain-making, Davy paints an idealistic portrait of the contemporary chemist, who is informed by a science that

> has given to him an acquaintance with the different relations of the parts of the external world; and more than that, it has bestowed upon him powers which may be almost called creative; which have enabled him to modify and change the beings surrounding him, and by his experiments to interrogate nature with power, not simply as a scholar, passive and seeking only to understand her operations, but rather as a master, active with his own instruments. (16)

Here Davy introduces the very distinction Mary Shelley wishes to draw between the scholar-scientist who seeks only to understand the operations of nature and the master-scientist who actively interferes with nature. But where Davy obviously prefers the master-scientist, Mary Shelley sees his instrumental activities as profoundly dangerous.

Davy sketches a visionary picture of the master-scientist of the future, who will discover the still unknown general laws of chemistry:

> For who would not be ambitious of becoming acquainted with the most pro-found secrets of nature: of ascertaining her hidden operations; and of exhibit-ing to men that system of knowledge which relates so intimately to their own physical and moral constitution? (17)

These are Waldman's chemists, who "penetrate into the recesses of nature and show how she works in her hiding places." The result of such activity, Davy confidently predicts, will be a more harmonious, cooperative and healthy society. True, he cautions, "We do not look to distant ages, or amuse ourselves with brilliant, though delusive dreams, concerning the infinite improveability of man, the annihilation of labour, disease, and even death" (22). But even as Davy apparently disavows the very dreams that would inspire Victor Frankenstein, Davy claims for his own project something very similar: "we reason by analogy from simple facts. We consider only a state of human progression arising out of its present condition. We look for a time that we may reasonably expect, for a bright day of which we already behold the dawn" (22). Having boldly stated the social benefits to be derived from the pursuit of chemistry, Davy concludes his *Discourse* by insisting on the per-sonal gratifications to be gained: "it may destroy diseases of the imagination, owing to too deep a sensibility; and it may attach the affections to objects, permanent, important, and intimately related to the interests of the human species," even as it militates against the "influence of terms connected only with feeling" and encourages instead a rational contemplation of the universal order of things (26).

In fairness to Davy, he had a great deal of skepticism about the very field that Victor Frankenstein chooses to enter, the new field of chemical physi-ology. Commenting on just the kind of enterprise Frankenstein pursues, the search for the principle of life itself, Davy warns

> if the connexion of chemistry with physiology has given rise to some visionary and seductive theories; yet even this circumstance has been useful to the public mind in exciting it by doubt, and in leading it to new investigations. A reproach, to a certain degree just, has been thrown upon those doctrines known by the name of the chemical physiology; for in the applications of them speculative philosophers have been guided rather by the analogies of words than of facts. Instead of slowly endeavouring to lift up the veil concealing the wonderful phenomena of living nature: full of ardent imaginations, they have vainly and presumptuously attempted to tear it asunder. (9)

Mary Shelley clearly heeded Davy's words, for she presents Victor Franken-stein as the embodiment of hubris, of that Satanic or Faustian presumption which blasphemously attempts to tear asunder the sacred mysteries of nature.

But in contrast to Davy, Mary Shelley doubted whether chemistry itself—insofar as it involved a "mastery" of nature—produced only good. She substituted for Davy's complacent image of the happy scientist living in harmony with both his community and himself the frightening image of the alienated scientist working in feverish isolation, cut off both physically and emotionally from his family, friends, and society. Victor Frankenstein's scientific researches not only bring him no physical or emotional pleasure but they also leave him, as Laura Crouch has observed, disgusted with the entire scientific enterprise.[7] Detached from a respect for nature and from a strong sense of moral responsibility for the products of one's research, purely objective thought and scientific experimentation can and do produce monsters. Mary Shelley might have found trenchant support for her view in Humphry Davy's praise for one of chemistry's most notable achievements: "in leading to the discovery of gunpowder, [chemistry] has changed the institutions of society, and rendered war more independent of brutal strength, less personal, and less barbarous."[8]

In contrast to Davy, Erasmus Darwin provided Mary Shelley with a powerful example of what she considered to be "good" science, a careful observation and celebration of the operations of all-creating nature with no attempt radically to change either the way nature works or the institutions of society. Percy Shelley acknowledged the impact of Darwin's work on his wife's novel when he began the Preface to the 1818 edition of *Frankenstein* with the assertion that "the event on which this fiction is founded has been supposed, by Dr. Darwin, and some of the physiological writers of Germany, as not of impossible occurrence" (1). To what suppositions, theories and experiments, by Erasmus Darwin and others, did Percy Shelley allude? Mary Shelley, in her Preface to the 1831 edition, referred to an admittedly apocryphal account of one of Dr. Darwin's experiments. During one of Byron's and Shelley's many long conversations to which she was "a devout but nearly silent listener," Mary Shelley recalled

> various philosophical doctrines were discussed, and among others the nature of the principle of life, and whether there was any probability of its ever being discovered and communicated. They talked of the experiments of Dr. Darwin (I speak not of what the doctor really did or said that he did, but, as more to my purpose, of what was then spoken of as having been done by him), who preserved a piece of vermicelli in a glass case till by some extraordinary means it began to move with voluntary motion. (227)

Even though Mary Shelley acknowledges that the animated piece of vermicelli is probably a fiction, Erasmus Darwin's theories have significant bearing on her purpose in *Frankenstein*.

Erasmus Darwin was most famous for his work on evolution and the growth of plants, and it is this work that Mary Shelley affirmed. Victor

Frankenstein is portrayed as a direct opponent of Darwin's teachings, as an anti-evolutionist and a parodic proponent of an erroneous "Creation Theory." The basic tenets of Erasmus Darwin's theories appear in his major works, *The Botanic Garden* (1789, 1791), *Zoonomia: or the Laws of Organic Life* (1793), *Phytologia* (1800), and *The Temple of Nature* (1803).[9]

Eighteenth-century scientists generally conceived of the universe as a perfect, static world created by divine fiat at a single moment in time. This universe, metaphorically represented as a Great Chain of Being, manifested myriad and minute gradations between species, but these relationships were regarded as fixed and permanent, incapable of change. As Linnaeus, the great eighteenth-century classifier of all known plant-life, insisted in his *Systema Naturae* (1735), "Nullae species novae"—no new species can come into existence in a divinely ordered, perfect world. But by the end of the eighteenth century, under pressure from Herschel's new discoveries in astronomy, Cuvier's paleontological researches, William Smith's studies of fossil stratification, Sprengel's work on botanical cross-breeding and fertilization, and observations made with an increasingly powerful microscope, together with a more diffuse Leibnizian "natural theology" that emphasized the study of nature's varied interactions with human populations, the orthodox Linnaean concept of an immutable physical universe had begun to weaken.[10]

Erasmus Darwin was inspired by the researches of Comte du Buffon, the "father of evolution,"[11] who in his huge *Histoire naturelle* (44 volumes, 1749–1804) had described myriads of flora and fauna and interspersed among them comments on the progressive "degeneration" of life forms from earlier and more uniform species, often caused by environmental or climatic changes. Although he adhered to the concept of the *scala naturae* and the immutability of species, Buffon was the first to discuss seriously such central evolutionary problems as the origin of the earth, the extinction of species, the theory of "common descent," and in particular the reproductive isolation between two incipient species.[12] Significantly, it was to Buffon that Victor Frankenstein turned after his early disillusionment with the alchemists, and Buffon whom he "still read . . . with delight" (36).[13] But it was Erasmus Darwin who for English readers first synthesized and popularized the concept of the evolution of species through natural selection over millions of years.

By 1803, Darwin had accepted, on the basis of shell and fossil remains in the highest geological strata, that the earth must once have been covered by water and hence that all life began in the sea. As Darwin concisely summed up this theory of evolution in *The Temple of Nature:*

> Cold gills aquatic form respiring lungs,
> And sounds aerial flow from slimy tongues.
> *(The Temple of Nature,* I, 11. 333–34)

Meditating on the suggestion that mankind descended from "one family of monkeys on the banks of the Mediterranean" that learned to use and strengthen the thumb muscle and "by this improved use of the sense of touch . . . acquired clear ideas, and gradually became men," Darwin speculated

> perhaps all the productions of nature are in their progress to greater perfection! an idea countenanced by modern discoveries and deductions concerning the progressive formation of the solid parts of the terraqueous globe, and consonant to the dignity of the Creator of all things. (*The Temple of Nature*, 54)

Darwin further suggested that such evolutionary improvement is the direct result of sexual selection:

> A great want of one part of the animal world has consisted in the desire of the exclusive possession of the females; and these have acquired weapons to bombard each other for this purpose, as the very thick, shield-like, horny skin on the shoulder of the boar is a defense only against animals of his own species, who strike obliquely upwards, nor are his tushes for other purposes, except to defend himself, as he is not naturally a carnivorous animal. So the horns of the stag are not sharp to offend his adversary, but are branched for the purpose of parrying or receiving the thrusts of horns similar to his own, and have therefore been formed for the purpose of combating other stags for the exclusive possession of the females; who are observed, like the ladies in the times of chivalry, to attend the car of the victor. (*Zoonomia*, 1794, I:503)

Erasmus Darwin anticipated the modern discovery of mutations, noting in his discussion of monstrous births that monstrosities, or mutations, may be inherited: "Many of these enormities of shape are propagated, and continued as a variety at least, if not as a new species of animal. I have seen a breed of cats with an additional claw on every foot" (*Zoonomia*, 1794, I:501).

In relation to *Frankenstein*, Erasmus Darwin's most significant evolutionary concept was that of the hierarchy of reproduction. Again and again, in *Zoonomia*, in *The Botanic Garden*, in *Phytologia*, and in *The Temple of Nature*, Darwin insisted that sexual reproduction is at a higher evolutionary level than hermaphroditic or solitary paternal propagation. As Darwin commented in his Note on "Reproduction" for *The Temple of Nature*:

> The microscopic productions of spontaneous vitality, and the next most inferior kinds of vegetables and animals, propagate by solitary generation only; as the buds and bulbs raised immediately from seeds, the lycoperdon tuber, with probably many other fungi, and the polypus, volvox, and taenia. Those of the next order propagate both by solitary and sexual reproduction, as those buds and bulbs which produce flowers as well as other buds or bulbs; and the aphis and probably many other insects. Whence it appears, that many of those vegetables and animals, which are produced by solitary generation, gradually become more perfect, and at length produce a sexual progeny.

A third order of organic nature consists of hermaphrodite vegetables and animals, as in those flowers which have anthers and stigmas in the same corol; and in many insects, as leeches, snails, and worms; and perhaps all those reptiles which have no bones . . .

And, lastly, the most perfect orders of animals are propagated by sexual intercourse only. (36–37)

This concept of the superiority of sexual reproduction over paternal propagation was so important to Darwin that it forced him to revise radically his concept of reproduction in his third, "corrected" edition of *Zoonomia* (1801). In 1794, Darwin had argued, following Aristotle, that male plants produce the seed or embryon, while female plants provide only nourishment to this seed, and by analogy, had contended "that the mother does not contribute to the formation of the living ens in normal generation, but is necessary only for supplying its nutriment and oxigenation" (*Zoonomia*, 1794, I:487). He then attributed all monstrous births to the female, saying that deformities result from either excessive or insufficient nourishment in the egg or uterus (497). But by 1801, Darwin's observations of both animal and vegetable hybrids had convinced him that both male and female seeds contribute to the innate characteristics of the species:

We suppose that redundant fibrils with formative appetencies are produced by, or detached from, various parts of the male animal, and circulating in his blood, are secreted by adapted glands, and constitute the seminal fluid, and that redundant molecules with formative aptitudes or propensities are produced by, or detached from, various parts of the female, and circulating in her blood, are secreted by adapted glands, and form a reservoir in the ovary; and finally that when these formative fibrils, and formative molecules, become mixed together in the uterus, that they coalesce or embrace each other, and form different parts of the new embryon, as in the cicatricula of the impregnated egg. (*Zoonomia*, 1801, II:296–97)

Interestingly, while Darwin no longer attributed monstrous births to uterine deficiencies or excesses, he continued to hold the *male imagination* at the moment of conception responsible for determining both the sex of the child and its outstanding traits:

I conclude, that the act of generation cannot exist without being accompanied with ideas, and that a man must have at this time either a general idea of his own male form, or of the forms of his male organs; or of an idea of the female form, or of her organs, and that this marks the sex, and the peculiar resemblances of the child to either parent. (*Zoonomia*, 1794, I:524; 1801, II:270)

The impact of the female imagination on the seed in utero is less intense, argued Darwin, because its impact lasts for a longer period of time and is therefore more diffuse. It follows that Darwin, in 1801, attributed the bulk of monstrous births to the *male* imagination, a point of obvious relevance to *Frankenstein.*

Erasmus Darwin's work on what he called "the economy of vegetation" has equally significant implications for *Frankenstein.* Darwin's comments in *Phytologia* on plant nutrition, photosynthesis, and the use of fertilizers and manures for the first time put gardening and agriculture on a sound scientific basis.[14] Again and again in this lengthy work, Darwin emphasized the necessity to recycle all organic matter. His discussion of manures runs to over twenty-five thousand words and is by far the largest section in this book on plant agriculture. The best manures, Darwin reports, are

> organic matters, which . . . will by their slow solution in or near the surface of the earth supply the nutritive sap-juice to vegetables. Hence all kinds of animal and vegetable substances, which will undergo a digestive process, or spontaneous solution, as the flesh, fat, skin, and bones of animals; with their secretions of bile, saliva, mucus; and their excretions of urine and ordure; and also the fruit, meal, oil, leaves, wood of vegetables, when properly decomposed on or beneath the soil, supply the most nutritive food to plants. (*Phytologia,* 254)

He urges every gardener and farmer to save all organic matter for manure, "even the parings of his nails and the clippings of his hair" (*Phytologia,* 241), and further urges the heretical notion that the soil nourished by the decomposition of human bodies ought to be available for growing plants. Mourning the waste of rich soil in churchyards and cemeteries, he argues that

> proper burial grounds should be consecrated out of towns, and divided into two compartments, the earth from one of which, saturated with animal decomposition, should be taken away once in ten or twenty years, for the purposes of agriculture; and sand or clay, or less fertile soil, brought into its place. (*Phytologia,* 243)

Mary Shelley was introduced to Darwin's thought by her father and again by her husband, who had been heavily influenced by Darwin's evolutionary theories while writing *Queen Mab.* Percy Shelley first read *The Botanic Garden* in July 1811, as he reported to Thomas Hogg, and in December 1812 he ordered Darwin's *Zoonomia* and *The Temple of Nature* from the booksellers Hookham and Rickman.[15] The extensive impact of Darwin's theories of evolution and agriculture and his poetic language on Percy Shelley's Notes to *Queen Mab,* "The Cloud," "The Sensitive Plant," and *Prometheus Unbound* has been well-documented.[16] It is clear that Darwin's work remained vivid in Percy Shelley's mind throughout the period in which Mary Shelley was writing *Frankenstein,* as his prefatory comment to the novel testifies.

Reading *Frankenstein* in the context of Darwin's writings, we can see that Mary Shelley directly pitted Victor Frankenstein, that modern Prometheus, against those gradual evolutionary processes of nature so well described by

Darwin. Rather than letting organic life-forms evolve slowly over thousands of years according to natural processes of sexual selection, Victor Frankenstein wants to originate a new life-form quickly, by chemical means. In his Faustian thirst for knowledge and power, he dreams:

> Life and death appeared to me ideal bounds, which I should first break through, and pour a torrent of light into our dark world. A new species would bless me as its creator and source; many happy and excellent natures would owe their being to me. (49)

Significantly, in his attempt to create a new species, Victor Frankenstein substitutes solitary paternal propagation for sexual reproduction. He thus reverses the evolutionary ladder described by Darwin. And he engages in a concept of science that Mary Shelley deplores, the notion that science should manipulate and control rather than describe, understand, and revere nature.

Moreover, his male imagination at the moment of conception is fevered and unhealthy; as he tells Walton:

> Every night I was oppressed by a slow fever, and I became nervous to a most painful degree; . . . my voice became broken, my trembling hands almost refused to accomplish their task; I became as timid as a love-sick girl, and alternate tremor and passionate ardour took the place of wholesome sensation and regulated ambition. (51)

Under such mental circumstances, according to Darwin, the resultant creation could only be a monster. Frankenstein has further increased the monstrousness of his creation by making a form that is both larger and more simple than a normal human being. As he acknowledges to Walton:

> As the minuteness of the parts formed a great hindrance to my speed, I resolved, contrary to my first intention, to make the being of a gigantic stature; that is to say, about eight feet in height, and proportionably large. (49)

Darwin had observed that nature moves "from simpler things to more compound" (*Phytologia*, 118). In defying nature's law, Victor Frankenstein has created not a more perfect species but a degenerate one.

In his attempt to override evolutionary development and to create a new species sui generis, Victor Frankenstein becomes a parodic perpetrator of the orthodox creationist theory. On the one hand, he denies the unique power of God to create organic life. At the same time he confirms the capacity of a single creator to originate a new species. By playing God, Victor Frankenstein has simultaneously upheld the creationist theory and parodied it by creating only a monster. In both ways, Victor Frankenstein has blasphemed against the natural order of things. He has moved down rather than up the evolutionary ladder—he has constructed his creature not only out of dead human organs collected from charnel houses and dissecting rooms, but also out of animal organs and tissue removed from "the slaughter-house" (50). And he has denied the natural mode of human reproduction through sexual procreation.

Victor Frankenstein has perverted evolutionary progress in yet another way. Despite Darwin's insistence that all dead organic matter—including decomposing human flesh and bones found in cemeteries—ought to be saved for compost-heaps and manure, Victor Frankenstein has removed human flesh and bones from graveyards. And he has done so not in order to generate life organically through what Darwin described as "spontaneous animal vitality in microscopic cells"[17] but to create a new life-form through chemical engineering. Frankenstein has thus disrupted the natural life-cycle. His attempt to speed up the transformation of decomposing organic material into new life-forms by artificial means has violated the rhythms of nature.

Mary Shelley's novel implicitly invokes Darwin's theory of gradual evolutionary progress to suggest both the error and the evils of Victor Frankenstein's bad science. The genuine improvement of the species can result only from the conjunction of male and female sexuality. In trying to have a baby without a woman, Victor Frankenstein has failed to give his child the mothering and nurturance it requires, the very nourishment that Darwin explicitly equated with the female sex. Victor Frankenstein's failure to embrace his smiling creature with parental love, his horrified rejection of his own creation, spells out the narrative consequences of solitary paternal propagation. But even if Frankenstein had been able to provide his child with a mother's care, he could not have prevented his creature's ostracism and misery. At best he would have produced another Elephant Man, a benevolent but still much maligned freak.

It is therefore a triple failure of imagination that curses Victor Frankenstein. First, by not imaginatively identifying with his creation, Frankenstein fails to give his child the parental support he owes to it. He thereby condemns his creature to become what others behold, a monster. Secondly, by imagining that the male can produce a higher form of evolutionary species by lateral propagation than by sexual procreation, Frankenstein defines his own imagination as profoundly anti-evolutionary and thus anti-progressive. Third, in assuming that he can create a perfect species by chemical means, Frankenstein defies a central tenet of Romantic poetic ideology: that the creative imagination must work spontaneously, unconsciously, and above all organically, creating forms that are themselves organic heterocosms.

Moreover, in trying to create a human being as God created Adam, out of earth and water, all at once, Victor Frankenstein robs nature of something more than fertilizer. "On a dreary night in November, . . . with an anxiety that almost amounted to agony," Victor Frankenstein infused "a spark of being into the lifeless thing that lay" at his feet (52). At that moment Victor Frankenstein became the modern Prometheus, stealing fire from the gods to give to mankind and thus overthrowing the established, sacred order of both earth and heaven. At that moment he transgressed against nature.

To understand the full implications of Frankenstein's transgression, we must recognize that Victor Frankenstein's stolen "spark of life" is not merely fire; it is also that recently discovered caloric fluid called electricity. Victor's interest in legitimate science was first aroused by the sight of lightning destroying an old oak tree; it was then that he learned of the existence of electricity and replicated Benjamin Franklin's experiment with kite and key to draw down "that fluid from the clouds" (35). In the late eighteenth century, there was widespread interest in the implications of Franklin's and Father Beccaria's discoveries of the existence of atmospheric mechanical electricity generated through such machines as the Leyden jar. Many scientists explored the possibility, derived from Newton's concept of the ether as an elastic medium capable of transmitting the pulsations of light, heat, gravitation, magnetism, and electricity, that the atmosphere was filled with a thin fluid that was positively and negatively charged and that could be identified as a single animating principle appearing under multiple guises (as light, heat, magnetism, etc.). Erasmus Darwin speculated that the perpetual necessity of the human organism for breathing suggests that "the spirit of animation itself is thus acquired from the atmosphere, which if it be supposed to be finer or more subtle than the electric matter, could not long be retained in our bodies and must therefore require perpetual renovation" (*Botanic Garden*, Canto I, Note to line 401). And Humphry Davy, founder of the field of electrochemistry, first gave authoritative voice to a theory of matter as electrically charged atoms. In his *Elements of Chemical Philosophy*, Davy argued:

Whether matter consists of indivisible corpuscles, or physical points endowed with attraction and repulsion, still the same conclusions may be formed concerning the powers by which they act, and the quantities in which they combine; and the powers seem capable of being measured by their electrical relations, and the quantities on which they act of being expressed by numbers. (57)

He further concluded that

it is evident that the particles of matter must have space between them; and . . . it is a probable inference that [each body's] own particles are possessed of motion; but . . . the motion, if it exists, must be a vibratory or undulatory motion, or a motion of the particles round their axes, or a motion of particles round each other. (95)

Reading Darwin and Davy encouraged Percy Shelley in scientific speculations that he had embarked upon much earlier, as a school-boy at Dr. Greenlaw's Syon House Academy in 1802. Inspired by the famous lectures of Dr. Adam Walker, which he heard again at Eton, Shelley began ten years of experiments with Leyden jars, microscopes, magnifying glasses, and chemical mixtures. His more memorable experiments left holes in his clothes and carpets, attempted to cure his sister Elizabeth's chilblains with a galvanic battery, and electrified a family tomcat. Shelley early learned to think of electricity and the processes of chemical attraction and repulsion as modes of a single polarized force. Adam Walker even identified electricity as the spark of life itself. At the conclusion of his discussion of electricity in his *A System of Familiar Philosophy,* Walker enthused

> Its power of exciting muscular motion in apparently dead animals, as well as of increasing the growth, invigorating the stamina, and reviving diseased vegetation, prove its relationship or affinity to the *living principle.* Though, Proteus-like, it eludes our grasp; plays with our curiosity; tempts enquiry by fallacious appearances and attacks our weakness under so many perplexing subtilties; yet it is impossible not to believe it the soul of the material world, and the paragon of elements![18]

Percy Shelley's basic scientific concepts had long been familiar to Mary Shelley, ever since the early days of our relationship when he ritually celebrated his birthday by launching fire balloons.[19] That Percy Shelley endorsed Adam Walker's identification of life with electricity is everywhere apparent in his poetry. The imagery of *Prometheus Unbound* explicitly associates electricity with love, light, and life itself, as in the final act of the poem where the Spirit of the Earth, earlier imaged as a Cupid-figure linked to his mother Asia/Venus, becomes a radiant orb—or "ten thousand orbs involving and involved"— of pure energy. And on the forehead of the spirit sleeping within this "sphere within sphere" is a "star" (or negative electrode) that shoots "swords of azure fire" (the blue flames of electrical discharges) or

> Vast beams like spokes of some invisible wheel
> Which whirl as the orb whirls, swifter than thought,
> Filling the abyss with sun-like lightnings,
> And perpendicular now, and now transverse,
> Pierce the dark soil, and as they pierce and pass,
> Make bare the secrets of the earth's deep heart.
> (*Prometheus Unbound,* IV, 241, 243, 270, 271, 274–79)

When Victor Frankenstein steals the spark of being, then, he is literally stealing Jupiter's lightning bolt, as Benjamin Franklin had proved. But in Percy Shelley's terms, he is stealing the very life of nature, the source of both love and electricity.

To appreciate fully the science that lies behind Victor Frankenstein's endeavors, however, we must remember that in the 1831 edition of *Frankenstein,* Mary Shelley explicitly associated electricity with galvanism. Victor Frankenstein is there disabused of his belief in the alchemists by a "man of great research in natural philosophy" who introduces him to "a theory which he had formed on the subject of electricity and galvanism" (238); and in her Preface, Mary Shelley linked the attempt to give life to dead matter with galvanism. After referring to Dr. Darwin's vermicelli experiment, she writes:

Not thus, after all, would life be given. Perhaps a corpse would be reanimated; galvanism had given token of such things: perhaps the component parts of a creature might be manufactured, brought together, and endued with vital warmth. (227)

In 1791 the Bolognese physiologist Luigi Galvani published his *De Viribus Electricitatis in Motui Musculari* (or *Commentary on the Effects of Electricity on Muscular Motion*)[20] in which he came to the conclusion that animal tissue contained a heretofore neglected innate vital force, which he called "animal electricity" but which was subsequently widely known as "galvanism." This force activated both nerves and muscles when they were connected by an arc of metal wires connected to a pile of copper and zinc plates. Galvani believed that his new vital force was a form of electricity different from both the "natural" form of electricity produced by lightning or by the torpedo fish and electric eel and the "artificial" form produced by friction (i.e. static electricity). Galvani argued that the brain is the most important source of the production of this "electric fluid" and that the nerves acted as conductors of this fluid to other nerves and muscles, the tissues of which act much like the outer and inner surfaces of the widely used Leyden jar. Thus the flow of animal electric fluid provided a stimulus which produced contractions or convulsions in the irritable muscle fibres.

Galvani's theories made the British headlines in December, 1802, when in the presence of their Royal Highnesses The Prince of Wales, the Duke of York, the Duke of Clarence, and the Duke of Cumberland, Galvani's nephew, disciple and ardent defender, Professor Luigi Aldini of Bologna University, applied a Voltaic pile connected by metallic wires to the ear and nostrils of a recently killed ox-head. At that moment, "the eyes were seen to open, the ears to shake, the tongue to be agitated, and the nostrils to swell, in the same manner as those of the living animal, when irritated and desirous of combating another of the same species."[21] But Professor Aldini's most notorious demonstration of galvanic electricity took place on January 17, 1803. On that day he applied galvanic electricity to the corpse of the murderer Thomas Forster. The body of the recently hanged criminal was collected from Newgate where it had lain in the prison yard at a temperature of 30 degrees Fahrenheit for one hour by the President of the College of Surgeons, Mr. Keate, and brought immediately to Mr. Wilson's Anatomical Theatre where the following experiments were performed. When wires attached to a pile composed of 120 plates of zinc and 120 plates of copper were connected to the ear and mouth of the dead criminal, Aldini later reported, "the jaw began to quiver, the adjoining muscles were horribly contorted, and the left eye actually opened."[22] When the wires were applied to the dissected thumb muscles they "induced a forcible effort to clench the hand"; when applied to the ear and rectum, they "excited in the muscles contractions much stronger . . . The action even of those muscles furthest distant from the points of contact with the arc was so much increased as almost to give an appearance of re-animation." And when volatile alkali was smeared on the nostrils and mouth before the Galvanic stimulus was applied, "the convulsions appeared to be much increased . . . and extended from the muscles of the head, face, and neck, as far as the deltoid. The effect in this case surpassed our most sanguine expectation," Aldini exulted, and remarkably concluded that "vitality might, perhaps, have been restored, if many circumstances had not rendered it impossible."[23] Here is the scientific prototype of Victor Frankenstein, restoring life to dead bodies.

In further experiments conducted by Aldini in 1804, the bodies of human corpses became violently agitated and one even raised itself as if about to walk; arms alternately rose and fell; and one forearm was made to hold a weight of several pounds, while the fists clenched and beat violently the table upon which the body lay. Natural respiration was also artificially reestablished and, through pressure exerted against the ribs, a lighted candle placed before the mouth was several times extinguished.[24]

Aldini's experiments on the severed heads of oxen, frogs legs, dogs' bodies, and human corpses were replicated widely throughout Europe in the early 1800s. His colleagues at Bologna, Drs. Vassali-Eandi, Rossi, and Giulio, reported to the Academy of Turin on August 15, 1802, that they had been able to excite contractions even in the involuntary organs of the heart and digestive system,[25] while applications of galvanic electricity to vegetables, animals, and humans were conducted in Germany by F. H. A. Humboldt, Edmund Schmück, C. J. C. Grapengiesser, and Johann Caspar Creve.[26] Their experiments were reported in 1806 by J. A. Heidmann in his *Theorie der Galvanischen Elektrizität,* while the theoretical implications of galvanism were expounded by Lorenz Oken in his influential *Lehrbuch der Naturphilosophie* (Leipzig, 1809–10). Oken argued that polarity is the first and only force in the world; that galvanism or electrical polarity is therefore the principle of life; and that organic life is galvanism in a state of homogeneous mass.[27]

Events so notorious and so widely reported in the popular press must have been discussed in both the Shelley and the Godwin households at the time and would have been recalled, however inaccurately, by Shelley and Byron in their conversations about the possibility of reanimating a corpse. Indeed, the popular interest in galvanic electricity reached such a pitch in Germany that a Prussian edict was passed in 1804 forbidding the use of decapitated criminals' heads for galvanic experiments. It is probably to these events, as well as to the experiments of Humboldt, Grapengiesser, and Creve and the expositions of Heidmann and Oken that Percy Shelley referred in his Preface to *Frankenstein* when he insisted that "the event on which this fiction is founded has been supposed, by Dr. Darwin and some of the physiological writers of Germany, as not of impossible occurrence" (6). Even though Erasmus Darwin never fully endorsed the revolutionary theory of Galvani and

Volta that electricity is the cause of muscular motion, he was convinced that electricity stimulated plant growth.[28]

Mary Shelley's familiarity with these galvanic experiments came not only from Shelley and Byron, but also from Dr. William Polidori. As a medical student with a degree from the University of Edinburgh, Polidori had been exposed to the latest galvanic theories and experiments by the famous Edinburgh physician, Dr. Charles Henry Wilkinson, whose review of the literature, *Elements of Galvanism in Theory and Practice,* was published in 1804. Dr. Wilkinson continued research on galvanism and developed his own galvanic treatments for intermittent fevers, amaurosis, and quinsy, with which he reported several successes.[29]

Mary Shelley based Victor Frankenstein's attempt to create a new species from dead organic matter through the use of chemistry and electricity on the most advanced scientific research of the early nineteenth century. Her vision of the isolated scientist discovering the secret of life is no mere fantasy but a plausible prediction of what science might accomplish. As such, *Frankenstein* has rightly been hailed as the first legitimate example of that genre we call science fiction. Brian Aldiss has tentatively defined science fiction as "the search for a definition of man and his status in the universe which will stand in our advanced but confused state of knowledge (science), and is characteristically cast in the Gothic or post-Gothic mold." And Eric Rabkin and Robert Scholes have identified the conventional elements of science fiction as "speculation and social criticism, hardware and exotic adventure."[30] We might expand these criteria to say that science fiction is a genre that (1) is grounded on valid scientific research; (2) gives a persuasive prediction of what science might be able to accomplish in the foreseeable future; and (3) offers a humanistic critique of either specific technological inventions or the very nature of scientific thinking.

Frankenstein is notable both for its grasp of the nature of the seventeenth-century scientific revolution and for its perspicacious analysis of the dangers inherent in that enterprise. Mary Shelley provides us with the first portrait of what the popular media has since caricatured as the "mad scientist," a figure that finds its modern apotheosis in Stanley Kubrick's Dr. Strangelove (1964). But Mary Shelley's portrait of Victor Frankenstein is both more subtle and more persuasive than subsequent media versions.

Mary Shelley recognized that Frankenstein's passion for his scientific research is a displacement of normal emotions and healthy human relationships. Obsessed by his vision of the limitless power to be gained from his newly discovered capacity to bestow animation, Victor Frankenstein devotes all his time and "ardour" to his experimental research, the creating of a human being. He becomes oblivious to the world around him, to his family and friends, even to his own health. As he admits, "my cheek had grown pale with study, and my person become emaciated with confinement" (49) as "a resistless, and almost frantic impulse, urged me forward; I seemed to have lost all soul or sensation but for this one pursuit" (50). In his compulsive desire to complete his experiment, he ignores the beauty of nature and stops corresponding with his father and Elizabeth. "I could not tear my thoughts from my employment, loathsome in itself; but which had taken hold of my imagination. I wished, as it were, to procrastinate my feelings of affection, until the great object of my affection was compleated" (manuscript version of 50:29–33). Frankenstein has clearly substituted his scientific research for normal emotional interactions. His only "object of affection" has become the experiment on the laboratory table before him.

In his ability to substitute work for love, a dream of personal omnipotence for a dream of familial interdependence, Victor Frankenstein possesses a personality that has recently been characterized by Evelyn Fox Keller as typical of the modern scientist. Keller argues from her psychological survey of physicists working at Harvard University that the professional scientific demand for "objectivity" often masks a prior psychological alienation from the mother, an alienation that can lead scientists to feel uncomfortable with their emotions and sexuality. The scientists she studied, when compared to the norm, typically felt more estranged from their mothers, were more emotionally repressed, had a relatively low sex-drive, and tended to feel more comfortable with objects than with people.[31] Their professional detachment often precluded a concern with ethics and politics in their research. They preferred to leave the problems resulting from the social application of their discoveries to others. Frankenstein's failure to take personal responsibility for the outcome of his experiment thus anticipates the practice of many modern scientists.

Mary Shelley developed the character of Victor Frankenstein as a calculated inversion of the eighteenth-century "man of feeling." Influenced by Shaftesbury's philosophical argument that sympathy is the basis of human morality and by the fictional treatments of this idea—Henry Mackenzie's *The Man of Feeling,* Godwin's *Fleetwood, or The New Man of Feeling,* Laurence Sterne's *A Sentimental Journey* and Rousseau's *La Nouvelle Héloïse* which she heard Percy Shelley read aloud that summer of 1816—Mary Shelley embodied in Victor Frankenstein the very opposite of the sentimental hero. Her isolated protagonist has given both "heart and soul" to his work, callously indifferent to the anxiety his silence might cause his father and his fiancée. As such he has truly "lost all soul" (50). He has cut himself off from all moral feeling, from the capacity either to perceive or to enact goodness, as Shaftesbury defined it.

That Mary Shelley endorsed the ideal of the man of feeling as a moral exemplar is revealed not only in her association of the alienated Victor Frankenstein with Faust and Satan but also in her cameo portrait of the Russian boat-master whom Walton employs. This character functions in the novel as a moral touchstone of disinterested sympathy from which to measure the fall of both Frankenstein and Walton. The master "is a person of an excellent disposition, and is remarkable in the ship for his gentleness, and the mildness of his discipline" (14). He is entirely altruistic. When the girl he had obtained permission to marry told him that she loved another man, he not only gave her up but bestowed his small fortune on his impoverished rival and then tried to persuade her father to consent to the love-match. When her father refused, thinking himself honor-bound to the sea-master, the master left Russia and refused to return until the girl had married her lover. But despite the master's noble character, Walton finds the master's sympathetic involvement in the communal life of the ship narrow and boring.

Walton is aware of his own emotional limitations. Throughout the novel, he desperately seeks a friend, some man who would "participate my joy, . . . sympathize with me, . . . approve or amend my plans . . . [and have] affection enough for me to endeavour to regulate my mind" (13–14). Walton's desire is modeled directly on Godwin's Fleetwood, who also desperately sought a friend:

> I saw that I was alone, and I desired to have a friend, . . . a friend . . . whose kindness shall produce a conviction in my mind, that I do not stand alone in the world . . . a friend, who is to me as another self, who joys in all my joys, and grieves in all my sorrows, not with a joy or grief that looks like compliment, not with a sympathy that changes into smiles when I am no longer present, though my head continues bent to the earth with anguish. . . . Friendship, in the sense in which I felt the want of it, has been truly said to be a sentiment that can grasp but one individual in its embrace.[32]

But Godwin's novel clearly demonstrates that Fleetwood's sentimental desire for a "brother of my heart" masks a selfish need to possess the beloved entirely. His jealousy leads to a paranoic suspiciousness that destroys the only genuine friendship Fleetwood ever finds, that with his wife Mary Macneil. In contrast, Mary Macneil articulates an ideal of true friendship, a concept that Godwin had learned from Mary Wollstonecraft:

> I am not idle and thoughtless enough, to promise to sink my being and individuality in yours. I shall have distinct propensities and preferences . . . In me you will have a wife, and not a passive machine. But, whenever a question occurs of reflection, of experience, of judgment, or of prudential consideration, I shall always listen to your wisdom with undissembled deference. In every thing indifferent, or that can be made so, I shall obey you with pleasure. And in return I am sure you will consider me as a being to be won with kindness, and not dictated to with the laconic phrase of authority.[33]

From the perspective provided by Godwin's *Fleetwood,* we can see that Walton's concept of friendship, which some have hailed as the positive moral value in the novel,[34] is badly flawed. Walton seeks an alter-ego, a mirror of his self who will reflect back his own joys and sorrows, adding only the wisdom that an older Walton would in time have discovered for himself. Rather than a relationship of genuine altruism and self-sacrifice, or a partnership of independent yet mutually supportive persons, Walton's concept of friendship is in fact another form of egoism. He is therefore given the friendship of his genuine alter-ego, Victor Frankenstein, a "friendship" that, being none, is found only to be lost. As Walton laments, "I have longed for a friend; I have sought one who would sympathize with and love me. Behold, on these desert seas I have found such a one; but, I fear, I have gained him only to know his value, and lose him" (209).

Both Walton and Frankenstein devote their emotional energy not to empathic feelings or domestic affections but to egoistic dreams of conquering the boundaries of nature or of death. Not only have they diverted their libidinal desires away from normal erotic objects, but in the process they have engaged in a particular mode of thinking which we might call "scientific." Frankenstein and Walton are both the products of the scientific revolution of the seventeenth century. They have been taught to see nature "objectively," as something separate from themselves, as passive and even dead matter—as the "object of my affection"—that can and should be penetrated, analyzed, and controlled. They thus accord nature no loving soul or "personhood" requiring recognition or respect.

Wordsworth had articulated the danger inherent in thinking of nature as something distinct from human consciousness. A reader of Wordsworth, Mary Shelley understood nature in his terms, as a sacred all-creating mother, a living organism or ecological community with which human beings interact in mutual dependence. To defy this bond, as both Frankenstein and Walton do, is to break one's ties with the source of life and health. Hence Frankenstein literally becomes sick in the process of carrying out his experiment: "every night I was oppressed by a slow fever, and I became nervous to a most painful degree" (51); and at its completion, he collapses in a "a nervous fever" that confines him to his sickbed for several months.

But Mary Shelley's critique of objective, rationalistic thought goes beyond Wordsworth's organicist notion that "we murder to dissect." Perhaps because she was a woman, she perceived that inherent in most scientific thought was a potent gender identification. Professor Waldman taught Frankenstein that scientists "penetrate into the recesses of nature, and shew how *she* works in *her* hiding places" (42, my emphasis). In Waldman's trope, nature is a passive female who can be penetrated in order to satisfy male desire. Waldman's metaphor is derived directly from the writings of the leading British scientists of the seventeenth and eighteenth centuries. Francis Bacon had heralded the seventeenth-century scientific revolution as a calculated attempt to enslave female nature. Bacon's metaphor of a passive, possessable female nature strikingly altered the traditional image of nature as Dame Kind, an "all-creating" and bounteous Mother Earth who single-handedly bore and nourished her children. But it was Bacon's metaphor that structured most of the new scientific writing in England in the eighteenth century. Isaac Barrow, Newton's teacher, declared that the aim of the new philosophy was to "search Nature out of her Concealments, and unfold her dark Mysteries,"[35] while Robert Boyle noted contemptuously that "some men care only to know Nature, others desire to command her."[36] Henry Oldenburg, a future Secretary of the Royal Society, invoked Bacon to support his assertion that the "true sons of learning" are those men who do not remain satisfied with the well-known truths but rather "penetrate from Nature's antechamber to her inner closet."[37] As Brian Easlea concludes, many seventeenth-century natural philosophers and their successors viewed the scientific quest as a virile masculine penetration into a passive female nature, a penetration that would, in Bacon's words, not merely exert a "gentle guidance over nature's course" but rather "conquer and subdue her" and even "shake her to her foundations."[38] This vision of nature was visually encoded in Ernest Barrias' large, bare-breasted female statue that in 1902 was placed at the entrance of the grand staircase of the Faculté de Médecine of the Université de Paris, bearing the inscription: "LA NATURE SE DEVOILANT DEVANT LA SCIENCE."

Carolyn Merchant, Evelyn Fox Keller, and Brian Easlea have drawn our attention to the negative consequences of this identification of nature as the passive female.[39] Construing nature as the passive Other has led, as Merchant shows, to the increasing destruction of the environment and the disruption of the delicate ecological balance between humankind and nature. Moreover, as Keller has suggested in her studies of how the social construction of gender has affected the making of science, the professional scientific demand for "objectivity" and detachment often masks an aggressive desire to dominate the female sex object. The results can be a dangerous division between what C. P. Snow called the "two cultures," between the power-seeking practices of science and the concerns of humanists with moral responsibility, emotional communion, and spiritual values. The scientist who analyzes, manipulates, and attempts to control nature unconsciously engages in a form of oppressive sexual politics. Construing nature as the female Other, he attempts to make nature serve his own ends, to gratify his own desires for power, wealth, and reputation.

Frankenstein's scientific project is clearly an attempt to gain power. Inspired by Waldman's description of scientists who "acquired new and almost unlimited powers" (42), Frankenstein has sought both the power of a father over his children, and, more omnipotently, of God over his creation. More subtly, yet more pervasively, Frankenstein has sought power over the female. He has "pursued nature to her hiding places" (49) in an attempt not only to penetrate nature and show how her hidden womb works but actually to steal or appropriate that womb. To usurp the power of reproduction is to usurp the power of production as such. Marx identified childbirth as the primary example of pure, or unalienated, labor. Victor Frankenstein's enterprise can be viewed from a Marxist perspective as an attempt to exploit nature or labor in the service of a ruling class. Frankenstein wishes to harness the modes of reproduction in order to become the acknowledged, revered, and gratefully obeyed father of a new species. His project is thus identical with that of bourgeois capitalism: to exploit nature's resources for both commercial profit and political control.[40]

Among these resources are animal and human bodies. Collecting bones and flesh from charnel-houses, dissecting rooms, and slaughter-houses, Frankenstein sees these human and animal organs as nothing more than the tools of his trade, no different from his other scientific instruments. In this sense he is identical with the factory owner who gathers men, his disembodied "hands" as Dickens's Bounderby would say, to manipulate his machines. We can therefore see Frankenstein's creature, as Franco Moretti has suggested, as the proletariat, "a *collective* and *artificial* creature,"[41] dehumanized by the mechanized modes of technological production controlled by the industrial scientist and, in modern times, by the computer. Elizabeth Gaskell first identified Frankenstein's monster with the nineteenth-century British working-class in *Mary Barton* (1848):

> The actions of the educated seem to me typified in those of Frankenstein, that monster of many human qualities, ungifted with a soul, a knowledge of the difference between good and evil.
>
> The people rise up to life; they irritate us, they terrify us, and we become their enemies. Then, in the sorrowful moment of our triumphant power, their eyes gaze on us with a mute reproach. Why have we made them what they are; a powerful monster, yet without the inner means for peace and happiness? (Chapter 15)

But this misshapen and alienated worker, Frankenstein's monster, has the power to destroy his maker, to seize the technology of production (the creature carries the secret of his own creation in his pocket) and force it to serve his own ends.

In the second edition of the novel, Mary Shelley further identifies Frankenstein's capitalist project with the project of colonial imperialism. Clerval here announces his intention to join the East India Company:

> He came to the university with the design of making himself complete master of the oriental languages, as thus he should open a field for the plan of life he had marked out for himself. Resolved to pursue no inglorious career, he turned his eyes toward the East, as affording scope for his spirit of enterprise. (243–44)

Frankenstein's enthusiastic affirmation of Clerval's plan signals Mary Shelley's recognition of the expanding and increasingly dangerous degree of cultural and scientific control over the resources of nature, whether dead matter or living races. Her awareness of the similarity between Frankenstein's scientific enterprise and Clerval's imperialist project may have been triggered by the Parliamentary Debates on the slave trade in 1824. The foreign secretary and leader of the House of Commons, George Canning, in a speech opposing the freeing of the Negro slaves in the West Indies, explicitly identified the slaves with Frankenstein's monster:

> To turn [the Negro] loose in the manhood of his physical strength, in the maturity of his physical passions, but in the infancy of his uninstructed reason, would be to raise up a creature resembling the splendid fiction of a recent romance; the hero of which constructs a human form, with all the corporeal capabilities of man, and with the thews and sinews of a giant; but being unable to impart to the work of his hands a perception of right and wrong, he finds too late that he has only created a more than mortal power of doing mischief, and himself recoils from the monster which he has made.[42]

Writing during the early years of Britain's industrial revolution and the age of Empire, Mary Shelley was aware of the damaging consequences of a scientific, objective, alienated view of both nature and human labor. Uninhibited scientific and technological development, without a sense of moral responsibility for either the processes or products of these new modes of production, could easily, as in Frankenstein's case, produce monsters. A creature denied both parental love and peers; a working class denied access to meaningful work but condemned instead, in Ruskin's words, to make the same glass bead over and over; a colonized and degraded race: all are potential monsters, dehumanized by their uncaring employers and unable to feel the bonds of citizenship with the capitalist society in which they live. Moreover, these workers can become more powerful than their makers. As Frankenstein's creature asserts, "You are my creator, but I am your master;—obey!" (165), a prophecy whose fulfillment might take the form of bloody revolutions in which the oppressed overthrow their masters.

Even more important is Mary Shelley's implicit warning against the possible dangers inherent in the technological developments of modern science. Although we have not yet discovered Frankenstein's procedure for reanimating corpses, recent research in biochemistry—the discovery of DNA, the technique of gene-splicing, and the development of extrauterine fertilization—has brought us to the point where human beings are able to manipulate life-forms in ways previously reserved only to nature and chance. The replacement of natural childbirth by the mechanical eugenic control systems and baby-breeders envisioned in Aldous Huxley's *Brave New World* or Marge Piercy's *Woman on the Edge of Time* is now only a matter of time and social will. Worse by far, of course, is the contemporary proliferation of nuclear weapons systems resulting from the Los Alamos Project and the political decision to drop atomic bombs on Hiroshima and Nagasaki in 1945. As Jonathan Schell has so powerfully reminded us in *The Fate of the Earth,* as such docudramas as

"The Day After" (1983) and "Threads" (1984) have starkly portrayed, a morally irresponsible scientific development has released a monster that can destroy human civilization itself. As Frankenstein's monster proclaims, "Remember that I have power; . . . I can make you so wretched that the light of day will be hateful to you" (165). Mary Shelley's tale of horror is no fantastical ghost story, but rather a profound insight into the probable consequences of "objective"—gendered—or morally insensitive scientific and technological research.

Notes

1. Benjamin Farrington, trans., "'Temporis Partus Masculus': an Untranslated Writing of Francis Bacon," *Centaurus* I (1951): 197. For a full discussion of Bacon's use of gender metaphors, see Evelyn Fox Keller, *Reflections on Gender and Science* (New Haven and London: Yale University Press, 1985), Chap. 2. [All page numbers for *Frankenstein* given in the body of the text refer to the 1818 edition unless otherwise noted.]

2. A marginal note on the Thomas copy of the 1818 *Frankenstein* beside this passage, probably in Mary Shelley's own hand, comments "you said your family was not sientific [sic]" (reported by James Rieger, ed., *Frankenstein*, p. 35 n8).

3. On the importance of this introductory lecture to Humphry Davy's career, see Sir Harold Hartley, *Humphry Davy* (London: Nelson, 1966), p. 41. Roger Sharrock has traced Davy's debt to William Wordsworth's "Preface to *The Lyrical Ballads* of 1800" in "The Chemist and the Poet: Sir Humphry Davy and the Preface to the *Lyrical Ballads*," *Notes and Records of the Royal Society* 17 (1962): 57.

4. *Mary Shelley's Journal*, ed. Frederick L. Jones (Norman, Oklahoma: University of Oklahoma Press, 1947), p. 67; Laura Crouch has persuasively argued that the "Discourse" is the book listed by Mary Shelley in her Journal under Books Read in 1816 as "Introduction to Davy's Chemistry" ("Davy's *A Discourse, Introductory to a Course of Lectures on Chemistry:* A Possible Scientific Source of *Frankenstein*," *Keats-Shelley Journal* 27 [1978]: 35–44). Mary Shelley would have known of Humphry Davy's work since childhood; she may even have been introduced to him when Davy dined with Godwin on February 16, 1801. See Samuel Holmes Vasbinder, "Scientific Attitudes in Mary Shelley's *Frankenstein:* Newtonian Monism as a Base for the Novel," *DAI* 37 (1976): 2842A (Kent State University).

5. *The Letters of Percy Shelley*, ed. Frederick L. Jones (Oxford: The Clarendon Press, 1964), I:319.

6. Sir Humphry Davy, *A Discourse, Introductory to a Course of Lectures on Chemistry* (London: John Johnson, 1802), pp. 5–6. All further references to this edition are cited in the text.

7. Laura Crouch, "Davy's *A Discourse*," p. 43.

8. Sir Humphry Davy, *Elements of Chemical Philosophy* (London, 1812), p. 58.

9. Erasmus Darwin, *The Botanic Garden* (London: John Johnson, Part I: "The Economy of Vegetation," 1791; Part II: "The Loves of the Plants," 1789); *Zoonomia: or The Laws of Organic Life* (London: John Johnson, 1794; third "Corrected" edition, 1801; *Phytologia: or the Philosophy of Agriculture and Gardening* (London: John Johnson, 1800); *The Temple of Nature* (London: John Johnson, 1803). All further references to these editions are cited in the text.

10. See Loren Eiseley, *Darwin's Century: Evolution and the Men Who Discovered It* (Garden City, New Jersey: Doubleday, 1958), Chaps. 1 and 2; and Ernst Mayr, *The Growth of Biological Thought: Diversity, Evolution, and Inheritance* (Cambridge: Belknap Press, 1982), pp. 301–41, for excellent summaries of pre-evolutionary and early evolutionary theories.

11.   Mayr, *Growth of Biological Thought,* p. 335.

12.   Mayr, *Growth of Biological Thought,* pp. 329–37.

13.   Percy Shelley also read Buffon attentively. In his journal letter to Peacock of July 23, 1816, Shelley alludes to the first volume of Buffon's work, *La Théorie de la terre,* in the course of describing the glaciers of Mont Blanc: "I will not pursue Buffons sublime but gloomy theory, that this earth which we inhabit will at some future period be changed into a mass of frost" (*Letters of Percy Shelley,* ed. Frederick L. Jones, I:499).

14.   Desmond King-Hele, *Erasmus Darwin* (London: Macmillan, 1963), p. 3.

15.   *Letters of Percy Shelley,* ed. Frederick L. Jones, I:129, 342, 345.

16.   For Erasmus Darwin's influence on Percy Shelley's thought and poetry, see Carl Grabo, *A Newton among Poets—Shelley's Use of Science in "Prometheus Unbound"* (Chapel Hill: University of North Carolina Press, 1930), pp. 22–74; Desmond King-Hele, *Erasmus Darwin,* pp. 144–51, and *Shelley—His Thought and Work* (London: Macmillan, 1960), pp. 162–64; Kenneth Neill Cameron, *The Young Shelley—Genesis of a Radical* (London: Victor Gollancz, 1951), pp. 121, 240; and Robert M. Maniquis, "The Puzzling *Mimosa:* Sensitivity and Plant Symbols in Romanticism," *Studies in Romanticism* VIII (1969): 129–55.

17.   Erasmus Darwin discusses this process in *The Temple of Nature,* Additional Note 1: "Spontaneous Vitality of Miscroscopic Animals," pp. 1–11.

18.   Adam Walker, *A System of Familiar Philosophy* (London, 1799), p. 391.

19.   Richard Holmes, *Shelley—The Pursuit* (New York: E. P. Dutton, 1975), pp. 150, 344.

20.   Luigi Galvani, *De Viribus Electricitatis in Motui Musculari. Commentarius* (Bologna, 1791); *Commentary on the Effects of Electricity in Muscular Motion,* trans. M. G. Foley, with notes and Introduction by I. Bernard Cohen (Norwalk, Conn.: Burndy Library, 1953).

21.   John Aldini, *An Account of the Late Improvements in Galvanism, with a series of Curious and Interesting Experiments performed before the Commissioners of the French National Institute and repeated lately in the Anatomical Theatres of London; to which is added, An Appendix, containing the author's Experiments on the Body of a Malefactor executed at New Gate* (London: Cuthell and Martin, and J. Murray, 1803), p. 54. This book is an English translation of the original French text, *Essay Théorique et Expérimentale sur le Galvanisme* published in Paris in 1802 and translated into German by F. H. Martens and published at Leipzig in 1804.

22.   Aldini, *Galvanism,* p. 193.

23.   Aldini, *Galvanism,* pp. 195, 194, 194.

24.   These results are reported by Paul Fleury Mottelay, in his *Bibliographical History of Electricity and Magnetism* (London: C. Griffin & Co., Ltd., 1922), which gives a complete set of references to Aldini's experiments, pp. 305–7.

25.   Reported by Dr. Giulio in Aldini, *Galvanism,* pp. 204–8.

26.   See F. H. A. Humboldt, *Sur Galvanisme,* trans. J. F. N. Jadelot (Paris, 1799); Edmund Joseph Schmück, "On the action of galvanic electricity on the *mimosa pudica,*" cited in Mottelay, *Bibliographical History of Electricity,* p. 332; C. J. C. Grapengiesser, *Versuche den Galvanismus* (Berlin, 1801, 1802); and Johann Caspar Creve, *Beiträge zu Galvanis versuchen* (Frankfurt and Leipzig, 1793).

27.   See Paul Mottelay, *Bibliographical History of Electricity,* pp. 402–4.

28.   Erasmus Darwin, *The Botanic Garden,* Part I, p. 463.

29.   Charles Henry Wilkinson, *Elements of Galvanism in Theory and Practice,* 2 Vols. (London, 1804), pp. 269–70. Wilkinson's treatise is heavily dependent upon the earlier dissertations on the subject of galvanism prepared by Johann C. L. Reinhold for his medical degree at Magdeburg in 1797 and 1798.

30.   Brian W. Aldiss, *Billion Year Spree—The History of Science Fiction* (London: Weidenfeld and Nicholson, 1973), p. 8. Cf. Robert Scholes and Eric S. Rabkin, *Science Fiction: History, Science, Vision* (New York: Oxford University Press, 1977), p. 38. Aldiss, Scholes and Rabkin concur that *Frankenstein* is the first legitimate example of science fiction. For an analysis of the

way *Frankenstein* has been misread by male science-fiction writers, see Judith A. Spector, "Science Fiction and the Sex War: A Womb of One's Own," *Literature and Psychology* 31 (1981): 21–32.

31. Evelyn Fox Keller, "Gender and Science," *Psychoanalysis and Contemporary Thought* I (1978): 409–33; see also her *Reflections on Gender and Science,* Chap. 4.

32. William Godwin, *Fleetwood, or The New Man of Feeling,* 3 Vols. (London, 1805; repr. New York and London: Garland, 1979), II:143–45.

33. William Godwin, *Fleetwood,* II: 278–79.

34. See, for example, Robert Kiely, *The Romantic Novel in England* (Cambridge: Harvard University Press, 1972), p. 166.

35. Isaac Barrow, *The Usefulness of Mathematical Learning Explained and Demonstrated* (London, 1734; repr. Frank Cass, 1970), pp. xxix–xxx.

36. Robert Boyle, *The Works of Robert Boyle,* ed. Thomas Birch, 6 Vols. (London, 1772), I:310.

37. Henry Oldenburg, *The Correspondence of Henry Oldenburg,* ed. A. R. Hall and M. B. Hall (Madison: University of Wisconsin Press, 1965), I:113.

38. Francis Bacon, *The Works of Francis Bacon,* ed. J. Spedding, R. L. Ellis, and D. N. Heath (new edn., 1879–90; Facsimile, Stuttgart-Bad Cannstatt, 1962, 7 Volumes), II:42, 373. For a discussion of the sexual metaphors utilized in much seventeenth- and eighteenth-century English scientific writing, see Brian Easlea, *Science and Sexual Oppression—Patriarchy's Confrontation with Woman and Nature* (London: Weidenfeld and Nicolson, 1981), p. 86; Chaps. 3, 4, 5.

39. Caroline Merchant, *The Death of Nature: Women, Ecology and the Scientific Revolution* (San Francisco: Harper and Row, 1980); see also Evelyn Fox Keller, *Reflections on Gender and Science,* Chaps. 4–9; and Brian Easlea, *Science and Sexual Oppression.*

40. As Caroline Merchant concludes, "The removal of animistic, organic assumptions about the cosmos constituted the death of nature—the most far-reaching effect of the Scientific Revolution. Because nature was now viewed as a system of dead, inert particles moved by external, rather than inherent forces, the mechanical framework itself could legitimate the manipulation of nature. Moreover, as a conceptual framework, the mechanical order had associated with it a framework of values based on power, fully compatible with the directions taken by commercial capitalism" (*The Death of Nature,* p. 193).

For a useful study of the way *Frankenstein* condemns bourgeois patriarchy and the concept of male motherhood, see Burton Hatlen, "Milton, Mary Shelley and Patriarchy," in *Rhetoric, Literature and Interpretation,* ed. Harry R. Garvin (Lewisburg, Pa.: Bucknell University Press, 1983), pp. 19–47.

41. Franco Moretti, *Signs Taken for Wonders—Essays in the Sociology of Literary Form,* trans. S. Fischer, D. Forgacs, and D. Miller (London: Verso, 1983), p. 85.

42. George Canning, "Ameliorization of the Condition of the Slave Population in the West Indies (House of Lords)," [Hansard's] *Parliamentary Debates,* n.s. 10 (March 16, 1824), cols. 1046–1198 [1103].

Mary Shelley's Daemon

ELLEN HERSON WITTMANN

Mary Poovey, in her landmark work *The Proper Lady and the Woman Writer,* discusses Mary Shelley as a prime example of a historically female and literary divided self, participating in a form of imaginative and critical self-effacement that tends to obscure the fact of her authorship:

> In preparing a preface for the revised edition of *Frankenstein,* Shelley shrank from "bringing [her]self forward in print." But she justified describing the origin of the novel by its distance from her real "personal" self: "as it will be confined to such topics as have connection with my authorship alone, I can scarcely accuse myself of a personal intrusion." This phenomenon, which is only one more manifestation of the indirection, or double consciousness, that we have already seen in women's social behavior, characterizes a remarkable number of women writers in the eighteenth and early nineteenth centuries. Women who wrote or achieved recognition in other "masculine" arenas frequently seemed unconscious of their accomplishment or, perhaps more accurately, thought of themselves in terms that simply did not fully acknowledge what they were doing.[1]

The attempts of feminist critics to reconstruct the Mary Shelley not merely hiding behind the male-centered text of *Frankenstein,* but in some sense obliterated by it, often rest on compensatory evidence culled from Mary Shelley's letters and journals. The telegraphic nature of Shelley's self-exposure in these documents, however, provides little basis for arguments concerning Mary's victimization by her husband and his humanist learning and ideals, such as Anne Mellor has disseminated.[2] U. C. Knoepflmacher and James O'Rourke have proposed two equally probable if not more likely objects of female rage informing Mary's narrative. They are Mary's father, William Godwin, and Jean-Jacques Rousseau, against whom Mary's mother, Mary Wollstonecraft, had polemicized in her 1792 *A Vindication of the Rights of Woman.* Both arguments are based primarily on literary as opposed to biographical sources.

This essay is a revised portion of the author's Ph. D. dissertation (Princeton University, 1994) and is published here for the first time by permission of the author.

O'Rourke's suggestion is grounded in a little-known article Mary Shelley wrote on Rousseau's literary production, in which she repeatedly criticizes him for abandoning his five children by his lifelong mistress.[3] Support for O'Rourke's thesis also comes from *Frankenstein,* in that it makes sense of the novel's setting: the creature is "born" outside the gates of Geneva, the home of both Victor and Rousseau, and the city from which Rousseau and Victor are eventually exiled. Knoepflmacher's alternative view, that Mary's narratives exact a fine revenge against her often cold, selfish, and manipulative father, is based on a convincing reading of *Frankenstein, Mathilda,* and "The Mourner," together with the biographical facts.[4] Because Shelley did, in fact, author *Frankenstein* independent of her husband's editorial involvement, the text of the novel, with supporting evidence from her letters and journals, is still the best locus of interpretation for Mary's meaning. For that reason, I will focus on Mary's use of the term "daemon" to describe her monster, working from the dual proposition that Mary and Percy not only collaborated on the use and meaning of that term prior to and after the composition of the novel, but also that Mary was a considerable influence on her husband's poetic career prior to his death, at which point she became his editor.

The term "daemon" is used to describe Victor Frankenstein's creation twice in Walton's letters to his sister, once in the opening letters and once in the closing letters. Victor uses the term twice in the first volume of the novel and thirteen times in the seventy-four page third and final volume. Volume two, consisting mainly of the creature's self-narrative, contains three uses of "daemon," two by Victor and one by the creature himself: "[I]t presented to me then as exquisite and divine a retreat as Pandæmonium appeared to the daemons of hell after their sufferings in the lake of fire."[5]

"Daemon" is the latinate transliteration of the Greek *daimôn,* a term used by Diotima in Plato's *Symposium* (202d) to characterize *erôs,* or love,[6] and again in Plato's *Apology* (31d) by Socrates when referring to the spirit that warns him against doing wrong.[7] While the English translation of *daimôn* from the New Testament into "demon" refers to an evil spirit,[8] prior to Christianity *daimôn* was a morally neutral term, ranging in meaning from spirit, as Alexander Nehamas and Paul Woodruff have translated it in the *Symposium,*[9] to genius, soul, fortune, divine power, and deity.[10] In this last sense, *daimôn* does not refer to a single dominant, or monotheistic, god, but rather to one of the many deities inhabiting nature, or, as William Blake claims in his *Marriage of Heaven and Hell,* who "reside in the human breast." "Daemon" is, of course, not the only term used to refer to the creature in the novel. "Fiend" and "devil" are commonly used, "monster," "creature," "wretch," and "the being" more rarely. "Daemon" is simply the most unexpected and evocative, given the morally neutralizing force of the latinate spelling, and given the fact that it becomes so prominent in the final third of the novel.

Percy Shelley's interest in Plato is well known. His early introduction to the *Symposium* by Dr. Lind at Eton, at a time when the influence of Plato was considered subversive as compared with that of Aristotle, made a lasting impression on Shelley—one which culminated in his own translation of the dialogue in 1818. Shelley writes in July, three months after the publication of *Frankenstein,* that he has taken on the translation of a dialogue that he had hitherto read only in translation "only as an exercise or perhaps to give Mary some idea of the manners & feelings of the Athenians—so different on many subjects from that of any other community that ever existed."[11] Unlike the Victorian Hellenists Linda Dowling discusses in her recent study of homosexuality at Oxford,[12] Percy Shelley's primary interest in the homosexual pederastic ethos of ancient Greece lies in its utter remoteness to, rather than its potential as a substitute for, the sexual mores of nineteenth-century England. Mary Shelley's journals lend support to the otherwise reasonable notion that some discussion of the *Symposium*, and the sexual practices it both valorizes and puts into question, preceded Percy's desire to share the actual language of the dialogue with his wife, who was subsequently to transcribe his translation.

Mary's journals show that she had her own relationship to the themes and language of ancient Greek literature prior to the nightmare in 1816 that produced *Frankenstein* and, hence, prior to Percy's *Symposium* translation in 1818, which followed the publication of Mary's novel. Shelley began her independent study of Greek in September of 1814,[13] less than two months after her elopement with Percy. Her study of Latin began somewhat later, in March of 1815, with the help of Thomas Jefferson Hogg.[14] Mary's entrance into classical studies is a significant move, in light of Percy's previous and yet, up to this point, superficial engagement with Greek. (Percy was already fluent in Latin.) It betrays a desire on Mary's part not merely to learn from Percy, but perhaps also to hold her own in an area where Percy had as yet little advantage. Mary Poovey, who does not comment on Mary Shelley's classical learning,[15] does, however, cite the incongruity of a woman learning languages beyond the feminine arena of polite discourse in the eighteenth-century example of Mary Wortley Montagu, "whose comment that a woman should 'conceal whatever Learning she attains' is sharply undercut by her mastery of Latin, German, Turkish, Spanish, and Greek and by her own publications."[16] Any engagement whatsoever with the classics in their original tongues was the mark of a learning in eighteenth- and nineteenth-century England that was almost strictly male. Rather than reject all things Greek as a result of the lack of university education available to women at the time, Mary chose to make some attempt to be a part of that tradition.

Mary's journals also show that in December of 1814, Mary read the Richardson translation of Wieland's novel *Geschichte des Agathon* (1766–1767),[17] a prototype of the German *Bildungsroman* that is explicitly, though loosely, based on the character Agathon in Plato's *Symposium*. Wieland blatantly contrasts the virtues of Platonism and Platonic love, as viewed through the contemporary lens of eighteenth-century Sensibility, to both the insensibilities of Stoicism, on the one hand, and the self-serving material and intel-lectual cunning of Sophism, on the other. Mary writes in her journal that she "dislike[s] his [Wieland's] opinions,"[18] suggesting that she is developing opinions of her own on what virtue is and how it ought to be represented in novels, based in part on Mary's and Percy's reading of her parents' writings (*Vindication* and *Caleb Williams*).

I would like to suggest that Mary's own exploration of the relationship between virtue and erotic love in *Frankenstein* gave some impetus to her hus-band's return to the Platonic dialogue, and, ultimately, to his further explo-ration of the power of love to effect good in *Prometheus Unbound*. We know from Mary's letters, in any case, that the *Symposium* translation comes to us in the form in which Mary put it, well after Percy's death, with some unhelpful and generally disregarded advice from Leigh Hunt. Hunt wanted Mary to change every occurrence of the word "love" in Percy's translation to "friend-ship," to prevent what Hunt thought would be the readers' misunderstand-ing.[19] In reality, the dichotomy "love versus friendship" is in itself opposite to the kind of love Mary and Percy had envisioned, which might be termed "ero-philic" in its attempt to unite interested and disinterested forms of love. Hence, friendship plays an equally important role in Mary's novel, because it is not terribly distinct from erotic love.

Diotima's discussion of *erŏs* as a *daimôn* in the *Symposium* is placed promi-nently at the center of a threefold nested narrative. Diotima is not present at the all-male banquet; in her stead, Socrates relates what he claims Diotima told him long before the banquet took place; Aristodemus then relates to Apollodorus what he and the others present at the banquet heard from Socrates and each other; finally, Apollodorus relates the highlights, or what he can remember of what he was told, to Glaucon. This structure is also used in *Frankenstein,* in which the creature's personal confession in the central sec-ond volume is related to Victor, who tells what he can to Walton, who writes what he can to his sister, Margaret Saville. In the *Symposium,* Socrates reveals that long ago Diotima had corrected his assumptions about love, much as Socrates now feels it necessary to correct Agathon, who holds the same opin-ions Socrates once held. In other words, Agathon represents the young Socrates, who in the *Symposium* is himself the embodiment of an *erŏs* that is determined to be rugged and barefooted rather than a spoiled beauty.

This indirect association of Agathon and *erŏs* is made explicit by Wieland, who casts Psyche as Agathon's beloved. Psyche is the female human beloved of the male god Eros in Apuleius's "Cupid and Psyche" tale, which appears as a nested narrative at the center of his longer work, *The Golden Ass* (mid-second century, A.D.). Mary Shelley partially translated the tale from the Latin in April of 1817,[20] but her earlier familiarity with the frame story of the transformed ass is evident from her allusion to beasts eating roses in a journal entry dated October 6, 1816: "On this day, Mary put her head through the door & said—Come and look, here's a cat eating roses—she'll turn into a woman. when beasts eat these roses they turn into men & women."[21] Apuleius's novel, like Wieland's, is a neo-Platonic work specifically dependent on the *Symposium* as its precursor, but it is distinct from Wieland and closer to Plato in its blend of high comedy and high mysticism. Low mysticism also abounds in *The Golden Ass*. Much of the gothic, or occult, quality of Shelley's narrative appears to be drawn from the darker side of the Apuleius novel, a narrative in which "filthy workshops" of witchcraft, not science, are commonplace.[22]

In Plato's *Symposium,* Diotima has told Socrates, much to his surprise and dismay, that love is "neither beautiful nor good" (201e),[23] in order to subvert his dualistic, "either/or," thinking on both love and virtue. The following quotation is from the Shelley translation, in which the term "daemon" is retained rather than translated:

> "Do not then say," she continued, "that what is not beautiful is of necessity deformed, nor what is not good is of necessity evil; nor, since you have confessed that Love is neither beautiful nor good, infer therefore, that he is deformed or evil, but rather something intermediate."
>
> "But," I said, "love is confessed by all to be a great God. . . ."—"You have confessed that Love, through his desire for things beautiful and good, possesses not those materials of happiness."—"Indeed such was my concession."—"But how can we conceive of God to be without the possession of what is beautiful and good?"—"In no manner, I confess."—"Observe, then, that you do not consider Love to be a God."—"What, then," I said, "is Love a mortal?"—"By no means."—"But what, then?"—"Like those things which I have before instanced, he is neither mortal nor immortal, but something intermediate."—"What is that, O Diotima?—"A great daemon, Socrates; and everything daemoniacal holds an intermediate place between what is divine and what is mortal." (202b–e)[24]

Diotima's "neither/nor" rhetoric helps to reinforce the premoral, nondualistic, or contemplative nature of the virtue of *erōs* as she understands it. The Shelley refusal to translate "daemon" into "demon," in both *Frankenstein* and the *Symposium,* is in keeping with Diotima's argument.

Diotima's insights are crucial, and yet, as the contemporary *Symposium* scholars Stanley Rosen, Martha Nussbaum, and Michel Foucault have stressed, hers is not the only truth contained in the dialogue, since it is convincingly challenged by competing and diametrically opposed views on the nature of love. Actually, these scholars argue against or shun Diotima altogether not on the basis of this passage, but rather with an eye to Diotima's notorious ladder of ascent from the sensual love of beautiful bodies to the spiritual love of beauty itself. In favoring the homosexual pederastic ethos of Pausanias and Phaedrus, as does Michel Foucault,[25] or the narcissistic self-absorption of Alcibiades, as does Martha Nussbaum,[26] over the ostensibly metaphysical idealism of Diotima, these scholars represent the postmodern reaction to all apparent forms of idealism and metaphysics. By contrast, Stanley Rosen's proposition that the truth of the dialogue may reside in the integration of the views and personae of Alcibiades and Diotima—what Martha Nussbaum has characterized as particular and universal (hence opposite and irreconcilable) modes of knowledge, respectively—is consistent with Diotima's own characterization of love as something intermediate between dichotomous extremes of good and bad, high and low. However, Rosen mentions this idea as a mere "playful suggestion" and does not pursue it.[27] David Halperin's essay "Why is Diotima a Woman" enriches our understanding of Diotima as a figure for mutual, as opposed to hierarchical, love and understanding but does not address the vital significance of the tension the interlocutors generate in opposition to Diotima's view.[28] Diotima's "neither/nor" should not be understood as an Aristotelian mean, or a strict avoidance of extremes, but rather as a Platonic *coincidentia oppositorum,* or meeting of opposites—neither/nor as a negation of either/or logic, one that maintains tension among divergent views while yoking them together. Diotima represents both an intensely idealizing view of love and this overarching perspective, which informs the structure of the whole dialogue. It is only by means of this perspective, placed at the center of the dialogue, that an unbiased view of erotic love can arise.

The creature at the center of *Frankenstein* enjoys a similarly privileged and complex viewpoint and symbolic status within the novel as a whole. The key passage in *Frankenstein* that is analogous to Diotima's is positioned at the very center of the novel (central volume, central page). It is the creature's response to the spectacle of the De Lacey family's loving interaction before they have become aware of the creature's presence. Bette London, in her work on masculine exhibitionism in *Frankenstein,* argues against the Mellorian retrieval of female identity from its obscure representation in the martyred monster and posits instead the general instability of the category "masculine" as the central allegory of the novel.[29] London does not discuss the novel's singular instance of male voyeurism in the creature's undiscovered viewing of the De Lacey family: "He raised her, and smiled with such kindness and affection, that I felt sensations of a peculiar and overpowering nature: they were a mixture of pain and pleasure, such as I had never before experienced, either from hunger or cold, warmth or food; and I withdrew from the window, unable to bear these emotions" (104). This "mixture of pain and pleasure" is a meeting of opposites that constitutes the creature's moral acme in the novel, because it represents a movement beyond attachment to either the pleasure or the pain of viewing or being viewed—either the unitary or discontinuous discourses of femininity or masculinity. The creature withdraws from the window "unable to bear these emotions"; nonetheless, he has consciously experienced the sort of internal tension that drives Victor to unconscious acts of destruction and madness. The window—one could argue in light of London's observations—functions here as a metaphor for the specular realm, with the creature's withdrawal representing a moral awakening, an awakening that is followed by the creature's acquisition of language.

Mary and Percy Shelley seek to subvert the inheritance of Western Christian morality by means of Platonic love. While Romantic Hellenism in general relies on a Platonic contemplative ethic to take the place of the Aristotelian material ethic that dominated Western Europe until the Enlightenment, Mary Shelley is reacting on a more immediate level to a culture that, in the words of William Blake, called her mother "a whore,"[30] and that was prepared, given her elopement with a married man, to call the daughter something worse, perhaps even a monster. In light of Mary Poovey's feminist-historicist analysis of women in the eighteenth and early nineteenth centuries, Mary Shelley must be seen as internalizing her culture's view of libidinous women (her mother and herself) and simultaneously reacting against it. In place of the virtue of erotic love, the Christian tradition, from its origins up to the present, and with the recent help of such scholars as C. S. Lewis, Anders Nygren, and Denis de Rougemont, has constructed *agapé,* or Christian charity, as a virtuous love diametrically opposed to the viciousness of *erōs.* Mary Shelley rejects this approach as thoroughly as does her husband. As a result, her creature, the daemon, repeatedly refers to virtue in terms of its extreme rarity or impossibility in the face of its opposition by vice. The novel, in kind, pursues a relentlessly divisive and destructive course of events, until the creature himself concludes: "No sympathy may I ever find. When I first sought it, it was the love of virtue, the feelings of happiness and affection with which my whole being overflowed, that I wished to be participated. But now, that virtue has become to me a shadow, and that happiness and affection are turned into bitter and loathing despair, in what should I seek for sympathy?" (218). Unlike Wieland's *Agathon,* in which the universal practicality of virtue is insisted upon (author's preface), Mary Shelley's novel is a commentary on the limits of virtue that reasserts the truth of her husband's contemplative humanism. *Frankenstein* demonstrates how—through the distortion of *erōs* into an evil demon, the displacement of *erōs* onto unattainable objects (the dead, the resurrected, mothers, maidservants, same-sex friends, small children, and sisterly fiancées), and the division of *erōs* into good and bad, selfless and selfish, spiritual and appetitive forms of love—virtue is degraded into vice.[31]

James Rieger has described Mary Shelley's creature as "erotically cut off" (xxx), citing an analogy between this aspect of the central narrative and the intellectual and geographic isolation that characterize the middle-frame and outer-frame narrators in the novel, Victor and Walton. A close reading of the text's use of "affection" and other key love-words demonstrates that the creature is the focal point for an erotic isolationism—also characterized by the continual evocation and absence, or death, of friends and family—that is pervasive throughout *Frankenstein.*

Percy Shelley makes a claim on Mary's behalf in the preface to *Franken-stein*: "I am by no means indifferent to the manner in which whatever moral tendencies exist in the sentiments or characters . . . [the story] contains shall affect the reader; yet my chief concern in this respect has been limited to avoiding the enervating effects of the novels of the present day, and to the exhibition of the amiableness of domestic affection, and the excellence of universal virtue" (7). The recurrence of the themes of affection and virtue within the novel suggests that Shelley's moral emphasis and his wish after the fact to efface some of the "enervating" effects of Mary's gothic tale were not far removed from his wife's intentions. The parallelism constructed in the phrase "the amiableness of domestic affection, and the excellence of universal virtue" already proposes an association between love and virtue, while the tension between the more particular homely forms of love, indicated by "amiable" and "domestic," versus the more abstract and imposing moral standards, suggested by "universal" and "excellence," is from the outset too great to be managed by simple rhetorical sleight of hand. This gesture signals a problematic within the novel: What is the meaning of "affection" as it is "exhibited" in its domestic form in *Frankenstein,* and what is its exact relation to a virtue that is universally practical?

Our first glimpse into the Frankenstein family circle informs us that Victor's father married a woman recently bereft of her father, who had left her "an orphan and a beggar" (28), a condition that inspires perhaps pity, perhaps a sense of obligation on the part of Victor's father. He then approaches the "poor girl" in the manner of a "protecting spirit" and eventually marries her after a two-year period of prenuptial abstention also required of Victor later in the novel. Victor's fiancée, Elizabeth, was also brought into the family as an orphan, we then learn, the daughter of Victor's father's sister, the sister being the one woman Victor's father is said to have "tenderly loved" (29).

The figurations of incest in this family portrait are obvious and, while significant in terms of Victor's sense of no escape from the slipknot that this loving family comes to represent, they should not obscure the fact that what we are witnessing is not an indiscriminate sexual desire that has transgressed social norms, but rather the directing of sexual desire away from socially acceptable relations toward those in which it cannot or will not be consummated. Victor's first description of Elizabeth dwells on her "uncommonly affectionate" (30) nature as chief among her virtues. She is "as gay and playful as a summer insect" (29). Some indication that erotic love is undergoing a process of caricature in the Frankenstein family is offered by Victor's explanation of his arranged marriage in terms of his mother's "desire to bind as closely as possible the ties of domestic love" (29) and his reference to his love for Elizabeth as a love "to tend on her as I should on a favorite animal" (30). The next instance of affection in the 1818 text[32] is a reference to the "dimpled cheeks" and "endearing manners" of the toddler William (37). The diminution of size, significance, intellect, and erotic interest already conveyed

by the comparison of Elizabeth with bugs and animals culminates in a parallel passage on the charms of tiny children and a summary passage on the subtly tyrannous effects of a system of "mutual affection" that is no model for
virtue. Here everyone is in everyone else's thrall simultaneously, with the
labors of inception and reception, intellection and enjoyment predictably
divided: "Such was our domestic circle, from which care and pain seemed for
ever banished. My father directed our studies, and my mother partook of our
enjoyments. Neither of us possessed the slightest pre-eminence over the
other; the voice of command was never heard amongst us; but mutual affection engaged us all to comply with and obey the slightest desire of each
other" (37). It is this emotional morass and the rejection and rage that it
inevitably produces, and not *erŏs,* that is most clearly associated with disease
and death in the novel. The mother contracts a fatal case of scarlet fever from
Elizabeth: "She died calmly; and her countenance expressed affection even in
death" (38). Victor's father closes his letter informing Victor of the murder of
William and the charge against Justine, "Your affectionate and afflicted
father" (68).

Victor's departure for the university represents a fall from the negative
paradise of his parental home, or a flight from hell; but the departure cannot
result in freedom. Instead, Victor experiences the unhappy division between
pleasure and desire that his emotional upbringing has so diligently prepared
him for:

> I threw myself into the chaise that was to convey me away, and indulged in the
> most melancholy reflections. I, who had ever been surrounded by amiable
> companions, continually engaged in endeavoring to bestow mutual pleasure, I
> was now alone. In the university, whither I was going, I must form my own
> friends, and be my own protector. My life had hitherto been remarkably
> secluded and domestic; and this had given me invincible repugnance to new
> countenances. I loved my brothers, Elizabeth, and Clerval; these were "old
> familiar faces;" but I believed myself totally unfitted for the company of
> strangers. Such were my reflections as I commenced my journey; but as I pro-
> ceeded, my spirits and hopes rose. I ardently desired the acquisition of knowl-
> edge. I had often when at home, thought it hard to remain cooped up in one
> place, and had longed to enter the world, and take my station among other
> human beings. Now my desires were complied with, and it would, indeed,
> have been folly to repent. (39–40)

"Mutual pleasure" within the family circle gives way to an "ardent desire" for
knowledge as Victor approaches the university, not because Victor is superla-
tively adaptive but rather for the opposite reason. He feels himself alone for
the first time, and, having no experience outside the family other than Clerval, he feels the lack of knowledge needed to "form friends," as he puts it.
Feminist discussion of *Frankenstein* has focused on the story as a birth myth.[33]
Victor's primary desire upon leaving home is not, however, to have a baby, as

Mary Shelley did, but to "make" a friend at college, as Mary Shelley could not have done. Certainly Victor cannot be accused of underestimating the difficulty of the task. Given Walton's repeated incantations of desire for a friend that open the novel, and that evoke the reader's sense of the rarity of such persons, as well as the fragility of friendship embodied in the fates of Clerval and Justine (the only two characters referred to as "beloved friend" [84, 153]), the emphasis on the importance of the capacity to make and keep friends, a key component of Aristotelian virtue, is marked in *Frankenstein*. The connection between friends and university education is made explicit in Walton's opening correspondence, in which he states that the only evil that exceeds his "want of a friend" is the fact that he is "self-educated" (13).

The friendship phase of human relationship represents the purgatorial aspect of Mary Shelley's inverted *Commedia*.[34] Clerval as a friend of the family is clearly the best thing that ever happened to Victor; he too escapes his own family circle (55) to join Victor at the university and to nurse Victor back to health; later, Clerval serves as his traveling companion in the "Northward journey." Just as the purgatorial journey represents a transition and connection between the pains of hell and the bliss of heaven, Clerval provides Victor with his only link between the repressively mild affections of his family life and the more extreme emotions, such as joy, that he seeks in the company of a genuine other. Victor's recovery after the strain of "giving birth" and what has been referred to as his "post-partum depression" figures a short-lived rebirth in the context of friendship: "It was a divine spring; and the season contributed greatly to my convalescence. I felt also sentiments of joy and affection revive in my bosom" (57). Victor's attributes his recovery from his "fatal passion" to Clerval's kindness. Prior to this juncture, Victor has enjoyed nature in isolation and shared affection with his family. Henry Clerval is Victor's only hope for a sustainable joy united with milder emotions.

It is the exclusion of joy from affection within the Frankenstein family and the parallel paradigm of the walled-in city of Geneva that has transformed *erōs* into a "fatal passion."[35] True *erōs*, on the other hand, is experienced by the unacculturated creature as a blend of joy and suffering, which can create intense emotional strain, a sense of mixed contraries that Ann Carson has termed in her translation of Sappho the quality of the "bittersweet."[36] As the "daemon" of the novel, the creature is the embodiment of an *erōs* that is denied access to all that it would seek, that cannot move freely, as it is wont to do, among people and between realms, except at night and in remote and frozen regions, where it is destined to destroy itself. Victor's destruction of the creature's mate, tearing it limb from limb even before its completion, is indicative of both Victor's and the creature's erotically deprived condition on a deeper level than that of lacking a partner, as poignant as that is in itself. In destroying the partner of Eros, Victor is tearing Psyche, the human soul, limb from limb. Neither *erōs* nor the virtuous soul can survive in isolation, which constitutes division against itself. The creature remonstrates with his creator: "My vices are the children of a forced solitude that I abhor; and my virtues will necessarily arise when I live in communion with an equal. I shall feel the affections of a sensitive being, and become linked to the chain of existence and events, from which I am now excluded" (143).

Deprived of the communion that Percy Shelley terms in *Queen Mab* "that sweet bondage which is freedom's self" (9.76), the creature in place of freedom enacts flight, and in place of Promethean inspiration self-immolation. From this standpoint, the creature's complaint that there is no virtue without love is not merely self-pitying, but rather a difficult, unpopular, and ethically serious claim for the virtue of erotic love in a post-Hellenic and post-Christian culture.

Notes

1. Mary Poovey, *The Proper Lady and the Woman Writer: Ideology as Style in the Works of Mary Wollstonecraft, Mary Shelley, and Jane Austen* (Chicago: University of Chicago Press, 1984), 40.

2. Anne K. Mellor, "On Romanticism and Feminism" and "Possessing Nature: The Female in Frankenstein," in *Romanticism and Feminism,* ed. Anne K. Mellor (Bloomington: Indiana University Press, 1988), 3–9, 220–32; and id., *Mary Shelley: Her Life, Her Fiction, Her Monsters* (New York: Methuen and Co., 1988), 62–88.

3. James O'Rourke, "'Nothing More Unnatural': Mary Shelley's Revision of Rousseau," *English Literary History* 56 (1989): 543–69.

4. U. C. Knoepflmacher, "Thoughts on the Aggression of Daughters," in *The Endurance of Frankenstein,* ed. George Levine and U. C. Knoepflmacher (Berkeley: University of California Press, 1979), 88–119.

5. The variant "demoniacal," which occurs once in Volume one and twice in Walton's closing letters, is not included in the above inventory. The words "demon" and "daemoniacal" do not occur in the text (Mary Wollstonecraft Shelley, *Frankenstein or, The Modern Prometheus: The 1818 Text,* ed. and introduction by James Rieger [Chicago: University of Chicago Press, 1982], 101). Subsequent citations are made parenthetically in the text from this edition.

6. Plato, *Symposium,* ed., with introduction by, Kenneth Dover (New York: Cambridge University Press), 52.

7. Plato, *Apology and Crito,* ed. Louis Dyer, rev. Thomas Day Seymour (New Rochelle, N.Y.: Orpheus, 1988), 84.

8. Liddell and Scott, *An Intermediate Greek-English Lexicon* (Oxford: Clarendon Press, 1989), 179, *sub verso* III.

9. Plato, *Symposium,* trans., with introduction and notes, Alexander Nehamas and Paul Woodruff (Indianapolis: Hackett Publishing Company, 1989), 47.

10. Liddell and Scott, *Greek-English Lexicon,* 172, sub verso I.1, I.2, II.

11. Percy Shelley, *The Letters of Percy B. Shelley,* ed. Frederick L. Jones (Oxford: Clarendon Press, 1964), 2:20.

12. Linda Dowling, *Hellenism and Homosexuality in Victorian Oxford* (Ithaca, New York: Cornell University Press, 1994).

13. Mary Shelley, *The Journals of Mary Shelley: 1814–1844,* ed. Paula R. Feldman and Diana Scott-Kilvert (Oxford: Clarendon Press, 1987), 1:27ff.

14. Ibid., 1:73ff.

15. Poovey does cite Mary's letter the following month in which Mary claims she will learn Greek to please her husband: "I will be a good girl and never vex you any more. I will learn Greek." This self-assigned motive seems as artificial as Percy's claim four years later that he is translating the *Symposium* for Mary's benefit.

16. Poovey, *Proper Lady,* 40.

17. Mary Shelley, *Journals,* 1:49.

18. Ibid., 1:49.

19. Mary Shelley, *The Letters of Mary Wollstonecraft Shelley,* 3 vols., ed. Betty T. Bennett (Baltimore: Johns Hopkins University Press, 1980), 2:319, 325, 327. These letters are dated July and October, 1839.

20. Mary Shelley, *Journals,* 1:169 n.4, 1:170.

21. Ibid., 1:139. This entry is in Percy Shelley's handwriting.

22. See A. D. Harvey, "Frankenstein and *Caleb Williams,*" Keats-Shelley Journal 29 (1980): 21–27, for the argument that "the details [of *Frankenstein*] do not seem very suggestive of a new scientific era" (22), but rather recall the era of alchemy and magic: "Frankenstein's grisly experiment, in the best alchemical tradition, leads to a *private* retribution."

23. Plato, *Symposium,* trans. in *Five Dialogues of Plato Bearing on Poetic Inspiration: "Ion" and "Symposium,"* trans. P. B. Shelley (New York: Dutton, 1910).

24. Ibid.

25. Michel Foucault, *The Use of Pleasure,* vol. 2 of *The History of Sexuality,* 3 vols., trans. Robert Hurley (New York: Vintage Books, 1985), 229–46.

26. Martha Nussbaum, *The Fragility of Goodness* (New York: Cambridge University Press, 1986), 165–99.

27. Stanley Rosen, *Plato's "Symposium,"* 2nd ed. (New Haven: Yale University Press, 1987), xviii.

28. David M. Halperin, "Why is Diotima a Woman," in *Before Sexuality: The Construction of Erotic Experience in the Ancient Greek World,* ed. David M. Halperin, John J. Winkler, and Froma Zeitlin (Princeton, N.J.: Princeton University Press), 257–308.

29. Bette London, "Mary Shelley, *Frankenstein,* and the Spectacle of Masculinity," *Publication of the Modern Languages Association* 108 (1993): 253–67. London is more openly critical of Rieger's textual work and commentary than of Mellor's biographical criticism, but she has discernibly strong reservations about both.

30. William Blake, "Mary," in *The Poetry and Prose of William Blake,* ed. David V. Erdman, with commentary by Harold Bloom (New York: Doubleday, 1970), 478–79.

31. The creature's "madness," or rage, is distinguished from insanity in my analysis of the effects of *erōs* divided. Kenneth Dover has commented on the ancient Greek formula that desire doubled equals *erōs,* and *erōs* doubled equals madness (Plato, *Symposium,* ed. Dover, 2). *Erōs* divided produces an opposite effect, which is justified wrath. I interpret the creature's actions, to use R. D. Laing's formulation, as a sane reaction to an insane society and believe that this view is perfectly consistent with that indicated by Mary's and Percy's experimentations in marital love.

32. The 1823 interpolation of a passage referring to "ardent affection" (31) is out of character with the 1818 text. Interestingly, the interpolation comes after Shelley's death and perhaps tends to efface some of the constraint Mary felt in the "family circle" constituted by Mary, Percy, Claire, et al.

33. This approach was initiated by Ellen Moers and has been taken up by a number of feminist critics, including Anne K. Mellor, who succinctly states the current significance of the reading: "On the cultural level, Frankenstein's scientific project—to become the sole creator of a human being—supports a patriarchal denial of the value of women and of female sexuality" ("Possessing Nature," 220). Moers' reading, in "Female Gothic," is a sensitive account of the representation of an aspect of female suffering in *Frankenstein,* "the trauma of the afterbirth" (*Literary Women* [New York: Oxford University Press, 1963], 93).

34.   Mary Shelley writes to Fanny Imlay nine days after Percy's and her arrival in Geneva and one month before the composition of *Frankenstein* (May 17, 1816): "We do not enter into society here, yet our time passes swiftly and delightfully. We read Latin and Italian during the heats of noon, and when the sun declines we walk in the garden of the hotel. . . . You know that we have just escaped from the gloom of winter and of London; and coming to this delightful spot during this divine weather, I feel as happy as a new-fledged bird . . ." (*Letters,* 1:18). The "Italian" is Dante's, which has influenced her imaginative rendering of winter in London versus spring in Geneva. Note the direct references to Dante, another neo-Platonic author like Apuleius and Wieland, in the text (53, 145). There are many more indirect references.

35.   Mary Shelley remarks in her second and last letter from Geneva (June 1, 1816), "The Genevese are also much inclined to puritanism. It is true that from habit they dance on Sunday, but as soon as the French government was abolished in the town, the magistrates ordered the theatre to be closed, and measures were taken to pull down the building" (*Letters,* 1:21).

36.   Anne Carson, *Eros: The Bittersweet* (Princeton, N. J.: Princeton University Press, 1986), 3–9.

"Did You Get Mathilda from Papa?":
Seduction Fantasy and the Circulation
of Mary Shelley's *Mathilda*

TERENCE HARPOLD

> In a dream, I saw myself descending toward my father, intending to join him
> in the library. But along the way, the little skeleton always snatched me from
> behind with its outstretched hand. And I continued to live with my night-
> mares, and would never dare, when night had fallen—and now even in the
> day—to go down alone to the library.
>
> This phobia was a too marvelous compromise between two powerful tenden-
> cies in my unconscious: to *be* my mother, in dying like her, which satisfied the
> most positive part of my oedipal complex: the love for my father; and to be
> *punished* with death by my mother, in reprisal for the death that I had caused
> her, which satisfied, in the other part of my oedipal complex, the unconscious
> sentiment of culpability attached to it.
>
> —Marie Bonaparte, "L'identification d'une fille à sa mère morte"[1]

Mary Shelley's entries to the journal dating from her elopement with Percy
in July of 1814 are interrupted in early June of 1819, near the end of the
Shelleys' brief stay in Rome. William, the Shelleys' first son, had fallen ill on
May 25. His condition wavered uncertainly for much of the following week,
and on June 4—when Mary broke off her journal—he seems to have taken a
sudden turn for the worse.[2] At noon of June 7, William died.[3] That William's
illness and death is marked by a discontinuity in her journal suggests the singular importance of this, the third such loss for Mary in four years. There are
only a few breaks in the journal before June 4, 1819: the death of Mary's
unnamed first child (a girl, d. March 6, 1815), and that of her third child,
Clara (d. Sept. 24, 1818), are recorded without any corresponding interrup-
tions (Feldman 73, 223; Jones 39, 105).[4] On June 27, three weeks after
William's death, Mary wrote to Amelia Curran about arrangements for his
tomb, "near which I shall lie one day & care not—for my own sake—how

Reprinted from *Studies in Romanticism* 28, no. 1 (Spring 1989): 49–67. Courtesy of Trustees of
Boston University.

soon—I shall never recover {*sic*} that blow . . . Everything on earth has lost its interest to me."[5]

Mary resumed her journal after the Shelleys moved to Leghorn, on August 4, 1819—Percy's twenty-seventh birthday—where she indicated that she was at work on the novel which in its final version was entitled *Mathilda*. It appears from her entries that she wrote out a first draft and corrected the fair copy through about September 12, revised it further on November 8, and finally, dated the manuscript on November 9.[6] The next day, November 10, there is again a break in her journal. On December 31, she wrote, "I have not kept my journal all this time; but I have little to say, except that on the morning of Friday, November 12, little Percy Florence was born" (Feldman 297; Jones 126).

It is evident from the first draft of *Mathilda* that the novel is, at least in part, Mary's response to William's death. In that draft, entitled *The Fields of Fancy,* Mathilda's autobiographical narrative is embedded in the account of an unnamed narrator.[7] "It was in Rome," the narrator begins, "that I suffered a misfortune that reduced me to misery & despair" (90). She is visited by a "lovely spirit" named Fantasia who, though unable to repair her loss ("those you love," she says, "are gone for ever & great as my power is I cannot recall them to you" {90}), offers to reassure her with a vision of the afterlife. She conveys the narrator to "the Elysian fields" (91), where they attend a circle of recently departed spirits recounting their earthly lives. Among these is Mathilda, a woman "of about 23 years of age" (94)—Mary was 22 in 1819—whose tale of "dark & phre[n]zied passions" (100) is directed to the narrator. Mathilda's story is strong stuff—a mother's death in childbirth, the father's incestuous love for the daughter, his suicide, her mourning and death—but the relation between the narratives is clearly one of lack and reparation: Mathilda's tragic history is presented to the narrator to fill the gap in her own history.

This narrative frame was discarded in the final version of the novel, in which the text is presented as Mathilda's written memoir, rather than another's record of her oral account. The discarding of the frame conflates the previously discrete levels of the narrative: the act of writing (reporting another's life or remembering one's own) and the experience recorded in writing belong in the final version of the novel to the same person. If, as I will argue, *Mathilda* is a profoundly autobiographical work, the collapse of the transparently autobiographical frame narrative into Mathilda's narrative is significant because it exemplifies a principle of identification at work across the structure of the novel. The events that frame the period in Mary's life during which she wrote *Mathilda*—the death of one son and the birth of another—invoke and sustain that principle. By way of Mathilda (by way of *Mathilda*), Mary reported or remembered a history of forbidden desire and death to repair a loss at the origin of that history. The composition of the novel and the circulation of its manuscript are inextricably bound to that history; they represent Mary's effort to revise, account for and neutralize its dangers.[8]

The death of Wollstonecraft ten days after her daughter's birth must have forever altered the course of Mary's psychological development. Her representations of her mother could be constituted only after the fact, drawing on the recollections of others—first among these being her father—and subject to the effects, *après-coup* (*nachträglich*),[9] of her subsequent experience. The well-documented preoccupation of the Godwin circle with the memory of Wollstonecraft would have reminded Mary at every turn that the figure of her mother was joined to that of her father. Moreover, this "memory" of Wollstonecraft—Mary's source of information for a woman that she herself could not have remembered—would have been, given Godwin's romantic proclivities, uniquely subject to reshaping by literary and sentimentalizing interests.[10] Mary's capacity for "pre"-oedipal identification with the mother—establishing both the model for subsequent development and the potential for rivalry at a critical stage of that development—would have been sharply restricted, in effect, *already* oedipalized, irreducibly subject to the imperatives of the father's desire.[11]

This is what happens in *Mathilda*. The passage relating the romance of her parents and her mother's death takes up fewer than three pages in the novel (4–6). Throughout this section, the mother, Diana, is portrayed only as the object of the father's passion, with no independent initiative or interest. The only independent sign for the mother appears in the discarded narrative frame of *The Fields of Fancy*, in the character of Diotima, "a woman about 40 years of age" (Wollstonecraft was thirty-eight at the time of her death), whose "eyes burned with a deep fire and every line of her face expressed enthusiasm & wisdom—Poetry seemed seated on her lips which were beautifully formed & every motion of her limbs although not youthful was inexpressibly graceful" (94). Diotima is clearly an idealized figure of Wollstonecraft, but she is, significantly, relegated to the frame of Mathilda's narrative, where she remains bound by the imperative to tell the story of the father's desire. Insofar as she represents the figure of the mother, it is a mother who acquiesces to that imperative: she is the one who presses Mathilda to tell her tale of "phre[n]zied passions" (100).

The daughter's account of herself is likewise shaped by the father's intervention in mother-daughter identifications. Because Mathilda can only represent the scene of her origin as already subject to her father's desire, her subsequent response to his love is already complicit with it. When she "chances" to mention her liking for Alfieri's "Myrrha," she is frightened and confused by the violence of his reaction (20), though her interest in a tragedy about a daughter's incestuous passion for her father can hardly seem to be the product of chance, in light of what she knows has happened when she records the event (20).[12] His equation of mother and daughter—"Diana dies to give her birth; her mother's spirit was transferred into her frame, and she ought to be as Diana to me" (40)—signifies as well Mathilda's sense of her succession to her mother's place. His despair at having "betrayed" his daughter's "confidence" (37) is also her despair at his having exposed their secret alliance.

The mutually implicating desires of father and daughter refigure Mary's compromised position in the oedipal configuration brought about by Wollstonecraft's death. The relations of Mathilda and Diana to the father represent, in this light, both Mary's chief inheritance from her mother and what she must make of that inheritance in order to find a place for herself in her mother's absence. After he confesses "the hell of passion" (40) that will burn in him until his death, Mathilda's father complains, "How dare I go where I may meet Diana, when I have disobeyed her last request; her last words said in a faint voice when all feeling but love, which survives all things else was already dead, she then bade me make her child happy" (40). His memory of Diana's final request revises Godwin's account of his last conversation with Wollstonecraft:

> I . . . affected to proceed wholly upon the ground of her having been very ill, and that it would be some time before she could expect to be well; wishing her to tell me any thing that she would choose to have done respecting the children [Mary and Fanny], as they would now be principally under my care. After having repeated this idea to her in a great variety of forms, she at length said, with a significant tone of voice, "I know what you are thinking of," but added, that she had nothing to communicate to me upon the subject.[13]

In *Mathilda,* the daughter missing from her mother's last wishes is written in as their principal concern. Moreover, the mother who commands the father to make their daughter "happy" provides in fantasy the maternal approval of oedipal succession that is possible for Mary only by implication in her relations with her father.

In a recent study of *Frankenstein,* Marc Rubenstein has suggested that the writing of that novel was motivated by Mary's "search" "for the mother of her origins."[14] He conjectures that Mary read the love letters of Godwin and Wollstonecraft from the period during which she was conceived, on a November evening much like the "dreary night of November" when Victor Frankenstein brings the monster to life.[15] The creation at the imaginative center of the novel, he concludes, refigures the scene of Mary's origin; the conflicting representations of the mother which spill out from that scene into the rest of the novel represent Mary's effort to rehearse and contain the dangers of motherhood signaled by Wollstonecraft's death.

Rubenstein's reading of *Frankenstein* suggests an analogous reading of *Mathilda.* Mary's fiction rehearses the problematic scene of her origin, and *Mathilda,* like *Frankenstein,* revises the elementary familial positions that emerge in that scene. It differs from the earlier novel in that the fantasy of origin it represents more actively foregrounds the oedipalization of the primal scene that is the effect of the father's intervention in the mother-daughter relation. The primal scene is refigured in *Mathilda* as a scene of *seduction,* between father and daughter, recasting Mary's emergence from her parents' embrace as a substitution of the daughter in the place of the mother, the object of (and responding to) the father's desire. The abstraction of the seduction fantasy over the entire novel is an accomplice to the seduction, because every position in the fantasy is cathected by the daughter who records it.[16] The narrator's story in *The Fields of Fancy* frame, Mathilda's story, her father's and her mother's stories—the structure of seduction that informs all of these stories—each of these is a version of Mary's story. These versions of Mary's story constitute, moreover, a revision of her family history in keeping with its oedipal interests and conflicts. In the family romance[17] as seduction fantasy, the revision of history is to the daughter's benefit; the mother is absent, or only implied, and the daughter's success in defining herself by supplanting the mother is made clear by her father's desire for her in her mother's place.

The mother's apparent absence from the seduction fantasy does not, however, lessen her influence on its structure. She returns from within it, as its limiting term—and with a vengeance. The contradictions of Mathilda's father's confession of his love signals Mary's internalization of the incest taboo and its implicit affirmation of the mother's continuing authority:

> "I hate you! You are my bane, my poison, my disgust! Oh! No" And then his manner changed, and fixing his eyes on me with an expression that convulsed every nerve and member of my frame—"you are none of these; you are my light, my only one, my life.—My daughter, I love you!" (30)

Mathilda's response to her father's confession is first pity, and then revulsion, the change so sudden that the repression is unmistakable:

> for the first time that phantom seized me; the first and only time for it has never since left me . . . I felt *her* fangs on my heart: I tore my hair; I raved aloud; at one moment in pity for his sufferings I would have clasped my father in my arms; and then starting back in horror I spurned him with my foot. (31, emphasis added)

This "phantom" appears nowhere else in the novel, though there can be little doubt as to her identity. Too-close an identification with the mother leads to death, as the daughter must conclude from the evidence of her own birth. The absent, usurped mother may still punish her rival; indeed, the rival will share her mother's fate if she takes her mother's place—she, too, will be subject to the fatal effect of the father's desire.[18] The problem that the seduction fantasy written into *Mathilda* must resolve is, how to enjoy the father's desire without suffering its consequences?[19]

The resolution described in *Mathilda* is a passive submission to the dangers of identification with the mother, a transformation of its penalty into a defense. After his confession of incestuous love, Mathilda's father flees from her, leaving behind a letter suggesting that he intends to cast himself into the sea. She sets out immediately in pursuit. As she nears the coast, a storm that began with nightfall grows more violent. The height of the storm coincides with a crisis of recognition:

> About two hundred yards distant, alone in a large meadow stood a magnificent oak; the lightnings shewed its myriad boughs torn by the storm. A strange idea seized me; a person must have felt all the agonies of doubt concerning the life and death of one who is the whole world to them before they can enter into my feelings—for in that state, the mind working unrestrained by the will makes strange and fanciful combinations with outward circumstances and weaves the chances and changes of nature into an immediate connection with the event they dread. It was with this feeling that I turned to the old Steward who stood pale and trembling beside me; "Mark, Gaspar, if the next flash of lightning rend not that oak my father will be alive."
>
> I had scarcely uttered these words than a flash instantly followed by a tremendous peal of thunder descended on it; and when my eyes recovered their sight after the dazzling light, the oak no longer stood in the meadow. (44)

The prophecy here is realized on several registers, for Mathilda has already dreamed of her father's flight to the sea and her unsuccessful effort to prevent his suicide, before she receives the letter describing his intentions (36).[20] Who is the victim of the blast (and who or what is responsible for it) is, moreover, unclear: the destruction of the oak fulfills Mathilda's earlier demand of her father that he "speak that word" (29) that will explain his suffering—"I demand that dreadful word; though it be as a flash of lightning to destroy me, speak it" (30).

Prophecy, like dreaming, is a form of wish-fulfillment; its utility in the work of fantasy is that it attributes the wished-for event to a necessity independent of the desires of the dreamer or prophet. Mathilda insists from the first paragraphs of the novel that her fate has been "governed by . . . a hideous necessity" (2). Mary's interest in that necessity is evident. It signals, on one hand, her acknowledgement within *Mathilda* of the irreversibility of the conditions of her birth and early childhood; on the other hand, it represents her defense against the sentiments of culpability produced by those conditions. The awkward syntax of Mathilda's cry (if . . . rend not . . . will be alive") suggests that, more than the father's life or death, what is at stake in the passage is a denial of responsibility for the event it predicts. The more straightforward, "if the next flash of lightning rend that oak my father will be dead," would imply a direct engagement of the speaker in that event. Mary's awareness that the daughter's innocence is compromised by her prediction is clear from Mathilda's explanation of the prediction, a striking formulation of the unconscious motivation of fantasy: "the mind working unrestrained by the will makes strange and fanciful combinations with outward circumstances and weaves the chances and changes of nature into an immediate connection with the event they dread." For Mary, for whom Mathilda's dream and prophecy are a defense, the consequences of the father's desire are more dreadful than his death. If father takes his own life, he takes with it the menace of his desire, leaving the daughter free of responsibility for his removal from the scene.

Were *Mathilda* to end with the father's suicide, that event would signal the priority of the phantom mother's menace over her daughter's need for identification with the mother. His death, however, comes only a little more than halfway through the novel. Mathilda's decision after his suicide to feign her own death, and then retreat into exile and decline, suggests that his removal not only defends her against the penalty of his love, but also prepares for her eventual identification with the mother.

> I who had before clothed myself in the bright garb of sincerity must now borrow one of divers colours: it might sit awkwardly at first, but use would enable me to place it in elegant folds, to *lie* with grace. Aye, I might *die* my soul with falsehood untill [*sic*] I had quite hid its native colour . . . My father, to be happy both now and when again we meet I must fly from all this life which is mockery to one like me. In solitude only shall I be myself; in solitude I shall be thine. (48–49, emphasis added)

As she wastes away in the last pages of the novel, she muses, "In truth I am in love with death; no maiden ever took more pleasure in the contemplation of her bridal attire than I in fancying my limbs already enwrapt in their shroud: is it not my marriage dress? Alone it will unite me to my father when in an eternal mental union we shall never part" (77–78),

A longing for death can represent a desire to dissolve the self, to return completely to the mother. For Mathilda, death is a doubly effective return: the mother is already dead, and to be like her in that respect is to be more with her than is possible in life. In death, moreover, the desired reunion with the father that compels her to take her mother's place is no longer forbidden. Death brings with it "mental" union—that is, asexual union—which can make a shroud into a wedding dress, and a daughter her father's bride, without fear of the mother's retribution.[21] The bride in her shroud is at once the mother, victim of the father's desire—the only mother the daughter has ever known—and the daughter who has taken her place.[22] The merging of mother and daughter frees the daughter from the menace of the phantom mother by embracing the menace and erasing the phantom. When Mathilda imagines the afterlife, it is a world in which the mother no longer has a place. She envisions the terrestrial paradise of the *Purgatorio*: "[I] thought it would be sweet when I wandered on those lovely banks to see the car of light descend with my long lost parent to be restored to me" (74). Only one lost parent is restored to her, and it is for *his* love that she embraces death.[23]

On May 2, 1820, Maria Gisborne left Leghorn for England, taking with her a copy of *Mathilda,* which Mary had asked her to convey to Godwin for his assistance in its publication.[24] Mary and Maria had met for the first time in Mary's adult life at La Scala, in May of 1818. Their very first meeting, however, had occurred long before. During the week following Wollstonecraft's death, Maria (then Maria Reveley) cared for the infant Mary while Godwin was occupied with the affairs of his dead wife. Maria's intimacy with Mary's parents dated from well before their marriage, and she appears to have been an early rival of Wollstonecraft for Godwin's affections. The three remained close friends during the marriage. After Wollstonecraft's death, Godwin took a renewed interest in Maria, though the jealousy of her husband, Willey Reveley, forced him to curtail his visits to her. In August of 1799, only one month after Reveley's death, Godwin proposed marriage to Maria. She received his offer coldly, no doubt put off by the impropriety of his advances. Shortly thereafter, she married John Gisborne. Godwin's letters to Maria during the courtship make it clear that Godwin intended (unconsciously?) for her to take Wollstonecraft's place in more ways than as simply his wife. "You have it in your power," he writes, "to give me new life, a new interest in existence, to raise me from the grave in which my heart lies buried."[25]

Mary was aware of her father's feelings for Maria—most of what is known, in fact, of her father's relations with Maria comes from Mary's unfinished biography of Godwin.[26] In Italy, Maria became Mary's closest female friend and confidant, a stepmother of sufficient grace and intellect to approximate the idealized figure of the mother she had never known, and to surpass the much inferior substitute—Mary Jane Clairmont—chosen by her father.[27]

During her visit to England, Maria and Godwin discussed *Mathilda*.[28] She writes in her journal,

> The subject he says is disgusting and detestable, and there ought to be, at least if [it] is ever published, a preface to prepare the minds of the readers, and to prevent them from being tormented by the apprehension from moment to moment of the fall of the heroine; it is true (he says) that this difficulty is in some measure obviated, by Matildas [*sic*] protestation at the beginning of the book, that she has not to reproach herself with any guilt; but yet, in proceeding one is apt to lose sight of that protestation; besides (he added with animation) one cannot exactly trust to what an author of the modern school may deem guilt.[29]

Godwin's misgivings about the compromised innocence of the novel's heroine screen his concern for the innocence or guilt of its author, and show his active engagement in his daughter's seduction fantasy. Whether or not he recognized himself in that fantasy, he could not have resisted the implication of his desire in not only its plot and Mary's writing of it, but also—perhaps most of all—in her having sent him the manuscript.

There is no evidence that Godwin made any effort to see that the novel was published. When it became clear that Godwin was not going to act on its publication, Mary undertook to recover the manuscript. Beginning in January, 1822, her letters to Maria repeat earnest requests that she retrieve the manuscript from Godwin and have it copied, but he appears to have resisted or ignored Maria's efforts to do so. Following a break between the Godwins and the Gisbornes in February, recovery of the manuscript became increasingly unlikely. Mary suggested Maria write for *Mathilda,* and herself wrote to Godwin at least once, but without result.[30] By late April, Maria had decided that the manuscript would never be recovered,[31] but Mary continued to hope otherwise. On June 2, she wrote to ask—and her question is informed by every identification that has shaped the novel and these letters—"Did you get Mathilda from Papa?"[32]

Godwin's refusal to return the manuscript breaks a sequence of identifications and defenses that can be traced back at least as far as William Shelley's death. These identifications and defenses inform the composition of the manuscript and its circulation between Mary, Maria and Godwin. They are multiform and autobiographical: the life they trace, the tale they write out, is Mary's. These are its major moments:

1. *Mathilda* represents a fantasy of seduction, Mary's refiguring of the scene of her origin, subject to the effects of the father's intervention in mother-daughter identifications. The fantasy responds to Mary's need for identification with her dead mother, to her feelings of culpability for her mother's death, to her guilt for the oedipal succession that is facilitated by it, and to the fantasy mother's punitive power over the daughter who succeeds to her mother's place.

2. The submission of the novel to Godwin signals Mary's effort to engage him in the seduction fantasy, but to acknowledge the authority of his desire in the primal scene which determines her understanding of herself and her relations with each of her parents. The daughter's need to acknowledge the father's authority is brought to crisis by the loss of the son whose name had previously signified that authority. The manuscript of the novel takes the place (for both daughter and father) of prior signs of submission to the father's desire. It is a substitute for at least two lost sons, the "William Godwin" that Mary could not be,[33] and the "William Shelley" who might have partially repaired that lack, had he survived.[34]

3. Mary submits the manuscript through Maria, who, acting in the place of the idealized mother (for both the daughter and the father),

figures the fantasy mother's acquiescence to the daughter's succession to the mother's place.

4. The loss of William requires a substitute sign of submission to the father's desire—the manuscript of *Mathilda*; Percy Florence's birth changes the daughter's relation to the father, and overdetermines the function of the manuscript. Just the name of her first son, "William," was a signal of the authority of the first father, so the name of her second son, "Percy," signifies the intervening authority of a second father. The seduction fantasy can serve not only to represent the daughter's submission to the father's desire, but also to restrict its authority to the fantasmatic scene of seduction. The writing of *Mathilda* and the naming of Mary's second son signal not only an effort to satisfy Godwin's desire and neutralize its dangers, but also to reshape the oedipal configuration that threatens the daughter with death. By satisfying the desire of one father—and restricting that satisfaction to its representation in fantasy—Mary is free to submit herself to the authority of another father's desire, and thereby assume the mother's place under conditions where she is less subject to the menace of that identification.[35] In *Mathilda*, the power of the family romance to remake the parents according to the daughter's desire remakes as well the daughter's sense of herself as parent, as mother and as wife.

5. Godwin, however, refuses to recognize Mary's revision of the family history. The seduction fantasy written into *Mathilda* would satisfy his unconscious need for the daughter's acknowledgement of his desire, but the submission of the manuscript, while on the one hand establishing his authority, would on the other hand signal Mary's effort to contain it. Godwin's refusal to aid in the publication of the manuscript, or even to return it to Mary, defends against the daughter's effort to alter the oedipal structure that defines her place as daughter, mother and wife, relative to the father.[36] To sanction her substitution of another father would have called into question his own position, complicit with the seduction; it would have hit too close to home.

Soon, however, another accident of history would render Mary's effort and Godwin's refusal of little consequence. Mary's hope of a father's love without mortal penalty would be ended by Percy's death in July of 1822. After that event, the overdetermination of the names in Mary's life increases: what remained after Percy's death of the revised oedipal configuration was the son, proof of a father's love, who could love a daughter and a mother in the father's name. She writes in her journal on October 2, 1822—her first entry after Percy's death, "Father, Mother, friend, husband, children— all made as it were the team that (dragged me) conducted me here; & now all except you, my poor boy & you are necessary to the continuance of my life, all are gone, and I am left to fulfil my task" (Feldman 405; Jones 181). In a journal entry later that month, she pleads with the spirit of Percy not to desert her: "Before when I wrote Mathilda, miserable as I was, the *inspiration* was sufficient to quell my wretchedness temporarily—but now I have no (rep) respite—& shall have none—I do not wish for any—the eternity of my sorrow is a pledge of our reunion & I would not barter it for ages of (a) more pleasurable feeling" (Feldman 414; omitted from Jones). Mary's pledge to Percy is too much like Mathilda's pledge to her father to mistake their common origin.

That origin, in fantasy and in reality, would shape Mary's sense of her destiny. She mentions *Mathilda* for the last time in a letter to Maria, May 3–6, 1823: "It seems to me that in what I have hitherto written I have done nothing but prophecy what has arrived to. Mathilda fortells [*sic*] even many small circumstances most truly—& the whole of it is a monument of what now is."[37]

Notes

I am grateful to Stuart Curran for his critical acumen and patience during the several revisions of this essay.

1. *Revue française de Psychoanalyse* 2.3 (1928): 541–65. Bonaparte's memoir of her childhood neurosis is worthy of more attention than it appears to have received. It is, as nearly as I have been able to determine, the only first-hand account in psychoanalytic literature of the oedipal conflicts of a daughter whose mother has died giving birth to her. It is one of the most important sources for my reading of the place and significance of *Mathilda* in Mary Shelley's life. Translations of passages from Bonaparte's memoir are my own.

2. *The Journals of Mary Wollstonecraft Shelley: An Annotated Edition,* ed. Paula Renée Feldman, diss., Northwestern University, 1974 (Ann Arbor: UMI, 1975. 7507910) 260. *Mary Shelley's Journal,* ed. Frederick L. Jones (Norman OK: U of Oklahoma P, 1947) 122. The heading "Friday 4th" is not followed by an entry, and there are no further daily entries in Book II of the journal (the remaining pages of Book II include transcriptions of poetry, fragments by Mary and Percy, lists of reading, clothing, etc., dating from a later period). Until recently, the only edition of Mary's *Journal* was that edited by Jones in 1947. The Jones text is marred by numerous omissions, and sometimes incorrect dates and annotations. Feldman corrects errors in the Jones text and restores omitted passages. In this essay, I follow Feldman's version of text and punctuation, but cite both editions, noting their differences when significant. Passages or words that are cancelled in the manuscript of the *Journal* are enclosed in parentheses, thus: ( ).

3. Clair [Clara Mary Jane] Clairmont, *The Journals of Claire Clairmont,* ed. Marion Kingston Stocking (Cambridge: Harvard UP, 1968) 113.

4. Only the entry for July 8, 1822, the day of Percy's death, is followed by a discontinuity comparable in length to that following William's death (Feldman 392; Jones 180). That entry, like that of June 4, 1819, is followed by no text, and is Mary's last entry in that journal book (Book III). The only other sizable gap in the published journal prior to Percy's death is attributed by Feldman and Jones to the loss of the journal book for May 14, 1815–July 20, 1816, which included the date of William Shelley's birth (January 24, 1816) (Feldman ix; Jones 50n1). Following Percy's death, Mary's entries to the journal were more irregular.

5. *The Letters of Mary Wollstonecraft Shelley,* 3 vols, ed. Betty T. Bennett (Baltimore: Johns Hopkins UP, 1980–88) 1: 100.

6.   Elizabeth Nitchie, "Mary Shelley's *Mathilda:* An Unpublished Story and Its Biographical Significance," *Studies in Philology* 40 (1943): 448–49. Mary's work on the novel took
altogether a little more than three months. In the final version of *Mathilda,* Mathilda's literary
effort also takes three months. Nitchie concludes that Mary finished copying the manuscript
on September 12 on the basis of the entry, "Finish copying my tale," which follows the heading
"Sunday 12" in the journal. Under the same heading, however, Mary also writes, "on friday
[that is, September 10]—S.[helley] sends his tragedy [*The Cenci*] to Peacock" (Feldman 292;
Jones 124). Jones notes in his preface that, "after neglecting her journal for a few days, Mary's
practice was to summarize the missing days, but she used only the one specific date for the
entry, usually (but not always) the date on which she wrote the summarizing entry" (xiii). The
next previous date heading in the journal is "Sunday 5th," followed by no entry. The entry for
"September 12" then, clearly records some events which occurred two days prior, and possibly
others of several days before that. Though the evidence is admittedly ambiguous, it is not
improbable that Mary finished copying the text of *Mathilda*—her "tale"—on September 10,
1819, the twenty-second anniversary of her mother's death. This would not have been the first
time that a landmark in Mary's writing coincided with the anniversary of Wollstonecraft's
death. Five years before, on September 10, 1814, she began her first attempt at a novel, now
lost, entitled *Hate* (Feldman 26; Jones 14).
      7.   *Mathilda,* ed. Elizabeth Nitchie, *Studies in Philology,* extra ser., 3 (Chapel Hill: U of
North Carolina P, 1959) 90–104. All subsequent references to *Mathilda* are to this edition.
      8.   The only substantive analysis of the work's biographical significance is Elizabeth
Nitchie's 1943 study of the then unpublished manuscript. (Her conclusions are repeated in an
abbreviated form, with some minor emendations, in her preface to the 1959 edition [*Mathilda,*
vii–xv], and in Appendix III of her biography, *Mary Shelley, Author of "Frankenstein"* (New
Brunswick, NJ: Rutgers UP, 1953; Westport, CT: Greenwood, 1970). While she concluded
that the novel is largely an autobiographical document, Nitchie seems reluctant to speculate
on the origin and significance of its central theme of father-daughter incest. She attributes the
incest there to Percy's interest in that subject and—improbably, I think—to Mary's "horror" of
her "unnatural and dreadful attitude" towards Percy after the death of Clara. "Mary may also,"
Nitchie continues, "have been recording, in Mathilda's sorrow over her alienation from her
father and her loss of him by death, her grief at a spiritual separation from her own father"
(457)—the estrangement resulting from Godwin's demands for money and attacks on Percy.
"Like Mathilda, she had truly lost a beloved but cruel father, a loss all the more poignant
because of what she later acknowledged to Mrs Gisborne was her 'excessive and romantic'
attachment to him" (459). That Nitchie does not make more of Mary's "excessive and romantic attachment" to Godwin seems to me a misjudgment.
      9.   On Freud's use of *nachträglich* (Nachträglichkeit; in the *Standard Edition,* infelici-
tously translated as "deferred action"), see Jean Laplanche and J.-B. Pontalis, *The Language of
Psychoanalysis,* trans. Donald Nicholson-Smith (London: Hogarth, 1973) 111–14.
      10.   Mitzi Myers has shown ("Godwin's *Memoirs* of Wollstonecraft: The Shaping of Self
and Subject," *Studies in Romanticism* 20.3 [1981]) that Godwin's *Memoirs of the Author of a Vindication of the Rights of Woman* (written in 1798, immediately after Wollstonecraft's death) is
deeply informed by such interests. Though Mary must have been familiar with the *Memoirs*
before she wrote *Mathilda,* the only evidence by her own hand indicating that she read them is
a journal entry dated eight months after the completion of the novel. Mary read the *Memoirs*
together with the *Posthumous Letters,* the *Letters from Norway and Mary, A Fiction* during the
period of June 1–7, 1820 (Feldman 314–15; Jones 133–34)—the first anniversary of William
Shelley's illness and death.
      11.   Mary Poovey's recent reading of *Frankenstein,* while it convincingly accounts for
Mary's conflicting desires for self-assertion and acceptance, is limited by its privileging of an
idealized mother. Poovey writes, "The motherless daughter's relationship with the father carries the burden of needs originally and ideally satisfied by the mother; in a sense, the relation-

ship with each father [Godwin and Percy] is only an imaginative substitute for the absent relationship with the mother" (*The Proper Lady and the Woman Writer: Ideology as Style in the Works of
Mary Wollstonecraft, Mary Shelley, and Jane Austen* [Chicago: U of Chicago P, 1984] 168). The
"needs originally and ideally satisfied by the mother" are, however, already subject to oedipal
defenses against the mother as the primary rival for the father's desire, because his desire is
already a principal element of any representation of the mother. This is true whatever the origin of the material for the representation (whether the daughter is told of her mother by her
father or by someone else), as the father is present by implication in every fantasy of the
mother.

12.   Alfieri's play could serve as a gloss to *Mathilda*. The eponymic heroine of "Myrrha"
is tortured by her incestuous desire for her father, brought to a crisis by her approaching marriage, and by the impossibility of responding truthfully to the repeated inquiries of her parents,
who recognize that she is in love with someone other than her intended husband. At the close
of the play, Myrrha reveals by a slip of the tongue made in her father's presence the name of
her beloved—*his* name. She seizes his dagger and kills herself. Percy read the play in translation
in 1815 (Feldman 97; Jones 49), as did Claire Clairmont, in 1819 (*Journals* 502). Percy encouraged Mary to translate the play (*The Letters of Percy Bysshe Shelley*, 2 vols., ed. Frederick L. Jones
[Oxford: Oxford UP, 1964] 2: 39, where it is misidentified by Jones as "Ariosto's 'Myrrha'").
Jean de Palacio concludes that the play was as influential as *The Cenci* on Mary's writing of
Mathilda, which he finds to be a "conjugation" of the two plays (*Mary Shelley dans son oeuvre:
Contributions aux études shelleyennes* [Paris: Editions Klincksieck, 1969] 135). William Veeder
notes that Thomas Medwin believed that Mary planned to write a father-daughter incest play
based on "Myrrha" ("The Negative Oedipus: Father, *Frankenstein,* and the Shelley's," *Critical
Inquiry* 12.2 [1986]: 388n17), but the "Tale probably suggested" by the play that Medwin
remembers is clearly *Mathilda* (Thomas Medwin, *The Life of Percy Bysshe Shelley,* rev. ed. H. Buxton Forman [London: Oxford UP, 1913] 252).

13.   William Godwin, *Memoirs of Mary Wollstonecraft* [*Memoirs of the Author of a Vindication of the Rights of Woman*], ed. W. Clark Durant (New York: Gordon, 1972) 122.

14.   "'My Accursed Origin': The Search for the Mother in *Frankenstein,*" *Studies in
Romanticism* 15 (1976): 187.

15.   Rubenstein 172.

16.   Cf. Laplanche and Pontalis: "The originary fantasy [*fantasme originaire*] . . . is characterized by an absence of subjectivization coincident with the presence of the subject *in* the
scene . . . "A father seduces a daughter" might perhaps be the summary formulation of the
seduction fantasy. The indication here of the primary process is not the absence of organization,
as is sometimes suggested, but the peculiar character of the structure, in that it is a scenario
with multiple entries, in which nothing shows whether the subject will be immediately located
in the term, *daughter,* it can as well be fixed as *father,* or even in the term *seduces*" ("Fantasy and
the Origins of Sexuality," *The International Journal of Psycho-Analysis* 49.1 [1968]: 13–14, translation slightly corrected).

17.   My use of "family romance" here and below is specific, and closer to Freud's use of
the term than is usually the case when it is invoked. A *Familienroman* is the *narrative* motivated
by oedipal conflicts, in which the history of the child's family is revised; "romance" refers to the
literary genre of the revision, rather than to the bond of affection between the child and one or
another of the parents. See Freud, *The Origins of Psycho-Analysis: Letters to Wilhelm Fleiss, Drafts
and Notes: 1887–1902,* eds. Marie Bonaparte, Anna Freud and Ernst Kris, trans. Eric Mos-
bacher and James Strachey (New York: Basic, 1954) 205, 256; "Family Romances," *The Standard Edition of the Complete Psychological Works of Sigmund Freud,* trans. and ed. James Strachey
(London: Hogarth, 1953–74) 9: 235–41.

18.   Cf. Bonaparte 547–48: "The place of my mother was empty, and I could perhaps
more easily than another little girl dream of occupying it. But the identification with the
mother encountered on the other hand a condition which did not exist for the other little girls

for whom the mother is the living rival: death . . . To be dead, for me, was to be identified with the mother, was to be in the place of the wife of my father, was, like my mother, to die—a kind of strange delight—by his agency [*par lui mourir*]." The last two chapters of Godwin's *Memoirs* would have provided Mary with ample evidence of the effect of the father's desire. Chapter IX begins, "I am now led, by the progress of the story, to the last branch of her history, the connection between Mary [Wollstonecraft] and myself" (97); chapter X begins, "I am now led, by the course of my narrative, to the last fatal scene of her life" (112).

19.   The structure of the seduction fantasy will be determined by the outcome of a struggle for predominance between idealizing and prohibitive functions of the super-ego. The fantasy objects that have replaced the dead mother can, on the one hand, provoke feelings of inferiority and resentment, as the daughter aspires forever unsuccessfully to match her ego-ideal. On the other hand, the fantasized mother can take on a sadistic, punitive character, strengthening the daughter's feelings of culpability for her mother's death, and enforcing the incest taboo from beyond the grave with the threat of the consequences of its violation. The content of these fantasies of the mother is likely to be in large part determined by the father's attitude towards his lost love object and the daughter that can be identified with that object: her idealization will be encouraged by his idealization, her experience of the prohibition of incest will be encouraged by his repression of the identification. The daughter is trapped by 1) the necessity of idealization in the absence of the mother, as a prerequisite to super-ego development on the basis of introjected imagos of the mother; and 2) the consequent threat of identification with the ideal, which, while it enforces the prohibitive function of the super-ego, does so at the expense of the socializing function of the identification. On the sadistic character of the daughter's fantasies of the dead mother, see Peter B. Neubauer, "The One-Parent Child and His Oedipal Development," *The Psychoanalytic Study of the Child* 15 (1960): 286–309; Otto Fenichel, "Specific Forms of the Oedipus Complex," *The Collected Papers of Otto Fenichel,* 2 vols., ed. Hanna Fenichel (New York: W. W. Norton, 1953). On the distinctions between idealizing and prohibitive functions of the super-ego, and the related question as to whether or not these operate independently or within a larger structure, see Laplanche and Pontalis, *Language,* 144–45; 435–38.

20.   Mathilda's pursuit (or her prophetic dream) is mentioned in Mary's letter (Sept. 2, 1822) to Maria Gisborne describing Percy's death: "It must have been fearful to see us [Mary and Claire]—two poor, wild aghast creatures—driving (like Mathilda) towards the *sea* to learn if we were to be for ever doomed to misery" (*Letters* 1: 247). The storm in *Mathilda* may refigure the terrific storm during the night of the Shelleys' elopement to the Continent (Feldman 3–5; Jones 3–4). The father's letter to Mathilda explaining his departure may then refigure the letter Mary left behind for Godwin, described by Godwin in a letter to John Taylor, August 27, 1814 (*The Elopement of Percy Bysshe Shelley and Mary Wollstonecraft Godwin as Narrated by William Godwin,* ed. H. Buxton Forman [Folcroft, PA: Folcroft Press, 1969] 11–12).

21.   The repression of the daughter's sexuality is a precondition for her passage into the afterlife and access to the father: the disguise Mathilda adopts in her exile is described variously as a "fanciful nunlike dress" (50), "a whimsical nunlike habit" (60), and "a close nunlike gown of black silk" (85n49).

22.   Cf. Bonaparte 544–45: "My dead mother, I had even seen her. In the great water-color hung by my grandmother in the salon, where my mother appeared lying on her back on her bed, in a white robe, looking like a bride—and pale, pale." Mary would have also seen her dead mother—in John Opie's portrait, which hung over the fireplace in her father's library (Glynn R. Grylls, *Mary Shelley: A Biography* [London: Oxford UP, 1938] 26; Claire Tomalin, *The Life and Death of Mary Wollstonecraft* [New York: Harcourt Brace Jovanovich, 1974] 231). The portrait, executed in April of 1797, shows Wollstonecraft in a loosely fitting light-colored gown, something like the shroud-wedding dress Mathilda envisages for herself. Mary is present implicitly in the portrait, as Wollstonecraft, in her fifth month of pregnancy, is noticeably plump. Godwin used a retouched engraving of the Opie portrait as the frontispiece of his *Mem-*

oirs (Tomalin, pls. 19–21). See also Durant's note on the Opie portrait in his *Supplement* to Godwin's *Memoirs,* 327–32.

23.   In *Purgatorio* XXVII, Matelda (clearly Mary's source for her heroine's name) directs the poet-voyager to the waters of forgetting of evil and of remembering of good (Lethe and Eunoë); she sings to him from Psalms 31[32]: 1, "Beati quorum tecta . . ." "Happy is he whose fault is taken away, whose sin is covered" (*Purgatorio* XXVII: 6ff). Only after drinking from these waters is Dante sufficiently purified to be able to enter Paradise. Palacio discusses at length the relation between *Mathilda* and the *Purgatorio,* finding (inappropriately, I think) Mathilda at fault for being incapable of a Matelda-like purification of her *father's* memory, and for that reason at least partially responsible for their separation (Palacio 42–46). He misses entirely the significance for *Mary* of the transition made possible by the memory-renovating springs tended by Matelda/Mathilda. Mary read the *Purgatorio* from August 4 to August 20, 1819, while she was writing out the first draft of *The Fields of Fancy* (Feldman 289–91; Jones 122–23).

24.   Maria's journal entry for May 9, 1820 records that she read the novel with approval: "This most s[ingu]larly interesting novel evinces the highest powers of mi[nd] in the author united to extreme delicacy of sentime[nt]. It is written without artifice and perhaps without [the] technical excellence of a veteran writer—There are [perhaps] some little inaccuracies which, up[on] revisal [*sic*], might have been corrected: but these are trifling blemishes [and] I am well persuaded that the author will one day be the admiration of the world. I am confident that I [should] have formed this opinion had I not been acquainted [with] her and loved her" (*Maria Gisborne & Edward E. Williams, Shelley's Friends: Their Journals and Letters,* ed. Frederick L. Jones [Norman, OK: U of Oklahoma P, 1951] 27). Others who were familiar with the novel (besides Maria, Godwin, and presumably, Percy) were Edward and Jane Williams, to whom Mary read from the copy she had retained in August and September of 1821 (Feldman 363–64; Jones 159–60). Nitchie concludes of Mary's submission of the manuscript to Godwin, "highly personal as the story was, [she] hoped that it would be published, evidently believing that the characters and the situations were sufficiently disguised" (*Mathilda* vii). Again, I think, Nitchie misses the significance of the "characters" and "situations" of the novel.

25.   *William Godwin: His Friends and Contemporaries,* 2 vols., ed. C. Kegan Paul (New York: AMS Press, 1970) 1: 335.

26.   *William Godwin: His Friends and Contemporaries* 1: 83, 162, 332–33.

27.   Entering Mary's life relatively late, after four years of an exclusive if distant relationship with Godwin, the second Mrs. Godwin must have appeared to the young Mary as proof of the mother's power to deprive the daughter of the father's love, and proof as well that the real stepmother could not equal the fantasy mother—encouraging in both Mary and Mrs. Godwin conflicting feelings of inferiority and superiority, and heightening their rivalry for the father's attentions. (See, for example, Mary's letter to Percy, September 27, 1817: "as to Mrs G. somthing [*sic*] very analogous to disgust arises whenever I mention her" [*Letters* 1: 43].) That Mrs. Godwin was Mary's rival in every sense to the privileged position occupied by the fantasy mother would have been made very clear by her name, *Mary Jane*; Mary always calls her "Mrs. Godwin." There were other women in the Godwin household whom Mary may have associated with the fantasy mother. Chief among these was Louisa Gray Jones, the servant assigned the task of caring for Mary and Fanny, who left the house when Mrs. Godwin arrived (Jane Dunn, *Moon in Eclipse: A Life of Mary Shelley* [New York: St. Martin's, 1978] 16–20). Grylls suggests (12) that Jones expected to marry Godwin.

28.   The Gisborne's visits to the Godwins were marked by confusion and increasing tensions (Maria Gisborne *Journals* 35–48). The strain was due in part, no doubt, to Godwin's discomfort with the memory of his unsuccessful courtship, but it was attributed by him to Mrs. Godwin's reaction to Maria's intimacy with Mary, whom she considered "the greatest enemy she has in the world." Mrs. Godwin was, Maria reports, so shocked at her first expressions of admiration for Mary that she thereafter refused to receive her (Gisborne *Journals* 39–40).

29. Gisborne *Journals* 44. Mary may never have known the details of Godwin's estima-
tion of the novel; there is no evidence that she ever read Maria's journal (Gisborne *Journals* 8n).

30. *Letters* 1: 224. Her letter and Godwin's reply, if any was made, are lost. She mentions the request to Godwin in a letter to Maria, April 6–10, 1822 (*Letters* 1: 229).

31. Gisborne *Journals* 82.

32. *Letters* 1: 237.

33. Wollstonecraft and Godwin expected their first child to be a boy, whom they would
name after his father (*Godwin & Mary: Letters of William Godwin and Mary Wollstonecraft,* 2 vols.,
ed. Ralph M. Wardle [Lawrence: U of Kansas P, 1966] 80, 82, 88, 92, 102; U. C. Knoepflmacher, "Thoughts on the Aggression of Daughters," *The Endurance of Frankenstein: Essays on
Mary Shelley's Novel,* eds. G. Levine and U. C. Knoepflmacher [Berkeley: U of California P,
1979] 92–93). When Godwin's first child with the second Mrs. Godwin, a boy
(b. 1802), was given his father's name, Mary must have perceived him as a rival, not only in
the way that any new child born into a family threatens the position of the older children, but
also in a very particular way signified by his name: William Godwin the Younger enjoyed a
privileged relation with his father that Mary (who could never be a "William") could not enjoy.
Cf. Mathilda's childhood fantasy of reunion with her father, in which the roles of daughter and
son are conflated: "*disguised like a boy* I would seek my father through the world. My imagination hung upon the scene of recognition; his miniature, which I should continually wear
exposed on my breast, would be the means and I imaged the moment to my mind a thousand
and a thousand times, perpetually varying the circumstances. Sometimes it would be in a
desart [*sic*]; in a populous city; at a ball; we should perhaps meet in a vessel; and his first words
constantly were, 'My *daughter,* I love thee!' " (11, emphasis added).

34. On the page preceding Mary's first journal entry following William's death, she has
written a fragment, evidently addressed to him:

> That time is Gone for ever—child—
> Those hours are frozen forever
> We look on the past, & stare aghast
> On the ghosts with aspects strange & wild
> Of the hopes whom thou & I beguiled
>   To death in life's dark river.
> The waves we gazed on then rolled by
> Their stream is unreturning
> We two stand, in a lonely land,
> Like tombs (m) to mark the memory
> Of joys & griefs that fade & flee
>   In the light of lifes [*sic*] dim morning
>   (Feldman 289; omitted from Jones)

The "ghosts with aspects strange & wild" must include the phantom of the fantasy
mother; the hopes that Mary and William might have beguiled would include the resolution of
the conflicts associated with the fantasy mother.

35. Mathilda addresses her memoirs to a character named Woodville, the one person
who befriends her during her exile. Woodville is clearly an idealized Percy (*Mathilda* xiii;
Nitchie, "Mary Shelley's *Mathilda*" 459), but his authority within the novel is extremely limited: his effort to dissuade Mathilda from her suicidal melancholy is ineffective, and he disap-
pears completely from the novel in its last pages. The primary function he fulfills in the novel
is, I suspect, to mark the transfer between oedipal configurations that the novel undertakes.
Mathilda is, in this respect, addressed to both men: to Godwin (Mathilda's father), as the father
in the originary configuration, for whom the narrative should represent a reassurance of his

continuing authority; to Percy (Woodville), as the father in the substitute configuration, for whom the narrative should represent a reassurance that the first father's authority is limited to the realm of fantasy.

36. The manuscript held by Godwin was never returned to Mary, and is, presumably, lost. The copy that Mary retained remained unpublished among the Shelley papers (Nitchie, *Mathilda* vii–viii; *Mary Shelley* 207). This manuscript is divided between two notebooks containing the finished draft of *Mathilda* and parts of *The Fields of Fancy,* in Lord Abinger's collection, the remainder of the rough draft in the Bodleian Library, and some fragments among the Shelley-Rolls papers in the Bodleian (Nitchie, *Mathilda* vii–viii; *Mary Shelley* 207). Among the Shelley-Rolls fragments is the conclusion to the *Fields of Fancy* narrative frame, which ends with Mathilda saying to Diotima, "I am here, not with my father, but listening to lessons of wisdom, which will one day bring me to him when we shall never part" (*Mathilda* 89n83).

37. *Letters* 1: 336.

Finding Mary Shelley in Her Letters

Betty T. Bennett

When the first volume of my edition of *The Letters of Mary Wollstonecraft Shelley* was published in 1980, one reviewer suggested that Mary Shelley's letters were not worth publishing: Anyone interested might have requested microfilm from the Bodleian or xeroxes from the Pforzheimer Library and read the manuscripts for themselves. Reality raises the more obvious challenges to this simple solution: the manuscripts are scattered throughout the world in public and private collections; portions of letters are sometimes in two repositories; Mary Shelley's letters are often only partially dated or completely undated, thereby eluding contextual understanding; even after one accustoms oneself to Mary Shelley's handwriting, single words and phrases are often difficult to decipher. Nevertheless, the reviewer's suggestion, by its very failure to understand either Mary Shelley or the nature of editing letters, inadvertently raised several important questions for Romantic studies: did past biographies of Mary Shelley reveal all we needed to know about the author? Was her place in Romanticism insufficiently recognized not because her works lacked a philosophic basis but because we had not noticed or understood it? Can an edition of letters portray an author's life story sufficiently to add substantial depth and context to her works?

At least one school of criticism argues that the words themselves should tell us all we need to know about an author. But the fact is that until recent years scholars have generally regarded Mary Wollstonecraft Shelley as a result: William Godwin's and Mary Wollstonecraft's daughter who became Shelley's Pygmalion. The story goes that she was inspired when she was with Shelley to write the extraordinary *Frankenstein,* but that when his life ended, so did hers—the actual event not occurring for her until twenty-nine years later. Unhappily for her and for us, this narrative leaves both *Frankenstein* and all her other works in an intellectual straitjacket. Perhaps the best demonstration of this impact is that despite the phenomenal interest in *Frankenstein* in the last ten years, explanations of so significant a Romantic work are still lim-

From *Romantic Revisions,* ed. Robert Brinkley and Keith Hanley (Cambridge: Cambridge University Press, 1996), 291–306. Copyright © Cambridge University Press. Reprinted with the permission of Cambridge University Press.

ited by biographical interpretations based on either a Victorian filter or a Freudian filter; one as confining as the other.[1] Fortunately, there is another story. It is Mary Shelley's own, written in her own words, in counterpoint with her own era. A major part of that story is contained in her letters.

Some 1276 letters are collected in the three volumes of *Letters,* approximately doubling the size of the largest past edition. There is no question that many letters are yet unlocated that well might add further to understanding Mary Shelley's life and works. Nor, in any limited space, can one do more than suggest the richness of material in the *Letters* that await biographical and critical consideration in depth, but the letters tell Mary Shelley's story in her own voices, her own commerce with the world. From them, a new complex, intellectual, political Mary Shelley has emerged—one that had been there all along.

To establish Mary Shelley biography through her letters means recognizing and exploring the countless facts of her life that shaped their own intricate context, both biographical and historical. Her story has not been readily available partially because her Romantic existence was washed in the mores of the remainder of the century and because women's lives tend generally to be lost in historical accounts. But Mary Shelley added to this mask because she was, first to last, a private, introspective person who lived much of her life in the inner world of her own imagination.[2] Finding Mary Shelley in her letters, therefore, has called for searching beyond that which all letter-editors undertake. To paraphrase her much-admired Coleridge, it has required the willingness to suspend, as far as possible, beliefs and disbeliefs, to allow a constant testing of earlier concepts about the author against the evidence provided in the letters themselves. This testing process proves critical to editing Mary Shelley's letters because the letters do not support the relatively pallid image of Mary Shelley offered in preceding studies.

Even a factual outline of her life suggests a more complex person than was previously understood. From her birth in London on August 30, 1797, Mary Shelley had the possibility of a remarkable heritage. Mary Wollstonecraft Godwin, writer and radical, died ten days after giving birth to her namesake, but left her a written legacy of reformist theory and practice. From William Godwin she had both the written legacy of reformist theory and the living example of an unconventional philosopher-writer who advocated an egalitarian new world and was never quite at home in the world assigned him. In 1814, when Mary Shelley was almost seventeen, she eloped with Shelley, poet, radical reformer, disciple of her parents—and already married, leaving a trail of scandal that would follow her until she died. After his first wife committed suicide in 1816, the Shelleys married. Of their four children, the first born seven months after they eloped, only Percy Florence, their last child, survived both his parents. When Shelley drowned in 1822, his twenty-five-year-old widow was left to support herself and her son until Shelley's father's death in 1844 brought them Shelley's inheritance. During those years, Mary Shelley constructed a life of her own, committed to raising her son, continuing her own writing, and establishing Shelley's reputation through the publication of his manuscripts. At her death on February 1, 1851, she had succeeded at all three. Her literary activity included five novels after *Frankenstein* (1818): *Valperga* (1823), *The Last Man* (1826), *Perkin Warbeck* (1830), *Lodore* (1835), and *Falkner* (1837); one novella, *Mathilda* (1819, pub. 1959); two travel books, *A History of a Six Weeks' Tour* (1817) and *Rambles in Germany and Italy* (1844); two mythological dramas, *Proserpine* (1820, pub. 1832) and *Midas* (1820, pub. 1922); five volumes of biographical *Lives* (1835–9) of Italian, Spanish, Portuguese, and French writers for Lardner's *Cabinet Cyclopedia;* more than two dozen short stories; essays; translations; reviews; poems; and the precocious satire *Mounseer Nongtonpaw,* published in 1808. As Shelley's editor, she brought out Shelley's *Posthumous Poems* (1824), and the monumental *Poetical Works* (1839, four volumes and one volume), and *Essays, Letters from Abroad, Translations and Fragments* (1839, dated 1840).

Mary Shelley's place as a writer and editor was recognized by her contemporaries, but since that time even scholars for the most part have been unaware that she wrote anything of value beyond her first novel. In the interest of understanding the Romantics, we need to re-evaluate the intellectual and artistic life of an author who was in community with the leading figures of the era and who made her own significant contribution to that world. Unfortunately, biographies of women writers are generally the product of gender-biased interpretations that emphasize emotions and family life, and largely ignore the intellectual and artistic. At best this provides a sympathetic reflection of the critic's opinions and at worst a denigration of the writer's artistry. The letters, in contrast, provide a voice through which to establish a genuine biographical context, one which in turn allows a solidly founded basis for analyzing and interpreting the author and her works.

This is not to suggest that the letters are in and of themselves necessarily true. Or that the editor's character does not intrude to some degree in the final product. In the most reductive terms, works of fiction—and autobiography—are written for a larger, impersonal audience. Letters (with the exception of "literary letters" also intended for an impersonal audience) are written for one person or for the expanded, but particular audience that their author has in mind. The "I" in the letters is the personal "I," whether in a love letter or a business letter, consciously engaging in dialogue with another person. Just as in oral conversation, that "I" may or may not be telling the truth; may be hiding or disguising intentions through style of diction; may only be partially aware of the implications of what is written. However, in compiling as many of the letters as possible, each separate voice, each separate "I," is set against another, finally bringing into focus the many facets that form their author.

Working with Mary Shelley manuscript letters provides two interdependent but distinct sources of information. The first, on the level of physical

detail; the second, building on the physical properties, the ultimately significant, larger portrayal that results from amassing, interweaving, and compar-
ing the contents of the letters. When accumulated and catalogued, the
physical properties of the letters play an important role in constructing the
sequence of a life. To begin with the most obvious: postmarks in Mary Shelley's lifetime reveal both the date a letter was mailed and the date received.
These timelines are often vital in establishing chronological order because
Mary Shelley omitted the year, and sometimes the numerical date and
month, on approximately one third of her letters. Because postmarks are
commonly only partially preserved or somewhat blurred and faded, working
with the original document rather than a photocopy allows one not only to
read more accurately but also affords the possibility, depending on the
fragility of the paper (and the co-operation of the archivist), to refold the letter and fit what remains of the date marks together. This, hopefully matched
with internal clues, can provide the otherwise missing information.

A brief example of how this methodology assists: In a one-line letter,
dated only January 6, to her publisher Edward Moxon, Mary Shelley encloses
"a letter to be inserted in the 2 Vol. of the Prose works at page 335." The
pink stamp on the letter was first used only after May 1840. This establishes
that the letter referred to the second, 1845 edition of the Prose, published
five years after the first, which on p. 335 includes a letter to Keats's devoted
friend Joseph Severn, with whom Mary Shelley had continued contact in the
1840s (III, January 6 [?1845]). Thus, the letter to Moxon establishes Mary
Shelley's continuing activity as Shelley's editor.

An inventory of stationery can also contribute to construction of the
chronological sequence. What color is the paper? The ink? What are its mea-
surements? Is it laid or woven? Plain, gold-edged, black-edged, or torn from
a larger sheet? Is there a watermark that includes the name of manufacturer
and, as quite common then, the date the paper was made? Are there samples
of a particular stationery that are dated, used only during particular years,
that can, together with context, establish when an undated letter was written? Through this approach the letters involved in George Byron's blackmail
sale of forged Shelley letters have gone through a process of considerable editorial correction since they were first published in 1944. The first, important
revisions, made in 1946, relied on matching stationery, thereby leading to
three quite different letters than had been originally presented.[3] Further
study of the stationery provided internal and external evidence that the
blackmail negotiations were not concentrated in a brief period in October
1845, and then completed in September 1846, as previously believed, but
that they stretched out throughout the period, one in which Mary Shelley was
severely ill (III, October 28, 1845).

Working with manuscripts allows a variety of other revisions of past
publications of the letter, illustrated in the following examples: (1) In the
George Byron forged letters already referred to, previous editors mistook the

number "8" for Mary Shelley's abbreviated "Yr" (for Your). As a result, they concluded that she had purchased and received eight Shelley letters early in the negotiation, confusing the possible provenance of those letters, miscounting the number of forged letters she actually received, and failing to appreciate Mary Shelley's assertive responses to George Byron's attempts to "borrow" further sums of money in exchange for additional Mary Shelley and Shelley letters. (2) Mary Shelley's concern for her son is quite differently interpreted when a comment that "the bustle of a school would develop his chances better" has been corrected to read that the bustle "would develop his character better" (II, May 5, 1831). (3) Her lengthy and informed letter to Abraham Hayward that discusses many contemporary issues both literary and political turns out to be an amalgam of two letters (III, 26 October 1840). (4) Mary Shelley's deleted passage at the end of her November 10, 1845 letter to Claire Clairmont, written after Mary Shelley had just escaped threatened blackmail by an Italian exile, repeats her injunction stated elsewhere to "Pray tell me that you [bu]rn our letters—the chief fear I have is there being other foreign [   ]." Clairmont replies that she does not reply sooner to Mary Shelley's letters because unless she responds at once, she forgets what is in them, being "obliged to burn your letters as soon as I have read them." Clairmont was obviously using this as an excuse and a bit of a complaint since actually—as in this case—she preserved almost all of Mary Shelley's many letters to her. The deleted passage results in another piece of evidence in the story of the troubled relationship between Mary Shelley and Claire Clairmont throughout most of their adult lives. A final example: (5) in a letter to Byron on [I, November 16, 1822] about *The Deformed Transformed*, which she had just copied for him, Mary Shelley writes that "The Critics, as they used to make you a Childe Harold, Giaour, & Lara all in one, will now make a compound of Satan & Caesar [   ] your prototype, & your 600 firebrands in Murray's hands will [   ] costume." The missing words "serve" and "be in" can only be supplied from snippets of the stationery that remain attached to the wax seal.[4]

The manuscripts also reveal Mary Shelley through a sentence structure that past editions of the letters have revised. In those editions, Mary Shelley's sentences almost always began with a capitalized word, have traditional punctuation in their expected place, and close with a period—all very proper. The manuscripts and her own testimony tell another tale. "A pen in hand my thoughts flow fast" (I, January 6 1825), Mary Shelley wrote, and her letters support her self-description. She moves quickly along, her pace reflected mostly in dashes between phrases and sentences rather than full stops. She sometimes omits letters in words that she has already demonstrated she can spell. Her deletions, except for the relatively few meticulously blocked out, can usually be retrieved, allowing her correspondent at the time to read the thoughts that she changed her mind about. When she completed a letter and had something more to say, she didn't rewrite—she added on. Her postscripts not only follow her signature, but appear in the margins of letters, upside down or right-side up at the beginning of letters, and when envelopes were invented, inside envelopes, and cross-written. In several letters she asked her correspondents not to cross-write to her because it made the letters difficult to read (I, March 7, 1823). This message she herself cross-writes. Does this indicate a contradictory character? A sense of humor? One should not make too much of such individual pieces of evidence in themselves. But taken together, such details help constitute the indices of a life.

Among the traces of Mary Shelley's life from the age of seventeen until a few months before her death, the letters offer the changes in her handwriting. Just after she eloped with Shelley, her handwriting was distinct for the squared nature of the individual character, but during the couple's years together her handwriting came to strongly resemble his. Shelley and Mary Shelley editors have noted this, and it has often produced confusion, but what has not been noted is that after Shelley's death, her handwriting evolved again, moving from both her own juvenile script and its later resemblance to Shelley's. No doubt some interesting biographical arguments might be founded on this information, as well as another handwriting issue. In the last twelve years or so of her life, her script began at times to noticeably, even severely, slur. Letters flattened; words sometimes ended in a series of small bumps. A sign of advanced age or carelessness? Hardly, since Mary Shelley was only fifty-three when she died and other letters belied the notion of indifference. What the letters give evidence of, and what has not been recognized in biographical studies, is that the illness, which began in 1839 and which was coincident with her editing of the monumental Shelley editions, was not an isolated incident. Rather, it was the beginning of the illness that finally took her life. During the next twelve years, she reported she was ill, then mending and well, constantly believing—or wanting to believe—herself fully recovered. But the frequency and degree of her disturbed writing establishes a narrative of its own and suggests why Mary Shelley was a less prolific writer during the period. Her handwriting indicates that one of the major reasons she wrote less was not because she had lost interest in writing but because for much of that time she was ill with a tumor on the brain that caused severe head pain and partial paralysis, and eventually led to her death.

Each letter is therefore important, though obviously not equally so, in allowing the final image to piece itself together. Even seemingly trivial letters may help establish chronology, geography, as well as otherwise unnoted relationships, and these are critical particulars in composing a larger, more accurate narrative that would either confirm old perspectives or substantiate new ones. Such compendiums provide the context to revise Mary Shelley's image from that of a passive, conventional Victorian lady into a multidimensional, complex Romanticist. Among these accumulated trails of evidence, perhaps the most important from her readers' perspective are those that lead to a portrayal of Mary Shelley, author.

From the letters emerges Mary Shelley's fundamental consciousness of herself as author. The 1814–27 letters trace her growth from her early works (Shelley arranged the anonymous publication of *Frankenstein,* and sent Sir Walter Scott a copy; Scott, who gave *Frankenstein* an excellent review, assumed Shelley was its author) through new-found self-reliance, after Shelley's death, to continue not only to write but to take on the responsibility of becoming Shelley's editor and her own agent. In her letters, she frequently speaks of projects finished and unfinished, aspirations, feelings of failure and satisfaction, efforts to publish, reactions to reviews and friends' opinions, exhaustion from overwork, deadlines, lost manuscripts, revisions, self-reappraisal. Through introductions and recommendations by Godwin and friends such as Charles Lamb, Horace Smith, Leigh Hunt, she began, as she would for the remainder of her life, to negotiate directly and persistently for herself and others with many of the leading publishers and editors of the day. To the author Bryan Waller Procter, she sends her dramas to arrange for possible publication (I, May 9, 1824); to James Hessey, publisher of the *London Magazine,* she offers an unsolicited tribute to Lord Byron (I, May [?24–31], [1824]); she requires the return of two of her articles that were not published for publication elsewhere (I, [?June 1824–27]). She arranged for the publication of her next four novels, biographical lives, and when publishers were slow, did not hesitate to remind that "an *immediate arrangement*" had been promised (II, December 12, 1829) or, on another occasion when kept waiting by a publisher, to wake him with a note beginning, "I hope your tiresome silence is not occasioned by your being dead" (II, [December ?28, 1830]).

When Shelley's death left her with no income, she expressed confidence, based on earlier authorship of *History of a Six Weeks' Tour, Frankenstein,* and *Valperga,* in her ability to earn a living through her writing: "I think that I can maintain myself, and there is something inspiriting in the idea" (I, March 7, 1823). She found solace in continuing her habits of writing and study: "I study—I write—I think even to madness & torture of the past—I look forward to the grave with hope—but in exerting my intellect—in forcing myself to real study—I find an opiate which at least adds nothing to the pain of regret that must necessarily be mine forever" (I, February 28, 1823). Protracted negotiations with Shelley's father, Sir Timothy Shelley, wrung from him, towards the close of 1823, only a modest allowance against Shelley's estate (I, see September 9–11, 1823 nn. 11 and 12). Dependent on her writing for additional income, Mary Shelley was aware, as professional authors necessarily are, that some works are motivated primarily by financial need. Her letters show, however, that she maintained her determination to develop and fulfill her understanding of herself as an artist. When she advised Leigh Hunt to write for magazines to earn the money he needed, she characterized her own situation: "I write bad articles which help to make me miserable—but I am going to plunge into a novel, and hope that its clear waters will wash off the [dirt] mud of the magazines" (I, February 9, 1824). Of *Rambles,* her last work, written when she was already a semi-invalid, she confidently asserted that her *History of a Six Weeks' Tour* had brought her many compliments and she had no doubt this new work would "procure me many more" (III, September 27, [1843]).

The years 1827–40 were Mary Shelley's most prolific as an author and editor. What do her letters present of her in these dual roles? Interactions with publishers are a pervasive theme. Her correspondence about *Lodore* is concerned mostly with efforts to find a publisher, negotiate a contract, and see the book through publication. New letters, however, reveal that a section of the book was lost, presumably in the mail or at the publishers, and that Mary Shelley was required to rewrite a considerable part of the novel. Other letters refer to Mary Shelley's many short stories, poems, reviews, and essays, and suggest that more shorter works were published than have been identified as hers. In dealing with matters of appropriate length of story, deadlines, payments, competing journals, contents, and editors, her letters provide considerable insight into contemporary publishing procedures and Mary Shelley's enterprise in that male-dominated world.

Another theme concerns her habits of reading and research, and complements the extensive records in her journals. Influenced by Godwin, Mary Shelley developed a lifelong habit of deep and extensive reading and research. The Shelleys had remained in Florence so she could locate Italian books for the materials she needed for *Valperga* (I, c. December 13, 1819, n. 4); when writing *Perkin Warbeck,* she wrote to Thomas Crofton Croker for his Irish sources (II, October 30, 1828); to Sir Walter Scott for references to Scottish source material (II, May 25, 1829); and to Godwin and others for additional factual details that she could distill into her fiction. When she contributed five volumes to Lardner's *Lives of the Most Eminent Literary and Scientific Men of Italy, Spain, and Portugal* (with others; 1835–7) and *Lives of the Most Eminent Literary and Scientific Men of France* (1838–9), the work occasioned many letters to contemporaries, such as Sir John Bowring and Gabriele Rossetti, from whom she sought sources for biographical, historical, and critical materials.

Letters that propose topics for books and essays, whether undertaken or not, also demonstrate Mary Shelley's self-confidence and broadly based knowledge, which critics so often have failed to recognize. Among the subjects that interest her are: full-length biographies of Mahomet, Josephine, Madame de Staël (about whom a chapter was included in *Lives*); a history of manners and literature; lives of the English philosophers; a geological history of the earth; a collection of the lives of celebrated women; a history of women; and regular articles for the *Court Journal.*

Of those authors to whom she was closest, her letters not surprisingly speak most of Shelley and his works. One month after his death, she wrote: "The world will surely one day feel what it has lost when this bright child of song deserted her—Is not Adonais his own Elegy—& there does he truly depict the universal woe wh[ich] should overspread all good minds since he has ceased to be [their] fellow labourer in this worldly scene. How lovely does he [ ] paint death to be and with what heartfelt sorrow does one repeat the line—'But I am chained to time & thence cannot depart' " (I, c. August 27, 1822). In 1824, she edited and published his *Posthumous Poems*. Eventually she synthesized her judgments and observations of Shelley's works and his literary significance in the introduction and notes to her 1839 Shelley editions. She also continued to comment on Byron, often in relation to Thomas Moore's Byron editions. Her letters to Moore seem not to be extant, but his to her and hers to those who might assist Moore (including Teresa Guiccioli and Sir John Bowring) illustrate how material a contribution she made to Moore's editions. In reviewing Moore's volume, she comments that Byron

> quitted England feeling himself wronged—an outcast & a mourner—his mind took a higher flight—It fed upon his regrets—& on his injuries . . . As his mind became more subdued—he became more critical—but his school of criticism being of the narrow order, it confined his faculties in his tragedies & Lord Byron became sententious & dull—except where character still shone forth . . . At Pisa he again belonged more to the English world—It did him little good . . . But, in the end, this war gave him a disgust to Authorship—and he hurried to Greece to get a new name as a man of action—having arrived at the highest praise as a poet. (I [June ?10, 1832])

Her opinions of Godwin's works she expressed in letters and in her laudatory memoir of him for the Colburn and Bentley 1831 reprint of *Caleb Williams* (written simultaneously with her new introduction for the revised 1831 *Frankenstein*) and in her review of *Cloudesley* in *Blackwood's Edinburgh Magazine* (II, May 4 [1830]).

Among projects left unfinished was her life of Godwin, who died on April 7, 1836. His will appointed Mary Shelley his literary executor and requested that she determine which of his papers and letters should be posthumously published (II, April 20, 1836). She accordingly signed an agreement with Colburn to publish his memoirs and correspondence, for the benefit of his widow, whom, despite their differences over the years, she greatly assisted after Godwin's death. In the course of preparing Godwin's manuscripts, Mary Shelley began to annotate his early memoirs and to solicit his letters from friends and acquaintances, including Bulwer-Lytton, Josiah Wedgwood, Thomas A. Cooper, William Hazlitt, Jr. (for letters to his father), and Henry Crabb Robinson. She also attempted to enlist Robinson's aid in obtaining letters from Wordsworth and from Coleridge's executors. On January 26, 1837, she informed Trelawny that her "sense of duty towards my father, whose passion was posthumous fame," had readied her to "become an object of scurrility & attacks." She was determined to defer publication, however, until the completion of arrangements for Percy Florence Shelley's matriculation at Trinity College, Cambridge, that following spring so that "a cry raised against his Mother" would not harm his career. She expected criticism not on the basis of politics but on that of religion, a subject that might well elicit public attack and scandal. Perhaps for this reason, the work was never completed. Or perhaps it was set aside in favor of first completing the Shelley editions and then was not resumed because she was unable to undergo again the acute physical and psychological stress that she endured in the preparation of her editions of Shelley's poetry and prose in 1838–9.

As editor, Mary Shelley became Shelley's collaborator, returning more than in kind the guidance he had given her when she wrote *Frankenstein* and other early works. She gathered and preserved his writings. She brought the experience of a professional author to the editing of his works. Finally, biographers and critics agree that Mary Shelley's commitment to bring Shelley the notice she believed his works merited was the single, major force that established Shelley's reputation as a poet during a period when he almost certainly would have faded from public view. Her intention to gather, preserve, and publish Shelley's works is repeatedly expressed in the letters, beginning almost immediately after his death.[5] After *Posthumous Poems,* her next major involvement with publishing Shelley was in 1829, when she assisted Cyrus Redding in editing Galignani's pirated *Poetical Works of Coleridge, Shelley and Keats*. Prohibited by Sir Timothy Shelley from bringing Shelley's name before the public in return for her repayable allowance, she obviously believed she could aid this French publication with impunity and thereby keep both her commitments: *she* would not bring Shelley forward, yet his works would be kept in the public notice. New letters and evidence supply fuller information than has formerly been available about the important contributions she made to the Galignani edition, including the fact that she read and gave her judgment of the Shelley memoir included:

> I have only made one correction in the MS—The whole tone of the Memoir is to my mind inaccurate—but if this is the guise it is thought right that it should assume of course I have nothing to say—since it is favorable in its way & I ought to be content—I should have written it in a different style—but probably not so much to the Publisher's satisfaction—It is a mere outline & is as communicative as a skeleton can be—about as like the (original) truth as the skeleton resembles the "tower of Flesh" of which it is the beams & rafters. ([? September–November 1829)

Ten years elapsed between the Galignani edition and Mary Shelley's 1839 editions. We have information now, however, from a previously unpublished letter that negotiations for her edition began at least as early as January 22, 1834, when she informed Edward Moxon of her willingness to publish with him once "family reasons" no longer prevented her. Mary Shelley's letters between 1834 and 1839 record the development of this project. They provide a wealth of information about the problems, constraints, editorial decisions, and exhaustive labor, as well as the ideals and objectives that shaped the volumes.

Among the most important aspects of these letters is how they illustrate the extent to which she went to try to prepare a text true to Shelley's intentions. For example, in trying to work with first editions when she did not have manuscripts, and at times finding herself without even those editions, she had to cajole grudging friends and strangers to borrow them. Thomas Jefferson Hogg said he had not a *Queen Mab*; but Mary Shelley asked,

> yet have you not? Did not Shelley give you one—one of the first printed . . . Will you lend me your Alastor also—it will not go to the printer—I shall only correct the press from it. Sir Tim forbids biography—but I mean to write a few notes appertaining to the history of the poems—if you have any Shelley's letters you would communicate mentioning his (author) poetry I should be glad & thank you; (I, December 11, 1838)

Has Miss Kent a *Queen Mab*? Has Charles Ollier? Who is Brookes; "two persons so uncivilized as to refuse to lend the book to *me* for *such a purpose* cannot exist" (II [December ?15, 1838]).

These letters also provide a far more accurate depiction than heretofore available of Mary Shelley's motives and actions and of contemporary publishing processes. For instance, Mary Shelley has been attacked almost universally for her omissions of the atheistical passages of *Queen Mab* in the four-volume *Poetical Works* (II, December 11, 1838). The letters disclose, however, that although she disagreed with atheism and believed that Shelley himself had changed his mind about this subject, she was persuaded by the publisher Edward Moxon to omit those passages to protect his copyright, which he could lose if found guilty of publishing a work containing blasphemy. Nor was her omission of the dedication to Harriet Shelley in *Queen Mab* the result, as critics have suggested, of her reluctance to relate Shelley's feelings for his first wife; rather, it was made on the reasonable editorial principle of authorial intent. Years before, she had decisive evidence that Shelley himself preferred the omission (II, February 11 [1839]).

The letters reveal Mary Shelley as a professional, deliberate editor. In addition to searching for first editions from which to publish and correct proofs, she inquired after additional manuscripts of Shelley's works and letters; and she sought advice and guidance from friends, including Leigh Hunt and Hogg. Her letters tell of her efforts in "turning over Manuscript books . . . scraps . . . unfinished half illegible" (II, November 11, [1839]); the questions of her claim to copyright (II, December 7, 1838; January 12, 1839); her impatience with the frustrations of the work; the injunction of her father-in-law, Sir Timothy Shelley, that she not include a biography of Shelley, which she circumvented through the notes she appended to the poems that trace their origins and history (II, December 11, 1838); the severe illness caused by the editorial and personal strains of preparing Shelley's manuscripts in context "chiefly produced by having to think of & write about the passed [past] . . . It has cost me a great deal" (II, May 2, [1839]).

Her labors resulted in the 1839 publication of the four-volume *The Poetical Works of Percy Bysshe Shelley,* the two-volume *Essays, Letters from Abroad, Translations and Fragments* by Percy Bysshe Shelley, and the one-volume *Poetical Works* (with the complete *Queen Mab* and other poems added). This achievement was not merely the work of a wife seeking posthumous fame for the writings of a beloved husband, as has been suggested or implied by many critics. As is true for all editors, some decisions she made are open to criticism. But the letters show that even her most serious error, the failure to use first editions consistently as copy-text when manuscripts were not available, was the result not of amateurishness or indifference but rather of the inability to procure copies to work from despite an intense search (II, December 11, 1838; December 12, [1838] ff.). In fact, Mary Shelley's letters reveal that her editorial principles, stated or implied, stand up well even by modern standards that undertake to preserve all of a writer's works and present them as much as possible as the author wished (see, for example, her letters regarding the omissions of the atheistical passages in *Queen Mab* and the dedication to Harriet Shelley; and her many efforts, continued as late as 1845, to locate and publish Shelley manuscripts, II, December 11, 1838 ff.).

After the Percy Shelley editions, Mary Shelley wrote only one more full-length work, her two-volume *Rambles in Germany and Italy* (1844), published just seven years before her death. Very little has been written about *Rambles* or their place in Mary Shelley's works. Her own comments regarding *Rambles* are fragmented among a number of different letters. Read separately, the letters show an author sometimes anxious to write and other times reluctant to. Taken together, the many letters about *Rambles* interact with each other in a duel that takes them beyond their individual reports to create a complex, somewhat ambivalent picture of the author. They contain not only the expression of her attitudes towards writing in the ten last years of her life; they stretch in a continuum backwards to the young Mary Shelley, and give perspective to the nineteen-year-old who wrote *Frankenstein,* the earlier *History of a Six Weeks' Tour,* and all the works that followed.

In the 1840s, constantly fighting illness, Mary Shelley's letters indicate that she generally felt too weak to write another book. Despite her condition, wanting money to establish a home for herself and Percy Florence (III, May 17, [1843]), and anxious to assist the Italian expatriate Ferdinand Gatteschi, who in 1845 would use her frank and supportive letters as the instruments of blackmail (III, August 30 [1843]), she marshalled her writer's energy. Though she claimed she "wished never again to publish" she also felt herself destined to write: "one must fulfil one's fate" (III, November 10 [1843]), a fate she acknowledged as hers in her grieving 1822 *Journal.*[6] To Edward

Moxon's invitation to write a new book, she indicated that her ill health at Florence had improved in Rome, and that she would be "glad to employ myself in that way this summer—but I [sca]rcely think I shall be able—we shall see" (III, May 7, [1843]). Mary Shelley did accept Moxon's offer and wrote at length about her journeys with Percy Florence Shelley and his friends to Germany (1840) and Italy (1841). Her first published book had been the *History of a Six Weeks' Tour* (1817), the record of her elopement with Shelley to the Continent. Now she came full circle, back to the Continent with another Shelley. Although the travelers, the events, and the years were different, throughout the *Rambles* there is an overlay of memories of earlier days with occasional explicit references to those beloved and lost from a time long gone.

Her letters written during her 1840–1 travels also reflect those memories: "There is something strange & dreamlike in returning to Italy after so many many years—the language the mode of life the people—the houses the vegetation are as familiar to me as if I had left them only yesterday—yet since I saw them Youth has fled—my baby boy becomes a man—& still I have struggled on poor & alone" (III, July 20 [1840]). Those dreamlike memories also include deep grief: In Venice she reflects on the death of her dear Clara (III, October 1–2 [1842]); in Rome, on William's death and her initial discomfort at moving into Via Sistina No. 64, with its 1819 sad memories of Italy.

Just as her memories circle back, so, too, do the *Rambles* reflect Mary Shelley's basic methodology of *History of a Six Weeks' Tour*. Then, she drew on her *Journal* observations and her letters. Now, again writing in the first person, she worked from observation, calling upon the letters she had written to supply her with specifics. For example, she indicated to Claire Clairmont: "I am writing some thing that requires that I should refresh my memory with regard to our tour in 1840. If you have any descriptive letters from Percy & myself at that time I wish you would send them to me with all possible speed" (III, October 13-[16] [1843]). Like many other nineteenth-century travel books, *Rambles* is meant to be an actual guide to the regions explored as well as a compendium of her reflections. But Mary Shelley goes beyond the ordinary events of travel and sightseeing to comment on political suppression and the need for reform and liberty. Her letters and *Rambles* together provide important evidence of Mary Shelley's unabated interest and support of reformist politics, an interest that past biographers claim died with Shelley but that in fact was a preoccupation throughout her life (see, for example, her commentary on French politics, III, November 18 [?1840]; her letters to Alexander Berry regarding British and Australian politics; and *Rambles* for a larger perspective on her belief in political liberty and its contemporary condition in Italy and Germany).

For Mary Shelley, to write about a foreign country required thorough knowledge about the country and its people. Her letters indicate a good number of the research sources she studied in giving historical and sociopolitical context to the *Rambles*. As important, the letters shed light on her writer's self-attitude some twenty-six years after *Frankenstein* was published. Perhaps most revealing was the pain she suffered when a close friend told her she should not write because "it does no good to any body" (III, October 13–[16] [1843]). Her friend's remarks may have resulted from concern for how ill Mary Shelley actually was; Mary Shelley herself reported that she continued to work though "suffering in my eyes" (III, January 28 [1844]). But Mary Shelley reacted to the comment by feeling "guilty & wretched," unable to "assert myself" and momentarily wishing "that never my name might be mentioned in a world that oppresses me" (III, October 13–[16] [1843]). Wounded, ill, she claimed she would continue with *Rambles* only to assist Gatteschi. But this was not the first time she had been discouraged by others about her writing and nevertheless continued, as her earlier letters demonstrate.

Collected, Mary Shelley's letters are in many ways unlike Lamb's, Byron's, Shelley's or Keats's in their inclusion of domestic concerns from a woman's perspective. But they do share with them a creativity, reflectiveness, and overall perspective that places their author solidly in the Romantic tradition. By adding a different, equally important, voice, they provide us with a new source for understanding Romanticism. Her interaction with her father and her idolized mother; her early writing; her elopement and life with Shelley; the independent life she created for herself in widowhood; her confidence in the reciprocity of nature; her occasional ambivalence rooted in conflict between the role she envisioned for herself and that which her society called for; her own writing career, and her publications of Shelley's works—all are rooted in the Romantic defiance of conventions intended to constrain. The letters, in her own voice, reflect an individual in the process of struggling against, revising, and defying those conventions.

Because of her own varied interests and her sensitivity to the concerns of her correspondents, Mary Shelley's letters (except when brief or about business) are generally not confined to any one topic. A passage about literature may follow one about housekeeping; a discussion of the Tuxcan landscape may precede an urgent request for combs or pencils. Though she occasionally played in her letters, she never posed. At times her self-awareness becomes maudlin, her candor chiding, her observations sentimental; but the voice that pervades is analytical, forthright, contemplative, and prophetic, at times darkly so.

Notes

1.   The Victorian filter interprets the work as free of the complex socio-political perspective that is fundamental to *Frankenstein*. The Freudian interprets the work as a *roman à clef*, with the creature and his creator interchangeably playing the role of Godwin and Shelley.

2. See, for example, December 2, 1834, *The Journals of Mary Shelley,* ed. Paula R. Feldman and Diana Scott-Kilvert (Oxford, 1987), Vol. 2, and her introduction to the second edition of *Frankenstein* (1823).

3. Theodore G. Ehrsarn, "Mary Shelley In Her Letters," *Modern Language Quarterly,* 7 (1946), 297–98.

4. Fredeick L. Jones (ed.), *The Letters of Mary W. Shelley,* 2 vols. (Norman, Oklahoma, 1944), Vol. 1, p. 202.

5. The first phase of this project, leading to the 1824 *Posthumous Poems,* is described in Vol. 1 of *Letters;* the 1827–40 letters in Vol. 2 detail the subsequent history of her plans that culminated in the 1839 editions.

6. See, for example, *Journals,* Vol. 2, pp. 431–2.

Mary Shelley, *Frankenstein,* and the Woman Writer's Fate

STEPHEN BEHRENDT

Frankenstein is a woman author's tale of almost exclusively male activity, a tale whose various parts are all told by men. Women are conspicuously absent from the main action; they are significantly displaced (Agatha de Lacey, Safie) or entirely eliminated (Justine, Elizabeth, and the Creature's partially constructed mate). The only woman truly *present* in the tale is paradoxically not "there" at all: the unseen, silent auditor/reader Margaret Walton Saville (MWS), who exists only in Walton's letters. Walton's letters make clear that Margaret figures into his part of the tale as both confidante and confessor, much as Walton himself serves Victor Frankenstein. Indeed, Walton's explanations to Margaret of his own behavior suggest that he casts her in a role as *sanctifier,* whose province it is to hear, understand, sympathize, and approve (see Letter 2, for instance), rather in the manner of the roles in which Dostoyevsky later casts Liza in *Notes from Underground* and Sonia Marmeladov in *Crime and Punishment.* Walton manipulates his sister much as William Wordsworth encircles and silences his sister Dorothy in "Tintern Abbey": the brother's own future viability (which the text explicitly demands) is to be engineered precisely by the resonance of his own words in his sister's consciousness (ll. 134–59).

As "silent bearers of ideology" in Western literature and art, women have traditionally been made "the necessary sacrifice to male secularity," which finds its expression in materialistic public activity in a world that cannot—indeed will not—accommodate the woman of action.[1] Ellen Moers sees in Ann Radcliffe an alternative to both the intellectual, philosophical woman typified by Mary Wollstonecraft and the super-domesticated image of the submissive wife and mother extolled by earlier eighteenth-century culture. Moers claims that Radcliffe's vision of female selfhood involved neither the wholly intellectual nor the traditionally "loving" nurturant role but rather

From *Romantic Women Writers: Voices and Countervoices,* ed. Paula R. Feldman and Theresa M. Kelley (Hanover, N.H.: University Press of New England, 1995), 69–87, 278–80. Copyright © University Press of New England. Reprinted with permission.

that of the traveling woman: "the woman who moves, who acts, who copes with vicissitude and adventure."[2] This very public role of the woman of action fits authors like Mary Darby Robinson and Helen Maria Williams, as well as the many Gothic heroines who, like Emily St. Aubert in *The Mysteries of Udolpho,* cope exceedingly well with continual reversals of fortune and circumstance. It is not, however, the model of experience embraced by Mary Shelley, who, despite her considerable travels and public activity, wrote in pointedly gender-specific terms in 1828 that "my sex has precluded all idea of my fulfilling public employments."[3] For modern readers her comment hints painfully both at the enculturated tendency of many women of the time— and today—to perpetuate women's oppression by discouraging public roles for women and at a narrowed and more biologically based rationalization of reserve on women's part.

In her important 1982 article, Barbara Johnson examines the troubled relationship among mothering, female authorship, and autobiography in *Frankenstein,* revealing some of the ways Mary Shelley associated authorship with monstrousness, and the products of authorship with the violent and unpredictable Creature. Anne Mellor has subsequently extended and refined the discussion in terms of Shelley's life and other writings.[4] My own reading is informed by their critical insights. I argue further that the initially well-intentioned and humane Creature resembles the idealistic author seeking to benefit her or his society, and so, tragically, does Victor Frankenstein. Both see their desires frustrated, however, as their intentions are first misunderstood and then misrepresented by others. Their interlaced histories thus pose a strong warning to authors—whether of literary texts or of cultural texts, such as revolutions—about the dangers of creating that which can destroy even its own author. The author must acknowledge the fact that her or his text's potential for mischief is at least as great as its potential for good. Because *Frankenstein*'s embedded lessons about the hazards of authorship bear particular relevance to the Romantic woman author, I shall here treat the novel as a touchstone as I examine some broader issues.

Although *Frankenstein* is a novel about *acts* and *actions,* it comes to us not in actions but in *reports* of actions, almost in the manner of classical theater, where much of the offstage action is represented only in verbal reports. The more contemporary parallel lies in Gothic fiction, in which the violence is often kept offstage and thereby rendered powerfully imminent, a menace whose physical manifestations are only barely held in abeyance by a combination of virtue, fortitude, coincidence, and plain good luck. In *Frankenstein* the reports are in fact frequently multilayered: they are reports of reports. The most heavily layered is Walton's report of Victor's report of the Creature's report of his self-education and experiences. Mary Shelley adds to this layering by beginning her novel in epistolary fashion, with a series of embedded reports that draw our attention to the writing acts of Walton and, by extension, to Shelley herself, both as original anonymous author and as the subsequently public, ex post facto authorial presence in the 1831 Introduction who reports on the novel's genesis. Moreover, in adopting the epistolary form of discourse, Walton adopts a genre long associated with *women's* writing. Just as he appropriates woman's procreative activity in creating his own "Creature," so does he appropriate the ostensibly uninhibited literary form (the letter form has been called "spontaneity formalized") that women—otherwise denied voice and hence access to male literary culture—"could practice without unsexing" themselves.[5]

To what extent does the nature of *Frankenstein* as a construct of words, rather than a direct representation of actions, embody the dilemma of the woman writer at the beginning of the nineteenth century? In what ways does the marginalization of women, their activities, and their perceived cultural worth figure in *Frankenstein's* elimination or destruction of them? And what relation do these questions bear to the circumstances and the literary productions of other women writers of the Romantic period? Inherent in *Frankenstein* are some telling reflections of the ways in which women figured in the public world. In Mary Shelley's novel, women are occasionally the *objects* of discourse—most notable Margaret Saville, who cannot respond (or is at least represented as not responding), but also Justine and Elizabeth, whose responses to discourse aimed at them are in each case truncated by their deaths at the hands (in Elizabeth's case, quite literally) of the violent system of male authority within which the narrative is inscribed. When they are the *subjects* of discourse, on the other hand, they fare little better, for every woman of any importance who is spoken of in the main narrative is likewise destroyed: Victor's mother, Elizabeth, Justine, and the Creature's mate (who dies before even being "born"). In the public literary world of the time, the story is much the same. As objects of discourse, women were continually reminded of their "proper" and "natural" place in private familial and public extrafamilial interaction. The woman writer (who becomes herself an originator of discourse by publishing) is "represented" within public culture as an object of discourse when her work is reviewed by the (generally male) critic. But she is also translated into the *subject* of discourse when her literary efforts are indiscriminately interchanged with, or substituted for, her self—her individual person—within the public discourse of criticism.

Mary Shelley's first novel demonstrates that men's actions are typically either overtly destructive and therefore disruptive of social bonding or simply so thoroughly counterproductive that they result in paralysis, much as Walton's ship becomes immobilized in the ice. This message is repeated in one form or another in her subsequent novels and tales, and it appears in perhaps its starkest terms in *Matilda,* where the psychological and sexual oppressions are so powerful that they resist language's capacity to record them at all. The writings of Shelley and others reveal the consequences of the cultural pressures exerted upon the woman author, pressures whose cumulative weight often served either to drive women to misrepresent themselves by adopting the masculinist culture's literary conventions or to silence them altogether.[6] In the case of Mary Shelley—daughter of politically radical philosophers, wife of a particularly notorious radical artist, and member of a glittering literary circle—the residue of this enculturated sense of inferiority is startling. The terrible cost of her search for personal fulfillment in a permanent, secure relationship based equally upon affection and intellectual equality have been documented by her biographers. Sufficiently telling are two comments from her letters to two women, the first of whom (Frances Wright [Darusmont]) was herself an active political and social reformer transplanted in 1818 to America:

> [W]omen are . . . per[pet]ually the victims of their generosity—& their purer, & more sensitive feelings render them so much less than men capable of battling the selfishness, hardness & ingratitude [which] is so often the return made, for the noblest efforts to benefit others.
>
> In short, my belief is—whether there be sex in souls or not—that the sex of our material mechanism makes us quite different creatures—better though weaker but wanting in the higher grades of intellect.[7]

The second remark, in which "weaker" clearly refers to physical strength and stature, comes from a letter that is unusual even for Mary Shelley in the violence of its self-deprecation. But Dorothy Wordsworth expressed her fear of disappointing Coleridge in much the same terms: "I have not those powers which Coleridge thinks I have—I know it. My only merits are my devotedness to those I love and I hope a charity towards all mankind."[8] John Stuart Mill expressed the nature of the dilemma when he wrote in 1861 that "all the moralities tell [women] that it is the duty of women, and all the current sentimentalities that it is their nature, to live for others, to make complete abnegations of themselves, and to have no life but in their affections."[9] Comments like Shelley's and Wordsworth's provide compelling evidence of the validity of Mary Jacobus's much more recent observation that women's attempts to gain access to a male-dominated culture tend often to produce feelings of alienation, repression, and division: "a silencing of the 'feminine,' a loss of woman's inheritance" (27).

Indeed, expressions of self-disgust and self-hatred recur in the personal, private statements of Mary Shelley and other women who indulged their ambition (or, like Mary Robinson, Charlotte Smith, Felicia Hemans, and Shelley herself, their plain financial *need*) to enter the public arena of authorship. Entering explicitly into competition with the dominant caste of male authors, the woman writer seemed to violate not just social decorum but also the nature and constitution of her own sex. Not surprisingly, her efforts generated both anxiety and hostility among the male literary establishment, particularly when the woman dared to venture outside genres such as Gothic fiction that were more or less reserved for the heightened emotionalism expected of women writers.[10] It is instructive to remember that when Percy Bysshe Shelley composed a review of *Frankenstein* in 1818 his language implied that the author was male (perhaps, as was believed, Shelley himself).[11] Although this may have been yet another instance of Shelley's exaggerated, chivalric protectiveness toward his wife, the result was nevertheless to strip her of her authorship, even as she had been stripped of her early literary efforts in 1814 when the trunk containing her papers was left behind in Paris and subsequently vanished.[12]

I do not mean to minimize the growing impact women had on the Romantic literary market, either as authors or as readers.[13] But for nearly two centuries their place has been defined largely in terms of their relation to sentimentalism, which has had the effect of stereotyping the majority and effectively silencing the rest. By the later Romantic period it was becoming apparent that men no longer held quite the stranglehold on the literary scene that we have generally assumed. While publishing and criticism remained male-dominated fields, publishers especially were shrewd enough to understand their markets and to cater to the apparent tastes of a growing female readership, in part by employing women authors who addressed that readership. Nevertheless, the literary woman's activity remained circumscribed. Although women were free to write the literature of sentiment and were, in fact, encouraged to do so, the invitation did not customarily extend to the literature of science or, for the most part, of philosophy, political science, or economics. Indeed, the criticism of the would-be intellectual woman typically turned on assumptions about both the proper "nature" of women and the attributes that make them desirable to men, who are still the ultimate "consumers." This comment is typical: "[T]his woman had utterly thrown off her sex; when nature recalled it to her, she felt only distaste and tedium; sentimental love and its sweet emotions came nowhere near the heart of a woman with pretensions to learning, wit, free thought, politics, who has a passion for philosophy and longs for public acclaim. Kind and decent men do not like women of this sort."[14] The woman is Charlotte Corday, the famous man-killer; the account, from a Jacobin newspaper of the time. Such terminology recurs repeatedly in the English press and in the culture it both reflects and molds, and it suggests the extent to which the male establishment feared the "monstrous" advances being made by women. Like other novels (Smith's *Desmond* or Wollstonecraft's *Maria,* for example) whose rhetorical and thematic threads include the political, *Frankenstein* at once trespasses on "forbidden" territory and at the same time comments on the nature and consequences of that incursion.

The Romantic reading public's voracious appetite could consume authors as easily as their works, but their lack of access to the male-dominated, symbiotic twin industries of publishing and criticism made women writers particularly vulnerable. When Joseph Johnson hired Mary Wollstonecraft in 1787, he was taking an unconventional step, even though his decision was undoubtedly rooted more in pragmatic economic reasons than in progressive, gender-sensitive political ones; just back from France, she offered him both a contact (as well as a translator and editor familiar with the Continental literary milieu) and an intelligent author in her own right. Mary Darby Robinson's work for the *Morning Post* (which placed her squarely in the company of—and partly in competition with—Coleridge and Southey) offers another exception to the all-but-universal rule of male dominance. This overall dominance inevitably lent publishers and critics an inordinate power to silence the woman writer by denying her access to an audience or by so characterizing her efforts as to render them wholly unattractive to the inquisitive reader and thus to the prospective publisher of any subsequent efforts. Both of these forces stood poised to strike as soon as the woman writer overstepped the boundaries of propriety; they stood ready to step in "the moment she appeared to them as too palpably a manifestation of that monstrously capricious readership that has given birth to her" (Ross, *Contours,* 232).

This is not to say, however, that women poets (and women writers in general) were not acknowledged. Indeed, women poets seem to have been anthologized more frequently in the nineteenth century than they have been until recently in the twentieth, whereas women novelists like Ann Radcliffe, Charlotte Turner Smith, Amelia Opie, Jane Austen, and Mary Shelley, who *began* on the margins, achieved a more immediate and lasting enfranchisement. But the *manner* of that acknowledgment of women poets and of that anthologization tells its own tale. Let us take one example: Frederic Rowton's 1853 edition of *The Female Poets of Great Britain: Chronologically Arranged with Copious Selections and Critical Remarks.*[15] An enterprising editor and publisher, Rowton was active in such liberal causes as the Society for the Abolition of Capital Punishment. His anthology achieved a wide readership, both in England and in America, and there is no question that the volume called attention to women's contributions to England's poetic heritage. Nevertheless, Rowton's "critical remarks" typify the narrow post-Romantic characterization of women's writing in terms analogous to those in which women's "domestic" work was being characterized at the outset of the Romantic period. Rowton's comments on Felicia Hemans, for example, are illustrative:

> She seems to me to represent and unite as purely and completely as any other writer in our literature the peculiar and specific qualities of the female mind. Her works are to my mind a perfect embodiment of woman's soul:—I would say that they are *intensely* feminine. The delicacy, the softness, the pureness, the quick observant vision, the ready sensibility, the devotedness, the faith of woman's nature find in Mrs. Hemans their ultra representative. . . . In nothing can one trace her feminine spirit more strikingly than in her domestic *home-*loving ideas. . . . No where, indeed, can we find a more pure and refined idea of home than that which pervades Mrs. Hemans's writings on the subject (Pp. 386–87)

The delicacy that Rowton so admires in Hemans is in fact a recessive, deferential attitude that is more a critical overlaying, an interpretive imposition, than an essential quality of Hemans's verse. Just as female subordinates are kept in their "place" at the office by being called by first name (frequently in a diminutive form, at that) by supervisors whom they are expected to call by formal surname, so too is Hemans (and many others) "placed" by Rowton's condescending but nevertheless firmly authoritarian language, shored up by his "selection" of verse, which guarantees that the reader will see in Hemans precisely what Rowton intends. Interestingly, when H. T. Tuckerman wrote an introduction for the American edition of Hemans's *Poems* that appeared in 1853 (the same year as Rowton's anthology), he employed many of the same critical tactics, engaging in a form of "psychic defense" under the guise of critical appraisal. Such tactics, as Marlon Ross has demonstrated, "enable the critic to perform the crucial cultural endeavor of putting women in their natural and social place while ostensibly simply going about the mundane task of literary criticism" (*Contours,* 237).

The deferential, self-deprecating introduction or preface was a familiar literary fixture, whether it was employed by a Wordsworth or a Shelley in offering the world works that were proposed to be somehow "experimental" or adopted by a Mary Tighe (as in *Psyche,* 1805). But while readers seem to have "seen through" the affected posture when men employed it, they were more likely to regard that disclaimer, when women adopted it, not as a mere convention but rather as a statement of fact. And if the woman author failed to make the expected apologies, others stood ready to do it for her. Thus, the editorial introduction addressed "To the Reader" in later editions of Tighe's *Psyche, with Other Poems* assigns gender-driven terms to Tighe—and Tighe to them: "To possess strong feelings and amiable affections, and to express them with a nice discrimination, has been the attribute of many female writers . . . [but Tighe is] a writer intimately acquainted with classical literature, and guided by a taste for real excellence, [who] has delivered in polished language such sentiments as can tend only to encourage and improve the best sensations of the human breast."[16] Notice that the praiseworthy features—nicety, amiability, polish, sentiment—are intimately associated with such archetypal attributes of the Western female as cleanliness, orderliness, softness, and pliability. Even the exceptional (i.e., unfeminine) attributes—strong feelings, classical learning—are tempered by their being assigned to the support of essentially "feminine" concerns, the nurturing of the best *sensations* of the human heart chief among them. This sort of bracketing commentary is the norm for the period, both for the woman authors themselves and for the (male) interlocutors who felt compelled to speak for them in order to "introduce" them to their audiences.

Ironically, the notions of "home-loving" domesticity that Tighe's publisher, Rowton, and others sought to impose on women's writing have been succinctly summed up a century and a half later in—of all places—an anthropological study of dining etiquette:

> If "a woman's place is in the home," her place implies all the "female" characteristics: interiority, quietness, a longing to nurture, unwillingness to stand forth, and renunciation of the "male" claims to authority, publicity, loudness, brightness, sharpness. These qualities have a multitude of practical applications; for example, they either make a woman altogether unfit and unwilling to attend feasts, or they influence the way she behaves while participating in them.[17]

Substitute "publish" for "attend feasts," and the fit is nearly perfect. Indeed, according to traditional Western (especially Anglo-American) etiquette, what could be less womanly, less feminine, that *public*-ation, which injects the woman into a visible world held to be as thoroughly and exclusively masculine an arena as that to which gentlemen adjourned after dining for cigars and port?

In exercises like Rowton's, ideology is represented as "natural" fact, and begging the question is then passed off as exposition. Elsewhere, Rowton observes of Hemans that "to *passion* she is well nigh a stranger." Unlike Byron (who is "indeed, of all others *the* poet of passion"), "affection is with her a serene, radiating principle, mild and ethereal in its nature, gentle in its attributes, pervading and lasting in its effects" (p. 388). And Letitia Landon (Maclean), whom Rowton explicitly compares (favorably) with Byron ("the Byron of our poetesses" [p. 424]) is nevertheless censured for treating materials and attitudes for which Byron was even in 1853 routinely praised—however cautiously. Rowton remarks of Landon's skill at portraying sorrow:

> Persons who knew her intimately say that she was *not* naturally sad: that she was all gaiety and cheerfulness: but there is a mournfulness of soul which is never to be seen on the cheek or in the eye: and this I believe to have dwelt in Mrs. Maclean's breast more than in most people's. How else are we to understand her poetry? We cannot believe her sadness to have been put on like a player's garb: to have been an affectation, an unreality: it is too earnest for that. We must suppose that she *felt* what she wrote: and if so, her written sadness was real sadness. (pp. 426–427)

Rowton's conclusions reveal a built-in ideological inability to credit the female poet with the imaginative capacity to *create* powerful moods or attitudes, a capacity attributed to a Wordsworth or a Byron without question. The male poet can create, invent; the female poet can only replicate and transcribe. Worse, Rowton extrapolates from his own faulty causal logic a narrowly moralistic (and predictably negative) literary-critical judgment: "This strong tendency towards melancholy frequently led Mrs. Maclean into most erroneous views and sentiments; which, though we may make what excuses we will for them out of consideration for the author, should be heartily and honestly condemned for the sake of moral truth" (p. 429).

We are dealing here with codes of behavior, with manners, considered within the sphere of literary production. Behaviors that are *tolerated* among male authors—even when they are disapproved—are intolerable in female authors. Morally reactionary critical responses to productions like *Don Juan, Prometheus Unbound,* or *Endymion* stemmed at least in part from a recognition that their authors were writers of substance and power, whose productions stood to shake up the conservative establishment on whose stability (and capital) the critical industry of the time had already come to depend. Women were writing powerful, socially volatile poetry, too; but rather than launch a comparable frontal attack on women writers like Mary Darby Robinson, Joanna Baillie, Charlotte Turner Smith, Letitia Landon, or even Hannah More, gender-driven criticism adopted the psychologically subtle device of *undermining* by misrepresentation, of assessing works in terms of their adherence to or deviation from presumed standards of "femininity." The male-dominated publishing industry and its accompanying critical establishment had, of course, a great store in preserving, codifying, *and enforcing* this construct of "the feminine" in writing, perhaps especially so in the field of poetry, which was, in the Romantic period, still the preeminent vehicle for "high" art. If the membership of the club could not be preserved indefinitely for males only, it could at least be stratified: separate, lesser rooms in the clubhouse could be apportioned to women to keep them out of the way.

Johnson and Mellor have helped us to see that Frankenstein's Creature shares the situation of Romantic women, marginalized and spurned by a society to whose patriarchal schemata they fail to conform. Moreover, the values and sensibilities typically assigned to women during the Romantic period are not unlike those that Shelley assigns the Creature, including instinctive responsiveness to Nature, the impulse toward emotional human bonding (especially apparent in the de Lacey episode), and an experiential rather than an abstract empirical way of "knowing"—all of which are the heritage of eighteenth-century sentimentalism. In the pursuit of all of these impulses the Creature is thwarted, both by his irresponsible creator and by the members of the society that has produced Victor and countless others like him. That the Creature is not "beautiful"—another attribute stereotypically associated with women—indicates the seemingly deforming nature of nonconformity as measured by the standards and sensibilities of the dominant majority. Ironically, as the representative of the masculinist culture that places such a premium on physical beauty among women (note especially his descriptions of Elizabeth), Victor Frankenstein creates a being whose hideousness contravenes any proper instinctive and loving parental response on his part to the Creature as "child." He has created that which he abhors, a situation entirely analogous to what the masculinist social and political establishment wrought upon women, writers or otherwise, and with the same consequences: the victim is led to self-deprecation and ultimately self-destructive behavior. Likewise, the author who thinks highly enough of her work to publish it nevertheless compromises herself in publishing with it self-effacing, apologetic, or temporizing prefaces that devalue or even destroy the work that follows. This is a necessary compromise, it would seem, for those who would be heard at all. But the cost in honesty and self-esteem to the author is considerable.

Victor renounces the product of his activities when the creative seeks to usurp the procreative. Hence, physically destroying the Creature's mate is only an emblem of the real act of devastation implicit in Victor's actions: the demolition of those who will not retreat to passive, silent existence on the margins of human experience. Silent neglect, however, is an equally powerful response. This fact lends particular significance to a literary project Mary Shelley proposed in 1830 to John Murray III and to which he apparently turned a (predictably) deaf ear. Suggesting topics on which she might write for publication, she says, "I have thought also of the Lives of Celebrated women—or a history of Woman—her position in society & her influence upon it—historically considered. [sic] and a History of Chivalry."[18]

Did Murray simply assume that the market-driven "buying public" (despite the very large number of women *readers* in it) would be uninterested in a volume of prose about women, perhaps especially one about "Woman"? The topic itself was certainly not prohibitively unpopular: Heman's *Records of Woman* had appeared in 1828, with a second edition the same year and a third in 1830, as Shelley must have known (although there is no mention of it, nor of Hemans, in her letters or journals of this period). The balance (or *im*balance) in Mary Shelley's query between the worthy and promising topic of the position *and influence* of women in society and the much "safer" "History of Chivalry" (in which women might be expected to figure as ornament rather than as agent) is unintentionally revealing of the cultural bind from which neither Mary Shelley nor any other woman writer of her generation could entirely escape. Certainly, when one considers the sentimental concessions to traditional expectations about gender and genre that mar *Records of Women,* one cannot help acknowledging the truth of what Jennifer Breen says about women writers' dilemma of creating in their works a woman's point of view: they were forced by social pressure "to conceal the split between what was expected of them and what they actually felt."[19] Hence, most of the women in *Records of Woman* are, in fact, reflections of male social and cultural expectations only slightly displaced from their customary passive, recessive, nurturant roles to relatively more aggressive ones whose activity is typically generated by default, by the disappearance, death, or the incapacitation of the male figure who would otherwise play the active role in the scenario (e.g., "Arabella Stuart," "The Switzer's Wife," or "Gertrude," whose subtitle, "Fidelity till Death," says it all).

One of *Frankenstein*'s lessons is that all creative activity (whether physically procreative or aesthetically/scientifically creative) drives individuals into seclusion and isolation and *away from* the salutary human interaction that is the proper objective of all human *action*. Shelley's introduction to the 1831 edition details the countersocializing aspect of her own experience as creative writer. That she chose to include that information and therefore to publicly detail her physical and psychological anxiety and her attempt to compete with the literary men who surrounded her is instructive, for her experience as a woman of words[20] ties her to contemporaries like Anna Letitia Barbauld, Jane Taylor, Mary Robinson, Ann Radcliffe, and Charlotte Smith, as well as to Dorothy Wordsworth, whose words were repeatedly appropriated by her brother in poems that for two centuries have blithely been regarded as "his." That still others, like Felicia Browne Hemans, unhesitatingly identified themselves by their married names (e.g., Mrs. Hemans, Mrs. Opie, or Mrs. Montolieu) indicates the extent to which they elected (whether freely or under cultural coercion) to reduce their actions and their identities to mere *words* (denoting marital status and recessive identity). What Stuart Curran says specifically of Felicia Hemans and Letitia Landon might be said of many of the women who were their contemporaries: In addition to the comfortable domesticity and sentimentality that may be glimpsed in their work, we can see also "darker strains," which include "a focus on exile and failure, a celebration of female genius frustrated, a haunting omnipresence of death."[21] This aspect of women's writing is as troubling today as it was two centuries ago, and it should not surprise us that intrusive contemporary commentators, editors, and anthologizers (like Frederick Rowton) attempted to deny the validity or even the meaningful presence of that aspect, either explicitly by branding it as subject matter inappropriate for women, in roundabout fashion by refusing to credit female authors with adequate imagination or intellect, or in slightly more covert fashion by calling their efforts on this front derivative from male models such as Byron.

Writing literature may be a form of communication, but it is decidedly not dialogue. Like Margaret Saville, the reader (or audience) is kept at a distance; functional interactive discourse with the author is precluded by the nature of the literary work of art. The one-sidedness of this arrangement is quite unlike the dialogic nature of the familiar letter (and I stress the adjective), a genre Mary Shelley seems to have much enjoyed.[22] The act of *literary* communication—the writing act and the production of a public, published text—distances both the writer and the reader from the subjective substance that the text mediates by means of language. In her preface to *Psyche* (1805), Mary Tighe presents a view of her work opposite to the one reflected in Shelley's 1831 reference to her "hideous progeny": "The author, who dismisses to the public the darling object of his solitary cares, must be prepared to consider, with some degree of indifference, the various receptions it may then meet."[23] Whether "hideous progeny" or "darling object," the fate of the published work is out of its author's hands, as is the author's private self, which soon becomes the property of critics and others who appropriate it by reading it both into and in the literary work, as is evident from this remark about Mary Darby Robinson's poetry:

> Of Mrs. Robinson's general character, it can only be added that she possessed a sensibility of heart and tenderness of mind which very frequently led her to form hasty decisions, while more mature deliberation would have tended to promote her interest and worldly comfort; she was liberal even to a fault; and many of the leading traits of her life will most fully evince, that she was the most disinterested of human beings. As to her literary character, the following pages, it may be presumed, will form a sufficient testimony.[24]

Here again are the terms we have seen applied to Hemans and Tighe; they include the standard catalog of "feminine" virtues of softness, tenderness, and pliability, as well as the converse (and therefore culpable) traits of independence, immaturity, hastiness, and lack of foresight. The concluding sentence of the "Preface" makes perfectly clear the writer's rhetorical strategy: having detailed for the reader a literary life characterized by failures to behave "properly," both in life and in print, the writer injects the works themselves ("the following pages") into this pejorative context. Co-opted into disapproving of the author's life and life-style, the reader is invited to carry along that sense of disapprobation while reading the poetry. It is a classic tactic of reader manipulation and an unusually effective one, as history affords us ample opportunities to observe.

To create literary art is ultimately to falsify both the person and the *act*—whether external and immediate or internal and imaginative—that motivates the verbal text. It is not just a matter of producing fading coals, as Percy Bysshe Shelley suggests in *A Defence of Poetry,* but rather of burning up the raw material entirely. In the process the individual self gets burned up as well, consumed and extinguished. For the woman writer, no less than for the man, who and what one *is* gets superseded in the process of publication by the *words* that may represent—but more likely *mis*represent—that individual private entity. Fame devours personhood, as Tennyson's Ulysses reminds us later when he ironically announces that "I am become a name." In a "man's world," which is very much what the Romantic era was in England despite the presence of literary women in it, men are better able to overcome this dissolution of the self because they are the principal *actors* (act-ors) on the public stage, as well as the controllers of language and other cultural determinants. But because of their social, political, and cultural marginalization, women have few resources for countering the extinguishing of the personal self. When they did write, as Susan J. Wolfson observes of Dorothy Wordsworth, their experiences frequently generated in their texts "countertexts and spectres of defeat."[25]

Wolfson reminds us that in professing to "detest the idea of setting myself up as author" (p. 140) Dorothy Wordsworth effectively accepted the marginalized and *un*authoritative female role assigned her by the masculinist society epitomized in her brother and valorized by his public audiences. As journal keeper and documenter of domestic affairs both personal and public, rather than self-promoting, publishing author, she played out the culturally conditioned expectations of woman as domestic engineer, historical and social housekeeper, and minder of minor details of order and appearance. Nevertheless, Dorothy Wordsworth did write, both in prose and poetry, and even her characteristic self-deprecating tone cannot entirely hide the clear strain in her writings of ambition and longing for a more authoritative and self-expressive voice.[26] Much the same might be said about Mary Shelley, whose letters are filled with protestations against public visibility: "There is nothing I shrink from more fearfully than publicity— . . . far from wishing to stand forward to assert myself in any way, not that I am alone in the world, [I] have but the desire to wrap night and the obscurity of insignificance around me."[27] Despite her very considerable oeuvre, she often deprecated both her literary talent and her intellectual acuity by referring to her writing, as she once did to John Murray, as "my stupid pen & ink labors."[28]

Part of the Romantic woman writer's predicament involves what Sandra Gilbert and Susan Gubar have called the "anxiety of authorship"—the woman's radical fear "that she cannot create, that because she can never become a 'precursor' the act of writing will isolate or destroy her."[29] This is a potentially and often an actually crippling anxiety. And yet this fear need not be gender-specific to women. Sonia Hofkosh has demonstrated that no less "male" a male writer than Byron exemplifies the author who "dreads, as he desires, being read by others—a reading that rewrites him and thus compromises his powers of self-creation."[30] The problem is particularly acute for the woman writer, however, who in the Romantic period was working with only the bare thread of a literary heritage. Battling the powerful forces that everywhere reminded her of her cultural and intellectual marginality and the impropriety of her artistic aspirations—forces that fed (and rewarded) timidity and submissiveness—the woman writer was very like Mary Shelley's Creature. This gender-driven cultural stifling both of experience and of expression lies behind what Mary Jacobus, among others, sees as the themes of "dumbness and utterance" and of the powerful quest to fulfill an impossible desire (*Reading Woman,* 28).

We do well to catch in the Creature's history a glimpse of the history of the woman artist during the Romantic period—and indeed during much of the history of Western culture. What is at issue, finally, is the ongoing radical marginalization of the unconventional, a phenomenon as much political as social and cultural. The dominant social milieu severs communication with the Creature because neither its appearance nor its acts conform to the expectations of that majority culture. The society in which Frankenstein and Walton alike opt for the isolation of individual pursuits over the socializing impulses of human interaction proves to be the real agent in redefining the parameters of creative activity. Acts are replaced by words, activity by passivity, responsibility by the irresponsibly ambivalent, and individuality by abstraction. The person is dissolved.

Mary Shelley's first major literary project after Percy's death was *The Last Man,* which presents itself as a set of fragmentary papers—Sibylline leaves—that trace the vanishing of an entire civilization in a prolonged universal cataclysm. Since the indifferent universe of time and history effectively ends in the skeptical intellectual framework of that novel, all that remains to lend meaning to mortal existence are human interaction and human language systems, both of which, being temporal, are themselves inevitably doomed to end. The alternative to this desolate picture lies in Shelley's frequently iterated commitment to "an ethic of cooperation, mutual dependence, and self-sacrifice" as the means for salvaging individual and collective dignity and meaning from the wreckage of temporal human existence. She argues in work after work that civilization can achieve its full promise only when "individuals willingly give up their egotistical desires and ambitions in order to serve the greater good of the community."[31] But this situation leaves the writer in a particularly precarious position, with her or his printed words dependent for value on a community of readers to whom the author is nevertheless a stranger, whose language and *identity* is subject to gross misconstruing over time. Mary Shelley's life of Alfieri offers insight into her view of authorship, which itself seems to echo both Wordsworth's and Percy Bysshe Shelley's views: "The author has something to say. . . . An Author . . . is a human being whose thoughts do not satisfy his mind . . . he requires sympathy, a world to listen, and the echoes of assent. [The author desires] to build up an enduring monument . . .[and] court the notoriety which usually attends those who let the public into the secret of their individual passions or peculiarities."[32] But this is risky business, surely, for even if the assenting voice is loud and unified, the author still exposes her or his own autonomous personhood ("individual passions or peculiarities") for public view and public reading—or misreading. As the daughter of Wollstonecraft and Godwin and wife of Percy Bysshe Shelley, she would have appreciated more than most that the "sympathy" of which she writes here could be a rare commodity indeed among the early-nineteenth-century English reading public.

At the same time, though, to write is not just to yield authority but also to *take* it, to exercise it. In the preface composed for the anonymous first edition of *Frankenstein,* Percy Bysshe Shelley claims that the author has gone beyond what Erasmus Darwin and other speculative physiologists have postulated about the nature of life and "the elementary principles of human nature." Indeed, the author is presented as having surpassed not only these *scientists* but also other culturally ensconced male *literary* luminaries, including Homer, the Greek dramatists, Shakespeare, and Milton, as well as the two "friends" to whose conversations the story is said to owe. In her own 1831 introduction to *Frankenstein,* Shelley pointedly reminds us that her story originated with a set of conversations between Percy Bysshe Shelley and Byron to which she was essentially a silent auditor. Yet *hers* is the story that was completed *and* published *and* that became sufficiently popular to demand republication. Making her claim of authorship explicit, Mary Shelley in the process claims possession not only of the novel's language but also of the material—the apparently unremittingly *male* material—of its subject matter. Moreover, the new introduction constitutes a gesture of authority by which her own authorial voice supersedes the ventriloquistic voice of her dead husband in the preface. By 1831 she had, after all, survived both Shelley and Byron, and the popularity of her novel had far exceeded that of her husband's works and had rivaled and in some quarters even surpassed that of Byron's.

The Last Man extends some of the issues I have already raised in terms of *Frankenstein.* Is the author's role (whether the author be female or male) merely to record the real or invented acts of others? That is, after all, what Mary Shelley turned to in her later years when she wrote the lives of eminent *men.* The *historian* characteristically steps *out* of the history she or he writes, functioning as nameless, invisible recorder, although even in the best of cases an element of fiction enters—or is inserted—into the writing of history. This ostensibly detached role appears to have become increasingly attractive to Mary Shelley, who in 1834, while working on her contributions to the *Lives of the Most Eminent Literary and Scientific Men of Italy, Spain, and Portugal,* wrote at length about her imagination's fleeing visitations and suggested that, as Wordsworth wrote in the "Intimations" ode, the years that bring the philosophic mind provide recompense (though not necessarily so "abundant" as the poet regards it in "Tintern Abbey") for the imagination's fading: "I hope nothing & my imagination is dormant—She awakes by fits & starts; but often I am left *alone* (fatal word) even by her. My occupation at present somewhat supplies her place—& my life and reason have been saved by these "Lives"—Yes—let the lonely be occupied—it is the only cure."[33]

And yet is not this consuming indulgence in words both the goal and the supermarginalizing consequence of authorship generally—to be reduced to *words,* to be captured, "pictured," and read not as person but as textual construct, as a sort of shadow existence, a phantasm of the reader's own distorting imagination?

The author constantly runs the risk of being made into a fiction by the reader who formulates or extrapolates the author from the text. The woman author is "read" within a system of culturally encoded patriarchal authority over which she has virtually no control but within which she is expected to express herself. She is thus deprived at once of subjectivity, creativity, and autonomy. The assessment not just of Romantic women's writing but also of the cultural and intellectual position of the woman writer in general underscores the urgency of Annette Kolodny's observation that what unites and invigorates feminist criticism is neither dogma nor method but rather "an acute and impassioned *attentiveness* to the ways in which primarily male structures of power are inscribed (or encoded) within our literary inheritance."[34] Worst danger of all, one runs the risk of becoming an accomplice to the substitutional fictionalization of the "real" (the actual, autonomous, personal, and historical individual) self by the very act of writing. For the text that results from that act contains the self that the reader may reformulate and reconstruct in a living lie that reflects not the author but the *reader*, who has, in the act of reading her, appropriated her and torn her to pieces, much as Victor Frankenstein first assembles and then tears to pieces the Creature's mate.

Virginia Woolf suggested that George Eliot's decision to combine womanhood and writing was very costly indeed; as Mary Jacobus observes, it was a mortally significant decision that entailed "the sacrifice not only of happiness, but of life itself" (*Reading Woman*, 29). Women writers are particularly sensitive to the conflict between the "domesticity" that society expects of them and their own authorial aspirations for public fame, Marlon Ross writes, precisely because "the conflict is so palpable in their private lives and in their poetic careers" (*Contours*, 289). Mary Shelley understood the personal cost of authorship, writing of it to Trelawny that "I know too well that that excitement is the parent of pain rather than pleasure."[35] Writing, especially for publication, is an act of society, of civilization: a surrender of the autonomous self and identity to, and ostensibly on behalf of, the collective public. But as Rousseau had foreseen, the impulse toward formal civilization brings with it a radical reduction of one's options and, for the writer, "an enclosure within the prisonhouse of language" (Mellor, *Mary Shelley*, 50). One becomes what one writes, to paraphrase Blake, even as one writes what one is. In this endlessly revolving cycle one becomes imprisoned in temporality and topicality; one is reduced, finally, to a cipher, to a sheaf of papers, to reports of actions—or to reports of *ideas* that purport to be actions.

Like her contemporaries, Mary Shelley wrestled with the assault upon the personal ego inherent in the public response to one's formal writing. She wrote—after 1822 primarily because she *had* to, to support herself and her son—and only occasionally did she allow herself to stare back at the potential uselessness of it all: "What folly is it in me to write trash nobody will read— . . . I am—But all my many pages—future waste paper—surely I am a fool—."[36] At more optimistic and self-assured moments she could at least find consolation in the *activity* of writing, even if it was merely a matter of filling the hours.

That Walton finally redirects his shop toward the south (and symbolically toward warmth and society) at the conclusion of *Frankenstein* might indicate that he has learned from his experience, were it not that Walton does not choose freely in the matter but rather accedes in the face of a mutiny. I suggest that the practical struggle to be true to oneself and to one's ideals and aspirations—for the woman writer as for the man Arctic explorer—inevitably involves compromise and with it the reduction and subjection of one's essential self to a report embedded in words. Literature traditionally introduces us not to authors but to their words, the words by which they represent impressions of their ideas and of the "selves" in which they live their days. Living with the diminished self whose record is the journal of papers that makes up the novel will haunt Walton, even as the Creature haunts the obsessive-compulsive Victor Frankenstein (who is no victor at all but the ultimate cosmic loser). But so too must the writer—woman or man—inevitably be haunted by the specter of herself or himself reduced to a cipher, to a construct of words, the work itself becoming a "hideous progeny" that dissolves the author as self, as living, acting entity. Whatever the inherent formal value of the literary product, it nevertheless both mutilates and misrepresents its author. In this sense, among others, it seems to me entirely valid to read in *Frankenstein,* as in much of Romantic women's writing, the enigmatic warning that creativity may be hazardous to one's health—indeed to one's entire existence.

Notes

1.   See Mary Jacobus, *Reading Woman: Essays in Feminist Criticism* (New York: Columbia University Press, 1986), 28.

2.   Ellen Moers, *Literary Women: The Great Writers* (1963; reprint, New York: Oxford University Press, 1985), 126.

3.   5 January 1828, *The Letters of Mary Wollstonecraft Shelley,* ed. Betty T. Bennett, 3 vols. (Baltimore and London: Johns Hopkins University Press, 1983), 2:22.

4.   Barbara Johnson, "My Monster / My Self," *Diacritics* 12 (1982): 2–10; Anne K. Mellor, *Mary Shelley: Her Life, Her Fiction, Her Monsters* (New York and London: Methuen, 1988).

5.   Moers, *Literary Women,* 163; Virginia Woolf, "Dorothy Osborne's 'Letters,' " in *The Second Common Reader,* ed. Andrew McNeillie (San Diego, Calif.: Harcourt Brace Jovanovich, 1986), 59–70.

6.   Deborah Cameron, *Feminism and Linguistic Theory* (New York: St. Martin's, 1985), 161. Mellor writes that "that unique phenomenon envisioned by Mary Wollstonecraft, the wife as the lifelong intellectual equal and companion of her husband, does not exist in the world of nineteenth-century Europe experienced by Mary Shelley" ("Possessing Nature: The Female in *Frankenstein,*" in *Romanticism and Feminism,* ed. Anne K. Mellor [Bloomington: Indiana University Press, 1988], 223).

7.   Shelley to Frances Wright [Darusmont], 12 September 1827, and to Maria Gisborne, 11 June 1835, *Letters* 2:4, 246.

8.   *The Letters of William and Dorothy Wordsworth,* ed. Ernest de Selincourt et al., 2nd ed., 6 vols. (Oxford: Clarendon Press, 1967–93), vol. 1, no. 239.

9.   John Stuart Mill, *The Subjection of Women,* ed. Sue Mansfield (Arlington Heights, Ill.: AHM Publishing, 1980), 15. Mill's essay was written in 1861 and published in 1869.

10.   See Mary Poovey, *The Proper Lady and the Woman Writer: Ideology as Style in the Works of Mary Wollstonecraft, Mary Shelley, and Jane Austen* (Chicago: University of Chicago Press, 1984); and Mellor, *Mary Shelley,* 56.

11.   Percy Bysshe Shelley's review may have been intended for Leigh Hunt's *Examiner.* It did not appear until Thomas Medwin published it in *The Atheneum* in 1832.

12.   See Mellor, *Mary Shelley,* 22–23, and Emily W. Sunstein, *Mary Shelley: Romance and Reality* (Boston, Toronto and London: Little, Brown, 1989), 85–86.

13.   Stuart Curran, Gaye Tuchman, and Marlon Ross have most notably reminded us of women's significant presence in the literary milieu. See Stuart Curran, *Poetic Form and British Romanticism* (New York: Oxford University Press, 1986); Gaye Tuchman, with Nina E. Fortin, *Edging Women Out: Victorian Novelists, Publishers, and Social Change* (New Haven: Conn.: Yale University Press, 1989); Marlon Ross, *The Contours of Masculine Desire: Romanticism and the Rise of Women's Poetry* (New York: Oxford University Press, 1989). See too Cheryl Turner, *Living by the Pen: Women Writers in the Eighteenth Century* (London: Routledge, 1992).

14.   Quoted in Rupert Christiansen, *Romantic Affinities: Portraits from an Age, 1780–1830* (London: Cardinal, 1988), 102.

15.   This volume, which is readily available in a facsimile edited by Marilyn Williamson (Detroit: Wayne State University Press, 1981), typifies the woman writer's treatment by the (male) Victorian anthologizer. Parenthetical page citations in this portion of my discussion refer to this facsimile.

16.   Mrs. Henry [Mary] Tighe, *Psyche, with Other Poems,* 5th ed. (London: Longman, 1816), iii–iv.

17.   Margaret Visser, *The Rituals of Dinner: The Origins, Evolution, Eccentricities, and Meaning of Table Manners* (New York: Grove Weidenfeld, 1991), 273.

18.   Shelley to John Murray III, 8 September 1830, *Letters,* 2:115.

19.   *Women Romantic Poets, 1785–1832: An Anthology,* ed. Jennifer Breen (London. J. M. Dent, 1992), xix.

20.   This is, in fact, the picture often painted of Mary Shelley: "Mary was never a woman of action. Her pursuits were intellectual, her pleasure domestic" (Jane Dunn, *Moon in Eclipse: A Life of Mary Shelley* [London: Weidenfeld and Nicolson, 1978], 278).

21.   Stuart Curran, "Romantic Poetry: The 'I' Altered," in *Romanticism and Feminism,* ed. Anne K. Mellor (Bloomington: Indiana University Press, 1988), 189.

22.   As Betty T. Bennett's three volumes of Shelley's letters amply demonstrate, she was an avid letter writer, and the style of those letters is richly interactive, inviting a variety of kinds of response from her correspondents. Even in letters from the years immediately following Percy Bysshe Shelley's death, letters in which postured self-pity mingles with spontaneous expresssions of genuine misery, the correspondent is never shut off from *communication* or from what Shelley clearly structures as an ongoing dialogue.

23.   [Mary Tighe], *Psyche, or the Legend of Love* (London, privately printed, 1805), ii.

24.   "Preface," in *The Poetical Works of the Late Mrs. Mary Robinson,* 3 vols. (London: Jones and Company, 1824), 1:4.

25.   Susan J. Wolfson, "Individual in Community: Dorothy Wordsworth in Conversation with William," in Mellor, *Romanticism and Feminism,* 162.

26.   The painful ambivalences about ambition, ability, and gender-related expectations that surface so frequently in what Dorothy Wordsworth's writings tell us about herself, her situation, and the life she led have at last been addressed in a number of sympathetic revisionist studies. See esp. Wolfson, "Individual in Community," Margaret Homans, *Women Writers and Poetic Identity: Dorothy Wordsworth, Emily Bronte, and Emily Dickinson* (Princeton, N.J.: Princeton University Press, 1980); and Susan M. Levin, *Dorothy Wordsworth and Romanticism* (New Brunswick, N.J.: Rutgers University Press, 1987).

27.   Shelley to Edward J. Trelawny, 1 April 1829, *Letters,* 2:72.

28.   Shelley to John Murray III, 10 February 1835, *Letters,* 2:223.

29.   Sandra M. Gilbert and Susan Gubar, *The Madwoman in the Attic: The Woman Writer and the Nineteenth-Century Literary Imagination* (New Haven, Conn., and London: Yale University Press, 1979), 49–50.

30.   Sonia Hofkosh, "The Writer's Ravishment: Women and the Romantic Author—the Example of Byron," in Mellor, *Romanticism and Feminism,* 94.

31.   Mellor, "Possessing Nature," 129, and *Mary Shelley,* 169, 215.

32.   Mary Shelley [with James Montgomery], *Lives of the Most Eminent Literary and Scientific Men of Italy, Spain, and Portugal,* 3 vols. (London: Longman, 1835), 2:351.

33.   Shelley, December 1834, *The Journals of Mary Shelley: 1814–1844,* ed. Paula R. Feldman and Diana Scott-Kilvert, 2 vols. (Oxford: Clarendon Press, 1987), 2: 543.

34.   Annette Kolodny, "Dancing through the Minefield: Some Observations on the Theory, Practice, and Politics of a Feminist Literary Criticism," in *The New Feminist Criticism: Essays on Women, Literature, and Theory,* ed. Elaine Showalter (New York: Pantheon Books, 1985), 162.

35.   Shelley to E. J. Trelawny, 27 July 1829, *Letters,* 2:82.

36.   Shelley, 30 January 1825, *Journals,* 2:489.

Mary Shelley on the
Therapeutic Value of Language

William D. Brewer

The therapeutic value of oral and written self-expression is a recurrent theme in Mary Shelley's works, particularly in those works, such as *Matilda* and *Valperga: or, the Life and Adventures of Castruccio, Prince of Lucca,* in which the heroines have been subjected to psychological trauma. For example, the eponymous heroine of *Matilda* refuses to tell her friend Woodville of her dead father's incestuous passion for her because she fears words, especially the word "incest," and, perhaps partially as a result of this self-censorship, she lives out her life in a state of chronic depression. In contrast, Beatrice, the brutalized prophet of *Valperga,* does relate her tale of suffering to the sympathetic (and aptly named) Euthanasia, but this narration provides only temporary relief. Mary Shelley's often garrulous characters frequently speak or write of their experiences, even when, as in the case of Frankenstein's monster, these narrations seem implausible. As Marc A. Rubenstein notes, "the author permits the monster an improbable series of digressions as he relates how he has passed the months since he wandered away from Frankenstein's laboratory" (168). There is, however, a psychological reason for the narrative, which Rubenstein touches on when he compares the monster to a "patient in psychoanalysis" (168)—the monster feels the need to work through and even validate his experience, and Frankenstein is the only person who will listen to him. In this essay I will argue that while Mary Shelley presents characters who are skeptical about the therapeutic value of verbal self-expression, she acknowledges the human need to put suffering into words, and the short-term relief that words can provide. Moreover, Shelley suggests that in the case of extreme trauma writing is sometimes more viable than speaking as a form of language therapy.

Mary Shelley's somewhat skeptical attitude toward the power of words was probably influenced by Percy Shelley's views on language.[1] In "On Life,"

From *PLL: Papers on Language and Literature,* Southern Illinois University, Volume 30, No. 4, Fall 1994.
Copyright © 1994 By the Board of Trustees, Southern Illinois University. Printed by Permission.

Percy writes: "How vain is it to think that words can penetrate the mystery of our being" (475); he goes on to argue that "the misuse of words and signs" prevents "the mind" from acting freely (477).[2] His frustration with the inadequacy of language is forcibly expressed in his note to "On Love": "These words are inefficient and metaphorical—Most words so—No help—" (474). Moreover, in *A Defense of Poetry*, Percy Shelley asserts that over time words decline into "signs for portions or classes of thought [i.e. abstract ideas] instead of pictures of integral thoughts"—if poets do not intervene to revitalize them, the language becomes "dead to all the nobler purposes of human intercourse" (482). Percy's concern about the inadequacy and abstraction of language is also expressed in his poetry. In *Prometheus Unbound* Prometheus repudiates his curse on Jupiter, declaring that "words are quick and vain" (IV.i.303), a sentiment echoed by the Maniac in "Julian and Maddalo," who exclaims "How vain / Are words!" (472–473). These declarations can be compared to many of the pronouncements in Mary Shelley's fiction regarding the effectiveness of language. For example, her meditation on the failure of words to improve the human condition in her historical novel *The Fortunes of Perkin Warbeck* recalls Percy's views on language's limitations:

> Oh, had I, weak and faint of speech, words to teach my fellow-creatures the beauty and capabilities of man's mind; could I, or could one more fortunate, breathe the magic word which would reveal to all the power, which we all possess, to turn evil to good, foul to fair; then vice and pain would desert the new-born world!
>   It is not thus: the wise have taught, the good suffered for us; we are still the same. (III: 18)

Moreover, Clifford, the villain of *Perkin Warbeck*, soothes "his evil passions with words," thus exemplifying "the misuse of words and signs" that Percy Shelley warns against in "On Life": "It was some relief to this miserable man to array his thoughts in their darkest garb, soothing his evil passions with words, which acted on them as a nurse's fondling talk to a querulous child" (II: 73–74). As I will demonstrate, many of Mary Shelley's works seem to support her husband's view that words are essentially inadequate, too metaphorical and easily misused to provide a reliable mode of self-expression.

While Mary Shelley's novels and stories often cast doubt on the effectiveness of words, her explorations of the theme of language therapy anticipate the preoccupations of modern psychoanalysis. According to Jacques Lacan, successful psychoanalysis relies exclusively on the spoken word: "Whether it sees itself as an instrument of healing, of training, or of exploration in depth, psychoanalysis has only a single medium: the patient's speech. . . . And all speech calls for a reply. . . . there is no speech without a reply, even if it is met only with silence, provided that it has an auditor" (40).[3] Without speech, or a linguistic relationship to "the other," the human subject can be reduced to what Lacan calls "the imaginary order," a self-regarding mental state in which the subject is prone to narcissistic fantasies. As Peter Brooks has noted, Frankenstein's monster learns language in an attempt to enter "the symbolic order," or "the cultural system into which individual subjects are inserted" (207), and escape his "monsterism": "only in the symbolic order may he realize his desire for recognition" (208).

While the monster fails in his attempt to be recognized by others, or to achieve membership in the linguistic community, Shelley's Mathilda and Ellen-Clarice (a character in her short story "The Mourner") choose to withdraw from the symbolic order, isolating themselves and thus refusing what has been called the "talking cure" (Lacan 46). In a number of her works, Mary Shelley suggests this kind of repression can lead to tragic consequences, an insight confirmed by modern psychology:

> The ultimate goal [of reconstructing the trauma story] is to put the story, including its imagery, into words. . . . The therapist should beware of developing a sequestered "back channel" of communication, reminding the patient that their mutual goal is to bring the story into the room, where it can be spoken and heard. Written communications should be read together. The recitation of facts without the accompanying emotions is a sterile exercise, without therapeutic effect. . . . At each point of the narrative, therefore, the patient must reconstruct not only what happened but also what she felt. The description of emotional states must be as painstakingly detailed as the description of facts. (Herman 177)

As I will show later in this essay, Mathilda and Ellen-Clarice refuse to talk about their traumatic experiences, and the result of this refusal is, in both cases, depression and premature death. Although these characters leave written records of their sufferings, these are to be read posthumously, and thus have little or no therapeutic effect. Like Lacan and Herman, Mary Shelley recognizes the human need to communicate and is aware of the psychological ramifications of words, whether spoken or unspoken. But, unlike Lacan and Herman, Shelley seems to believe that trauma victims have neither the desire nor the ability to speak to others about their experiences.

Perhaps more than any of Shelley's other characters, Frankenstein's monster realizes the importance of oral communication.[4] His hideous and terrifying appearance inspires fear and hatred in others, but when he overhears cottagers conversing with one another, he learns that relationships can have a linguistic basis: "I found that these people possessed a method of communicating their experience and feelings to one another by articulate sounds. I perceived that the words they spoke sometimes produced pleasure or pain, smiles or sadness, in the minds and countenances of the hearers. This was indeed a godlike science, and I ardently desired to become acquainted with it" (83). He has complete faith in the "godlike" powers of language, which he thinks will create a bond between him and the cottagers: "I formed in my imagination a thousand pictures of presenting myself to them, and their reception of me. I imagined that they would be disgusted, until, by my gentle demeanour and conciliating words, I should first win their favour, and afterwards their love. These thoughts exhilarated me, and led me to apply with fresh ardour to the acquiring the art of language" (85). But language fails to live up to the monster's expectations: although he succeeds in impressing the blind De Lacey, De Lacey's son Felix returns and violently attacks the monster before he can say a word in his own defense. His need to communicate with other intelligent beings remains unsatisfied.

The monster refuses, however, to give up in his quest to form a relationship through language, and asks Frankenstein to create a female monster: "my virtues will necessarily arise when I live in communion with an equal. I shall feel the affections of a sensitive being, and become linked to a chain of existence and events, from which I am now excluded" (109). But when Frankenstein destroys the unfinished female, the monster is condemned to perpetual linguistic isolation—he is convinced that he will never experience the consolation of expressing his thoughts and feelings to a sympathetic "equal." Only in the last scene of the novel, after Frankenstein has died, can the monster express his powerful emotions to an attentive listener, and the extravagance of his language does seem to give him some relief: "'But soon,' he cried, with sad and solemn enthusiasm, 'I shall die, and what I now feel be no longer felt. Soon these burning miseries will be extinct. I shall ascend my funeral pile triumphantly, and exalt in the agony of the torturing flames' " (164). Before Walton, the monster can play his final part "with sad and solemn enthusiasm." While language cannot in and of itself enable the monster to have the relationships he craves, he can finally experience the satisfaction of confessing his crimes and articulating his miseries before a man who, if not totally sympathetic, is at least torn between "curiosity and compassion" (161). But, despite his last impassioned monologue, the monster is never truly admitted into the symbolic order—from the moment he sees his own hideous visage reflected in "a transparent pool" (84), he is condemned to remain in the mirror-stage, irrevocably cut off from the linguistic community.

Mary Shelley's speculations about language and therapy may have begun when she was a child and her father allowed her to hear Coleridge recite "The Rime of the Ancient Mariner." In the epigraph to her short story "Transformation," she quotes from the section of Coleridge's poem in which the Ancient Mariner is compelled to tell his tale, and "Transformation" begins with the protagonist wondering about his motivation for narrating his story:

> Forthwith this frame of mine was wrench'd
>   With a woeful agony,
> Which forced me to begin my tale,
>   And then it set me free.

> Since then, at an uncertain hour,
>   That agony returns;
> And till my ghastly tale is told
>   This heart within me burns.
>   (Coleridge's Ancient Mariner)

I have heard it said, that, when any strange, supernatural, and necromantic adventure has occurred to a human being, that being, however desirous he may be to conceal the same, feels at certain periods torn up as it were by an intellectual earthquake, and is forced to bare the inner depths of his spirit to another. . . . in spite of strong resolve—of a pride that too much masters me—of shame, and even of fear, so to render myself odious to my species—I must speak. (286)[5]

This passage describes both the innate human need "to bare the inner depths of [one's] soul" and the sense that the consequences of this self-exposure could well be devastating and could, in fact, make one appear "odious" to one's entire species. These contradictory urges to reveal and conceal are typical of a number of Shelley's traumatized characters and create a dialectic that she explores extensively in the figures of Mathilda and Beatrice, both of whom are modeled on Percy Shelley's tragic protagonist Beatrice Cenci. Like Beatrice Cenci, Mary Shelley's heroines can find no words to heal their psychic wounds. Both Mathilda and Beatrice Cenci are confronted with the horror of father-daughter incest, and Mathilda also resembles Beatrice in her fear of forbidden words, or, more specifically, in her repression of words signifying incest, the "guilt that wants a name" (*Mary Shelley Reader* 239). Thus a comparison of *Mathilda* and *The Cenci* allows us to see how Mary Shelley's treatment of the theme of logophobia builds on her husband's dramatic portrayal of post-traumatic word repression.

In Percy's *The Cenci,* after Cenci has struck and cursed Beatrice, Lucretia asks her what is wrong, and the stunned Beatrice forces herself to say: "It was one word, Mother, one little word" (II.i.63). That unspeakable word has, however, put Cenci in the position of power. While before it was Cenci who left Beatrice uttering "inarticulate words" (II.i.112), after Cenci's threat it is she who is afraid to speak. Moreover, following her father's rape of her, Beatrice is unable to give the act a name. In response to Lucretia's questions she repeatedly equivocates: "What are the words which you would have me speak?" (III.i.107); "Of all words / That minister to mortal intercourse, / Which wouldst thou hear?" (III.i. 111–113). All victims of incest, she suggests, are compelled to leave "it . . . without a name" (III.i.117). As Anne McWhir notes, Beatrice's repression of the word incest results in the word's revenge: "rejected as a way of dealing with passion, [the word] returns as a means of suggesting perverse, excessively literal action" (148).[6] Because she could not give her horror a name, Beatrice feels compelled to have her father murdered.

Like Beatrice, Mathilda struggles with unutterable words, but, unlike Beatrice, Mathilda precipitates her own tragedy by begging her father to speak "that dreadful word" (201). Whereas Beatrice's mistake may be her refusal to give Cenci's crime a name, Mathilda's initial error is to insist that her father tell her his dark secret, and his confession of incestuous passion is what leads to their destruction. Mathilda passionately demands that her father "Speak that word," and his "strange words" (200) are fatal to him and, eventually, to her. In fact, in the scene in which Mathilda confronts her moody and evasive father, "word" and "words" are repeated with obsessive regularity. She replies to her father's "terrific words": "the sword in my bosom [is] kept from its mortal wound by a hair—a word!—I demand that dreadful word; though it be as a flash of lightning to destroy me, speak it" (201). Her father resists uttering the "strange words" of his confession, but Mathilda's "words [he] cannot bear" (200), so his secret is extracted: "My daughter, I love you!" (201). In his subsequent ravings he tells her that he foolishly believed that "these words . . . would blast her to death" (201). Unfortunately, those words, once uttered, can never be taken back, and inevitably lead to the father's death and Mathilda's decline. Thus, after learning the fatal consequences of certain words, Mathilda becomes, like Beatrice Cenci, logophobic: her thoughts become "too harrowing for words" (219), and, although her narrative is ostensibly written for Woodville, she is never able to "give words to [her] dark tale" (239).

In its skepticism about the therapeutic value of spoken words, *Mathilda* is somewhat different from the section of *The Fields of Fancy,* an earlier draft of *Mathilda,* in which Diotima persuades Mathilda to tell her story. In *The Fields of Fancy,* Mathilda asks: "Are there in the peaceful language used by the inhabitants of these regions [the Elysian Gardens]—words burning enough to paint the tortures of the human heart—Can you understand them? or can you in any way sympathize with them[?]" (Nitchie 100).[7] But even in *The Fields of Fancy* the implication is that a tale like Mathilda's can only be told in some visionary realm; on earth, Mathilda chooses to repress the words that might help her to exorcize her mental demons. Her tale is left as a manuscript to be read posthumously.

In fact in the final chapters of the novella Mathilda makes the mental error that Shelley describes in his notes to *Queen Mab:* "the vulgar mistake of [confusing] a metaphor for a real being, . . . a word for a thing" (Ingpen & Peck I: 145; McWhir 148–149). She has an almost superstitious awe of words, which seem to have the power to destroy. While she is searching for her suicidal father, Mathilda gazes at "a magnificent oak" in the midst of a lightning storm and declares to her servant that "if the next flash of lightning rend not that oak my father will be alive." Her father is dead, and the tree is accordingly obliterated: "I had scarcely uttered these words than a flash instantly followed by a tremendous peal of thunder descended on it [and] the oak no longer stood in the meadow" (213). While the word incest has the power to damn Mathilda to mental hell, her words in this scene appear to have the power to command the forces of heaven. In light of these events, it is not surprising that Mathilda changes from a woman who demands that her father "Speak that word" to a secretive recluse. Mathilda's logophobia is such that she refuses (while alive) to reveal the secret of her despair to Woodville, although he begs her to allow "complaint and sorrow" [to] shape themselves into words" (231). She remembers all too clearly her devastation after her father shaped his "complaint and sorrow" into language.

Although Mathilda represses the words which would explain the cause of her sorrows, she nevertheless finds a kind of consolation in complaining to Woodville, in clothing her "woe in words of gall and fire" (231). Moreover, Woodville's soothing conversation shows Mathilda the positive power of words: "Woodville's hands had magic in them" (232), she writes, admitting that "His words are sweet" (234). Unfortunately, however, "the influence of Woodville's words [is] very temporary" (240), and in his absence Mathilda again succumbs to despair. As long as she fails to "give words to [her] dark tale" she will not be able to exorcize it, and death comes to her as a relief. Mathilda recognizes the "magic" of language but comes to believe that its consolatory effect is too ephemeral to provide any lasting benefit. Moreover, Mathilda's remorse over her father's death leads her to blame herself for his unnatural passion: "I alone was the cause of his defeat and justly did I pay the fearful penalty" (197). In fact, Mathilda even questions her motivation for writing her story: "Perhaps a history such as mine had better die with me, but a feeling that I cannot define leads me on and I am too weak both in body and mind to resist the slightest impulse" (175). Although her conscious mind seems to favor repression, her unconscious, or that "feeling that [she] cannot define," moves her to perform at least one act of linguistic therapy. She can accept the fact that incestuous passion can be written about, but refuses to believe that it can be *spoken* about—thus *Mathilda* suggests that writing can be used as a therapy in cases in which speaking is not an option.

Ten years after she composed *Mathilda*, Shelley returned to the themes of father-daughter love and linguistic repression in a short story entitled "The Mourner." In "The Mourner" a young woman, Clarice Eversham, is obsessively devoted to her father: "He appeared to her like an especial gift of Providence, a guardian angel—but far dearer, as being akin to her own nature" (Robinson 92). When she and her father are caught in a shipwreck, she refuses to leave her father when the women are being put on boats, even though the angry captain expostulates with her: "You will cause your father's death—and be as much a parricide as if you put poison into his cup—you are not the first girl who has murdered her father in her wilful mood" (94). She remains with her father because she has the "fearful presentiment" (93) that if she leaves her father he will die; ironically, however, she does indirectly cause his death when the one boat that returns for them has room for only one person. Her father tosses her aboard it and is drowned (like Mathilda's father)—

during the homeward voyage Clarice hears reproaches from her fellow passengers who, rather harshly, conceive "a horror of her, as having caused her father's death" (94). In essence, "The Mourner" is a reworking of *Mathilda* without the incest theme: like Mathilda, Clarice responds to her father's death by isolating herself and ultimately dying in that isolation. Clarice even goes so far as to change her name to Ellen and pronounce her earlier self (Clarice) dead. She befriends Horace Neville, who, like Woodville, is a Percy Shelley surrogate (the names of both characters end in "ville"), and who, again like Woodville, must persuade her not to commit suicide.

As Ellen, Clarice is characterized by "wordless misery"—instead of telling Neville her story, she generalizes on the subject of sorrow: "She recited no past adventures, alluded to no past intercourse with friend or relative; she spoke of the various woes that wait on humanity" (89). This relatively abstract form of therapy does not alleviate her suffering, and she occasionally begins to tell her story, but then breaks off: "Sometimes she gave words to her despair . . . and every pulsation of her heart was a throb of pain. She has suddenly broken off in talking of her sorrows, with a cry of agony—bidding me to leave her" (89). This fragmentary type of language therapy does not seem to help in the least, and she soon falls ill, refusing medical help and doing "many things that tended to abridge [her life] and to produce mortal disease" (91). Her ultimate confession, like Mathilda's, is in the form of writing, but even here she fragments the word that describes her "crime." In her final letter she asks Neville to give the following message to her erstwhile lover, Lewis Elmore: "Tell him . . . it had been destruction, even could he have meditated such an act to wed the parrici—. I will not write that word" (98). Like Mathilda, she has made "the vulgar mistake of [confusing] . . . a word for a thing"—she represses the word parricide just as Mathilda represses the word incest, but neither woman is truly guilty of what she accuses herself. They leave writings that will be read posthumously and seek to escape both life and fearful words in death. And, like Mathilda, Ellen-Clarice prefers written revelations to oral confessions, even though she is unsure of the justification for her final document. As Ellen-Clarice muses, "Perhaps it is a mere prevarication to write," but write she does, and she seems to gain some measure of consolation from the fact that she has bid those who loved her "a last farewell" (98). Again, while spoken words are rejected as a possible form of communication, written words are at least posthumously acceptable.

Moreover, in both *Mathilda* and "The Mourner" the psychologically unbalanced female protagonists are provided, in a sense, with amateur psychoanalysts: the Percy Shelley surrogates, Woodville and Neville, are faithful and supportive listeners who intervene successfully when their friends contemplate suicide. The auditors are clearly present; what is wanting is that one indispensable element, speech. The brusque way in which Mathilda and Ellen-Clarice reject the catharsis of oral self-expression—that catharsis that Coleridge's Mariner must repeatedly experience—suggests a somewhat masochistic desire to preserve their lonely sufferings from outside observation and interference. In memory of their dead fathers, they do not want to be relieved of their guilt until they expiate that guilt in death. Tragically, they remain in the "imaginary order."

While Mathilda and Ellen-Clarice are traumatized by their inability to deal with their dead fathers, the Beatrice of *Valperga* is emotionally shattered by her lover's rejection and her subsequent abuse by a band of sadists. Her sufferings, like those of Percy's Beatrice Cenci, have a physical as well as emotional component,[8] but unlike Mathilda and Ellen-Clarice, she deals with her terrible memories in an outspoken way. An orphan raised by the Bishop of Ferrera in fourteenth-century Italy, Beatrice is considered a prophet, or *Ancilla Dei,* until she is seduced and then deserted by Castruccio, Prince of Lucca. Broken-hearted, she wanders as a penitential pilgrim, troubled by a recurrent dream which features a flood, "a dreary, large, ruinous house" (*Valperga* III: 82), and a mysterious and evidently traumatic event: "Then something happened, what I cannot now tell, terrific it most certainly was . . . there is something in this strange world, that we none of us understand" (III: 83). Her dream becomes reality when she actually catches sight of "an old, large, dilapidated house islanded in the flood" (III: 84), and she faints. When she awakens, she finds herself in the house of a Cenci-like psychopath who is like a "god of evil" (III: 87). As she represses the horrific event of her dream, she refuses to specify all of what happens to her in that house of torture: "It was a carnival of devils, when we miserable victims were dragged out to—Enough! enough!" (III: 86). And although she speaks about her subsequent madness, she feels unable to dwell on it: "But I must speak of that no more; methinks I again feel, what it is madness only to recollect" (III: 88). In telling Euthanasia of her terrible experiences, she proves far more willing than either Mathilda or Ellen-Clarice to speak of what troubles her, but there are obvious limits to what even she is able to articulate: her dream and the accounts of her abuse and later insanity are partially censored.

In *Valperga* there are, however, indications that Beatrice's words are therapeutic not only to Beatrice but also to her listener, Euthanasia. Both Beatrice and Euthanasia feel a special kinship for one another because they have loved, and had their hearts broken by, the same man, a power-obsessed tyrant named Castruccio. Under Beatrice's influence, Euthanasia is able to break out of her state of emotional paralysis: "Beatrice again awoke [Euthanasia] to words, and these two ladies, bound by the sweet ties of gratitude and pity, found in each other's converse some balm for their misfortunes" (III: 59). And Beatrice, like several of Mary Shelley's other characters, feels the urge to communicate the tragic events of her life, even though Euthanasia advises her to forget the past (III: 68). It is important to note that Beatrice, unlike Mathilda and Ellen-Clarice, tells her story to a sympathetic *woman*—however supportive Woodville and Neville may appear, their masculinity may well present a barrier to communication, although in the case of Mathilda's logophobia it is unlikely that anyone would be able to penetrate her reserve. Together, however, the two patriarchal influences on Mathilda and Ellen-Clarice—first the excessively loving and guilt-inspiring fathers, second the younger men who seek to "save" them from their suicidal depressions—work effectively to silence these extremely sensitive women. In *Valperga,* however, Castruccio, the oppressive masculine influence in that novel, allows his female victims to find at least a temporary peace in each other's company.

And, as Mary Shelley asserts, Beatrice's narrative has a positive effect on her: "Euthanasia had feared, that the reviving the memory of past sorrows, might awaken the frenzy from which [Beatrice] before suffered; but it was not so. She had pined for confidence; her heart was too big to close up in secrecy all the mighty store of unhappiness to which it was conscious; but, having now communicated the particulars to another, she felt somewhat relieved" (III: 98). Although this seems like an unambiguous affirmation of the therapeutic value of spoken words, the qualifying "somewhat" indicates that Beatrice's cure is not complete, and it turns out to be temporary indeed. In fact, like the modern analysand who becomes overly dependent on his or her psychoanalyst, Beatrice is lost when Euthanasia and Padre Lanfranco, her spiritual advisor, leave her alone in Lucca: "she was left without a guide to the workings of her own mind" (III: 118). She encounters a corrupt priest named Tripalda, one of her former torturers, and falls senseless; she dares "not speak to any . . . and the deep anguish she [feels is] no longer mitigated by the converse with her friend" (III: 121).

In this emotionally fragile state, Beatrice falls under the influence of Fior di Mandragola, a self-proclaimed witch, and she describes to Mandragola her recurrent dream of the flood-islanded house, which now includes a confrontation with a doppelgänger: "I was transported into a boat which was to convey me to that mansion . . . a woman sate near the stern aghast and wild as I . . . It was myself; I knew it; it stood before me, melancholy and silent;. . . I can tell no more" (III: 132). In Lacanian terms, Beatrice is trapped in the mirror-stage, "in which the I is precipitated in a primordial form, before it is objectified in the dialectic of identification with the other, and before language restores to it, in the universal, its function as subject" (2). Her specular dream epitomizes her alienation from the symbolic order. As in its earlier incarnations, this dream is inconclusive, and word repression is again suggested: "a few moments, and I distinctly remembered the words it spoke; they have now faded" (III: 132). Unfortunately, Mandragola, unlike Euthanasia, uses Beatrice's words to manipulate her, misinterpreting the dream as a divine sign of Beatrice's mystical powers, and promising Beatrice that she will be able to use these powers to command Castruccio, whom Beatrice still loves. Thus Shelley shows how exposing one's inner self to the wrong person can be psychologically devastating: the witch raises false hopes in Beatrice, and then makes her swear never to reveal what has transpired.

As in the cases of Mathilda and Ellen-Clarice, Beatrice decides to remain silent because of the man she loves, and this silence proves fatal. When Euthanasia returns, she notices a change in Beatrice: "She was much disappointed . . . to find her friend far worse both in body and in mind, than when she left her. More than all wildness of words and manner, she feared her silence and reserve, so very unlike her latest disposition" (III: 142). Beatrice approaches Euthanasia for comfort, but cannot speak: "I have sworn, and I will not tell—. . . I shall sleep now; so not a word more" (III: 146). Later the witch drugs her with henbane and arranges for her to encounter Castruccio on the road; when Castruccio and her former abuser Tripalda approach, Beatrice falls down in convulsions and later dies, insane. She is no longer able to separate nightmare from reality.

Thus Shelley balances her presentation of positive language therapy, Beatrice's narration before the loving and sensitive Euthanasia, with an example of how baring one's psyche before a manipulative and unscrupulous person can lead to madness. Moreover, Beatrice's dependence on Euthanasia, and her rapid decline into insanity after she decides to stop confiding in her friend, suggest that although spoken words can be therapeutic, a traumatized person's prognosis depends on the availability of a sympathetic and supportive listener. And in an oppressively patriarchal world, a psychologically disturbed woman needs another woman to hear her—in *Mathilda* and "The Mourner" women refuse to tell their emotionally-charged stories to men, no matter how well-intentioned the men may be, but Beatrice gains at least a temporary respite when she relates her tale to Euthanasia. In every case, however, there are some words which must remain unsaid.

Although Shelley does not explicitly deal with the theme of language therapy in two of her later novels, *The Fortunes of Perkin Warbeck* and *Lodore,* she does address the issue of language's power to effect positive change. In *Perkin Warbeck,* for example, Monina de Faro uses words to entrance one of the novel's villains, the treacherous Robert Clifford: "They spoke of the desolate waste of waters that hems in the stable earth—of the golden isles beyond: to all these subjects Monina brought vivid imagery, and bright painting, creations of her own quick fancy. [Robert] Clifford had never before held such discourse. . . . The melodious voice of Monina, attuned by the divine impulses of her spirit, as the harp of the winds by celestial breezes, raised a commotion in his mind, such as a prophetess of Delphi felt, when the oracular vapour rose up to fill her with sacred fury." But Monina only succeeds in enchanting (and, significantly, feminizing) Clifford for a moment: "A word, a single word, was a potent northern blast to dash aside the mist, and to re-apparel the world in its, to him, naked, barren truth" (II: 26). Her praise of Richard of York (Perkin Warbeck) inspires Clifford's jealous hatred, and "a single word" is enough to recall him to his evil nature. While Monina is, like Woodville in *Mathilda,* a poetic and spellbinding speaker, both characters fail in their efforts to use words to inspire others. Not even the most powerful and imaginative discourse can wean Clifford and Mathilda away from their self-destructive passions. In *Perkin Warbeck,* Shelley suggests that words cannot convert—they can only reinforce tendencies and beliefs already present. Thus Monina is able to inspire Edmund Plantagenet because he thinks as she does: "her bold, impetuous language had its effect on Edmund: it echoed his own master passion" (III: 67).

Fanny Derham, a minor character in Shelley's *Lodore,* believes passionately in the power of words to cause change. She declares her convictions to Ethel Villiers, the novel's heroine: "Words have more power than any one can guess; it is by words that the world's great fight, now in these civilized times, is carried on; I never hesitated to use them, when I fought any battle for the miserable and oppressed. People are so afraid to speak, it would seem as if half our fellow-creatures were born with deficient organs; like parrots they can repeat a lesson, but their voice fails them, when that alone is wanting to make the tyrant quail" (153). Moreover, when Ethel and her husband are in need of help, Fanny's conversation with Ethel's estranged mother, Lady Lodore, saves her friend from much suffering. But Shelley repeatedly undercuts Fanny's idealistic sentiments by presenting her as other-worldly and unrealistic; after the speech quoted above, Fanny asserts that "while [she] converse[s] each day with Plato, and Cicero, and Epictetus, the world . . . passes from before [her] like a vain shadow" (153). And when Fanny inherits a fortune, she cannot grasp its significance: "Fanny was too young, and too wedded to her platonic notions of the supremacy of mind, to be fully aware of the invaluable advantages of pecuniary independence for a woman. She fancied that she could enter on the career—the only career permitted to her sex—of servitude, and yet possess her soul in freedom and power" (206). Thus, although Shelley presents a character in *Lodore* who steadfastly believes in the power of language, Fanny is too inexperienced and bookish to be taken as a reliable authority on this subject. In fact, Shelley suggests that life will test Fanny's idealism: "One who feels so deeply for others, and yet is so stern a censor over herself—at once so sensitive and so rigidly conscientious—so single-minded and upright, and yet open as day to charity and affection, cannot hope to pass from youth to age unharmed" (228). Even in this late novel, Shelley seems skeptical about the efficacy of words, particularly when they are employed by a naive idealist.

As we have seen, Mary Shelley's fictions return repeatedly to the predicament of a suffering human being torn between the impulse to communicate and the urge to retreat into isolation and death. More often than not, the result is psychic paralysis, the opposite of the meliorism championed by Percy Shelley. But ultimately an ephemeral sort of consolation can be found in the act of writing, as Lionel Verney discovers at the end of Mary Shelley's apocalyptic *The Last Man.* Since he is the last man on earth, Lionel Verney's compositions seem the most futile of all self-expressions—no one will read them. But in writing his narrative, Verney rejoins, temporarily, all of the people he has loved: "I lingered fondly on my early years, and recorded with sacred zeal the virtues of my companions. They have been with me during the fulfillment of my task. I have brought it to an end—I lift my eyes from my paper—again they are lost to me" (339). Even Mary Shelley's most repressed characters, such as Mathilda and Ellen-Clarice, find themselves compelled to express themselves in writing, just as Shelley herself, mourning the deaths of her husband and two of her children, and facing the prospect of social ostracism and emotional deprivation, was moved to present her state of mind in *The Last Man*. In a May 14, 1824, journal entry she wrote: "The last man! Yes I may well describe that solitary being's feelings, feeling myself as the last relic of a beloved race, my companions, extinct before me" (II: 476–477).

Moreover, in her October 2, 1822, journal entry, her first journal entry after Percy's death, Mary clearly states her need for the therapy provided by written rather than spoken self-expression: "Now I am alone! . . . The stars may behold my tears, & the winds drink my sighs—but my thoughts are a sealed treasure which I can confide to none. White paper—wilt thou be my confident [*sic*]? I will trust thee fully, for none shall see what I write" (II: 429)? While in her bereavement Mary Shelley finds social "intercourse with others extremely disagreable [*sic*]," she feels compelled to record her emotions in her journal: "coming home I write this, so necessary is it for me to express in words the force of my feelings" (II: 440). Although the acts of speaking or writing may not cure psychological problems or bring the dead back to life, these forms of self-expression can provide some comfort, and as Mary Shelley's fiction and life seem to suggest, that momentary comfort often is the only consolation allowed to suffering humanity.[9]

Notes

1. For a more extensive presentation of Percy Shelley's attitudes toward language, see Keach 1–41.

2. All references to Percy Shelley's works are from the Reiman and Powers edition.

3. Freud also stresses the importance of words in psychoanalysis: "Nothing takes place in a psycho-analytic treatment but an interchange of words between the patient and analyst. The patient talks, tells of his past experiences and present impressions, complaints, confesses to his wishes and his emotional impulses. . . . Words were originally magic and to this day words have retained much of their ancient magical power. . . . Words provoke affects and are in general the means of mutual influence among men. Thus we shall not depreciate the use of words in psychotherapy and we shall be pleased if we can listen to the words that pass between the analyst and the patient" (17).

4. For a analysis of the monster's acquisition of language, see Brooks 208–213.

5. In another short story, "The Parvenue," Mary Shelley has a character begin the tale by asking: "Why do I write my melancholy story?" (Robinson 266).

6. Worton argues that "Beatrice's inability to speak coherently of her sufferings indicates that language cannot codify extreme emotion" (110).

7.   In *The Fields of Fancy* draft edited by Murray, Mathilda's faith in the therapeutic value of relating her story is even more evident. Mathilda says: "Never on earth was that fearful tale unfolded—here among the shadows of the dead It may be—And I feel that the bonds that in this existence as well as in that past weigh heavily on me, will be broken" (I: 271).

8.   Mary Shelley's Beatrice is specifically compared to the historical Beatrice Cenci: see *Valpenga*, II: 17–18.

9.   It should be noted that as Mary Shelley's sense of isolation following her husband's death deepened, even writing failed her as a form of therapy: "I can speak to none—writing this is useless—it does not even soothe me—on the contrary it irritates me by shewing the pityful [*sic*] expedient to which I am reduced" (*Journal* II: 485).

Works Cited

Brooks, Peter. " 'Godlike Science/Unhallowed Arts': Language, Nature, and Monstrosity." In *The Endurance of Frankenstein: Essays on Mary Shelley's Novel*. Ed. George Levine and U. C. Knoepflmacher. Berkeley: U of California P, 1979. 205–220.

Freud, Sigmund. *The Complete Introductory Lectures on Psychoanalysis*. Trans. and Ed. James Strachey. New York: Norton, 1966.

Herman, Judith Lewis. *Trauma and Recovery*. New York: Basic, 1992.

Ingpen, Roger and Walter E. Peck. Eds. *The Complete Works of Percy Bysshe Shelley*. 10 vols. New York: Gordian, 1965.

Keach, William. *Shelley's Style*. New York: Methuen, 1984.

Lacan, Jacques. *Écrits: A Selection*. Trans. Alan Sheridan. New York: Norton, 1977.

McWhir, Anne. "The Light and the Knife: Ab/Using Language in *The Cenci*." *Keats-Shelley Journal* 38 (1989): 145–161.

Murray, E. B. Ed. *A Facsimile of Bodleian MS. Shelley d. 1*. Vol. 4 of *The Bodleian Shelley Manuscripts* in 2 parts. New York: Garland, 1988.

Nitchie, Elizabeth, ed. *Mathilda*. By Mary Wollstonecraft Shelley. *Studies in Philology* extra ser. 3. Chapel Hill: U of North Carolina P, 1959.

Robinson, Charles E., ed. *Mary Shelley: Collected Tales and Stories*. Baltimore: The Johns Hopkins UP, 1976.

Rubenstein, Marc A. "*Frankenstein*: Search for the Mother." *Studies in Romanticism* 15 (1976): 165–194.

Shelley, Mary Wollstonecraft. *The Fortunes of Perkin Warbeck, a Romance*. 3 vols. London: Henry Colborn and Richard Bentley, 1830.

———. *The Journals of Mary Shelley: 1814–1844*. Ed. Paula R. Feldman and Diana Scott-Kilvert. 2 vols. Oxford: Clarendon, 1987.

———. *The Last Man*. Ed. Hugh J. Luke, Jr. Lincoln: U of Nebraska P, 1965.

———. *Lodore*. New York: Wallis & Newell, 1835.

———. "Transformation." *The Mary Shelley Reader*. Ed. Betty T. Bennett and Charles E. Robinson. New York: Oxford UP, 1990. 286–300.

———. *Valperga: or, the Life and Adventures of Castruccio, Prince of Lucca*. 3 vols. London: G. and W. B. Whittaker, 1823.

Shelley, Percy Bysshe. *Shelley's Poetry and Prose*. Ed. Donald H. Reiman and Sharon B. Powers. New York: Norton, 1977.

Sunstein, Emily W. *Mary Shelley: Romance and Reality*. Baltimore: The Johns Hopkins UP, 1989.

Worton, Michael. "Speech and Silence in *The Cenci*." In *Essays on Shelley*. Ed. Miriam Allott. Totowa: Barnes & Nobles, 1982. 105–124.

Exile, Isolation, and Accommodation in *The Last Man*: The Strategies of a Survivor

VICTORIA MIDDLETON

The Last Man is a watershed in Mary Shelley's career, both politically and aesthetically. In this first novel written after Shelley's death, her feeling of engulfment by tragic events, her guilty apprehension of further "punishment" for living audaciously, cause her to resign her quest for self-knowledge. The order of things—in the family, the state, the universe—exacts submission rather than rebellion. Always before, the nature of life was a subject that prompted interrogation. In the original version of *Mathilda, called The Fields of Fancy,* the unhappy heroine is counselled by Diotima, instructress of Socrates, that human happiness "depends upon [one's] intellectual improvement . . ." in order to "become more like that beauty which I adore. . . ."[1] Mathilda's response to this Shelleyan idealism is an unanswered question: "If knowledge is the end of our being why are passions and feelings implanted in us that hurries [*sic*] us from wisdom to selfconcentrated misery and narrow selfish feeling?" (p. 99). In *The Last Man,* Mary Shelley schools herself in acceptance of the riddle of existence, without demanding an answer to it:

> What would become of us? O for some Delphic oracle, or Pythian maid, to utter the secrets of futurity! O for some Oedipus to solve the riddle of the cruel Sphynx! Such Oedipus was I to be—not divining a word's juggle, but whose agonizing pangs, and sorrow-tainted life were to be the engines, wherewith to lay bare the secrets of destiny, and reveal the meaning of the enigma, whose explanation closed the history of the human race. (*The Last Man,* pp. 310–311).

This is no version of Keatsian negative capability, a conscious acceptance of the mystery, but really a withdrawal of the question posed in *Mathilda.*

After *The Last Man,* the protagonists in Mary Shelley's novels do not quarrel with their makers, nor does their author quarrel with herself. In the

From *Elektra in Exile: Women Writers and Political Fiction,* ed. Victoria Middleton (New York: Garland, 1988), 32–76. Reprinted with the permission of Garland Publishing Inc.

late novels, the egocentricity of the narrative point of view is reduced even as the Promethean protagonist is domesticated and reconciled, if not to the whole of society, at least to the microcosmic society of his family. Mary Shelley's conception of the self and its relation to society changes, and the narrative structure of her novels reflects this change.

The use of first-person narration conspicuously stops. (Falkner's first-person confession . . . is the exception that validates the rule.) This signifies, I believe, a decision against the study of the consciousness of a single protagonist as he simultaneously reveals and makes himself. In its place we find the bilateral monologues and the dialogues—rather awkwardly executed—of the realistic *Perkin Warbeck, Lodore,* and *Falkner. The Last Man* reveals Mary Shelley's motivation for shifting from the "self-centered" to the objective in narrative modes.

In this novel, Lionel Verney speaks for the author through his aesthetic credo as well as his philosophical and political opinions. We must understand Verney's story—his survival of the plague that destroys not only civilization but (almost) the entire human species—and, more importantly, his attitude toward the telling of his story, in order to appreciate how and why Mary Shelley lost the liberal faith of her youth. . . .

The very journal entry that records her despair at the failure of her imagination [after Shelley's death] also contains the seed of her next novel: "The last man! Yes, I may well describe that solitary being's feelings, feeling myself as the last relic of a beloved race, my companions extinct before me" (*Mary Shelley's Journal,* ed. Frederick L. Jones [Norman, Okla.: University of Oklahoma Press, 1947], p. 193, 14 May 1824 [hereafter cited in text as *Journal*]. Mary Shelley uses the energizing emotions of grief and loneliness to make a final effort to "become something," to assert herself in the act of writing.

In *The Last Man* [she draws] upon the longstanding conflict between her desire to know herself independent and her desire to please others. It is her last novel to use first-person narration, in which the teller of the tale creates a self or persona in the process of telling it, where the narrative mode becomes an object of scrutiny in its own right. In the course of the novel, Lionel Verney's conception of his task undergoes a change that is symbolic of Mary Shelley's. Verney's definitions of himself, his relation to society, and his role as creator and historian represent the transformation of Mary Shelley's own roles.

In *The Last Man,* she chooses a narrator whose life history has less symbolic affinity with her own than the betrayed and disconsolate orphans of *Frankenstein* and *Mathilda.* Although both Mary Shelley and Lionel Verney are left widowed and childless, Verney does not express her sense of loss as well as the monster and Mathilda. Possibly Mary Shelley felt that a male observer would add verisimilitude to the novel's depiction of political exchanges. At the same time, however, using a man as narrator distanced her from the experience described. In a sense, the maleness of the victimized hero may have intensified Mary Shelley's conflict—for she resented being left alone by male guardians as much as she mourned it. . . .

Intellectual freedom becomes an emotional burden in *The Last Man* because it entails exile from human fellowship. *The Last Man* depicts varieties of exile and gives both private and political causes for them. Ultimately, however, the root cause of all alienation is the insolubility of the metaphysical mystery, why do we live, if destined to die? The novel asks, not "How live?" but "Why live at all?" The former question requires an answer in terms of personal choices, social responsibilities, political decisions. The latter, for Mary Shelley, proves unanswerable. Because she cannot teleologically justify why we live, the activity of living becomes an end in itself. This outcome, paradoxically, influences possible choices of how best to live.

Besides being the primary theme of *The Last Man,* exile is a fact confronted in the very narrative mode of the novel. That is, Lionel Verney's attitude toward his story—his conception of his role as narrator—is as much a revelation of the artist's role as of the relation of a single self to society. Mary Shelley depicts the artist's transformation from a (Romantic) sublime egotist, proudly superior to society if tragically alienated from it, into a (Victorian) scribe for whom writing becomes life-preserving, Carlylean *work.* This transition from a Romantic to a Victorian narrator is inextricably bound up with Lionel Verney's discovery about the ultimate isolation of the self.

Verney's history, related in *The Last Man,* includes at least three distinct phases. As her modern editor points out, Mary Shelley ironically reverses the Wordsworthian triadic progression of innocent unity; experiential alienation; higher, maturer oneness with the universe. Instead, she "presents us with the pattern of a life beginning in alienation, temporarily achieving a sense of union, and then returning to an intensified isolation."[2] Verney's first and final states of isolation are different in kind as well as intensity. He undergoes a change from political to social exile, which is remediable, to existential exile, for which there is no solution. Through Verney's career, Mary Shelley demonstrates her new belief that political solutions to the problem of human unhappiness are not ineffectual but rather meaningless, a more radically pessimistic view of the human social condition.

Verney's initial social exile was brought on by his noble father's being exiled from the royal court for his recklessness and lack of self-control. The father's political sins being visited on the innocent child, Lionel grows up orphaned and neglected. He becomes rebellious and arrogant, conscious of some innate social superiority to his rustic friends: ". . . I knew I was different and superior to my protectors and companions, but I knew not how or wherefore" (*The Last Man,* p. 8). He is an incipient radical—"The sense of injury, associated with the name of king and noble, clung to me . . ." (p. 8)— angry at unjust or irresponsible authority figures who have deprived him of paternalistic nurturing. Exclusion from power brings about desire for illegitimate power: "I associated with others friendless like myself, I formed them into a band, I was their chief and captain" (p. 8); ". . . finding that my chief superiority consisted in power, I soon persuaded myself that it was in power only that I was inferior to the chiefest potentates of the earth" (p. 9). The exiled boy, disinherited by the royal "father" and left orphaned by his real parents, represents the growth of disaffection in the childlike or primitive lower classes of a society whose leaders fail their subjects.

Mary Shelley does not recommend, as a solution to Verney's incipient rebelliousness and to popular unrest, a more humane and benevolent paternalism. Nor does she heroicize man in his natural, primitive condition and advocate complete self-rule. Instead, she gives Verney a friend, Adrian, himself a rebel against aristocratic tyranny in his own royal family. Adrian (the novel's surrogate for Shelley) is a Platonist and a philanthropist. Eventually, he governs England in time of crisis as a philosopher-king. As a boy, his "active spirit of benevolence" (p. 18) wins a peaceful contest over Lionel's belligerence. Adrian's gentle personality converts Lionel to a political philosophy of good will: "'This,' I thought, 'is power! Not to be strong of limb, hard of heart, ferocious, and daring; but kind, compassionate and soft'" (p. 19). Showing the "'fervour of a new proselyte'" (p. 19), Verney feels transformed, "as much changed as if I had transmigrated into another form" (p. 21).

This internal revolution, a type of Godwinian intellectual change that must precede institutional change, produces admirable results—for a while. From social rebelliousness, Lionel Verney's energy is channeled into scholarship. . . . Verney exalts intellectual enlightenment over political activism. His scholarship takes a seemingly passive course. Books, he says, ". . . stood in the place of an active career, of ambition, and those palpable excitements necessary to the multitude. The collation of philosophical opinions, the study of historical facts, the acquirements of languages, were at once my recreation, and the serious aim of my life" (p. 112). Yet for Verney, knowledge represents power. His ardent enthusiasm makes him hope for a future of intellectual achievement: "Life is before me, and I rush into possession. Hope, glory, love, and blameless ambition are my guides, and my soul knows no dread. What has been, though sweet, is gone; the present is good only because it is about to change, and the to come is all my own. . . . my eyes seem to penetrate the cloudy midnight of time, and to discern within the depths of its darkness, the fruition of all my soul desires" (p. 25). With Wordsworthian (and Adamic) exultation, he anticipates constructing a brilliant future. He will become a ". . . citizen of the world, a candidate for immortal honors, an eager aspirant to the praise and sympathy of my fellow men" (p. 113). In thinking, Lionel conceives of himself—creating an identity as a scholar.

Verney's research, like Mary Shelley's autobiographical fiction, involves rescuing from obscurity and infamy "favourite historical characters, especially those whom I believed to have been traduced, or about whom clung obscurity and doubt" (p. 133). He sees himself as a heroic agent rather than as a transcriber of others' past deeds: "As my authorship increased . . . my point of sight was extended, and the inclinations and capacities of all human beings became deeply interesting to me. Kings have been called the fathers of their people. Suddenly I became as it were the father of all mankind. Posterity became my heirs. My thoughts were gems to enrich the treasure house of man's intellectual possessions . . ." (p. 133). Lionel's intellectual ambition is not destructive as was the Faustian drive of Victor Frankenstein. Without question, however, it is in his eyes a heroic and audacious activity. What he says about his sister Perdita's discovery of philosophy might be true of him as well: she was "questioning herself and her author, moulding every idea in a thousand ways, ardently desirous for the discovery of truth in every sentence" (p. 114). In short, the seemingly passive occupation of scholarship is, for Verney, a Promethean activity. Like Prometheus, he transmits wisdom to mankind, while at the same time "questioning . . . [his] author."

Verney's closest companions in a Promethean circle include Adrian and Raymond, both aristocrats with political interests that are, however, antagonistic. Adrian is a "philanthropist" who feels sympathy "with the universe of existence"; Raymond is a "politician" motivated by "self-gratification" and worldliness (p. 31). Both agree that England (a republic since 2073) is a nation of servile and vulgar citizens—"willing slaves, self-constituted subjects" (p. 41)—incapable of the "erect and manly" self-rule that would make the republic glorious. The chance to implement their different utopian visions comes to Raymond and Adrian by turns, with Mary Shelley demonstrating through them the benefits and limitations of political practice.

Raymond becomes Protector, chief governor of England, when the self-serving popular leader Ryland sells his candidacy for personal profit. Raymond's plan is to effect a utopia through the example of his own personality: ". . . men were not happy, not because they could not, but because they would not rouse themselves to vanquish self-raised obstacles. Raymond was to inspire them with his beneficial will, and the mechanism of society, once systematized according to faultless rules, would never again swerve into disorder" (p. 76). Unfortunately, Raymond's lack of self-rule makes it impossible for him to succeed politically, to provide an heroic example. He admits to being the "slave" of his own heart (p. 45), ruled by his passions (his love for Perdita; his fascination with Evadne, which precipitates his political ruin).

Mary Shelley implies that Raymond's political downfall stems from his disbelief in free will. He argues with Lionel and Adrian on this subject, insisting that our lives are determined both by nature and by nurture: " ' . . . this cultivation, mingling with our innate disposition, is the soil in which our desires, passions, and motives grow' " (p. 47). Not feeling free to govern himself, Raymond ultimately cannot set the example of "beneficial will" that he hoped would inspire the people.

In contrast to the fatalistic Raymond, both Lionel and Adrian have faith in some degree of freedom of volition. Adrian enthusiastically believes in humanity's capacity to make the ideal real by willing it. Able to conquer his own passions, to rule himself as Raymond is not, Adrian overcomes his grief at Evadne's refusal to return his love and dedicates himself to humanitarian causes. He believes that man's ability to conceive of utopia ensures its realization, such is the power of the human mind: " 'The choice is with us; let us will it, and our habitation becomes a paradise. For the will of man is omnipotent, blunting the arrows of death, soothing the bed of disease, and wiping away the tears of agony' " (p. 54). For Adrian (as for Shelley), nothing exists but as it is perceived. The ideal is more real (and more realizable) than what is actual.

Adrian is a pragmatic idealist, a philosopher-king who leaves the Platonic cave of philosophy to return to public service. His political ambition is vitiated by neither the greedy self-interest of the lower-class Ryland nor the aristocratic egotism of Raymond. Adrian is devoted to moral, aesthetic, and intellectual excellence. Despite his idealism, he does not aim at the establishment of an English utopia. He enters politics only in time of crisis and imperative public need, when the plague has devastated the citizenry and threatened to destroy civilization itself:

> "This is my post: I was born for this—to rule England in anarchy, to save her in danger—to devote myself for her. The blood of my forefathers cries aloud in my veins, and bids me be first among my countrymen. Or, if this mode of speech offend you, let me say, that my mother, the proud queen, instilled early into me a love of distinction. . . . I cannot, through intrigue and faithlessness, rear again the throne upon the wreck of English public spirit. But I can be the first to support and guard my country, now that terrific disasters and ruin have laid strong hands upon her." (p. 185)

Adrian's language is formal, abstract, remote from practical experience and application; it reveals Adrian's self-consciousness, more naive than self-interested. His failure to save England, despite his great talents and noble motives, proves the ultimate futility of heroism in politics.

Mary Shelley feels ambivalent about heroic individualism. On the one hand, pride of rank is artificial and "worse than foolish." "False was all this— false all but the affections of our nature. . . . There was but one good and one evil in the world—life and death" (p. 212). But if pride based on birth, rank, wealth is fallacious, the loss of individual heroism wrought by the plague is lamentable:

> The pomp of rank, the assumption of power, the possessions of wealth vanished like morning mist. One living beggar had become of more worth than a national peerage of dead lords—alas the day! than of dead heroes, patriots, or men of genius. There was much of degradation in this: for even vice and virtue had lost their attributes—life—life—the continuation of our animal mechanism—was the Alpha and Omega of the desires, the prayers, the prostrate ambition of human [sic] race. (p. 212)

Mary Shelley regrets the passing not of aristocracy itself but of heroes—the individual patriots or philosophers or artists that the caste system is capable of producing. She sympathizes with an aristocracy of talent ("nature's true nobility," p. 161) and with the Promethean greatness that it makes possible.

Mary Shelley equates the anarchy caused by the plague that sweeps the entire earth with democratization. England is contaminated because of its increasingly unheroic mercantilism: "Our own distresses, though they were occasioned by the fictitious reciprocity of commerce, encreased in due proportion" (p. 169). In one description, the plague is explicitly likened to the French Revolution: "As at the conclusion of the eighteenth century, the English unlocked their hospitable store, for the relief of those driven from their homes by political revolution; so they were not backward in affording aid to the victims of a more widespreading calamity" (p. 171). Mary Shelley regarded revolution in the social fabric with dread, even horror. In a letter inspired by the Revolution of 1848, she commented:

> . . . these are awful times. The total overthrow of law, the dislocation of the social system in France presents a fearful aspect. In Italy and in Germany the people aim at political rather than social change—but the French will spare no pains to inculcate their wicked and desolating principles—and to extend the power of their nefarious Provisional Government all over Europe. . . . their measures are so tyrannical—so ruinous that they must be looked upon as the worst engines of a bad system. There is no doubt that a French propaganda is spread among all nations—they are raising the Irish and even exciting the English Chartists. . . . I do believe that in England law and the orderly portion of the community will prevail. God grant it. God preserve us from the tyranny and lawlessness now oppressing France. . . .[3]

Even as early as 1826, when writing *The Last Man,* Mary Shelley echoed her father's fear of "social" revolution as opposed to political, institutional reform. She reacted to changes in the social fabric—relationships between people in the state or in the family—with outrage and fear. It was natural for her to advocate paternalistic custodianship of social bonds based on emotions.

Adrian's governing plan is benevolently paternalistic. The state will be governed like a well-ordered family unit. As his lieutenant, Lionel Verney decides that in rural England, "each small township [would be] directed by the elders and wise men. . . . Each village, however small, usually contains a leader, one among whom they venerate, whose advice they seek in difficulty, and whose good opinion they chiefly value" (p. 195). These "rustic archons," reminiscent of Wordsworth's wise solitaries, rule their tiny kingdoms like loving parents.

Like the nineteenth-century capitalist, the plague victim is advised to seek spiritual restoration in the boson of his family. Lionel Verney's revulsion from public life, following his return from the war between the Greeks and Turks, sets a reactionary example: "I cannot describe the rapturous delight with which I turned from political brawls at home, and the physical evils of distant countries, to my own dear home, to the selected abode of goodness and love; to peace, and the interchange of every sacred sympathy" (p. 163). Lionel calls for retreat from the world, repudiation of political action altogether:

> How unwise had the wanderers been, who had deserted its shelter, entangled themselves in the web of society, and entered on what men of the world call "life,"—that labyrinth of evil, that scheme of mutual torture. To live, according to this sense of the word, we must not only observe and learn, we must also feel; we must not be mere spectators of action, we must act; we must not describe, but be subjects of description. Deep sorrow must have been the inmate of our bosoms; fraud must have lain in wait for us; the artful must have deceived us; sickening doubt and false hope must have chequered our days; hilarity and joy, that lap in the sole in ecstacy, must at times have possessed us. Who knows what "life" is, would pine for this feverish species of existence? . . . shut the door on the world, and build high the wall that is to separate me from the troubled scene enacted within its precincts. Let us live for each other and for happiness; let us seed peace in our dear home. . . . (p. 158)

The wall that Verney wants to erect between his family—his own little kingdom—and the larger world becomes a model for the organization of the state.

Adrian and Lionel exhort people to accept social order, including a hierarchic division of society, as the best means of controlling the spread of the plague: ". . . it became our part to fix deep the foundations, and raise high the barrier between contagion and the sane; to introduce such order as would conduct to the well-being of the survivors, and as would preserve hope and some portion of happiness to those who were spectators of the still renewed tragedy" (p. 195). The wall of separateness and order is a reactionary measure necessary to diffuse the power of political contagion.

Adrian's and Lionel's proposal is also conservative in that it is atavistic. It attempts to restore the lost harmony of the fabled Golden Age that was the object of much nostalgia in the increasingly industrialized eighteenth and nineteenth centuries. The devastation brought by the plague inspires paternalistic benevolence in other aristocrats as well as in Adrian. Mary Shelley cites many modestly heroic responses to anarchy:

> Among some these changes produced a devotion and sacrifice of self at once graceful and heroic. It was a sight for the lovers of the human race to enjoy; to behold as in ancient times, the patriarchal modes in which the variety of kindred and friendship fulfilled their duties and kindly offices. (p. 223)

Young noblemen perform rustic chores while noblewomen provide them with "the simple and affectionate welcome known before only to the lowly cottage—a clean hearth and bright fire . . ." (p. 223). The political ideal is a pastoral idyll—peopled by happy children under a benevolent guidance that is paternal. . . .

The domestic idyll briefly achieved in the home and in the state proves an ineffectual antidote to anarchy. Mary Shelley, though she may believe them possible or desirable in 1848, undercuts political solutions in *The Last Man*. Because the plague does not merely symbolize democratization and commercialism, political and social levelling, no political solutions—radical *or* conservative—can forestall its destructive advance.[4]

What the plague ultimately represents to Lionel Verney and Mary Shelley can best be deduced from its effects. Its destructiveness is so undiscriminating, so widespread, so irrevocable that survival becomes the highest goal of every human being. Mere animal life comes to have greater value than genius, moral worth, and other excellences esteemed by civilized man:

> Now life is all that we covet; that this automaton of flesh should, with joints and springs in order, perform its functions, that this dwelling of the soul should be capable of containing its dweller. Our minds, late spread abroad through countless spheres and endless combinations of thought, now retrenched themselves behind this wall of flesh, eager to preserve its well-being only. We were surely sufficiently degraded. (p. 230)

The plague represents, in essence, death: the metaphysical fact. "We were all equal now; but near at hand was an equality still more levelling, a state where beauty and strength, and wisdom, would be as vain as riches and birth. The grave yawned beneath us all . . ." (p. 231). Humanity, which had seemed a fertile "flood," "a vast perennial river," is now seen to progress toward "the ocean of death" (p. 300)—there is no greater end.

Death by plague comes to all, even to individuals who seek to isolate themselves for safety. The radical sectarians who follow a Methodistic "prophet" all succumb: "At length the plague, slow-footed, but sure in her noiseless advance, destroyed the illusion, invading the congregation of the elect, and showering promiscuous death among them" (p. 296). Justice is apparently served when the ranting religious despot is defeated. Yet the plague is not the instrument of an intelligible providence. It "promiscuously," indiscriminately, attacks benevolent as well as egocentric politicians and their dependents. It cruelly—or with indifference—kills children before their fond parents.

Perhaps worst of all, death in this virulent form seems *meaningless*. The human mind—Lionel Verney's, Mary Shelley's—cannot make sense of the effects of the plague: ". . . it appeared as if suddenly the motion of the earth was revealed to us—as if no longer we were ruled by ancient laws, but were turned adrift in an unknown region of space" (p. 270).

Lionel Verney's (and Adrian's) original brave faith in the human imagination is undercut by such unforeseeable, even unimaginable destruction. Verney had optimistically believed that the mind of man could effect anything it willed: "So true it is, that man's mind alone was the creator of all that was good or great to man, and that Nature herself was only his first minister" (p. 5). He had argued against Raymond's determinism: ". . . nature always presents to our eyes the appearance of a patient: while there is an active principle in man which is capable of ruling fortune, and at least of tacking against the gale, till it in some mode conquers it" (p. 46). Verney learns that man, individual or species, cannot conquer nature, at least not the (natural) fact of death.

The illusion of human progress is undercut in public life and in private as well. Civilization is exposed as an evanescent fiction, a hopeful creation of man's imagination that has no substantial or absolute reality. "England, late birth-place of excellence and school of the wise, thy children are gone, thy glory faded! Thou, England, wert the triumph of man!" (p. 235). Without its heroes, the political and cultural glories of England are ephemeral.

One private illusion that the plague exposes is the natural though irrational faith of the parent that his children will survive to continue his life in theirs: ". . . we call ourselves lords of the creation, wielders of the elements, masters of life and death, and we allege in excuse of this arrogance, that though the individual is destroyed, man continues for ever" (p. 167). "Thus, losing our identity, that of which we are chiefly conscious, we glory in the continuity of our species, and learn to regard death without terror. But when any whole nation becomes the victim of the destructive powers of exterior agents, then indeed man shrinks into insignificance, he feels his tenure of life insecure, his inheritance on earth cut off" (p. 167). Lionel Verney is forced to realize, as he watches his children die before him, the delusion in his optimistic belief in posterity ("Willingly do I give place to thee, dear Alfred! advance, offspring of tender love, child of our hopes; advance a soldier on the road to which I have been the pioneer! I will make way for thee . . ." (p. 165). The blunt fact of death defeats this naive hope, as Mary Shelley learned when watching three of her own children die. In 1820 she wrote Leigh Hunt, ". . . you, my dear Hunt, never lost a child or the ideal mortality w[oul]d not suffice to your immagination [*sic*] as it naturally does thinking only of those whom you loved more from the overflowing of affection, than from their being the hope, the rest, the purpose, the support, and the recompense of life."[5]

Verney is progressively shorn of his human ties and props. With the death of his wife Idris, "the talisman of my existence" (p. 44), Lionel feels "as if all the visible universe had grown as soulless, inane, and comfortless as the clay-cold image beneath me. I felt for a moment the intolerable sense of struggle with, and detestation for, the laws which govern the world . . ." (p. 260). Lionel regains his resignation to fate, his hope that they will be reunited in an unearthly incarnation. But his response to Idris's death clearly emulates Mary's reaction to Shelley's. The world suddenly seems robbed of meaning. Even individual death (like Adrian's accidental drowning at the end of *The Last Man*) is senseless, random, absurd. Obviously it is not nature, in all its mutability and unpredictability, that is senseless or dead. It is man's mind that imbues the animate and inanimate universe with meaning; the "death" of the universe signifies the failure of man's imagination, its defeat by unbearable facts.

Lionel continues to hope—fantastically—that spiritually they can survive and continue to know each other: "We talked of what was beyond the tomb; and, man in his human shape being nearly extinct, we felt with certainty of faith, that other spirits, other minds, other perceptive beings, sightless to us, must people with thought and love this beauteous and imperishable universe" (p. 248). . . . For a time, Lionel behaves as if this belief sustains him, retrieves his faith in the self-sufficient creativity of the human mind. He addresses the reader, for example, as one of this race of spiritually superior beings who have replaced humanity: "Patience, oh reader! whoever thou art, sprung from some surviving pair, thy nature will be human, thy habitation the earth . . ." (p. 291).

Really, however, Verney has no hope; the message that he wishes to transmit to this hypothetical posterity is negative: "Beware, tender offspring of the re-born world—beware, fair being, with human heart, yet untamed by care, and human brow, yet unploughed by time—beware, lest the cheerful current of thy blood be checked, thy golden locks turn grey . . ." (p. 318). "Seek a cypress grove, whose moaning boughs will be harmony befitting; seek some cave, deep embowered in the earth's dark entrails, where no light will penetrate, save that which struggles, red and flickering, through a single fissure, staining thy page with grimmest livery of death" (p. 318). Lionel advocates retreat from life—from the sun—to the depths of isolation and self-exploration. . . .

In advocating a retreat to a cave of solitude and self-communion, Lionel Verney is prescribing not self-discovery but quiescence, a passivity that is deathlike. In one particularly despairing mood, in fact, he advises his readers to seek rather than wait for death:

> Surely death is not death, and humanity not extinct; but merely passed into other shapes, unsubjected to our perceptions. Death is a vast portal, an high road to life: let us hasten to pass; let us exist no more in this living death, but die that we may live! (p. 310)

What must die is the illusory belief that not only man but also his fictions are indestructible, immortal, absolute.

Chief among man's fictions is his belief in free will and its power. When arguing against Raymond's fatalism, Lionel insists, "'There is much truth in what you say' said I, 'and yet no man ever acts upon this theory. Who, when he makes a choice, says, Thus I choose, because I am necessitated? Does he not on the contrary feel a freedom of will within him, which, though you may call it fallacious, still actuates him as he decides?'" (p. 47). Man's feeling of free will is his chief weapon against death: ". . . in times of misery we must fight against our destinies, and strive not to be overcome by them" (p. 233). The impact of the plague is enervating; it saps the will of the survivors. The very fact that their dwindling number ensures greater wealth individually makes ambition unnecessary: ". . . there was no need of labour, no inquisitiveness, no restless desire to get on" (p. 279).

Confronting death forces the survivors to realize that the fictions by which they have lived are irrelevant to the mysterious laws of the universe. Action, even the act of willing, cannot prevent death; only resignation and submission to fate are possible:

> Would you read backwards the unchangeable laws of Necessity? Mother of the world! Servant of the Omnipotent! eternal, changeless Necessity! who with busy fingers sitting ever weaving the indissoluble chain of events!—I will not murmur at thy acts. If my human mind cannot acknowledge that all that is, is right; yet since what is, must be, I will sit amidst the ruins and smile. Truly we were not born to enjoy, but to submit, and to hope. (pp. 290–291)

At the last, living becomes an end in itself, a process of getting from point to point in time and space (just as Adrian leads his dwindling band of survivors across the Continent, believing that only endless motion will alleviate suffering and prolong life).

At the novel's end, Lionel Verney is the last man, and he longs for death. (It is most assuredly the "Friend" whom he adjures, "'Friend, come! I wait for thee!'" [p. 322].) He wants to die, either to rejoin his beloved friends or else simply to escape the enormous pain of being "alone of my race" (p. 234). At the same time, he has also, involuntarily, an imperative will to live. He survives the boating accident which kills Adrian and Clara because "instinctive love of life animated me, and feelings of contention, as if a hostile will combated with mind (p. 323). Almost in spite of himself, Lionel is a survivor. Because of this strong will—"I, lord of myself"—he clings to life, half resentful at his instinct for self-preservation. (p. 323).

The achievements of the human will are ephemeral, but the will of individual man is tenacious. Lionel Verney turns this fundamental fact into its own justification. Like Tennyson's Ulysses, he voyages ceaselessly, having no goal beyond that of staving off despair and panic: "How dreadful it is, to emerge from the oblivion of slumber, and to receive as a good morrow the mute wailing of one's own hapless heart . . ." (p. 325); ". . . I would not

believe that all was as it seemed—The world was not dead, but I was mad
..." (p. 327). As for the Victorian Ulysses, Verney's traveling is an end in
itself:

> ... to endless time, decrepid and grey headed—youth already in the grave
> with those I love—the lone wanderer will still unfurl his sail, and clasp the
> tiller—and, still obeying the breezes of heaven, for ever round and another
> promontory, anchoring in another and another bay, ploughing seedless ocean,
> leaving behind the verdant land of native Europe, adown the tawny shore of
> Africa, having weathered the fierce seas of the Cape, I may moor my worn skiff
> in a creek, shaded by spicy groves of the odorous islands of the far Indian
> ocean. (pp. 341–342)

The Romantic or Promethean hero has suffered a sea change into a Victorian. Work for its own sake, existence for its own sake, submission to the
incomprehensible ways of a "dead," godless universe: all characterize Lionel
Verney at the novel's end:

> I form no expectation of alteration for the better; but the monotonous present
> is intolerable to me. Neither hope nor joy are my pilots—restless despair and
> fierce desire of change lead me on. I long to grapple with danger, to be excited
> by fear, to have some task, however slight or voluntary, for each days fulfil-
> ment. I shall witness all the variety of appearance, that the elements can
> assume—I shall read fair augury in the rainbow—menace in the cloud—some
> lesson or record dear to my heart in everything. (p. 342)

This endless motion for its own sake anticipates the last line of "Ulysses,"
with its goalless activity: "To strive, to seek, to find, and not to yield." Verbs
without direct objects, actions that can have no satisfactory punctual end: the
will to create a personality, a civilization, a universe, is subdued and reduced
to sheer willing-ness.

This purposelessness is brought about not by exile or conscious, deliberate estrangement from society, but by solipsism. The novel closes with an
image of intense isolation, with Lionel Verney's "tiny bark" dwarfed by an
alien universe, neither malign nor benignant, only watchful:

> Thus round the shores of deserted earth, while the sun is high, and the moon
> waxes or wanes, angels, the spirits of the dead, and the ever-open eye of the
> Supreme will behold the tiny bark, freighted with Verney—the LAST MAN.
> (p. 342)

His initial social exile has been superseded by an existential isolation. Mary
Shelley portrays Verney as the last survivor of a species, surrounded by alien
beings and *watched*—not guided, protected, nurtured—by the Creator of this
mystifying universe.

When the survivor of devastation undergoes transformation—encounters death and climbs back up from the cavern depths into the sunlight—there is no society left for him to rejoin. Nevertheless, Verney records his story for posterity. He counsels quiescence, resignation, submission to the incomprehensible ways of fate. Lionel Verney's *life* is, in essence, the lesson: it exemplifies the futility of exertion, the need for resignation. There is another message in Verney's story, too, besides the purposelessness of present action. Nostalgia for past glory—for the dead heroes and the lost treasures of civilization—is as strong as submissiveness. Verney presumes that his hypothetical readers will "seek to learn how beings so wondrous in their achievements, with imaginations infinite, and powers godlike, had departed from their home to an unknown country" (p. 339). Verney dedicates his history "To the illustrious DEAD," bidding them, "Shadows, Arise and Read Your Fall!" (p. 339). In *The Last Man,* there is a Fall which precipitates man's exile from Paradise:

> Alas! to enumerate the adornments of humanity, shews, by what we have lost, how supremely great man was. It is all over now. He is solitary; like our first parents expelled from Paradise, he looks back towards the scene he has quitted. The high walls of the tomb, and the flaming sword of the plague, lie between it and him. Like to our first parents, the whole earth is before him, a wide desart. (p. 234)

Yet this fall is not sexual or social in nature. Not one human being's crime toward another, but the incontrovertible, morally neutral fact of death, brings the end of innocence—and with it, the end of hope, desire, will.

The destruction of civilization through the plague is an emblem for Mary Shelley's fear and outrage at political anarchy. The death of the heroic individual, the consequences of levelling revolutions in the social order, is similarly regretted. For Mary Shelley, however, the ineluctability of death is more terrifying than any political or social destruction. Her subject is as much the death of the human personality as it is the end of heroic individuality and civilized life. Hers is not the conservatism of T. S. Eliot, who held that "only those who have personality . . . know what it means to want to escape from" it. Escape into culture or other comforting fictions of and about the human mind eventually becomes impossible for Mary Shelley. Her imagination *cannot get beyond* the fact of death.

Yet it is not fear of her own death that makes Mary Shelley retreat to a conservative posture and console herself with society, in real life and in her novels.[6] Rather, death brings a terrible isolation, whose image is Verney's engulfment by the indifferent universe at the end of *The Last Man.* Shelley's death deprived Mary of her strongest social tie and, consequently, of a reflection of her own existence. There is no one, no event, no object to which Lionel Verney can feel himself bound, for good or ill. Unlike

Frankenstein's monster and Mathilda, Lionel Verney cannot even complain to his Creator. Death is not crime, not an injustice; rather it is the quintessential fact of life.

Lionel Verney's response to this discovery is to retreat. He is not a coward withdrawing from a contest—in fact, he has lost his combatants; his ambition and will have no outlet. (In much the same way, Mary Shelley's pursuit of self-definition could not continue in a vacuum, in utter isolation.) Nevertheless, Lionel detaches himself from his own experience. This is clear in his attitude toward his role as narrator, which illuminates Mary Shelley's evolving conception of her own creative function.

The self-reflexive action of writing nullifies the pain of consciousness. As Lionel discovers while eulogizing his dead wife, mere articulation brings relief: "With ardent and overflowing eloquence, I relieved my heart from its burthen, and awoke to the sense of a new pleasure in life, as I poured forth the funeral eulogy" (p. 262). The act of writing the history, similarly, is anaesthetizing: "I had used this history as an opiate; while it described my beloved friends, fresh with life and glowing with hope; active assistants on the scene, I was soothed; there will be a more melancholy pleasure in painting the end of all" (p. 193). Like Lionel Verney, the author of *The Last Man* professes to find solace in the act of writing:

> Will my readers ask how I could find solace from the narration of misery and woeful change? This is one of the mysteries of our nature, which holds full sway over me, and from whose influence I cannot escape. I confess, that I have not been unmoved by the development of the tale; and that I have been depressed, nay, agonized, at some parts of the recital, which I have faithfully transcribed from my materials. Yet such is human nature, that the excitement of mind was dear to me, and that the imagination, painter of tempest and earthquake, or, worse, the stormy and ruin-fraught passions of man, softened my real sorrows and endless regrets, by clothing these fictitious ones in that ideality, which takes the mortal sting from pain. (p. 4)

Writing brings a distancing from pain rather than an engagement with it—even, paradoxically, when one is writing about the causes of that pain. Consolation comes from idealizing the past rather than contending with it. Lionel's role, as he defines it, is to organize reality into bearable form:

> All events, at the same time that they deeply interested me, arranged themselves in pictures before me. I gave the right place to every personage in the groupe [*sic*], the just balance to every sentiment. This undercurrent of thought, often soothed me amidst distress, and even agony. It gave ideality to that, from which, taken in naked truth, the soul would have revolted: it bestowed pictorial colours on misery and disease, and not unfrequently relieved me from despair in deplorable changes. (p. 126)

Later in his narrative he recurs to the idea that the act of giving form diminishes rather than augments reality:

> Time and experience have placed me on an height from which I can comprehend the past as a whole; and in this way I must describe it, bringing forward the leading incidents, and disposing light and shade so as to form a picture in whose very darkness there will be harmony. (pp. 192–193)

. . . Besides the consolation of the writer, narration has a second purpose in *The Last Man,* one that is equally centrifugal in its direction. The narrator's organizing function has been re-defined from Mary Shelley's earlier novels. The narrator of *Frankenstein* was an active artificer ("seizing on the capabilities of a subject and . . . moulding and fashioning ideas suggested to it") who sought to move his audience by manipulating the form of his materials. Narration in *The Last Man* has as its second goal the reduction of experience to static "pictures." Action is Victorianized aesthetically. Mary Shelley anticipates Matthew Arnold's dictum of *showing* right action rather than the workings of an individual mind. . . . This impulse to show pictures rather than to tell stories prompts Mary Shelley's movement away from first-person, toward third-person, narration.

The solitary exiles who narrate Mary Shelley's earliest novels speak directly to their auditors and readers, more actively soliciting a response than subsequent characters whose stories are related in third-person narration or direct discourse. Paradoxically, despite their alienation, the first-person narrators reach out to their audience—like the Ancient Mariner, who is compelled to make an impact on his auditor. Unlike the correspondents in *Frankenstein* and *Mathilda,* who write to particular readers, Lionel Verney writes to an unknowable audience, an unembodied "posterity." . . . He doesn't aim at effecting psychologically radical change. Instead, for Verney, writing—like voyaging, striving, living—is an activity pursued for its own sake. . . .

Mary Shelley's interest passes from psychic doubling—the projection of emotionally conflicting aspects of her self—to relationships between protagonists. The constitution of the social group, the establishment of a happy family to compensate for a myriad of childhood deprivations, replaces the configuration of the single self as the primary object of Mary Shelley's fiction.

The conquest of the Promethean hero by death, marriage, or symbolic emasculation parallels the retrenchment from first-person narration. Static pictures of experience take the place of narrative complexity. From telling to showing; from self-realization to self-absorption; from imaginative isolation to assimilation: *The Last Man* enacts these transitions. . . .

In the end, Mary Shelley's defection from the liberalism of the Godwin circle represents her own version of "independence of mind." By allying herself with the orthodox social community rather than with the enclave of intellectual exiles (as Virginia Woolf would do in Bloomsbury), Mary Shelley chooses rather than accepts a superior authority. Deference is given, not owed; her role is selected, not inherited. The act of renouncing her intellectual and political inheritance brings with it a kind of self-acceptance. Yet there is a sad falling off, one felt and tacitly acknowledged by Mary Shelley herself, in this. Mary Shelley's political "independence" or apostasy really follows from her failure to achieve emotional independence. Imposed isolation removes the desire for self-sufficiency. The contentious, emotionally rebellious exile comes to identify herself as a follower, a party member, a dependent. . . . Her protest against and interrogation of authority in the early novels lose their force when Mary Shelley loses her audience. In the end, apology conceals reproach, assimilation conceals the desire to "be something." These tactics make it possible for Mary Shelley to survive, but only at the expense of the self she once sought to fashion.

Notes

1. Mary Shelley, *The Fields of Fancy*, in *Mathilda*, ed. Elizabeth Nitchie (Chapel Hill: The University of North Carolina Press, 1959), pp. 93, 98. Hereafter cited parenthetically in the text.

2. Hugh J. Luke, Jr., "Introduction," *The Last Man*, ed. Hugh J. Luke, Jr. (Lincoln: University of Nebraska Press, 1965), p. xviii. Subsequent references will be cited parenthetically.

3. *The Letters of Mary W. Shelley*, ed. Frederick L. Jones (Norman: University of Oklahoma Press, 1954), II, 28 March 1848, 313–314.

4. In "*The Last Man:* Anatomy of Failed Revolutions," *Nineteenth-Century Fiction* (1978), Lee Sterrenburg analyzes Mary Shelley's use of nature metaphors to render a "pessimistic and apocalyptic" view of a world where political reform and revolution are futile (p. 328). Sterrenburg says that *The Last Man* is "an antipolitical novel" (p. 328).

5. *Letters,* I, 29 Dec. 1820, 122.

6. In her journal on 21 Oct. 1838 Mary writes: "I like society; I believe all persons who have any talent (who are in good health) do. The soil that gives forth nothing, may lie ever fallow; but that which produces . . . needs cultivation, change of harvest, refreshing dews, and ripening sun. Books do much; but the living intercourse is the vital heat. Debarred from that, how have I pined and died!" (*Journal*, p. 205). In a letter to Maria Gisborne on 17 July 1832 Mary complained: ". . . I live in a silence and loneliness—not possible any where except in England where people are so *islanded* individually in habits—I often languish for sympathy— and pine for social festivity" (*Letters*, II, 82). A negative view of her desire for society is taken by the editor of her *Letters* and *Journal*, Frederick L. Jones, in his "Appendix II" to Volume II of the *Letters:* "Mary had an insatiable desire to associate herself with people of talent and genius" (pp. 350–351); "Throughout Mary's whole life, her constant cry was for friendship. There is even something morbid in her desire for affection—a certain lack of self-confidence, of self-sufficiency" (p. 351).

MARY SHELLEY,
A "PRODIGIOUS GENERATOR"

◆

Monsters of Empire: Conrad and Lawrence

Chris Baldick

Wells may have brought the Frankenstein myth's fictional exploitation to one kind of dead end in *The Invisible Man,* but in *The Island of Doctor Moreau* he had opened it out in another direction already foreshadowed by the colonial setting of Butler's *Erewhon.* Moreau's island settlement, like Prospero's before it, is a colony, and his efforts to "raise" his Beast Folk to his own condition reflect in macabre form the cruelties and dangers of late-Victorian imperialism and its "civilizing mission." In English fiction the most powerfully imaginative extension of the Frankenstein myth to this imperialist period and to the forces at work in it, which would spill out of control in the wars and revolutions of 1914–18, are to be found in the work of Joseph Conrad and D. H. Lawrence.

Conrad had read *The Time Machine* and *The Island of Doctor Moreau* in the mid-1890s, and it seems quite possible that he lifted the narrative frame of his *Heart of Darkness* from Well's use of a group of anonymous professionals sitting in darkness listening to the Time Traveller. Conrad was repeatedly concerned, too, with the theme of transgression, especially in the form of "that immoral detachment from mankind . . . fostered by the unhealthy conditions of solitude" which the Editor in "The Planter of Malata" condemns.[1] But the solitaries and transgressors in his fiction are not scientists or inventors; these latter meddlers he held responsible for unforgivable destruction to the ships and men of his own beloved profession, and he dismissed them with harsh sarcasm. On the inventors of modern armaments he wrote, in his memoir *The Mirror of the Sea,*

> The learned vigils and labours of a certain class of inventors should have been rewarded with honourable liberality as justice demanded; and the bodies of the inventors should have been blown to pieces by means of their own perfected explosives and improved weapons with extreme publicity as the commonest prudence dictated. By this method the ardour of research in that direction would have been restrained without infringing the sacred privileges of science.[2]

Conrad's most memorable transgressors go to their remote hideouts not to invent or experiment like Moreau, but to exploit raw materials and cheap labour. They seek gold, silver, or ivory, not in the alchemist's crucible but by means of colonial pillage.

The remaining link in Conrad's fiction between the quest for heroic discoveries and the sordid scramble for raw materials is that they are both conducted by deluded men who imagine themselves to be benefactors of the human race. Charles Gould in *Nostromo* disobeys his father's instruction not to reopen the "cursed" San Tomé silver-mine (which has afflicted him with dreams of vampires), in the belief that the weight of "material interests" will stabilize the chaotic state of Costaguana. At first, this civilizing ideal appears to have been realized, but by the end of the novel we are obliged to conclude with Dr. Monygham that "There is no peace and no rest in the development of material interests. They have their law, and their justice. But it is founded on expediency, and is inhuman."[3] The inhuman logic of the silver-mine and the railway (and by extension, that of capitalist development in general) will come, Monygham predicts, to oppress the people of Costaguana as heavily as the barbaric misrule from which Gould has intended his enterprise to liberate them. An imperialist Adam, Gould has literally undermined the "paradise of snakes" at Sulaco, setting in motion an inhuman logic beyond his control, which in true Frankensteinian fashion separates him and his obsession from his wife.

> Mrs. Gould continued along the corridor away from her husband's room. The fate of the San Tomé mine was lying heavy upon her heart. It was a long time now since she had begun to fear it. It had been an idea. She had watched it with misgivings running into a fetish, and now the fetish had grown into a monstrous and crushing weight. It was as if the inspiration of their early years had left her heart to turn into a work of silver-bricks, erected by silent work of evil spirits, between her and her husband. He seemed to dwell alone within a circumvallation of precious metal, leaving her outside . . .[4]

The corrupting lure of the silver-mine here is in part a more restrained version of Hoffmann's "The Mines at Falun," a fable of industrial transgression presented as a Fall from the Paradise of snakes into unwitting idolatry, which leaves Gould and Nostromo morally compromised and Martin Decoud, like Judas, fatally weighed down by his pieces of silver. The pacific ideal of material progress has engendered an industrial monster which crushes it under the full weight of commodity fetishism.

Similar ideals are overtaken by their own creatures in *Heart of Darkness,* a novella which bears a number of uncanny resemblances to the design of *Frankenstein.* The equatorial equivalent of Walton's voyage, Marlow's expedition to the Congo is likewise a young man's quest for the limits of the known world, which becomes, in his encounter with the central transgressor-figure, a revelation of moral chaos and uncertainty. Like *Frankenstein,* and like *Moby Dick* too,[5] *Heart of Darkness* takes the path of masculine adventure and exploration to its self-destructive terminus, self-consciously excluding the world of women ("We must help them to stay in that beautiful world of their own," Marlow insists[6]), to whom the true story cannot even be told. In the narrative structure of *Heart of Darkness* we have another case of that concentric design favoured by high Romantic fiction: Kurtz's vision of horror is distanced by a third-hand account, as if it were too scorching to be met directly, while at the same time some of its implications can be brought home through the conduit of Marlow to disturb his civilized auditors in London, thus bringing the Heart of Empire into correspondence, complicity, even equivalence, with the Heart of Darkness.

Kurtz is unmistakably the typical Transgressor. The wilderness has "beguiled his unlawful soul beyond the bounds of permitted aspirations (*HD,* 107), but the apparent point of divergence from the Frankenstein tradition is that neither Marlow nor Kurtz creates anything: Kurtz is nearer to Captain Ahab, in that he is both an ungodly-godlike transgressor and a factitious and miscreated agent of civilized trade who runs destructively out of his masters' control. Like Ahab, he does his job too well, too single-mindedly and obsessively for the comfort of his Starbucks and Pelegs; his ghastly surplus of ivory exposing too openly the barbaric nature of the pillage they have undertaken. The excess of his productivity in looting ivory is the mocking counterpart to that excess of idealism over mere trade which Kurtz has brought to Africa, and which distinguishes Gould and Ahab too. Kurtz at first tells the other managers that "Each station should be like a beacon on the road towards better things, a centre for trade of course, but also for humanizing, improving, instructing" (*HD,* 65). But it is just this surplus of civilizing zeal which is the real danger in Kurtz, since it already gives him a role he imagines to be that of a god; that he should come to be worshipped idolatrously is the fulfilment of his missionary presumption. For all his high ideals, he is reduced to the position of a "pitiful Jupiter" (*HD,* 100), a mere "voice," a hollow mouthpiece for the existing fetishism of ivory.

Kurtz is a factitious "god," made up of bits of European civilization, like the harlequin suit of his Russian follower, or like the multicoloured map over which Marlow pores. "His mother was half-English, his father was half-French. All Europe contributed to the making of Kurtz" (*HD,* 86). And Kurtz eventually returns to confront his creators in Marlow's narrative. Marlow's function—like Walton's—is to hear the dying words of the transgressor and report them back to the heart of civilization, his own early zeal for exploration now chastened (as a boy, Marlow has a passion for exploring the map's blank spaces at the North Pole and the Equator). Moreover, he is able to bring home from the Congo, like some contaminated cargo, an unsettling acknowledgement of kinship with the monstrous. The connection stretches from the untamed nature of the jungle—"monstrous and free," as Marlow describes it—through the natives ("what thrilled you," he explains, "was just the thought of their humanity—like yours—the thought of your remote kinship with this wild and passionate uproar" (*HD*, 69), via Kurtz and Marlow in a chain of such recognitions which ends with the Accountant, the Lawyer, the Director of Companies, and finally the reader. As Frankenstein's monster demands acknowledgement of kinship from his creator, who is in turn recognised as a brother by Walton in his letters home to his sister, so the impossibility of disavowing the monstrous consequences of imperialism is brought home to the metropolis itself, to London, "the monstrous town" (*HD*, 29).

It is in this London that Alvan Hervey, the protagonist of Conrad's tale "The Return," has a vision of monstrosity beginning with the shock of his wife's desertion and spreading to embrace the whole of that civilized urban life of which he is the polished representative.

> The contamination of her crime spread out, tainted the universe, tainted himself; woke up all the dormant infamies of the world; caused a ghastly kind of clairvoyance in which he could see the towns and fields of the earth, its sacred places, its temples and its houses, peopled by monsters—by monsters of duplicity, lust, and murder. She was a monster—he himself was thinking monstrous thoughts . . . and yet he was like other people.[7]

Monstrosity is again brought home from the "criminal" fringe, and revealed in the ordinary, the quotidian, and the domestic. Conrad himself shows just such a "ghastly kind of clairvoyance" in his fiction, stripping away his characters' illusions with his acid skepticism, to expose them as disconnected jumbles of monstrous impulses.

Like Dickens, Conrad peoples his novels with characters who have hardened into corpse-like automata. He sets *The Secret Agent* in a darker and more artificial version of Dickens's London, "a monstrous town more populous than some continents and in its man-made might as if indifferent to heaven's frowns and smiles."[8] This London is itself a man-made monster set apart from any natural morality. Its own mad scientist, the Professor, directs his "frenzied puritanism of ambition" (*SA*, 102) towards the perfecting of an explosive charge which will reduce himself and all those around him to fragments. In the same novel Mr. Verloc—another agent who has gone blunderingly and destructively beyond his masters' intentions—is presented as an absurd monstrosity: "Mr. Verloc [moved] woodenly, stony-eyed, and like an automaton whose face has been painted red. And this resemblance to a mechanical figure went so far that he had an automaton's absurd air of being aware of the machinery inside of him" (*SA*, 186). Verloc belongs to a large family of such Dickensian effigies in Conrad's works: Kayerts and Carlier in "An Outpost of Progress" are puppets of Society's routines, who "could only live on condition of being machines,"[9] while in *Victory* Wang has an "unreal cardboard face" which we see "grimacing artificially," and Morrison too moves "like an automaton."[10] In the same novel Mrs. Schonberg is described repeatedly as a mechanism, automaton, or dummy capable only of nodding its head, and Heyst sees the people around him as "figures cut out of cork" (*V,* 150). His antagonist, Jones, is constantly referred to as a spectre (accompanying the "tame monster" Pedro), his appearance being "gruesomely malevolent, as of a wicked and pitiless corpse" (*V,* 306). The first mate Burns in *The Shadow-Line* looks like a scarecrow or an "animated skeleton," while in *The Nigger of the "Narcissus"* James Wait "looked as ridiculously lamentable as a doll that had lost half its sawdust."[11]

Several other Conrad characters have this appearance of being dolls—Babalatchi in *An Outcast of the Islands,* Laspara's daughters in *Under Western Eyes,* and Heemskirk's warrant officer in "Freya of the Seven Isles," who appears, like Wait, to have been stuffed. It is the idea of losing one's stuffing that gives a clue to the function of these Conradian marionettes. Conrad's use of monstrosity follows a traditional moral convention, as we shall see below, and in the case of his dolls and automata, the lack of an organic interior figuratively presents a moral evacuation: lacking any coherent moral purpose or ideal around which their actions can be organized, these people are hollowed out into a crustacean stupidity, their lives reduced to a repertoire of meaningless gestures. The horror of which Kurtz speaks is already hinted at and given disturbing concreteness by Marlow when he describes the company agent at Central Station as a "papier-mâché Mephistopheles." As Marlow tells us, "it seemed to me that if I tried I could poke my forefinger through him, and would find nothing inside but a little loose dirt, maybe" (*HD,* 56). This character is a mere social machine, like his counterparts Kayerts and Carlier—all of them as brittle as the ivory they worship, all hollow men.

It is the hollow women, though, who are more alarming still in Conrad's eyes. In the short story "Because of the Dollars," the wild laughter of the former prostitute Anne startles Captain Davidson "like a galvanic shock to a corpse"; while the irresistible flesh of Hermann's niece in "Falk" provokes the narrator to describe her with a nervous jocularity as if she were a ship: "All I know is that she was built on a magnificent scale. Built is the only word. She was constructed, she was erected, as it were, with regal lavishness."[12] A more macabre (and again nameless) female construction, bearing some resemblance to Mrs. Skewton in *Dombey and Son,* is Madame de S——— in *Under Western Eyes.* Conrad's intense discomfort with women and with democratic politics expresses itself here (under the guise of Rasumov's revulsion) in repeated violent dismemberments of this character.

> At that moment he hated Madame de S———. But it was not exactly hate. It was more like the abhorrence that may be caused by a wooden or plaster figure of a repulsive kind. She moved no more than if she were such a figure; even her

eyes, whose unwinking stare plunged into his own, though shining, were life-less, as though they were as artificial as her teeth.[13]

In Razumov's vividly disordered perception, this salon anarchist confronts him as a "grinning skull," a "painted mummy," and worse still, "like a galvanized corpse out of some Hoffmann's Tale" (WE, 182). As she speaks of extirpating the Czar and his family, she is again presented as a hardened type of inauthenticity: "Her rigidity was frightful, like the rigour of a corpse galvanized into harsh speech and glittering stare by the force of murderous hate" (WE, 187). The force of hatred here is more likely to be Razumov's, the rigidity that of Conrad's resistance to democratic "fanaticism," above all in women. When other writers want to scare themselves and their readers, they introduce a ghost; Conrad brings in a woman, for him the most fearful figure of ghastly artificiality.

Conrad's monstrosities are, clearly enough, traditionally allegorical representatives of inner moral faults, projected in the form of physical deformity and horror. The clearest such case, and one which carries some echoes of Mary Shelley's description of her monster in *Frankenstein*, is the account of Cesar, a treacherous villain involved in one of Conrad's first smuggling voyages as recalled in his *Mirror of the Sea:*

> His parchment skin, showing dead white on his cranium, seemed to be glued directly and tightly upon his big bones. Without being in any way deformed, he was the nearest approach which I have ever seen or could imagine to what is commonly understood by the word "monster." That the source of the effect produced was really moral I have no doubt. An utterly, hopelessly depraved nature was expressed in physical terms, that each taken separately had nothing positively startling. You imagined him clammily cold to the touch, like a snake. (MS, 165–6)

This clammy and rather artificial-looking person advertises in his bodily appearance the fact that he is morally a monster of disloyalty who betrays his fellow-sailors. This is a straightforward and recognizable use of the idea of monstrosity; but what is more curious in Conrad is that, while he readily attributes monstrosity to depraved human hearts and to nature itself (as in *Heart of Darkness*), he will not extend it to human artefacts in the way that Carlyle, Dickens, and so many other writers did in the nineteenth century. On the contrary, while Conrad makes some familiar observations on the subordination of people to their products, his reflections on this problem are quite at odds with that tradition. He writes in *Mirror of the Sea* that "we men are, in fact, servants of our creations. We remain in everlasting bondage to the productions of our brain and to the work of our hands" (MS, 25). To Carlyle or Emerson this state of affairs was cause for lamentation and protest, but for Conrad it is a basis—perhaps the only basis—for hope: his pessimism about human behaviour, almost pretentiously cosmic in its scope, attributes a limitless depravity to all human action and a boundless capacity for self-deception to all human thought, but it exempts our artefacts from blame. It is we who are the monsters; our innocent creatures are our betters, particularly if they be ships, and certainly if they be sailing ships. As Conrad explains, "a ship is a creature which we have brought into the world, as it were on purpose to keep us up to the mark" (MS, 28). Men have betrayed their ships, but no ship can betray a man—it can only offer him the chance of redemption, calling on his capacities for loyalty and duty to test themselves in its service. If we do not serve the productions of our hands and brains, Conrad suggests, then we would only revert to serving our vain and egotistical selves; only our works can call us out of our inner moral chaos towards some higher purpose.[14] There are common features in Conrad's attitudes to seamanship and to art which endorse this ideology of service, just as there is an equivalence between the workmanlike truthfulness of Marlow's navigation and that of his narration—both of them leading him out of the temptation represented by Kurtz.

The irony of all this is that the writer who so powerfully presented and condemned imperialism's commodity fetishism in the ivory-looting of Heart of Darkness should have done so from within an ideological position which is itself deeply fetishistic in conception. With Conrad's ideology of service, as with the Carlylean gospel of Work which prefigures it, there are serious problems. A code of duty to the task at hand and of unswerving loyalty to the collective yet hierarchical effort against the sea's perils is, by its unquestioning and immediately demanding nature, a palliative to certain kinds of cosmic skepticism; yet it only raises, beyond its immediate imperatives, the uncomfortable question, what further end does such maritime service itself serve? The depressing answer, and one which drags down (often literally) the basis of the sailor's enviable ethical certainties, is that the beloved creatures of which Conrad writes too often serve the contaminating greed and violence of the landlubber: murderous warfare, unscrupulous trade, and imperialist plunder. As surely as the old sailing craft of the Indian ocean succumbed to steam and the Suez Canal, so the clear moral directives of seamanship are sullied by piracy in its various forms, the pure ideals of maritime service being mocked by the unclean idols which call upon its devotion: ivory, silver, potatoes, rotten hippopotamus-meat, the dangerously smouldering coal in Youth, the dollar-crazed Chinamen in Typhoon. By serving that floating creature which Conrad casts as his better angel, the sailor becomes at the same time the servant of those fetishized "material interests" which drag him back towards the bestial, and towards the monstrosity of imperialism's organized greed. Describing the imperialism of "our modern Conquistadores" to his friend R. B. Cunninghame Graham, Conrad wrote that "Their achievement is monstrous enough in all conscience—but not as a great human force let loose, but rather like that of a gigantic and obscene beast."[15] From this enormous monster the ideology of service was hardly likely to offer any escape.

The equivalent devotion and selflessness of the artist was unstable too: Conrad was slow to come to writing, but then quick to discover that alarming sense of the printed word's alien and independent life which had disturbed Mary Shelley. The first time he saw his words in print—on receiving the proofs of *Almayer's Folly*—he was "horrified by the thing in print," and disconcerted by a "fear of the ghosts which one evokes oneself and which often refuse to obey the brain that has created them."[16] Conrad felt the Frankensteinian problem as an artist confronted by his own products, and he gave us, in *Nostromo* and *Heart of Darkness,* powerful images of Frankensteinian transgression; but he was too complicit with prevailing forms of fetishism to have recognized, behind his conveniently isolated maritime model of "service," the greater problem of who was serving what. In this sense, his attention to the unleashing of monstrous forces in the modern world is damagingly distracted, compromised in ways which make it far inferior to that of D. H. Lawrence.

Poles—not the Joseph Conrad sort, of course, but the magnetic, geographical, and conceptual—were as important to the thinking of D. H. Lawrence as they were to the dreams and ambitions of Mary Shelley's Walton. In Lawrence's formative years as a writer, Polar exploration again captured the world's attention as the old hopes of reaching the North and South Poles were at last realized by Peary in 1909 and Amundsen in 1911. Of this achievement Lawrence observed that "the supreme little ego in man hates an unconquered universe. We shall never rest till we have heaped tin cans on the North Pole and South Pole, and put up barb-wire fences on the moon. Barb-wire fences are our sign of conquest. We have wreathed the world with them."[17] Writing in 1915, Lawrence could see in retrospect the connection between the barbed-wire wreaths of the Great War and the preceding scramble for territorial conquest symbolized by these Polar expeditions. In 1912, when Lawrence himself was exploring the North/South contrasts of European culture on his route from Germany to Italy, the British Empire suffered two humiliating and instantly legendary disasters, both of them inflicted by ice and cold: the death of Captain Scott's Antarctic team, and the sinking by an iceberg of the "unsinkable" liner *Titanic* with the loss of more than 1,500 lives. In the enormous public impact of these events one can detect, so to speak, a new "ice age" of the imagination threatening the expansive certainties of the great industrial empire. To the superstitious (among them Thomas Hardy in his poem "The Convergence of the Twain"), the *Titanic* disaster revived the familiar conservative warnings about tempting fate or titanically transgressing the limits to human control over the elements. The exertion of the human will (specifically, of the British will) had been humbled in exemplary symbolic spectacle.

Out of this symbolic ice age of British imperial decline emerges Lawrence's most ambitiously representative fictional character, Gerald Crich in *Women in Love*. Gerald embodies the world-conquering will of the British industrial bourgeoisie, depicted in its agony of disorientation and self-destruction, drifting to an appropriately icy death. Our first ominous sight of Gerald Crich, through the eyes of Gudrun Brangwen in the opening chapter of the novel, fixes him inescapably in his polar identity: "There was something northern about him which magnetized her. In his clear northern flesh and his fair hair was a glisten like cold sunshine through crystals of ice. And he looked so new, unbroached, pure as an arctic thing."[18] Gerald is, as we shall see, a creature of northern mechanical will-power, and his trajectory in the novel is an almost exact reversal of the career of Frankenstein's monster: the latter is unleashed in the Alps and finally wanders off to the North Pole to kill himself, while Gerald makes his first appearance as an "arctic thing" and dies after walking off into the snows of the Alps. It is quite possible that this design was not directly or consciously adapted by Lawrence from Mary Shelley, but it is clear that Lawrence is employing a Romantic vocabulary of geographical symbols derived from the Shelley-Byron circle's Alpine obsessions, and that his equation of Alpine and Arctic zones parallels Mary Shelley's in reinforcing the symbolic impact of ice: for both novelists, these zones represent the dangers of unfeeling isolation which are courted by the mentality of challenge, aspiration, and the conquering will. To be born from one and to die in the other is to bind (even to define) the intervening north-European world in an embrace of death, wherein ashes return to ashes, ice to ice.

Gerald's "arctic" nature and Alpine fate function partly to enhance his representative status as Northern Man, although Gudrun's very sudden recognition of this is well in advance of the reader's in the opening chapter. Only later does Lawrence's symbolic design emerge; while the world of *The Rainbow* is built with geometric and architectural figures (arches, columns, circles, portals), that of *Women in Love* is charged with electrical and magnetic imagery. Gudrun, as we have seen, is magnetized by Gerald, while Birkin's notorious loins of darkness are "electric" in their power, and Lawrence even goes to the trouble of making Gudrun's previous lover an electrician. At a deeper level, Lawrence is working with an idea of magnetic attraction and repulsion, of basic polarity, which works through to his characters from the very sources of life itself. The cosmology which he had evolved in *The Study of Thomas Hardy* and *The Crown* in 1914 and 1915 had been built upon polarities of female and male, dark and light, power and love, flesh and spirit, which in their necessary opposition correspond broadly with the polarity of North and South in *Women in Love*.

There is some possible confusion in that now, the polar opposite of the Arctic is the Equatorial or African, not the Antarctic (Lawrence's horizons had not yet stretched as far as the antipodean *Kangaroo*); but the exposition of this polarity in Chapter XIX still clarifies considerably the initial mystery of

Gerald's arctic attributes. As Birkin meditates on the African statuette he has seen at Halliday's flat, he sees the impending collapse of civilization as a fission in which the vital polar opposition of northern (male/rational/light) and southern (female/instinctual/dark) principles falls apart into separate processes of decomposition, one of which has already run its course in Africa:

> There remained this way, this awful African process, to be fulfilled. It would be done differently by the white races. The white races, having the arctic north behind them, the vast abstraction of ice and snow, would fulfil a mystery of ice-destructive knowledge, snow-abstract annihilation. Whereas the West Africans, controlled by the burning death-abstraction of the Sahara, had been fulfilled in sun-destruction, the putrescent mystery of sun-rays. . . .
>
> Birkin thought of Gerald. He was one of these strange white wonderful demons from the north, fulfilled in the destructive frost-mystery. And was he fated to pass away in this knowledge, this one process of frost-knowledge, death by perfect cold? Was he a messenger, an omen of the universal dissolution into whiteness and snow? (WL, 331)

The polar extremes, Arctic and African, figure forth the destinations allotted to the disseevered halves of European civilization as they burst apart in the self-destruction of the Great War. Gerald as the harbinger of the northern process of dissolution is made to return to his chosen element, in that Alpine territory which Gudrun recognizes as "the centre, the knot, the navel of the world" (WL, 492), as if to deliver at this central junction of Latin and Germanic cultures his prophecy of Europe's conquest by ice.

As a messenger of northern abstraction and destructive knowledge, Gerald represents a process which is no longer a term in a vital polarity, but a sheer negation of life. As William Blake had insisted, there is a difference between contraries which are necessary to life, and negations which are flatly opposed to it; the qualities embodied in Gerald "the denier" are terms of this latter kind of opposition, best formulated in Lawrence's description of his industrial modernization as "the substitution of the mechanical principle for the organic" (WL, 305). This pair of opposites stands, of course, as the central terms of the Romantic critique of modern society since Schiller, Coleridge, and Carlyle, and they are drawn into even more violent and repeated confrontations throughout Lawrence's work. Gerald is the champion and avatar of the mechanical principle in its insistent subordination of the organic, not just in his industrial aims, but in his very person. Like Kurtz, and like Captain Ahab (another "northern monomaniac"[19]), he resembles both Victor Frankenstein in the enormity of his transgression and the monster in his artificially assembled nature. He confesses that his life has no centre but is "artificially held together by the social mechanism"; he feels emptily inert "like a machine that is without power"; and the repetitive rhythms of "his clenched, mechanical body" finally repel Gudrun, who likens them to the clockwork regimentation of modern society: "He, his body, his motion, his life—it was the same ticking, the same twitching across the dial, a horrible mechanical twitching forward over the face of the hours" (*WL*, 109, 344, 554, 564). Gudrun recognizes here the same mechanical motion which she had felt, upon her return to Beldover, in the "half-automated colliers" whose voices had sounded to her like strange machines (*WL*, 174). She is reminded of its power when listening to Loerke (himself a kind of Morlock or "obscene monster of the darkness" born from "the underworld of life" [*WL*, 522]) as he explains the fairground design on his frieze as an interpretation of modern industry. "What is man doing," asks Loerke, "when he is at a fair like this? He is fulfilling the counterpart of labour—the machine works him instead of he the machine" (*WL*, 519). This inversion certainly applies to Gerald, who is the God of the Machine, and at the same time its creature and victim.

Gerald's automatism is echoed in the repeated mechanical images applied to people in Lawrence's other early works. Lawrence's own first direct experience of modern industry was, unusually for the son of a mining village, not down t'pit but in a factory which made—of all things—artificial limbs. In *Sons and Lovers* he makes Paul Morel undergo the same initiation into monstrosity: "It seemed monstrous," to Paul, "that a business could be run on wooden legs."[20] While the colliery, as Lawrence believed, still allowed some physical integrity to the miners, this kind of "light" industry seemed more directly and visibly to subordinate human life to the mechanical principle. As Paul watches Clara Dawes working at her spinning jenny, "her arm move[s] mechanically, that should never have been subdued to a machine" (*SL*, 321). The same principle extends beyond the industrial to the military mechanism, when Mrs. Morel defines a soldier as "nothing but a body that makes movements when it hears a shout" (*SL*, 234), and to the education system in *The Rainbow*, where Ursula sees the other teachers at Brinsley Street School as machines. Applying this diagnosis more widely, Lawrence has Ursula look down on her fellow-citizens from her new-found position of dark fecundity, seeing the passengers in the trains and trams as "only dummies exposed . . . And all their talk and all their behaviour was sham, they were dressed-up creatures. She was reminded of the Invisible Man, who was a piece of darkness made visible only by his clothes."[21] Her lover Anton similarly despises the people around him as "so many performing puppets, all wood and rag," equipped with "man's legs, but man's legs become rigid and deformed, mechanical" (*R*, 500). At the centre of this pervasive mechanizing of human life is the colliery which Ursula sees on her visit to Uncle Tom in Wiggiston. The pit has become the governing principle of this town, reducing all life outside it to a mere side-show, "human bodies and lives subjected in slavery to that symmetric monster of the colliery" (*R*, 397). To Ursula's horror, Winifred and Uncle Tom worship this "impure abstraction," feeling happy and free only in its service, hypnotized by the power of "the monstrous mechanism that held all matter, living or dead, in its service" (*R*, 397–8).

At this inclusive level of his social criticism, Lawrence assails modern industrial society as a monstrous machine, or as a huge deformed body devoted and enslaved to the machines it has created. America, he writes in *Studies in Classic American Literature,* has been "mastered by her own machines" (*SCAL*, 27); and in earlier drafts of the same work he defines the organizing principle of American society as "the perfect mechanical concord, the concord of a number of parts to a vast whole, a stupendous productive mechanism."[22] Lawrence is referring not simply to the new assembly-line factory systems, but to the fearsome political monster of democracy itself. "This thing, this mechanical democracy, new and monstrous on the face of the earth" (*SM*, 28) is for Lawrence a new Burkean nightmare of popular self-assertion, now equipped with overwhelming industrial power. Europe's domination was now, as Lawrence and many others saw, giving way to that of its American child, this "monstrous reflection of Europe," this "mechanical monstrosity of the west" (*SM*, 28, 29).

Confronted by the enormous body politic of modern democracy, Lawrence is driven to account for the existence of such a monster. From his standpoint of radical individualism, a human collectivity is a contradiction in terms: Ursula is terrified of her class of schoolchildren in *The Rainbow* "because they were not individual children, they were a collective, inhuman thing" (*R*, 426). Larger and more powerful industrial collectives are still more inhuman, drawing their power from the masses' blasphemous and self-destructive longing to become superhuman. Gerald's miners commit this sacrilege by accepting the new order of their "high priest":

> The men were satisfied to belong to the great and wonderful machine, even while it destroyed them. It was what they wanted. It was the highest that man had produced, the most wonderful and superhuman. They were exalted by belonging to this great and superhuman system which was beyond feeling or reason, something really godlike. (*WL*, 304)

Gerald's modernized industry can proceed only on the basis of this perverse submission to an inhuman mechanical collectivity which seems godlike, but to Lawrence is monstrous.

The miners willingly make (in a sense, make up) the very power which outgrows and dominates them, in a Frankensteinian process that recurs often in Lawrence's writings on democracy and modern civilization. In *The Rainbow* Will Brangwen feels awed and threatened by the massive artificial superstructure that is London: "The works of man were more terrible than man himself, almost monstrous" (*R*, 235). And in a letter to Lady Cynthia Asquith in 1915 Lawrence remarks that "we have created a great, almost overwhelming incubus of falsity and ugliness on top of us, so that we are almost crushed to death."[23] Again, Lawrence's reference is less to the physical bulk of industrial technology in itself than to the concomitant worship of an abstract democratic deity, whom he analyzes in his essay on "Democracy" as the Average Man. "The average human being: put him on the table, the little monster, and let us see what his works are like. He is just a little monster. . . . What a loathsome little beast he is, this Average, this unit, this Homunculus."[24] Horrified at the creation of a democratic prodigy which would challenge his own natural superiority over the herd of other people, Lawrence is driven straight back into the arms of Edmund Burke, denouncing democracy as a monstrous and mechanical threat to the organically-given hierarchy of human life.

Lawrence blames the existence of a monstrous democracy upon the subordination of instinctual life to a false ideality—above all, to the predominance of *will* (Lawrence frequently italicizes the word, mimetically). Attempting to account for the modern disease which has led to war, Lawrence claims in his 1917 article, "The Reality of Peace," that "we have been filled with a frenzy of compulsion, our insistent will has co-ordinated into a monstrous engine of compulsion and death."[25] The monstrous mechanism of modern society originates in this insistent will, in the subordination of the individual's real self to an ideal self, "that fancy little homunculus he has fathered in his own brain."[26] The will forces the instinctual life relentlessly into the service of mechanically-conceived ideals, just as Gerald forces his mare to confront the speeding train in *Women in Love*. As in so many other respects, Gerald embodies the northern disease in this monomaniac wilfulness too. Lawrence's analysis of Gerald in his capacity as Industrial Magnate insists monotonously upon his obsession with the power of his will. Gerald glories in the fact that the miners are instruments subordinated to his will, and in his subjection of nature to human control. Ultimately, his motive in the mining enterprise is not money, Lawrence claims, but purely the fulfilment of his own will; the transforming of people into pure instrumentality. Living under this obsession, Gerald himself becomes a creature of the process he has willed. Gudrun recognizes that he is "a pure, inhuman, almost superhuman instrument" (*WL, 511*).

The will-driven Gerald resembles not just Ahab, in his lust for conquest over nature, but Frankenstein too. In a series of essays written in 1918 and later revised for *Studies in Classic American Literature*, Lawrence devoted one essay to Benjamin Franklin, in which he fulminated against the predominance of the will in the "self-made" American. After inaccurately presenting William Godwin's supposed doctrine of perfectibility as the recipe for a "perfect" man, Lawrence holds up Franklin as the image of what such a creature would be like. "He was, perhaps, the most admirable little automaton the world has ever seen, the invention of the human will, working according to good principles. So far as affairs went, he was admirable. As far as life goes, he is monstrous" (*SM,* 46). Franklin is monstrous, of course, because his life is the pure product of an imposed will, not an organic growth from instinctual sources. "This deliberate entity, this self-determined man, is the very Son of Man, man made by the power of the human will, a virtuous Frankenstein monster" (*SM,* 43). Franklin is interpreted as a mock Saviour, made not begotten, consubstantial with the godlike idealism and rationality of the Enlightenment, yet truly an Antichrist in the pride and conceit of his self-making.

Lawrence's commentary upon *Frankenstein* in the Benjamin Franklin essay is subsumed into his larger warnings against the tyranny of the will:

> The magicians knew, at least imaginatively, what it was to create a being out of the intense *will* of the soul. And Mary Shelley, in the midst of the idealists, gives the dark side to the ideal being, showing us Frankenstein's monster.
> The ideal being was man created by man. And so was the supreme monster. (*SM,* 36)

Recent interpretations of *Frankenstein* which read it as a covert critique of Godwinian idealism are foreshadowed here, although Lawrence's use of the story is barely an interpretation, more a polemical appropriation of the idea of the monster to emphasize his point about the imposition of human will on nature. The picture of Frankenstein's creature as "the supreme monster," for example, does not faithfully reflect the suffering and initially benevolent being whose story appears in Mary Shelley's novel. There are several more frightening, and certainly more inhuman monsters in ancient mythology who could contend for the monstrous supremacy of which Lawrence writes, but only Frankenstein's, mild as it is, will fit Lawrence's diatribe against deliberate efforts to remake the human world from a conscious design.

It is something of an irony that a writer who has long been regarded not just as an example but as the great modern champion of human creativity actually argued himself into a position from which that same creativity is denied as a monstrous blasphemy:

> This has been the fallacy of our age—the assumption that we . . . can create the perfect being and the perfect age. . . . But we can *create* nothing. And the thing we can make of our own natures, by our own will, is at the most a pure mechanism, an automaton. So that if on the one hand Benjamin Franklin is the perfect human being of Godwin, on the other hand he is a monster, not exactly as the monster in *Frankenstein,* but for the same reason, viz., that he is the production or fabrication of the human will, which projects itself upon a living being, and automatises that being according to a given precept. (*SM,* 37)

Lawrence understands the monstrous quality of Frankenstein's creature not as the result of a noble aspiration gone disastrously wrong, but as the sign of an inherent perversion in the aspiration itself, in the assertion of will. It is the same sin with which Lawrence charges Ahab when he interprets the voyage of the *Pequod* as the "ideal will" of the white race rushing to self-destruction. This northern racial will "sank in the war," Lawrence writes, "and we are all flotsam" (*SCAL*, 169).

Lawrence's belief that a life lived from the ideal will rather than from the blood and the body is only a mockery of life helps to account for his use of the Frankenstein monster in the Benjamin Franklin essay, as it does for the frequent resort to Gothic or ghostly images in his early works. The life of the ideal will which is maintained by strangling the life of the body is the life of ghosts, vampires, and the walking dead. In a letter to Henry Savage in 1913, Lawrence wrote that "all Englishmen are swathed in restraint and puritanism and anti-emotion, till they are walking mummies."[27] In *The Study of Thomas Hardy*, a year later, Lawrence characterized the excessively spiritual relationship between Jude Fawley and Sue Bridehead as "a *frisson* of sacrilege, like the Frenchman who lay with a corpse."[28] Over this necrophilic world of the mechanical will broods the shade of Edgar Allan Poe, whose vampires Lawrence had also interpreted as monomaniacs of the spirit (Poe's Raven makes unexpected appearances in both *The White Peacock* and *Sons and Lovers*). It is a world in which the dead "cling to the living, and won't let go," as Birkin puts it in *Women in Love* (*WL*, 253). Gerald comes to Gudrun's bedroom at night with the clay of his father's grave still clinging to his feet (and, Lawrence adds, "on his heart" [*WL*, 424]); his need to draw sustenance from Gudrun is distinctly vampiric, and, not surprisingly, he confronts her and Loerke in his final scene "like a ghost" (*WL*, 571). The will-driven and hyperconscious Hermione is described insistently as a ghost, a corpse, a ghoul, a *revenant,* or as sepulchral, and she is only one among many. Ursula and Birkin meet whole crowds of "spectral people" (*WL*, 480) at Ostend and Ghent, who correspond to the spectral colliers Ursula sees at Wiggiston in *The Rainbow,* and to the "corpse-like inanation" of Anton Skrebensky, who feels "like a corpse that is inhabited with just enough life to make it appear as any other of the spectral, unliving beings which we call people in our dead language" (*R,* 501, 508). Ursula's task in seeking her independence is to fight clear of the clammy embrace of corpses: her disobedient pupil Vernon Williams has a "half transparent unwholesomeness, rather like a corpse," while Winifred Inger and Uncle Tom seem to her to be "ghoulish" in their worship of the monstrous colliery (*R,* 452, 397).

It is worth noticing in connection with this last attribution of ghoulishness to Tom and Winifred that these characters are scientists. In describing Ursula's lesbian affair with her teacher, Lawrence has taken care to inform us that "Winifred had had a scientific education," and he tells us that Tom Brangwen has converted the front room of his house into a laboratory which looks out over the "abstraction" of the town to "the great mathematical colliery" beyond (R, 388, 394). The ghoulishness and the scientific abstraction in the relation of this couple to the industrial system merge together, Lawrence's purpose being to force the laboratory and the tomb, the scientist and the graverobber, into the kind of equivalence they have in *Frankenstein*. It is no accident that at the training college (itself a "laboratory for the factory" [R, 485]), Ursula's physics teacher is called Dr. Frankstone; she refuses to acknowledge any special mystery in life, regarding it only as a complex of physical and chemical processes. Ursula, who prefers botany, clings to the mystical and religious conception of life as she watches it gleaming under the microscope, and dismisses Dr. Frankstone's view as a reduction of this supreme mystery to the merely mechanical.

Science is always portrayed in Lawrence's work as a reductive, corrosively impersonal dismantling of life into mechanical components, always substituting the mechanical principle for the organic. In this, Lawrence is of course restating some long-standing Romantic anxieties in even more harshly polarized terms, and appealing, through echoes of *Frankenstein*, to the received reduction of all scientific rationality to anatomical dissection. In an often-quoted distillation of Romantic arguments Lawrence claimed that "Analysis presupposes a corpse," recalling Wordsworth's line, "We murder to dissect."[29] Lawrence's Romantic proverb is literally true only in so far as the rapid advances in medicine in the preceding century could not have been achieved without examining cadavers; but by including all Analysis—chemical, physical, philosophical, cultural—Lawrence makes an absurd reduction which implies further that analysis and organic life are incompatible. As a matter of fact, physicians of all kinds spend much of their daily practice in analyzing living beings—often without that religious veneration for life which Lawrence would demand, it is true, but also without resorting to murder. Lawrence's attempt to equate all scientific enquiry with ghoulishness is a version of the Mad Scientist stereotype (albeit in rather different terms than H. G. Wells's), pushing our attitude to the scientist back through the Frankenstein myth all the way to Edmund Burke. Every scientist—and Lawrence would add, every democrat too—is an anatomist who hacks her or his parent in pieces just for the sake of the experiment.

If Lawrence's attitudes to science look back across a century to Anti-Jacobinism and the Gothic novel, his vision of modern civilization's self-destructive capacities appears to look forward prophetically, with Gudrun and Loerke in *Women in Love*:

> As for the future, that they never mentioned except one laughed out some mocking dream of the destruction of the world by a ridiculous catastrophe of man's invention: a man invented such a perfect explosive that it blew the earth in two, and the two halves set off in different directions through space . . . (WL, 551)

If this looks like prophecy, it is not because of any uncanny powers of Lawrence's—he was writing about the world of 1916—but because Lawrence's nightmare is one that we still inhabit.

Notes

1. Joseph Conrad, *Within the Tides* (Harmondsworth, 1978), 33–4.

2. Joseph Conrad, *The Mirror of the Sea; with A Personal Record* (London, 1947), 150. Subsequent page references in the text are to this edition, abbreviated as MS.

3. Joseph Conrad, *Nostromo: A Tale of the Seaboard,* ed. Martin Seymour-Smith (Harmondsworth, 1983), 423.

4. Ibid., 204–5.

5. Conrad dismissed *Moby Dick* as a strained and wholly insincere work (letter to Humphrey Milford, 15 Jan. 1907, cited by Harold Beaver in *Moby Dick,* 20). None the less, *Heart of Darkness* is his version of Melville's tale, just as *The Shadow-Line* is his version of "The Rime of the Ancient Mariner."

6. Joseph Conrad, *Heart of Darkness,* ed. Paul O'Prey (Harmondsworth, 1983). Subsequent page references in the text are to this edition, abbreviated as HD. The function of women in Conrad's fiction is very often to be told soothing lies.

7. Joseph Conrad, *Tales of Unrest* (Harmondsworth, 1977), 126.

8. Joseph Conrad, *The Secret Agent: A Simple Tale,* ed. Martin Seymour-Smith (Harmondsworth, 1984), 40–1 (Author's Note). Subsequent page references in the text are to this edition, abbreviated as SA.

9. Conrad, *Tales of Unrest,* 87.

10. Joseph Conrad, *Victory: An Island Tale* (Harmondsworth, 1963), 278, 25. Subsequent page references in the text are to this edition, abbreviated as V.

11. Joseph Conrad, *The Shadow-Line: A Confession,* ed. Jeremy Hawthorn (Oxford, 1985), 86; *The Nigger of the "Narcissus," Typhoon, and Other Stories* (Harmondsworth, 1963), 67.

12. Conrad, *Within the Tides,* 159; *Nigger,* 263.

13. Joseph Conrad, *Under Western Eyes* (Harmondsworth, 1957), 190. Subsequent page references in the text are to this edition, abbreviated as WE.

14. Conrad transfers to ships the role allotted by many Victorian writers to women: that of inspiring men to overcome their baser selves through a pure devotion.

15. *Joseph Conrad's Letters to R. B. Cunninghame Graham,* ed. C. T. Watts (Cambridge, 1969), 148–9 (26 Dec. 1903).

16. *The Collected Letters of Joseph Conrad, Volume 1: 1861–97,* ed. Frederick R. Karl and Laurence Davies (Cambridge, 1983), 425 (20 Dec. 1897).

17. D. H. Lawrence, *Phoenix II: Uncollected, Unpublished and Other Prose Works,* ed. Warren Roberts and Harry T. Moore (London, 1968), 391.

18. D. H. Lawrence, *Women in Love,* ed. Charles L. Ross (Harmondsworth, 1982), 61. Subsequent page references in the text are to this edition, abbreviated as WL.

19. D. H. Lawrence, *Studies in Classic American Literature* (Harmondsworth, 1971), 166. Subsequent page references in the text are to this edition, abbreviated as SCAL.

20. D. H. Lawrence, *Sons and Lovers,* ed. Keith Sagar (Harmondsworth, 1981), 133. Subsequent page references in the text are to this edition, abbreviated as SL.

21. D. H. Lawrence, *The Rainbow,* ed. John Worthen (Harmondsworth, 1981), 498. Subsequent page references in the text are to this edition, abbreviated as R.

22.   D. H. Lawrence, *The Symbolic Meaning: The Uncollected Versions of "Studies in Classic American Literature,"* ed. Armin. Arnold (Arundel, 1962), 27. Subsequent page references in the text are to this edition, abbreviated as *SM*.

23.   *The Letters of D. H. Lawrence, Volume 2: June 1913–October 1916,* ed. George J. Zytaruk and James T. Boulton (Cambridge, 1981), 379 (16 Aug. 1915).

24.   *Phoenix: The Posthumous Papers of D. H. Lawrence,* ed. Edward D. McDonald (London, 1936), 699.

25.   Ibid., 674.

26.   Ibid., 712.

27.   Lawrence, *Letters II,* 102 (15? Nov. 1913).

28.   Lawrence, *Phoenix,* 505.

29.   Lawrence, *Phoenix II,* 391; William Wordsworth, "The Tables Turned," *Lyrical Ballads* 1798.

Sweetheart of Darkness: Kurtz's Intended as Progeny of Frankenstein's Bride

MARY LOWE-EVANS

The Queen is most anxious to enlist everyone who can speak or write to join in checking this mad, wicked folly of "Women's Rights" . . . *with all its attendant horrors,* on which [the feminist's] poor feeble sex is bent, forgetting every sense of womanly feeling and propriety. . . . It is a subject which makes the queen so furious that she cannot contain herself.[1]

So long as Englishmen retain at once their migratory instinct, their passion for independence and their impatience of foreign rule, they are bound by a manifest destiny to found empires abroad, or in other words, to make themselves the dominant race in the foreign countries to which they wander.[2]

I

Chris Baldick has noted numerous parallels between *Frankenstein* and several of Conrad's works, including *Heart of Darkness*:

> Like *Frankenstein,* . . . *Heart of Darkness* takes the path of masculine adventure and exploration to its self-destructive terminus self-consciously excluding the world of women . . . to whom the true story cannot even be told.

> Marlow's function—like Walton's—is to hear the dying words of the transgressor and report them back to the heart of civilization, his own early zeal for exploration now chastened. . . .

> As Frankenstein's monster demands acknowledgement of kinship from his creator, who is in turn recognised as a brother by Walton in his letters home to his sister, so the impossibility of disavowing the monstrous consequences of imperialism is brought home to the metropolis itself, to London, "the monstrous town."[3]

This essay was written specifically for this volume and is published here for the first time by permission of the author.

As Baldick makes clear in his essay, the reach of *Frankenstein* is long. Mary Shelley's tale of ill-considered, excessive ambition resonates especially in the technological and colonialist "advances" of the late nineteenth and early twentieth centuries. My focus in this essay, however, will be the suggestive power of *Frankenstein* with regard to the representation of woman as the moral arbiter, the "heart," of civilization in Conrad's novel. Baldick's observation that *Heart of Darkness,* like *Frankenstein,* excludes women from the arenas of masculine adventure and exploration is accurate up to a point. I will argue, however, that Conrad *does* involve women in male enterprises in somewhat the same compromised, peripheral, yet paradoxically *necessary,* way that Mary Shelley did. Conrad's women, though, show signs of having internalized three-quarters of a century's worth of lessons about both their debt and their moral superiority to the field of commercial progress, a field kept healthy by imperialist projects.

As I have argued at some length in the introduction to the present collection of essays, Victor Frankenstein, his creature, and their associates project Mary Shelley's fears and hopes about the direction that gender politics were taking in early-nineteenth-century England. Mary Shelley asks readers, in the person of her surrogate, Margaret Walton Saville, to witness and judge the exotic proceedings fully recounted in her brother's letters. But, like many another female relative of a male explorer, Margaret Saville must judge from afar and must consider only mediated evidence shaped by masculine perceptions. Elizabeth Lavenza, Victor Frankenstein's fiancée and short-lived bride, dies a bewildered innocent, ignorant of the scientific business that her genius-fiancé engages in. But Margaret lives to pass on to us the letters recounting the cautionary tale of Victor's sin and destruction, Elizabeth's wedding-night murder, and Walton's redemption. Her tacit partnership with Walton makes Margaret "Saville" the "civil" servant of the text, the requisite female preserver of civilized values. As Stephen Behrendt observes, "Walton's explanations to Margaret of his own behavior suggest that he casts her in the role of sanctifier, whose province is to hear, understand, sympathize and approve."[4]

Eighty-four years later, in *Heart of Darkness,* Joseph Conrad, a colonized aristocrat, a multinational seafaring man, assigns to Marlow, in some respects Conrad's alter ego, the "heavenly mission to civilise."[5] Delivering Kurtz's letters and lying to Kurtz's Intended about her fiancé's last words, yet confessing his lie to a company of men, Marlow apparently fulfills his assignment. The civilizing mission, then, has become a rather more complicated conspiracy by the end of the nineteenth century than it had been when *Frankenstein* was produced.

Kurtz's Intended, like Margaret Saville and Elizabeth Lavenza, is the recipient of letters by or about an ambitious male genius who recounts some portion of his enterprise. But the Intended is more closely related to Elizabeth, an ignorant innocent, since the Intended is kept under interdiction by Marlow's lie from the action and "horror" of Kurtz's story. Having been restricted to her own beautiful world, she is also apparently not privy to the "attendant horrors" of the real-world women's rights movement to which Queen Victoria so vehemently objected. But the mysterious "slim packet of letters" (89) that Marlow delivers is never publicized to the reader. In her ignorance (and ours) the Intended takes on characteristics of a degenerate Elizabeth Lavenza, a feckless descendant of Frankenstein's bride who contributes to the "horror" of Kurtz's tale by default or, in her anxious *desire* for the lie ("I want—something—something—to—to live with" [93]), as a conspirator with Marlow who purposely "unspeaks" the "colossal scale of [Kurtz's] vile desires" (90). Either way, as Johanna M. Smith argues, by substituting the Intended's name for Kurtz's last words, "The horror! The horror!" Marlow "equates the two."[6] If the Intended is a Dorian Grayish replica of Elizabeth Lavenza, Marlow's aunt is the activist antitype of Margaret Saville, providing not only moral support but political influence for her "questing" male relative. "She was determined," Marlow says, "to make no end of fuss to get me appointed skipper of a river steamboat if such was my fancy" (23).

By 1890, when Conrad made his journey into the Congo, the apparently simpler, scientifically more pure urge in Mary Shelley's day to explore uncharted territories had changed with the expediencies of empire. Patrick Brantlinger explains that "in the 1870s Germany, Belgium, and the United States began an intense imperial rivalry against the older colonial powers, above all Great Britain. . . . Imperialism as an element in British culture grew increasingly noisy, racist, and self conscious as faith in free trade and liberal reformism declined. The militant imperialism of the late Victorian and Edwardian years thus represents a national (indeed, international) political and cultural regression, a social atavism."[7] By 1902, it had become "a commonplace of history [that governments use] foreign wars and the glamour of empire-making in order to bemuse the popular mind and divert rising resentment against domestic abuses" (J. A. Hobson, as quoted in Brantlinger, 35). Middle-class women, still philosophically relegated to separate spheres of activity from men (though increasingly taking their places in the workforce), were cajoled, reasoned, bribed, distracted, and flattered into an even greater ideological investment in imperialism. Yet, with the exception of missionary wives and nurses, they remained at a great remove from the major arenas of political and economic activity, especially those ventures undertaken outside the country.

In "Ministers of the Interior," Judith Newton reveals how women had been prepared for their roles in expanding the empire. Among the numerous voices in the culture telling women how to fulfill their part of the nation's mission were two women whose widely circulated pamphlets on the "Woman Question" of the 1830s and 1840s "resolved . . . tensions . . .

between narratives promoting and narratives criticizing commercial society . . . through the figure of the middle class woman, a figure [like Kurtz's Intended] *produced* and *sustained* by a commercial progress that she assumes a *superior* and *correcting* relation to" (emphasis added).[8] Sarah Lewis's *Woman's Mission* and Sarah Ellis's *Women of England* (both published in 1839 and reprinted several times) "represent feminine virtues as superior to masculine [and also work] to establish the cultural superiority of 'the middle class' and to identify middle class values with national identity and national identity with successful imperialist ventures" (Newton, 132). As imperialism required a new definition of Englishness, so Englishness required a new—or modified—definition of its moral center, the woman. "We claim for [women]," Lewis insisted, "no less an office than that of instruments (under God) for the regeneration of the world" (quoted in Newton, 128). And Ellis wrote, "If to grow tardy or indifferent in the [commercial] race were only to lose the goal, many would be glad to pause; but such is the nature of commerce and trade, as at present carried on in this country, that to slacken in the exertion is altogether to fail" (quoted in Newton, 130).

Paradoxically, the need for women's civilizing influence had proportionally increased as the business of imperialism had widened the gap between them and the men who ventured into foreign territories to carry the faith and expand the market. In 1859 Harriet Martineau, drawing on the census of 1851, pointed out that there were "over half a million more women than men in Britain" who could not depend on marriage partners for their livelihood.[9] Her point was that women should be released from the strictures of the domestic and allowed to enter the workforce more freely (as indeed they began to do; see Holcombe, 11). But the number of middle-class English women continued increasingly to outnumber the men in the years leading up to World War II, and "the chief reason given to explain this surplus of middle-class women was the excessive emigration of men of their class, who were responding to the calls of far flung empire" (Holcombe, 11).

Among ways to maintain the moral fiber of the nation, women were expected to write encouraging letters to the increasing numbers of brothers, nephews, cousins, and sweethearts who became involved in empire building. For most middle-class women, then, the empire-ical world was indeed a darkness, relieved only by the filtered, tightly focused light of return letters and sensational journal accounts of their men's adventures. Robin Gilmour notes the glamour of these "stories of incredible survival in alien environments spiced with danger and controversy."[10] Among them were David Livingstone's *Missionary Travels and Researches in South Africa* (1857), a tremendous bestseller that, along with Henry M. Stanley's *How I Found Livingstone, Adventures and Discoveries in Central Africa* (1872), impressed Conrad to the extent that he may have used these two explorers as prototypes for Kurtz and Marlow, respectively. Interestingly, Dr. Livingstone had an Intended much like

Kurtz's, who viewed him as "the wonder of the age," a man who devoted his life to making an "open path for commerce and Christianity."[11] A letter that Livingstone wrote to one of his earlier marriage prospects from "on board the barque George" in February 1841 as he was about to begin his lifelong "affair" with Africa conveys a tone similar to that of Robert Walton's early letters to his sister Margaret: "Please write to me and ask any questions you choose. I don't know very well what kind of information you would like. Name the different subjects you should like to know and I will give you all the information in my power. Is it the difference in the mode of life? . . . You know I am not very well acquainted with the feelings of those who have been ladies all their lives."[12] Here Livingstone volunteers to educate his Intended about the exotic world he is entering while admitting that he is "not very well acquainted" with the feelings of ladies. Livingstone has a particularly high stake in enticing his correspondent into the exigencies of empire, since he hopes that she will eventually become his wife and share—in a limited way—his mission.

In a later letter to a male correspondent Livingstone makes clear the precise role of women in imperial projects. In describing the relationship between the British and the Portuguese explorers (on the Zambezi Expedition of 1858–1864), Livingstone assesses the Portuguese as "the lowest of the low—there is not half a dozen upright men of that nation in Africa. Their establishments are small penal settlements and not colonies, no women are sent out, and the moral atmosphere is worse than that of the valley of Siddim."[13] British women, then, whether exerting their influence from at home (where the vast majority remained) or on site, were consistently enlisted by imperialist rhetoric (which subsumes missionary "texts") to provide moral sanctions for exploration, trade and often exploitation of foreign lands.

II

ELIZABETH LAVENZA'S HIDEOUS PROGENY

Percy Shelley composed his preface to the first edition of *Frankenstein* in Marlow, a town roughly halfway between London and Oxford. The coincidence of this place name with the name of Conrad's "narrator's narrator" in *Heart of Darkness* begins the kinship chain that links not only the works themselves but one end of the century with the other. Both novels treat the theme of the social responsibility that is assigned the educated, intellectually superior man—the genius—a question of concern throughout the Victorian era. Each also addresses the problem of recognizing and controlling the divided self. In addition to these philosophical, political, and psychological emphases, each employs a complicated narrative frame that involves the in/exclusion of women in the imperialist agenda. For my purposes, the similarities and differences between these frames invite careful attention. One might say that *Frankenstein* is a domestic tragedy framed by imperialist comedy while *Heart of Darkness* is an imperialist tragedy framed by domestic farce, an adjustment of emphasis that mirrors the restructuring of Victorian patriarchal priorities.

Frankenstein's Robert Walton writes to his married sister in England as his outward-bound ship carries him further and further toward the Arctic Circle. Walton seeks Margaret's moral support for this journey into uncharted territory, where he hopes to discover "a passage near the pole" or to ascertain "the secret of the magnet."[14] He will continue to seek that support through letters that fully disclose Victor Frankenstein's bizarre adventure, even though Walton knows Margaret had regarded his enterprise with "evil forebodings" from the start (59).

Walton reminds Margaret that she had "been tutored and refined by books and retirement from the world and [is] therefore somewhat fastidious." Paradoxically, he concludes that her reclusive book learning qualifies her "to appreciate the extraordinary merits of [Victor Frankenstein]" (74). The inherent contradictions in and seductiveness of bourgeois domestic feminism intrude on this passage. Margaret's refinement and exclusion from the world of patriarchal business should disqualify her for such a mentoring role, yet Walton insists (as did both male and female feminists in the first half of the nineteenth century) that her woman's education and retirement enhance her critical powers.

The reader loses sight of both Robert Walton and Margaret Saville as the narratives of Victor Frankenstein and his Creature take over. Nonetheless, in the end, Walton and Margaret come back into focus as Walton haltingly decides to give up his dangerous quest—despite Victor Frankenstein's powerful influence—in the interests of his men. Walton and crew listen to Victor's deathbed rallying cry, an echo of speeches delivered at geographical or missionary society fund-raisers: "[This is] an honourable undertaking. You [will be] hailed as the benefactors of your species . . . brave men who encountered death for honor and the benefit of mankind" (253). As Philip Corrigan and Derek Sayer point out, "It took a national culture of extraordinary self-confidence and moral rectitude to construe . . . imperialism as a 'civilizing mission', " and, as Judith Newton demonstrates, it took the cooperation of influential women to see the imperialist venture through (Newton, 145). Eighty-one years after Victor Frankenstein's parting shot, Kurtz's contention that each Company station in the Congo "should be like a beacon on the road toward better things, a centre of trade, of course, but also for humanizing, improving, instructing" (47) sounds a familiar but hollow ring.

Mary Shelley's Walton, exhibiting a failure of such imperialist self-confidence on board his ice-bound ship, threatened with mutiny, and responding to Margaret's early training in refined sympathies, reluctantly consents to turn back: "I have lost my hopes of utility and glory. . . . I will . . . detail these bitter circumstances to you, my dear sister; and while I am wafted towards England and towards you, I will not despond" (254). Margaret Saville's apparent "triumph" over Victor Frankenstein's hold on Walton's imagination and over Walton's excessive ambition and the implicit success of what I will call "informed domesticity" over imperialism saves the novel from being an apocalyptic vision of unbridled male egoism. Margaret Saville's moral surveillance of her brother's enterprises seems to have kept him from destroying both himself and his crew. Fantastic though Mary Shelley's vision be in this frame narrative, it synthesizes the hopes of women like herself who accepted an idealized version of a symbiotic separate spheres philosophy.

Framing the Creature's story and within Victor's, however, is the biography of Elizabeth Lavenza, Victor's "more than sister—the beautiful and adored companion of all [his] occupations and [his] pleasures" (80). From her adoption into the Frankenstein household, "everyone loved Elizabeth"; and it was Madame Frankenstein's dying wish that Elizabeth and Victor marry. During Victor's six-year absence, Elizabeth thinks of her own domestic activities as "trifling occupations" for which she is rewarded by "seeing none but happy kind faces around [her]" (109). Her idyllic world anticipates the Intended's "too beautiful" realm. We're told that Elizabeth is "saintly" and "selfless" and that Victor believes her existence "bound up with [his]" (133). All these protestations render incredible Victor's criminal negligence that leads to Elizabeth's nuptial-bed murder by the Creature. But Elizabeth is guilty, too.

Even when confronting Victor in a letter about his erratic behavior, she has been painfully tentative and self-effacing. Expressing her "disinterested . . . affection," she begs Victor not to let her become an "obstacle to [his] wishes" (228). Her letter anticipates the conciliatory tone of another letter, one from Emily Davies to Barbara Bodichon 47 years after *Frankenstein*'s publication. Davies disapproves a radical feminist friend's references to "the arguments [of male conservatives as] 'foolish.' Of course they *are,* but it does not seem quite polite to say so. . . . You see . . . nothing irritates men so much as to attribute tyranny to them . . . many . . . really *mean well,* and . . . it seems fair to admit it and to show them that their well intentioned efforts are a *mistake,* not a crime."[15] It is because Elizabeth Lavenza believes that Victor Frankenstein *means well,* and is confident that he has committed no crime, that she obediently enters the nuptial chamber alone while Victor paces distractedly about outside. I am convinced that Mary Shelley "murdered" Elizabeth, using an alter ego, the Creature, as hit man because Elizabeth's variety of woman had become outdated—if only briefly so—for the daughter of William Godwin and Mary Wollstonecraft. Margaret Saville, on the other hand, was more to Mary Shelley's taste. Having kept informed, Margaret had challenged her brother's obsessions, and her early imprinting saved him from destruction. Margaret thus epitomizes the optimism, and Elizabeth Lavenza the pessimism, in discourses about complementary but separate roles for men and women during, roughly, the first half of the nineteenth century.

Had the optimism about woman's civilizing influence inherent in Margaret Saville's position in *Frankenstein* proved well-founded, Marlow's aunt and Kurtz's Intended might never have been created. Instead, Charlie's "excellent aunt," gets carried away in a rush of capitalist rhetoric (26), while the Intended glides "forward, all in black, with a pale head, floating toward [Marlow] in the dusk," for all the world like the vampire of Elizabeth Lavenza, metaphorically eviscerated and lobotomized by imperialist propaganda. Her enigmatic assertion, "I have survived," uttered with a deep catch of the breath (91), eerily reinforces for me her identity as Elizabeth's ghost.

Both Marlow's aunt and the Intended are pushed so far out into the margins of Conrad's novel that most readers don't even remember them. Whereas Mary Shelley had added Margaret Saville to her cautionary tale in order to contain and control Walton's obsessive tendencies by hearing them out, Conrad's women promote Marlow's discipleship and Kurtz's "unspeakable rites," even as they seem to insist that those rites remain unspoken. *Heart of Darkness* is emphatically a thinking *man's* adventure story. Women resist "understanding" the excesses carried out there as a number of my own women friends avoid confronting the atrocities depicted in its cinematic descendant, *Apocalypse Now.* Furthermore, the very resistance the novel sets up to women readers replicates women's resistance to understanding imperialist politics, a resistance both planned by men and agreed upon by women.

Operating "outside the common pathways of men" to find a passage to the North Pole, Mary Shelley's Walton had sought *moral* support from his sister. On the other hand, Charlie Marlow—the "glamour's [now being] off" the North Pole, as he says (22)—uses his aunt's political influence to get command of a Congo River steamer. The glamour is, of course, emphatically "on" Africa during the later nineteenth century. Marlow's aunt is both removed from and complacent about the business of exploitation. From her room "that most soothingly look[s] just as you would expect a lady's drawing room to look" (26), she smugly speaks the colonizer's language, babbling about "weaning those ignorant millions from their horrid ways" (26). Her vehemence discomfits even Marlow, whose admission that "the Company [is] run for profit" (27) belies his earlier "heavenly mission to civilise" (22).

With his aunt in mind, Marlow, unlike Robert Walton, finds women neither "fastidious," that is, hypercritical, nor "retir[ed] from the world" (*Frankenstein,* 74), which implies a voluntary move away from some former connection, but completely, astoundingly "out of touch with truth [and living] in a world of their own" (27). The ingenuous comment that elicits this response, however, shows clearly the aunt's connectedness with the patriarchal "truths" of political economy: "You forget, dear Charles, that the labourer is worthy of his hire." Continuing to muse about the altogether "too beautiful" world of women, Marlow gets "embraced," reminded to "write often, and so on" and then leaves (27). Unlike the correspondence between Robert Walton and Margaret Saville, Marlow's and his aunt's letters, we suspect, will be filled with reports of commercial success or exotic adventures that *conceal* the unspeakable wrongs of the enterprise they both support.

Marlow's memory later juxtaposes "that beautiful world" of women (64) to the "one immense jabber, silly, atrocious, sordid, savage . . . mean, without any kind of sense" (63) world of his Kurtzean quest. The Intended's image enters that world, unbidden, only to have Marlow banish it: "We must help them to stay in that beautiful world of their own, lest ours get worse" (64). As Johanna Smith observes, "The patriarchal ideology of separate spheres which underpins imperialist ideology could hardly be better formulated" (192). But the Intended's presence, even though only a shadow in Marlow's memory, suggests Marlow's belief or suspicions about her collusion in both Kurtz's and Marlow's enterprises.— Remembering how Kurtz had spoken of his "Intended," Marlow assures his company of men that they "would have perceived . . . how completely she was out of it." Then by some quirky associative train of thought, Marlow is prompted to exclaim, "And the lofty frontal bone of Mr. Kurtz!" (64), conjuring an image that anticipates the Intended's appearance in the closing frame of Marlow's memoir, in which "only her forehead, smooth and white, remained illumined by the inextinguishable light of belief and love" (91). The subtle invocation of phrenology, the pseudoscience of skull reading that reinforced the theory that males and females had decidedly different mindsets, suggests how the scientific seal of approval on theories of separateness could be enlisted to authorize imperialist attitudes.

That understanding the Intended is requisite to understanding Conrad's apocalyptic tale is established by her kinship to the "meaning of an episode" as defined by Marlow through the narrator: "The meaning of an episode was . . . outside, enveloping the tale which brought it out as a glow brings out a haze, in the likeness of one of these misty halos . . . made visible by the spectral illumination of moonshine" (19–20). The Intended's "fair hair . . . pale visage [and] pure brow [which seem] surrounded by an ashy halo" (90) identify her with the enigmatic meaning of the story as does her joint position with Marlow's aunt in the "envelope" of the tale. That meaning, impenetrable as it is, has to do with the undefined "horror" that Marlow replaces with the unspoken name of the Intended and may in turn be interpreted as the self-loathing all the participants in the lie must feel. For in the final analysis, Marlow, his aunt, the Intended, and Marlow's audience on board the Nellie must face their kinship with Kurtz, a man who could "get himself to believe anything" (88).

Seated ill-at-ease in the Intended's drawing room, observing her changing expressions, Marlow "saw [Kurtz and the Intended] together . . . heard them together." Admitting that they both knew Kurtz well, Marlow agrees that the Intended "knew him best." Marlow's "strained ears seemed to hear distinctly, mingled with her tone of despairing regret, the summing up whisper of [Kurtz's] eternal condemnation" (91). Seized with panic, Marlow wonders what he is doing there, but, like Coleridge's startled wedding guest, he stays. Indeed, in Marlow's imagination Kurtz seems to have posthumously *wed* his Intended, but in this union of exploitive experience and willful ignorance Marlow becomes the surrogate groom consummating the union and impregnating the Intended with his lie, a lie he "hates and detests." The lie elicits from the Intended "an exulting and terrible cry . . . of inconceivable triumph and of unspeakable pain" (93). She will surely nurture it and set it loose in the world where it will continue to engender "hideous progeny."

Notes

1. Queen Victoria, paraphrased in Margaret Cole, *Women of Today* (London: Thomas Nelson, 1946), 150–51.

2. E. V. Dicey, a liberal lawyer, quoted in "Mr. Gladstone and our Empire," *Nineteenth Century* 11 (1877): 292–308, 294.

3. Chris Baldick, "Monsters of Empire: Conrad and Lawrence," in *In Frankenstein's Shadow: Myth, Monstrocity, and Nineteenth-Century Writing* (Oxford: Clarendon Press, 1987), 165, 166, 167. This chapter of Baldick's work is reprinted in the present collection.

4. Stephen Behrendt, "Mary Shelley, *Frankenstein*, and the Woman Writer's Fate," in *Romantic Women Writers: Voices and Countervoices,* ed. Paula R. Feldman and Theresa M. Kelley (Hanover: University Press of New England, 1995), 69. This essay is reprinted in the present collection.

5. Joseph Conrad, *Heart of Darkness: A Case Study in Contemporary Criticism,* ed. Ross C. Murfin (New York. St. Martin's Press, 1989), 22. Subsequent references to *Heart of Darkness* are made to this edition parenthetically within the text.

6. Johanna M. Smith, " 'Too Beautiful Altogether': Patriarchal Ideology in *Heart of Darkness,"* in *Heart of Darkness: A Case Study in Contemporary Criticism,* 179–89, 193. Subsequent references to this work are made parenthetically within the text.

7. Patrick Brantlinger, *Rule of Darkness: British Literature and Imperialism, 1830–1914* (Ithaca, N.Y.: Cornell University Press, 1989), 33. Subsequent references to this work are made parenthetically within the text.

8. Judith Newton, " 'Ministers of the Interior': The Political Economy of Women's Manuals," in *Starting Over: Feminism and the Politics of Cultural Critique* (Ann Arbor: University of Michigan Press, 1994), 125–27, 132. Newton derives the title of this essay from a phrase used in the *Edinburgh Review,* 1833, as part of an argument for "excluding women from formal political power" (126). Newton observes that the phrase "ministers of the interior . . . insinuates as many parallels between women and men, domestic and public, as it does differences,

and, as part of an argument for excluding women from formal political power, it also politicizes the domestic sphere" (126).

9. Quoted in Lee Holcombe, *Victorian Ladies at Work* (Hamden, Conn.: Archon Books, 1973), 10–11. Subsequent references to this work are made parenthetically within the text.

10. Robin Gilmour, *The Victorian Period: The Intellectual and Cultural Context of English Literature, 1830–1890* (London: Longman, 1993), 180–81.

11. For more on the connections between the saga of Stanley and Livingstone and *Heart of Darkness,* see Mary Golanka, "Mr. Kurtz I Presume? Livingstone and Stanley as Prototypes of Kurtz and Marlow," *Studies in the Novel* 17, no. 2 (1985): 195–202, 196.

12. Livingstone, David, *Letters and Documents 1841–1872* (London: James Currey, 1990), 10; Letter to Catherine Ridley, 24 February 1841.

13. Livingstone, *Letters,* 65; Letters to James Young, 28 January 1860.

14. Mary Shelley, *Frankenstein,* ed., with introduction by, Maurice Hindle (New York: Viking Penguin, 1985), 60.

15. Rosamund Billington, "The Dominant Values of Victorian Feminism," in *In Search of Victorian Values,* ed. Eric M. Sigsworth (Manchester: Manchester University Press, 1988), 116–30, 124.

Frankenstein and Its Cinematic Translations

TRACY COX

To grasp the genuine relationship between an original and a translation requires an investigation analogous to the argumentation by which a critique of cognition would have to prove the impossibility of an image theory. There it is a matter of showing that in cognition there could be no objectivity, not even a claim to it, if it dealt with images of reality; here it can be demonstrated that no translation would be possible if in its ultimate essence it strove for likeness to the original. For in its after life—which could not be called that if it were not a transformation and a renewal of something living—the original undergoes a change.

—Walter Benjamin, "The Task of the Translator"[1]

Alas! Victor, when falsehood can look so like the truth, who can assure themselves of certain happiness?

—Mary Shelley, *Frankenstein*[2]

Benjamin's "The Task of the Translator" addresses the difficulties of translating a work from one language to another. One might aptly apply Benjamin's observations to cinematic adaptations of novels: The written language of the novel is translated into the cinematic language of the film. The heated debates over a given film's fidelity to the original literary work prove that "there can be no objectivity" and that a translation is ultimately a transformation. The process of cinematic adaptation inevitably involves a filtering of the original novel through a variety of lenses shaped by technological, cultural, aesthetic, and economic considerations. The many film adaptations of Mary Shelley's *Frankenstein* exemplify the process Benjamin describes, as they respond to different aspects of Shelley's rich novel, extending the legend and creating new meanings for new generations.

The popularity of Mary Shelley's story with filmmakers is overwhelming. Donald Glut's *The Frankenstein Catalog*[3] (1984) references more than 200

This essay was written specifically for this volume and is published here for the first time by permission of the author.

movies based on *Frankenstein,* and new adaptations continue to emerge each year. Some of these films purport to directly present Shelley's story (*Mary Shelley's Frankenstein,* 1994), while others parody the story (*Frankenstein's Great Aunt Tillie,* 1964; *Young Frankenstein,* 1974), loosely adapt or exploit the subject matter (*Blackenstein,* 1974; *Frankenhooker,* 1990), appropriate a theme (*The Vindicator,* 1986; *Extreme Measures,* 1996), appropriate the cinematic creature (*Abbott and Costello Meet Frankenstein,* 1948; *Frankenstein Meets the Space Monster,* 1965), or even represent the novel's genesis (*Gothic,* 1987; *Haunted Summer,* 1988). In discussing the *Frankenstein* films, critics must confront this unwieldy list and impose a methodological frame to significantly narrow the scope.

Critics of the *Frankenstein* films typically frame their discussions around a film's ability to capture the themes of the novel. Wheeler Winston Dixon separates the films of Frankenstein into four periods: 1910 (Edison's *Franken-stein,* the first film adaptation), 1931 (Universal Pictures' *Frankenstein,* starring Boris Karloff), 1957 (*The Curse of Frankenstein,* the first of the British Hammer Frankenstein series starring Christopher Lee), and 1976 (*Victor Frankenstein,* made by the low-budget Swedish company Aspekt Film). Dixon maintains that these films merit critical attention because "[in these four films], the essence of [Shelley's] novel survives the many emendations made to her plot."[4] Harriet Margolis similarly recommends a selection of films that capture the novel's themes, but she frames her inquiry somewhat differently. Assuming that the viewer/reader first knows *Frankenstein* through the cinema, she examines "Hollywood's influence over contemporary consumptions of the *Frankenstein* text," limiting her scope to three popular film versions: Universal's 1931 *Frankenstein,* Universal's 1935 *The Bride of Frankenstein,* and Mel Brooks's 1974 parody *Young Frankenstein.*[5] In each of these films, Margolis finds "the same crucial philosophical questions about creation, science, and social responsibility" that mark the novel.[6]

In a discussion of the films on their own terms, William Nestrick proposes that "in *Frankenstein* the filmmaker finds a story that offers a narrative analogy to film itself."[7] His attention to cinematic terms enables a more accommodating reading of many of the films, as he embraces avant-garde appropriations of the Frankenstein myth exemplified by *Frank Film* (1973) and *Andy Warhol's Frankenstein* (1974). Though these obscure films were hardly box-office successes, Nestrick argues that their reflexive commentary on the nature of film narrative warrants critical attention.

Other critics look to the many stage versions of *Frankenstein* that preceded the film productions. Albert J. Lavalley explains how nineteenth-century stage conventions influenced the novel's frequent condensations and alterations, resulting in the melodramatic simplifications often repeated in the films.[8] He also provides an illuminating account of various international influences that figured into the cinematic representations.

Steven Forry similarly surveys the stage productions "in an effort to elucidate [Frankenstein's] transformation from a grotesque travesty of nineteenth-century prototypes to a powerful cult image that eclipsed all previous interpretations."[9] He shows how two popular stage versions—Peggy Webling's *Frankenstein: An Adventure in the Macabre* (1927) and John Balderston's 1931 revision of that script—"culminate over one hundred years of dramatizations" and influence subsequent films, most notably the 1931 Universal production.[10]

My examination similarly proposes to explain the somewhat consistent condensation of Shelley's themes, as I examine the mechanics of film adaptation and uncover the particularly cinematic qualities of the story that the films continue to repeat. I will limit my scope to three significant American film versions of *Frankenstein* that represent pregnant moments in the history of the adaptation: the Thomas Edison Company's 1910 production (the first *Frankenstein* film), Universal's 1931 production starring Boris Karloff (the classic Hollywood version, which remains the locus classicus of all *Frankenstein* films), and Kenneth Branagh's 1994 production (which declares its intentions to faithfully represent the novel). For all their differences, these three films similarly exploit the novel's thrill and gore potentials, at the cost of its more subtle arguments about education, sympathy, and social intolerance.

Though the context of each of these films manifests itself in different representations, I maintain that the cinema's origin as a spectacular visual attraction (wherein "falsehood can look so like the truth") largely determines each film's transformation of Mary Shelley's novel. Each film seizes upon the spectacle-potential of the creature in its inevitable condensation of the novel. Indeed, the treatment of the creature in each film ultimately determines the success or failure of the film. Though the 1910 and 1931 films eliminate much of the creature's story, they both manage to offer an appropriately ambiguous and cinematically interesting tale of the creature. The 1994 version restores much of the creature's story, but ironically fails to leave the viewer with an appreciation of the creature's suffering; rather, Victor's story overpowers the creature's as the viewer is bombarded with grandiose scenes of Victor's noble (albeit misguided) attempt to defeat death.

THE ISSUE OF ADAPTATION

The films of *Frankenstein* represent certain theoretical problems of adaptation in general. On the one hand, film theorists wish to maintain that cinema should not be evaluated according to the criteria of the literary critic: Cinema represents a distinct medium, subject to its own grammar and rules of signification.[11] On the other hand, the critic who is familiar with the literary source cannot avoid making comparisons when confronted with a film bearing the same title. And surely such comparisons have merit.

Theorists of intertextuality have argued that texts continually recycle previous texts and have demonstrated that an examination of the various networks of intertextual references reveals much about both the texts in question and their cultural contexts. The usefulness of intertextuality lies in its shifting of focus from the text as an essential, closed entity to the text as one manifestation in a cultural discourse. In his discussion of adaptation, Dudley Andrew argues for an intertextual comparison of films and novels: "Filmmaking, in other words, is always an event in which a system is used and altered in discourse. Adaptation is a peculiar form of discourse but not an unthinkable one. Let us use it not to fight battles over the essence of the media or the inviolability of individual art works. Let us use it as we use all cultural practices, to understand the world from which it comes and the one toward which it points."[12] Andrew points to the cinema's unique status as a translator of "systems." The cinematic adaptation, then, performs the task of translation (and hence transformation) on many levels, ultimately altering the system it used as its source: It translates the people/objects before the camera into images on a screen (transforming the people into "stars," the objects into mise-en-scène), even as it translates the novel into film.

Rather than provide a point-by-point comparison of the films' failures to capture the "essence" of the novel, I will examine the films in their own cinematic terms and their own cultural contexts, heeding Andrew's warning that "the most frequent and most tiresome discussion of adaptation . . . concerns fidelity and transformation."[13] Exploring the *Frankenstein* films' historical contexts—including technological innovations, popular tastes, and aesthetic conventions—reveals much about the cinematic treatments of the novel and largely explains the somewhat consistent condensation of the novel's themes. Like Shelley's novel, the films in question reveal much about the cultures that spawned them, and their treatments of the novel represent significant links in the chain of signification that one might call the discourse of *Frankenstein*. Following Andrew, "[W]e need to study the films themselves as acts of discourse. We need to be sensitive to that discourse and to the forces that motivate it."[14]

THE 1910 EDISON PRODUCTION: CINEMA AS SPECTACLE

The first cinematic production of *Frankenstein* introduces two significant features that characterize many of the subsequent films: the creation scene's propensity for sensationalism and gore, and the moralistic fable of man's intemperate ambition.[15] That the filmmaker would condense the novel into these two features seems logical, considering cinema's status as a life-producing technology (spawn of Edison's ambition),[16] capable of trick effects that render the supernatural real, the false true. As Nestrick states, "If Victor follows in the footsteps of Magnus, Paracelsus, and Agrippa to learn about the 'raising of ghosts or devils,' the first filmmakers also saw themselves in the role of magician."[17] The cinema offered an unprecedented capacity to trick the eye, and the *Frankenstein* story offered an opportunity to exploit that capacity and simultaneously allegorize cinema's status as a death-defying invention.[18]

Histories of early cinema show that Edison's *Frankenstein* arose in a context of vaudeville, peepshows, and fairground entertainments.[19] In 1910, cinema remained largely a proletarian diversion, not yet co-opted by the bourgeois novel and "legitimate" theater. Edison's *Frankenstein* exists on the cusp of cinema's "narrativization," still rife with elements of what Tom Gunning calls the "cinema of attractions": "The cinema of attractions directly solicits spectator attention, inciting visual curiosity, and supplying pleasure through an exciting spectacle. . . . [I]ts energy moves outward towards an acknowledged spectator rather than inward towards the character-based situations essential to classical narrative."[20] Typical of these early spectacles were such Edison productions as the muscle-flexing strongman Sandow and the "serpentine dance" of Annabelle. Soon these spectacles adopted expedient narratives to sustain them, as exemplified by the works of George Méliès, whose classic *A Trip to the Moon* exploits cinema's spectacular capacity to render trick effects. Yet even as these "attractions" began to rely upon narrative, the narrative remained subservient to the ostentatious visual displays.[21] Spectacle certainly dominates the 1910 *Frankenstein,* and character development remains superficial at best.

The 1910 production presents an interesting contradiction: Though the publicity materials for the film assure viewers that the Edison rendition of *Frankenstein* has excised from the novel its "repulsive" potentials, viewers describe a shockingly graphic scene of creation and an equally lurid portrayal of the creature. This contradiction represents the unique status of cinema in 1910: It had not yet learned how to combine the literary with the spectacular, as classic Hollywood cinema would later master. *Frankenstein's* 1910 press materials read: "In making the film the Edison Company has carefully tried to eliminate all the actually repulsive situations and to concentrate its endeavors upon the mystic and psychological problems that are to be found in this weird tale. Wherever, therefore, the film differs from the original story it is purely with the idea of eliminating what would be repulsive to a moving picture audience."[22] Yet the novel represents the "repulsive" appearance of the creature primarily through other characters' reactions. The creature's horrific appearance is important to the novel only to demonstrate his unjust rejection and subsequent evil deeds. It discusses the specifics of the monster's creation only once, and even then it leaves much to the imagination.[23] Yet, subsequent films exploit the gore potentials of the creation to the hilt, raiding graveyards, splattering brains, sewing together body parts. Even the 1910 production is by all accounts more graphically "repulsive" than either the novel or the stage productions.

Like its descendants, the 1910 film places much emphasis on the scene of creation, an episode entirely absent from the novel. As Méliès's experiments with such film techniques as stop-substitution (stopping the camera, rearranging the scene, and then restarting the camera, giving the impression that one object has transformed into another) and superimposition (layering one film image onto another) proved, cinema was the perfect medium for bringing the impossible to life. Wheeler Winston Dixon describes the 1910 creation scene:

> The use of reverse-motion footage allows the skeletal form of the monster to assemble out of nothingness. . . . Watching the monster being created from the slime and mire of a gigantic, steaming tub, we see flesh compose on bone, eyes find sockets, limbs take on human aspect. . . . Despite the Edison Company's professed intention to bowdlerize *Frankenstein,* this is a graphic, harrowing, and convincing sequence. Many exhibitors found the film too horrid to show their patrons: it is easy to see why.[24]

Thus the film exploited both its potential to render the fantastic and its ability to shock audiences with scenes of gore. One 1910 review declared, "no film has ever been released that can surpass it in power to fascinate an audience. The scene in the laboratory in which the monster seemed gradually to assume human semblance is probably the most remarkable ever committed to a film."[25]

With the Edison production, the creature begins his transformation from a sympathetic (albeit unsightly) outcast to a horrifying, bloodthirsty monster. Like numerous previous stage productions, the film renders the creature mute, vastly decreasing his chances of gaining audience sympathies by telling his own story. The film differs from the stage productions, though, in visualizing the monster. The creature of the film is not just unattractive and bizarre but hideously misshapen and menacing. Steven Forry describes the creature: "His Kabuki-like expression, deformed visage, and protruding bulbous eyes instill fright, and his misshapen body, malformed—or unformed—hands, patches of mangy hair sprouting from cadaverous arms, and tattered clothing all suggest a Creature from beyond the grave. Once again, Shelley's intentions are sacrificed to the exigencies of mass appeal."[26] As Forry indicates, "mass appeal" dictates the creature's transformation— though the production claims to render the "psychological problems" of *Frankenstein,* accounts of the film situate it firmly in the tradition of a cinema of attractions.

As one would imagine, the first cinematic production of *Frankenstein* was considerably influenced by the various nineteenth-century stage dramatizations that preceded it. Though the film is of course silent, it does rely upon musical pieces popularly used in the stage productions. Perhaps more significant, though, is the film's use of the melodramatic convention of stock characters: Elizabeth becomes the damsel in distress, while Victor Frankenstein embodies the hero who must overcome his tragic flaw (excessive ambition) in order to restore a harmonious union by marrying Elizabeth. Further, Frankenstein's bumbling assistant, who does not appear in the novel, first appears in one of the stage dramatizations, representing "the classic servant figure of popular comedy."[27] Most significantly, the conventions of melodrama require the tidy moral of "man playing God" that has been the hallmark of most cinematic adaptations.

Edison's brief, one-reel film narrows the scope of *Frankenstein*'s themes to focus on the monstrous consequences of overextended ambition. Subsequent films of *Frankenstein* likewise focus on this theme, often specifying the monstrous consequences of overextended technologies. The 1910 film uses a sophisticated film technology to embody this theme, in one of the film's most interesting scenes: We learn that the creature is only a doppelgänger of Victor Frankenstein; when Victor forgets his ambitions and remembers his love for Elizabeth, the creature will disappear. This climactic scene occurs as Victor gazes into a mirror only to see the monster's image; then, gradually, "under the effect of love and his better nature,"[28] the monster's image fades and Frankenstein's image is restored. This scene exemplifies the filmmakers' use of cinema's unique ability to immediately capture a complex theme that would require much spilled ink to establish in print. This theme is in fact planted in the novel; Mary Shelley goes to great pains to establish that Victor and the creature are in fact two sides of the same coin. Yet the 1910 film eloquently portrays the doppelgänger theme in one "magical" superimposition.

This fable of the mad scientist becomes refigured in the classic Hollywood film 20 years later. Yet by 1930, cinema had developed its own elaborate conventions that enabled a more harmonious mixture of narrative and spectacle.

Universal's 1931 Production: Hollywood Horror

By the 1930s, the Hollywood moviemaking industry had established an elaborate system in which the major film studios functioned like assembly-line factories, turning out profitable products at the rate of almost one film a week.[29] Each of the major studios developed its own "speciality" genres, enabling more efficient, highly regulated productions. Universal Studios narrowed its production scope to concentrate on moderate-budget, formulaic genres with wide popular appeal. The greatest of these proved to be the horror film.

The genre formula of the Hollywood horror film conceals the potentially discordant combination of spectacle and narrative that remained a problem in the 1910 production. By cleverly suturing together the nineteenth-century stage melodrama, the Gothic novel, contemporary aesthetic sensibilities, and cinematic innovations, Universal Studios created a genre in which spectacular effects complemented the narrative. One could even say that spectacle exploited the narrative. Hollywood producers quickly learned that the public would line up, money in hand, to experience the thrills and horrors of the cinema, even in the midst of the Depression. The Hollywood publicity machine promised via posters and advertisements to "surpass in thrills even *Dracula*."

Another publicity stunt involved the warning from Edward Van Sloan (who plays Dr. Waldman in the film) that appears before the film begins. Mr. Van Sloan directly addresses the theater audience:

> Mr. Carl Laemmle feels it would be a little unkind to present this picture without a word of warning. We are about to unfold the story of Frankenstein, a man of science who sought to create life after his own image, without reckoning on God. It is one of the strangest tales ever told. It deals with the two great mysteries of creation—life and death. I think it will thrill you. It may shock you. It may even . . . horrify . . . you. So, if any of you feel you'd not care to subject your nerves to such a strain, now's your chance to . . . er . . . well, we warned you.

This speech is interesting for several reasons: Unlike the introduction to the 1910 film found in the *Edison Kinetogram,* this introductory speech offers no pretensions of literary adaptation and instead openly declares an intention to thrill; its anomalous direct address to the theater spectators confuses the boundaries between "film-world" and "audience-world," which contributes to the thrill-potential; and it states its intentions and establishes audience expectations much as Shelley's own preface(s) did for the novel.

The film continues to establish its intentions and reveal its sources of inspiration even as the credits roll. The background scenery for the credits displays a whirling collage of eyeballs and superimposes the image of an ominous, bald, pointed head. These two images, in fact, reference two German horror films that preceded Universal's *Frankenstein* and greatly influenced its presentation of Shelley's themes. The whirling collage of eyes first appears in Fritz Lang's *Metropolis* (1926), another science-fiction narrative that involves the creation of a life, and the ominous head resembles the now legendary image of Max Schreck in Friedrich Murnau's expressionist masterpiece *Nosferatu* (1922). The incorporation of these images is a cinematic "tipping of the hat" to German expressionism, the dark, silent genre that greatly influenced the Hollywood horror film, most evident in the mise-en-scène.[30] The opening graveyard scene of the 1931 film, for example, displays the off-kilter sets and chiaroscuro lighting typical of expressionist sets initiated by the groundbreaking *Cabinet of Dr. Caligari* (1919).

In referencing these classic German horror films and prominently displaying the eyes even as the credits roll, *Frankenstein* comments on its own status as a predominantly visual discourse. In fact, much of the film's dialogue references the power of sight, evoking the cliché "seeing is believing." When Henry Frankenstein (the scriptwriters changed the name from Victor to Henry) leaves for his laboratory, his pining fiancée Elizabeth worries about his extended absence and decides that she must see him in order to determine the status of their relationship. She receives letters from Henry but laments, "I've read this over and over again . . . they're just words . . . I can't understand." She reads a portion of Henry's letter that hints at his covert activities: "There is no one here. Prying eyes can't peer into my secret." Elizabeth resolves, "I must see him." Whereas the 1910 film remained ambivalent about its visual rendering of a literary classic, the classic Hollywood film knows that its chief asset (i.e., selling point) is its capacity to stage spectacular effects and portray the creature's horrifying countenance.

In addition to the intertextual references to German expressionism, the film introduces other innovative ways to visually capture elements of the novel. For example, after the monster innocently (and fatally) tosses little María into the water, we see María's father carrying her limp body through the village. These parallel scenes suggest associations: Like the creature, the father walks narcotized, with arms outstretched, carrying the girl. Yet whereas the scene by the lake is highly staged, the village scene represents an aesthetic of realism, filmed in a long take by a somewhat shaky camera, incorporating realistic images and sounds of the crowds gathered in the streets to celebrate Frankenstein's wedding. In fact, the scene anticipates the famed street scenes of De Sica's neorealist masterpiece *The Bicycle Thief* (1948). This cinematic handling reinforces the real consequences and tragedy of the fanciful creature's misguided actions.

The film builds toward the creation, wherein the creature reveals himself in calculated gradations. The famed scene resembles the creation of the robot in *Metropolis* (1926): Both Frankenstein's creature and Rotwang's robot receive life from electrical currents conducted through shining orbs. Strapped to a metal platform, Frankenstein's creature slowly descends from the heights of the laboratory where he has received electrical currents from a flash of lightning. A turgid movement of his hand first signifies life. The audience's initial sight of the creature's visage occurs as he appears in a doorway from behind, then slowly turns to reveal himself, heightening the dramatic effect.

The face he reveals is, of course, the now legendary metal-clamped, Neanderthal forehead and bolted neck of Boris Karloff. The creature remains mute, as in the 1910 film. The 1931 creature is given a criminal's brain, which should clarify any ambiguity regarding his evil nature. Yet, despite his muteness and despite his criminal brain, Karloff's creature remains one of the most sympathetic monsters rendered on film. The reasons for his sympathetic portrayal are complex. The creature's makeup largely resembled the makeup of Cesare from *The Cabinet of Dr. Caligari,* yet Cesare remains a much more menacing creature.

The film's plot—often inconsistent with the switched brain episode— contributes to the creature's sympathetic portrayal. We see little evidence of innate evil tendencies in the creature. In fact, his initial violence results from Fritz's provocation with torches. The only innate quality we see in the creature, in fact, is his fear of fire—an innately *human* quality that makes the final scene of his destruction all the more affecting. Many of his further outbursts are similarly provoked, with the exception, of course, of the little girl's drowning, which is clearly accidental. The creature assumes that the girl, like the flowers, will float in the water as he playfully tosses her in. These scenes problematize any tidy declaration of the creature's evil nature.

But perhaps the most significant—and most speculative—source of the creature's humanity comes from the actor himself. Karloff's earnest counte- nance and his careful gestures render the monster almost lovable. He is a far cry from Shelley's eloquent and benevolent creature who actively seeks the love of others, yet something gentle and tragic emerges in his awkwardness. His maladroit gestures seem to reach toward acceptance. Even within the tightly regulated Hollywood studio, cinema's visual capabilities can remain somewhat ungovernable and unpredictable, as a certain actor can elicit com- plex and varied audience responses, often altering the film's narrative inten- tions. Even as the audience's initial introduction to the creature is directed to incite horror, most critics agree that Karloff eventually brings a tragically human quality to the creature, causing ambivalence in spectators' responses to the final scene of his violent demise. It is this ambiguous nature of the crea- ture that makes the film successful. Like the Edison production, the Universal production provides a cinematically complex creature to reflect the themati- cally complex creature of Shelley's novel.

Frankenstein (1931), like *Frankenstein* (1910), incorporates the conven- tions of nineteenth-century melodrama, which require a hero, a sensational climax, and a happy ending. Whereas the creature accounts for the film's excessive, sensational scenes, Henry Frankenstein remains the center of the narrative. By centering the narrative around Frankenstein and shaping it into a story about one man's hubris, the film greatly simplifies the novel's themes and eliminates the complexities of the creature. The creature's unjust suffer- ing, his lack of and desire for education, and the other characters' varying responses to both the creature and each other recede in order that the "man playing God" theme can emerge, eliminating thematic ambiguity.[31]

Despite the crude plot alterations, the film remains laudable for Karloff's careful portrayal of the creature and for the expressive appropriation of uniquely cinematic flourishes. The film indicates from the beginning, through Van Sloan's preface and the credit sequence, that this is a story about seeing. The film recognizes its own capability to exploit the story's visual potentials. At the very least, one must acknowledge that the film honestly exposes its intentions to render visual thrills. Nowhere does it assume literary pretentions. The case of Kenneth Branagh's 1994 version of *Frankenstein,* however, remains an entirely different matter.

KENNETH BRANAGH'S 1994 VERSION: PRETENTIOUS NOSTALGIA

The 1994 production *Mary Shelley's Frankenstein* might have been titled "Kenneth Branagh's Frankenstein" or, as James Wolcott suggests, "Kenneth Branagh's ego run amok."[32] Though the film's publicity promised to restore Shelley's novel, capturing the subtleties neglected by previous films, the literary pretentions remain just that, pretentions. Despite the occasional inclusion of original plot elements (e.g., the frame of Walton's sea expedition, the creature's stay with the De Lacey's), the result is less a restoration than a symptom of both its nostalgia-ridden cultural context and its ostentatious director/star.

Mary Shelley's Frankenstein arose as a specific genre of "period films" had become popular. These films, initiated by the famed Merchant/Ivory productions, arose as a backlash against the popular action thrillers characterized by huge budgets and overblown special effects. These "period dramas" appropriate the ethos of "high art," frequently employing British stage actors rather than American movie stars. *Mary Shelley's Frankenstein,* directed by and starring Shakespearean stage actor Kenneth Branagh, attempts to update and upgrade the horror genre to the realm of such films; yet, it fails where many of the other "literary" films succeed. Whereas other literary adaptations, such as *Howard's End* (1992), *Remains of the Day* (1993), or even *Bram Stoker's Dracula* (1992), are both sensationally melodramatic and tolerable, *Mary Shelley's Frankenstein* is burdensomely sensational and at times, even considered solely in terms of the horror genre, unbearable.

Like Edison's 1910 *Kinetogram* and Van Sloan's 1931 warning, *Mary Shelley's Frankenstein* employs a preface to direct audience expectations. This time, however, the preface consists of an excerpt from Mary Shelley's own preface to her novel. Unlike the 1931 film, this film is framed as "the real thing." Yet Mary Shelley's words are carefully selected: "I busied myself to think of a story . . . which would speak to the mysterious fears of our nature, and awaken thrilling horror—one to make the reader dread to look round, to curdle the blood, and quicken the beatings of the heart." Consider how the following words (found in the novel's original preface, written by Percy Shelley) would alter the film's introduction:

> The event on which the interest of the story depends is exempt from the disadvantages of a mere tale of spectres or enchantment. It was recommended by the novelty of the situations which it develops; and, however impossible as a physical fact, affords a point of view to the imagination for the delineating of human passions more comprehensive and commanding than any which the ordinary relations of existing events can yield.[33]

Clearly, Branagh chooses an excerpt that will allow him to revel in scenes of gore, as evident in the film's opening scene, which shows the violent and bloody slaying of the sled dogs. Though Branagh promises Mary Shelley's *Frankenstein,* we see from the outset that he will similarly pillage the novel to suit his own purposes. This appropriation of the novel is not in itself grievous (on the contrary, it is inevitable); however, Branagh's lofty declarations render the predictable transformations particularly distasteful.

Though the monster (played by Robert De Niro) retains many of the characteristics of the novel's creature (most notably, a voice), his potential for engendering thematic complexities is overshadowed by Victor Frankenstein's overblown, melodramatic scenes. De Niro offers a sensitive portrayal of the creature as an abandoned child, longing for acceptance and affection. Yet, each of his scenes is followed by a grandiose scene centered on Victor. One critic commented that "Branagh plays the hapless doctor obsessed as a Marlovian figure, to whom he adds his *Henry V* modus operandi: big hammy gestures, exaggerated emotions and loud speech."[34] One might even suggest that the creature exists only as an excuse for Victor to labor about his laboratory shirtless, as he does throughout a considerable portion of the film. Unlike the 1910 or 1931 films, the 1994 version foregrounds Victor's role at the expense of the creature's.

Perhaps the most disappointing aspect of the 1994 film involves its unmotivated and uninteresting camerawork. In this respect, both the 1910 and the 1931 films remain far more innovative for their times in translating written language into film language. The 1994 film resorts to baroque camerawork that attempts to enact in style what the film lacks in substance, namely its claim to "high art." The proliferation of 360-degree tracking shots creates a profoundly dizzying effect and, far from enhancing the narrative, actually distracts from it.

Another aspect of the film that appears to restore Shelley's original plot but in fact distorts it involves the establishment of Victor's motive for creating the monster. The novel, in fact, provides little explanation for Victor's actions. Victor abandons home and family to throw himself into solitary, obsessive labors. The reader draws a parallel to Walton's obsessive search for the North Pole: Walton wants to go where no man has gone before. Similarly,

Victor wants to create life because no man has done it before. Whereas the novel questions Victor's pompous motives, the film goes to great lengths to show that Victor's ambitions are indeed noble. Yet, once again, the film goes too far and lapses into sentimentality as Victor writhes in agony over the untimely death of his mother. He vows to defeat death. This vow haunts not only Victor but also the viewer, for it enables a most unfortunate and unintentionally over-the-top twist in the film's narrative conclusion. After the creature murders Elizabeth, Victor uses his forbidden knowledge to reanimate her, as the film enlists yet another addition to compete with De Niro's creature. The restored Elizabeth appears as grotesquely pieced-together as the first creature. Yet, upon her reanimation, Victor and his scabrous bride waltz majestically around the laboratory (captured in the ubiquitous 360-degree tracking shots). With this scene, any dignity the film might have salvaged is eradicated. Victor, far from appearing noble or even sympathetic, is by now merely laughable.

CONCLUSION

This examination of three film representations of Shelley's novel illuminates some specific problems of the literary adaptation. Certainly, films should not be critiqued solely according to literary standards. And, as Branagh's film shows, an attempt to faithfully represent a novel can prove monstrous indeed. Cinema must rely on its own devices to visually engender the subtleties we often find in novels.

As an artistic practice, cinema is uniquely bound by a variety of forces— cultural, technological, aesthetic, and economic—that differentiate it in many ways from literature. With every technological innovation comes another possibility for rendering a narrative, a possibility that is often exploited with varying results—for example, the expressionistic mise-en-scène enhances Universal's *Frankenstein,* whereas the 360-degree tracking shots distract the viewer in the 1994 *Frankenstein.* In addition, films cost a great deal to produce and must therefore guarantee a popular response (especially in Hollywood cinema). Filmmakers rely on genres that have already proven themselves and thus guarantee an audience—Universal's *Frankenstein* was billed as a horror film, Branagh's *Frankenstein* as a "period" horror film— but genres, of course, demand specific renderings of the narrative that shift points of emphasis and alter the original novel. The filmmaker, then, is bound by a wide variety of determinants that often increase the difficulties of adapting literature for the screen.

All three films demonstrate the continued presence of a "cinema of attractions," as each adaptation exploits its own devices to vivify the spectacular aspects of the novel. In fact, each film can be judged according to the efficacy of these devices. Though the promotional materials from the 1910 version suggest a guilty conscience on the part of the filmmakers, its sensational creation scene and uniquely cinematic rendering of the doppelgänger theme comprise a complex and effective portrayal of the creature. The 1931 Hollywood production represents a more harmonious marriage of narrative and spectacle, as the two combine to form the genre of the classic horror film. Openly declaring its status as a primarily visual discourse, the film uses its cinematic potentials to successfully capture Shelley's ambiguous creature. Despite its lofty claims, the 1994 version grows dizzy with its own nobility as Victor's exalted motive overshadows the creature's story and undermines the film's potential to provide a technologically sophisticated and thematically complex rendering of the creature.

Notes

1.   Walter Benjamin, "The Task of the Translator," in *Illuminations* (New York: Schocken Books, 1968), 73.

2.   Mary Shelley, *Frankenstein: A Case Study in Contemporary Criticism,* ed. Johanna M. Smith (New York: St. Martin's Press, 1992), 85.

3.   Donald F. Glut, *The Frankenstein Catalog* (Jefferson: McFarland & Company, 1984).

4.   Wheeler Winston Dixon, "The Films of *Frankenstein,*" in *Approaches to Teaching Shelley's Frankenstein,* ed. Stephen C. Behrendt (New York: The Modern Language Association of America, 1990), 178.

5.   Harriet E. Margolis, "Lost Baggage, or the Hollywood Sidetrack," in *Approaches to Teaching Shelley's "Frankenstein,"* ed. Stephen C. Behrendt (New York: The Modern Language Association of America, 1990), 290.

6.   Margolis, "Lost Baggage," 165.

7.   William Nestrick, "Coming to Life: *Frankenstein* and the Nature of Film Narrative," in *The Endurance of "Frankenstein": Essays on Mary Shelley's Novel,* ed. George Levine and U. C. Knoepflmacher (Berkeley: University of California Press, 1979), 294.

8.   Albert J. Lavalley, "The Stage and Film Children of Frankenstein: A Survey," in *The Endurance of "Frankenstein": Essays on Mary Shelley's Novel,* ed. George Levine and U. C. Knoepflmacher (Berkeley: University of California Press, 1979), 243–89.

9.   Steven Earl Forry, *Hideous Progenies: Dramatizations of "Frankenstein" from Mary Shelley to Present* (Philadelphia: University of Pennsylvania Press, 1990), 80.

10.   Forry, Hideous Progenies, 100.

11.   Consider, for example, Alexandre Astruc's 1948 proclamation that cinema should cease attempting to reproduce the novel and become its own art form. This proclamation sounded a clarion call for the French New Wave. Astruc writes, "The cinema is quite simply becoming a means of expression, just as all the other arts have before it, and in particular painting and the novel. After having been successively a fairground attraction, an amusement analogous to boulevard theatre, or a means of preserving the images of an era, it is gradually becoming a language. By language, I mean a form in which and by which an artist can express his thoughts, however abstract they may be, or translate his obsessions exactly as he does in a contemporary essay or novel. That is why I would like to call this new age of cinema the age of caméra-stylo." (Quoted in James Monaco, "Introduction," in *The New Wave: Truffaut, Charbrol, Rohmer, Rivette* [New York: Oxford University Press, 1976], 5.)

12. James Dudley Andrew, *Concepts in Film Theory* (Oxford and New York: Oxford University Press, 1984), 106.

13. Andrew, *Concepts,* 100.

14. Andrew, *Concepts,* 106.

15. Since 1980 Edison's *Frankenstein* has been on the American Film Inventory (A.F.I.) lost film list. The film does exist but has not been officially registered in any archive. The copy is owned by a private collector and has been transferred to videotape.

16. In his discussion of nineteenth-century conceptions of the robot, Peter Wollen likens Frankenstein's monster to "Edison's Future Eve" as conceived in Villiers de L'Isle Adam's novel *Ève Future* (1886). In this science fiction novel, Thomas Edison creates human life. Prophetically, this work anticipates Edison's 1891 invention of the kinetoscope, a peepshow device that for the first time reanimates human motion and, in Edison's words, "does for the eye what the phonograph does for the ear." Wollen explores the gender implications of Edison's fictional robot creation which prefigures the cinema in *Raiding the Icebox: Reflections on Twentieth-Century Culture* (Bloomington: Indiana University Press, 1993), 41–47.

17. Nestrick, "Coming to Life," 291.

18. In "Charles Baudelair versus Doctor Frankenstein," film historian Noël Burch discusses journalists' responses in 1895 to the first projected moving pictures. In these responses he finds a consistent affirmation of cinema's capacity to defeat death. One reviewer writes, "Speech has already been collected and reproduced, now life is collected and reproduced. For example, it will be possible to see one's loved ones active long after they have passed away." Another writes, "When these cameras are made available to the public, when everyone can photograph their dear ones, no longer in a motionless form but in their movements, their activity, their familiar gestures, with words on their lips, death will have ceased to be absolute" (Life to Those Shadows [Berkeley: University of California Press, 1990], 20–21).

19. See, for example, Charles Musser's discussion, "Thomas Edison and the Amusement World," in *The Emergence of Cinema* (Berkeley: University of California Press, 1990), 55–89.

20. Tom Gunning, "The Cinema of Attractions: Early Film, Its Spectator and the Avant-Garde," in *Early Cinema: Space Frame Narrative,* ed. Thomas Elsaesser and Adam Barker (London: BFI, 1990), 58–59.

21. Gunning writes of these attractions that "the role narrative plays is quite different from in traditional film. Méliès himself declared in discussing his working method: 'As for the scenario, the fable, or tale, I only consider it at the end. I can state that the scenario constructed in this manner has no importance since I use it merely as a pretext for the stage effects, the tricks, or for a nicely arranged tableau' " (Gunning, "The Cinema of Attraction," 56–57).

22. The page of the Edison Kinetogram (15 March 1910) from which this text derives is reproduced in Forry, *Hideous Progenies,* 82.

23. Victor tells of his labors: "I pursued nature to her hiding-places. Who shall conceive the horrors of my secret toil, as I dabbled among the unhallowed damps of the grave, or tortured the living animal to animate the lifeless clay? My limbs now tremble, and my eyes swim with the remembrance. . . . I collected bones from charnel-houses; and disturbed, with profane fingers, the tremendous secrets of the human frame. . . . The dissecting room and the slaughterhouse furnished many of my materials. . . ." Shelley, *Frankenstein,* 56.

24. Dixon, "Films of *Frankenstein,*"167.

25. This review is excerpted in Donald F. Glut's *The Frankenstein Legend* (Metuchen, N.J.: The Scarecrow Press, 1973), 63.

26. Forry, *Hideous Progenies,* 81.

27. Lavalley, "Stage and Film Children," 250.

28.   As quoted from the synopsis of the March 15, 1910 *Kinetogram*. See Forry, *Hideous Progenies*, 84.

29.   For a detailed discussion of filmmaking in an era of the factory-studios, as well as an account of Universal's co-opting of the horror genre, see Thomas Schatz's *The Genius of the System: Hollywood Filmmaking in the Studio Era* (New York: Pantheon Books, 1988).

30.   David Cook writes of German expressionism: "the screen of German Expressionism was indeed a haunted one; but its terrors were those of morbid psychological states and troubled dreams rather than the more concrete horrors that Hollywood's Universal Studios was to offer us in the thirties (although Universal's horror films were the lineal descendants of Expressionism, created in many cases by the same artists). The nightmarishly distorted decor of German Expressionist films and their creation of *stimmung* ("mood") through shifting chiaroscuro lighting were expressive of the disturbed mental and emotional states they sought to portray" (*A History of Narrative Film*, Second Edition [New York: W. W. Norton, 1990], 119).

31.   For a discussion of *Frankenstein*'s cinematic evolution into a cautionary tale of the dangers of breaching God's natural order, see Stephen Jay Gould, "The Monster's Human Nature: When Filmmakers Adapt Books for the Screen, They Often Dumb Down the Subtle Themes," *Natural History*, July 1994, 14–21. Gould proposes that "Hollywood knows only one theme in making monster movies," that this theme begins with its 1931 treatment of *Frankenstein* and continues into such contemporary movies as *Jurassic Park*.

32.   James Wolcott, "Nice Guys Finish Last," *New Yorker*, February 12, 1996, 85.

33.   Shelley, *Frankenstein*, 24.

34.   Amanda Lipman, "Mary Shelley's *Frankenstein* [reviewed]," *Sight and Sound*, December 1994, 51.

Mary Shelley: Romance and Reality

EMILY W. SUNSTEIN

One of Mary Shelley's valid prophecies turned out to be the predilection of her alter ego in *The Last Man,* Lionel Verney, for historical figures who had "been traduced, or about whom clung obscurity and doubt." For she is a striking example of a posthumous reputation bent out of shape by admirers and, more lastingly, by traducers.

This situation derives from Mary Shelley's association with Shelley, and is loaded with instructive ironies. Whether, as Keats said, writers lead allegorical lives, the issue in the Shelleys' case has been the nature of the allegory. Mary Shelley's daughter-in-law, Lady Shelley, has borne the brunt for liberal Victorian sentimentalization of Shelley, and she could likewise be charged about Mary Shelley. But this obscures the fact that both idealizers and defamers of controversial figures select qualities relevant to larger arguments of their own times. For nineteenth-century conservatives the Shelleys exemplified immoral, subversive views enacted in a liaison that drove his first wife to suicide. Shelley engendered his own legend in reaction to such opprobrium; Mary Shelley, Hunt, the Cambridge Apostles, and innumerable others developed aspects of it to counter his critics, and after her death in 1851 liberal Victorians incorporated her in the legend—before her adoring children, themselves liberals, spearheaded the cause. Sentimentality, moreover, can be an expression of genuine feelings and longing for the ideal that made strong men weep over Rousseau's and Richardson's novels in the eighteenth century, Dickens's in the nineteenth, and that manifests itself today in tragic situations, fictional and real.

As Victorian liberals apologized for or overlooked Shelley's radicalism, so they excused Mary Shelley's liaison with him and her early radicalism, romanticized their union, took for granted her punishment by society, and ignored the social and political content of her works. Indeed, progressives also romanticized the pair. A few weeks after Mary Shelley's death, George Lewes's and Thornton Hunt's *Leader* published "Lines on the Death of Mrs. Shelley" by

From Emily W. Sunstein, *Mary Shelley: Romance and Reality.* Copyright © 1989 by Emily W. Sunstein. Pages 387–403, 455–56. Reprinted by permission of the Johns Hopkins University Press.

"E.W.L.," eulogizing her as a genius among blessed immortals; Shelley's beloved, inspiration, and inconsolable mourner:

> Another, yet another, snatch'd away,
> By death's grasp, from among us! Yet one more
> Of Heaven's anointed band,—a child of genius,—
> A peeress, girt about with magic powers,—
> That could at will evoke from her wild thought
> Spirits unearthly, monster-shaped . . .
>
> Mourn her not, Earth! her spirit, disentrall'd,
> No more shall droop in lonely widowhood . . .
>
> Mourn her not, Earth! She is at rest with him,
> The mighty minstrel of the impassion'd lay,—
> The Poet-martyr of a creed too bright,
> Whose lofty hymnings were so oft attuned
> Unto the music of her own pure name,
> The theme and inspiration of his lyre . . .

This was Sir Percy and Lady Shelley's favorite eulogy. The couple could have lived a peaceful uncomplicated existence in "Moon-country," as neighbors called the coastscape near Bournemouth. Their spacious Boscombe Manor was sited in woods that thinned near the heathered cliff tops into dwarfed wind-slanted thickets, with hillocks of sand dunes descending to the sea. Jane became a yachtswoman, sailing with Percy off Bournemouth, and in 1853 took her first cruise with him to the Mediterranean, which he described in a newspaper article. They made a number of such voyages until she hurt her neck in a boating accident. Between 1854, when Percy was elected to England's premier sailing club, the Royal Yacht Squadron, and 1887, he owned a total of ten cruising yachts and boats for cup-racing, two of which, *Genevra* and *Queen Mab,* he named for his father's poems.[1] Jane encouraged his dilettante talents in a perfect vocation; he built a beautiful little theater at Boscombe, painted the curtain with a scene of Casa Magni, and put on plays, sometimes writing book and music, in which he and Jane acted. In time, their stage productions grew so professional that they gave benefits for charities at their Chelsea house on the Embankment—and were legally enjoined to cease. Being unable to have children, they adopted Jane's niece Bessie Florence Gibson.

An endearing eccentric in conventional surroundings, Percy had the shrewdness of an innocent child, a quaint wit, and "a curious strain of a somewhat furtive, illusive, inarticulate fantasy, almost as far removed from the everyday world as was his father's soaring poetic imagination."[2] At one point he retired to Chelsea in some disgrace, having painted the ribs of several greyhounds white and let them run around the area looking like skeletons. He was also prone to melancholia (his half sister, Ianthe Esdaile, ended a melancholic recluse), "vigorously met" by Jane.[3]

Their mission, however, for which Jane rightly said they suffered much, was the Shelleys. Jane had a romantic temperament of the Trelawny type; she was a fierce lover and hater who heightened and masked reality, though she did not make things up as Trelawny did. But Percy felt just as strongly about his parents, and if he let his wife take the lead and had a drier tone, they were partners. Add to this the couple's unworldliness, and the fact that the more, sometimes unscrupulous, opposition their tactics evoked, the more fanatic Jane grew.

The ugly incident at St. Peter's over burying Mary Shelley started them off in a beautifying reaction. They commissioned Henry Weekes for a large memorial sculpture à la Michelangelo's *Pieta*: Mary on one knee clasping Shelley's drowned body. St. Peter's refused to install the work; they placed it at nearby Christchurch Priory. Jane made her boudoir into a museum displaying relics, manuscripts, and portraits, an entirely appropriate undertaking if she had not called it "the sanctum" and expected admittees to be church-reverent. Jane Hogg thought this ludicrous, yet she herself stood up and bowed whenever Shelley's name was spoken.

Percy and Jane made a survey of Mary Shelley's great cache of manuscripts, her own, her parents', and Shelley's, a trove in private hands perhaps unequaled in the world. Their priorities approximated hers: first, a life of Shelley, which would serve as well as a partial biography of her until they authorized a complete life; then a biography of Godwin incorporating and modeled upon her unfinished memoir of her father, in which she had also begun to rehabilitate her mother; and additional restitution of Wollstonecraft in some form.

Near the sixth anniversary of Mary Shelley's death, in early 1857, they invited Hogg, Peacock, and Trelawny to a reunion, in order to choose the Shelley biographer who would present the poet according to their own lights. Trelawny declined to attend (and began his own book); Peacock was too cool, and besides mentioned that Mary had sometimes annoyed him in the early days of their association. Hogg was entrusted with the task, assuring Percy that he would give Mary, whose life and Shelley's had been "blended," due importance. His first two volumes, ending before Shelley's separation from Harriet, came out in 1858, a vivid but facetious, self-servingly manipulated work that so offended Percy and Jane they refused Hogg access to their papers for the sequel. Peacock agreed with that prohibition for reasons of his own: Hogg intended to hint that Peacock had been Harriet's lover—and had already so misinformed Boscombe Manor.

That same year, Trelawny published his *Recollections of the Last Days of Byron and Shelley*, in which Mary Shelley is a highly gifted personage, attrac-

tive woman, and a deeply loving if individual mate to an eccentric genius.*
Percy and Jane were quite pleased. It would be a quarter of a century before
they were to authorize another biographer, however. Instead, they decided to
publish *Shelley Memorials,* a biography of both Shelleys, with selected papers.
Jane was editor-in-chief; as her aid they engaged twenty-four-year-old
Richard Garnett, who had been working with Anthony Panizzi, Librarian of
the British Museum, for eight years. A precocious scholar, Garnett had much
to learn about public relations. Leigh Hunt and John Touchet also helped
with *Shelley Memorials,* which was published in 1859.

There is a natural antagonism between family and other parties whose
job or pleasure it is to ferret out problematic information, or who must
defend themselves. *Shelley Memorials* combined illumination, defense, manipulation of truth, and hagiography, and set off a long train of consequences. It
was not too far off the mark to state, for example, that while Shelley never
deviated from championing "the poorer classes," Mary's sympathy, encour-
agement, and entire "self-devotion" divested him of hostile bitterness in his
attacks on social and political abuses. ("The editor, Lady Shelley, is quite a liberal," observed Crabb Robinson.)[4] But the work minimized the Shelleys' marital problems, and Christianized his religious views. As for Mary Shelley's
career after his death, *Shelley Memorials* skimmed over it, leaving out its het-
erodox aspects, while noting her "noble energy of character" in struggles with
poverty and loneliness, and her major works, with expurgated correspondence and extracts from her journals.

In the vital matter of Shelley's treatment of Harriet Shelley, *Shelley
Memorials,* like Hogg's life of Shelley, defended the poet by implying that she
had been unfaithful to him. Boscombe Manor had Shelley's letters so stating,
plus Hogg's "information" about Peacock and Harriet, but published no
specifics—as Mary and Shelley had not—to protect Harriet's daughter,
Ianthe Esdaile. *Shelley Memorials* also duplicitously reinforced Hunt's "fiction,"
which Mary had deplored, that she and Shelley began their liaison only after
the separation.

Infuriated, and threatened, the aged Peacock published his corrective
"Memoirs of Shelley" in *Fraser's Magazine* between 1858 and 1860, in which
he introduced a fiction of his own: that Shelley had been happy with Harriet
until he met Mary, and that Harriet had been a faithful wife. He went so far
as to include Eliza Westbrook's deposition for the Chancery court suit of
1817, stating that Mary had "cohabited" with Shelley before the separation,
and Shelley's letter telling Eliza that she could excusably consider Mary the
cause of Harriet's ruin.

---

*Though Trelawny had been responsible for the unseaworthy design of Shelley's *Don Juan,* in this
work he blamed it entirely on Edward Williams, even declaring that he himself had objected to it.

Now Jane felt engaged in holy war, and was probably worried as well about her susceptible husband's distress. A believer in spiritualism, she "received" messages from Mary Shelley in automatic writing: "Don't mind Mr. Peacock—he wont live another year you will get more letters more papers by waiting dear Janey. . . . Dear Love Never pray me to come to you but I charitably wait for our meeting . . .[5]

Meantime, in *Fifty Years' Recollections* Cyrus Reding had praised Mary Shelley's truthfulness and assistance for the biographical sketch of Shelley he wrote for his 1829 edition of Shelley's poems. Another of her old friends, Eliza Rennie, published *Traits of Character* with a chapter on Mary Shelley in widowhood, in the liberal Victorian mold; emphasizing her character and integrity, her sadness and shrinking from notice, her "correct" behavior, her supposed belief that publishing was "unfeminine," and giving no glimpse of her complexity, depth, or ambition.

In 1863 the radical Thornton Hunt gave a truer and yet partly unfortunate picture of Mary Shelley in the *Atlantic Monthly.* "She was, indeed, herself a woman of extraordinary power, of heart as well as head," he wrote, with her mother's magnaminity, "a masculine capacity for study" all her life, command of history, imaginative power and daring originality in her fiction. Moreover, "While the biographers of Shelley are chargeable with suppression, the most straightforward and frank of all of them is Mary . . . while she has nobly abstained from telling those things that other persons should have supplied . . ."[6] Informed by his parents, aided by Lady Shelley, who was avid to get back at Peacock despite Ianthe Esdaile's feelings, and making deductions from Mary Shelley's fiction, Thornton gave the most accurate story of Shelley and Harriet yet published.

He affirmed both Mary Shelley's community of spirit with Shelley and her "stubborn" independent outlook. But he reported what he had absorbed from his father, Leigh Hunt (Thornton had been about seven when he knew the Shelleys as a couple); that in youth she was physically unattractive, a bit of a sloven, given to "peevishness" (Leigh Hunt had referred to her "irritability" in his condolence letter to Sir Percy), and not fully appreciative of Shelley until after his death, though he added that Shelley had not fully appreciated her either.

Furthermore, he suggested that her education had been spotty, making her subsequent achievement overly dependent on Shelley and adding a new dimension of credence to her own self-denigration in that regard. Here Thornton was misled by Lady Shelley, who out of hatred for the Clairmonts claimed to one and all that young Mary had been a Cinderella, relegated to household drudgery while Claire enjoyed all the advantages. Thus, Thornton wrote, Shelley was Mary's "great school." And thus, noting that *Frankenstein*'s "leading idea has been ascribed to her husband," Thornton said only, "but, I am sure, unduly." In 1876, the "fact" that Godwin had neglected her education was established in *William Godwin* by C. Kegan Paul, the Godwin biog-

rapher chosen by Boscombe Manor—and authorized to republish Mary Wollstonecraft's letters to her lover Gilbert Imlay.*

Two years later Trelawny transmogrified these misinterpretations and
introduced worse in a brutal character assassination. William Michael Rossetti had begun interviewing him for a memoir of Shelley in 1869. The current generation considered Trelawny *the* authority, since by now Hunt, Peacock, and Hogg were dead, and no one had any idea that Trelawny had not
been as close to Shelley as he claimed, nor a consistent friend of Mary Shelley's. Then a reclusive, ignored old bear, Trelawny was simmering with ani-
mus against her that had been reignited by the "cant" about both Shelleys (to
which he himself admittedly had bowed in his *Recollections*) and by his
loathing of Jane Shelley, a "nasty devil," he told Rossetti, and Percy, "a beer-
swilling lout." Pumped for information, he gave it slashingly, and decided to
write another book himself.

He knew little about the Shelleys prior to Pisa, so he got that information from Claire Clairmont, who had converted to Catholicism and was living
with her niece in Florence.† Shortly after Mary Shelley's death Claire had considered writing her own memoirs, and more recently thought of writing
about Shelley in order to deplore his sexual theories, which had wreaked such
havoc in her life. That Mary Shelley was in malign hands is clear from Claire
and Trelawny's correspondence and appallingly so in his *Records of Shelley,
Byron, and the Author,* published in 1878. He got added ammunition from
H. Buxton Forman's recent publication of Mary Shelley's poem "The Choice,"
in which she accused herself of "cold neglect" of Shelley.

Reared "perfectly orthodox" by Godwin, Trelawny's Mary Shelley never
believed in her mothers views and never had sympathy with any of Shelley's,
while she conformed to the rules of the world as wife and widow, longing only
to be respectable and accepted into society. (After his cremation she indifferently gave Shelley's heart to Leigh Hunt.) Whenever she could she went to
church, partly to show that she did not agree with his atheism. Her torso was
too long for her legs. She was shrewish, jealous, a bad housewife. Shelley
stayed with her, enduring "the utmost malice of fortune," for fear she would
commit suicide.

> Mrs. Shelley was of a soft, lymphatic temperament, the exact opposite of Shel-
> ley in everything; she was moping and miserable when alone, and yearning for
> society. Her capacity can be judged by the novels she wrote after Shelley's
> death, more than ordinarily commonplace and conventional. . . . The memory

---

*Paul was an Anglican cleric who left holy orders to become a publisher, and who had ties to the
Christian Socialist movement.
†Ferdinando Luigi Gatteschi called on Claire, Pauline reports, "a most fascinating man—old now &
fat . . . & rather deaf—but clever!—amiable and cultivated"; whereupon Claire furiously demanded
that Pauline choose between them. (*CC Journals,* p. 220, fn. 56.)

of how often she had irritated and vexed him tormented her after-existence, and she endeavoured by rhapsodies of panegyric to compensate. . . .[7]

Records has reverberated from that day to this. Though many readers were disgusted by Trelawny's coarseness, his book entered a vastly disproportionate wedge between the Shelleys, shifted the ground so that the woman renowned for heterodoxy, character, and talent came to be thought conventional and more or less deficient, and bombed Boscombe Manor into defensive measures that made correction impossible.

Garnett answered Trelawny's charges (and at more length exposed his inaccuracies about Shelley and Byron) in an article in the *Fortnightly Review*. He asserted that Mary Shelley had eminently understood and sympathized with Shelley, conceded that the poet at times was dissatisfied, and concluded that her initial overwrought self-reproach had been moderated by a "chastened" heart.[8] "The charge of excessive orthodoxy is very new, and calculated to excite inextinguishable hilarity," he stated simply. What was self-evident to him, however, required proof twenty-seven years after Mary Shelley's death. Only a full biography by an independent, forthright author who had access to all of Boscombe Manor's primary source material could definitely have refuted Trelawny and set the record straight.

And now was the time, while the Romantic Mary Shelley still had life. George Eliot's hero in "The Lifted Veil" (1859) possesses her gift of prevision; the heroine of *Daniel Deronda* (1876), Gwendolyn Harleth, is reminiscent of Mary Shelley. Bulwer-Lytton's futurist *The Coming Race* (1871) owes something to *The Last Man*. In 1880 Eliza Lynn Linton published *The Rebel of the Family,* whose auburn-haired, hazel-eyed heroine, Perdita, is a modernized Mary Godwin; "that complex and bewildering Perdita, whom no one understood, and whom so many afflicted": tactless, alternately silent and impassioned, a republican and democrat, who is saved from a man-hating feminist "Illuminati" by love for a plebeian whom she marries against her family's wishes.

Tributes to Mary Shelley's intellect and liberalism were published by Robert Dale Owen in the early 1870s. *Perkin Warbeck* had been republished in 1857, and *Frankenstein* remained in print; in an 1887 dramatization the monster was manufactured by a girl named Mary Ann. Mary *Shelley* was included in the French encyclopedias, in the American Sarah Josepha Hale's *Woman's Record; Or, Sketches of all Distinguished Women, From 'The Beginning' Till A.D. 1850.* A passage from *Valperga* was printed in S. Austin Allibone's *Prose Quotations: From Socrates to Macaulay,* published in Philadelphia in 1876.

Lady Shelley, to whom Sir Percy had given carte blanche with the family papers, took the precise wrong course. "I believe that your hands alone are pure enough to touch her,"[9] she had told Garnett. When he got out of writing Mary Shelley's life on grounds that he would be discounted as a special pleader, Jane spent five years editing the Shelley's major correspondence and the journals and privately printing some dozen copies of this censored material, titled *Shelley and Mary,* on which biographers would have to depend. She omitted about a fifth of the journals dating in Mary Shelley's widowhood, all references to "A" (Aubrey Beauclerk), and two passages that she had already printed in *Shelley Memorials,* which she now considered too revealing and cut out of the original notebooks with a penknife. It was probably she who also cut out other such segments, though Mary Shelley herself might have destroyed some.

To give credit where credit is due, nevertheless, Jane preserved the vast majority of the original manuscripts—unlike Cosima Wagner or Albertine de Staël or Hallam Tennyson and others who destroyed quantities of their relatives' private papers—except for giving some holographs to admirers of the Shelleys. Percy purchased additional material as it became available, excepting Claire Clairmont's; they remained on such bad terms that he refused her offer to sell him her papers.

Claire died in 1879 and was buried in a shawl Shelley had given her. (The contest for her papers, which Buxton Forman eventually won, would inspire Henry James's *The Aspern Papers.*) Trelawny died in 1881, having rewarded his wife Augusta for all she had undergone for him by bringing a young mistress into their home, been honored as Shelley's magnificent old rebel friend by Swinburne, and been painted by Millais. He capped his mendacity in the epitaph on his tombstone next to Shelley's: "let not their bones be parted. / For their two hearts in life were single-hearted." Shelley would have been startled, to say the least.

In 1882, on Garnett's recommendation, Lady Shelley chose Edward Dowden to write Shelley's life and Florence T. (Mrs. Julien) Marshall to write Mary Shelley's. By then, although they did not swallow Trelawny whole, these biographers and most of Mary Shelley's admirers were influenced by him. This applied to the American Helen Moore, who published *Mary Shelley,* the first biography, in 1886. Lady Shelley, meanwhile, insisted that Mary Shelley had been a saint, claiming, for instance, that a pencil portrait of Mary that Sir Percy and she found at Casa Magni had been worshiped as the Virgin by a local peasant. Moore quoted extensively from *Shelley Memorials* and included passages from Thornton Hunt and Trelawny, along with Lady Shelley's statement that Mary Shelley was the most tender, gentle, pure, and noble woman who ever trod this earth, and that no thought of self had ever occurred to her. In Moore's interpretation, Mary Shelley had no life separate from Shelley, and, like de Staël and Wollstonecraft, was the kind of female author who influences her male colleagues but whose works have no lasting importance.

Similarly, in Dowden's *Life of Shelley,* which was also published in 1886, Mary Shelley plays, often behind the scenes, the role of Shelley's steadfast, loving pupil and best friend, herself devoid of genius. From girlhood "naturally more conservative" than Godwin and Wollstonecraft, she exercised wholesome restraint on Shelley. Claire Clairmont was far more vivid. (Ironically, a hostile conservative, John Cordy Jeaffreson, gave a truer picture of Mary's youthful dissidence in *The Real Shelley*.) That same year William Michael Rossetti stated in a memoir of Shelley that Mary Shelley contributed to the development of Shelley's poetic power, but judged her "essentially simple." Hereafter, many people would say that a separate biography was unwarranted.

Mary Shelley's son may not have read her biography by Mrs. Marshall, as Sir Percy died after an extended illness on December 5, 1889, not long after the work appeared. Lady Shelley buried him with his mother and grandparents, with Shelley's heart in a silver urn. A charming eulogy came from Samoa from Robert Louis Stevenson, with whom the couple had been intimate during his residence in Bournemouth, and who loved Percy for his sweet nature and "strange, interesting, simple thoughts; . . . he had the morning dew upon his spirit . . .," Stevenson wrote, "so a poet's son—to the last."[10] In fact, Percy was much like his mother. Stevenson had already done Mary Shelley poetic justice, however, for at Bournemouth he too had a fertile nightmare that inspired his *Dr. Jekyll and Mr. Hyde,* in the Frankenstein genre.

Florence Marshall opened her *Life and Letters of Mary Wollstonecraft Shelley* with a cogent review of her subject's status: "She has been variously misunderstood . . . idealized as one who gave up all for love, and to be condemned . . . for the very same reason . . . extolled for perfections she did not possess, and decried for the absence of those she possessed in the highest degree . . . lauded as a genius, and depreciated as one overrated. . . . To her husband she has been esteemed alternately a blessing and the reverse."[11] But being restricted to *Shelley and Mary,* dogged by Lady Shelley, and herself a product of her times, Marshall furthered her subject's eclipse. She stated that Mary Shelley abdicated her individuality for Shelley, offered up her whole life as the shrine of one "transcendently greater." She gave Godwin little credit as Mary's educator, and claimed that Shelley had adversely affected her because their early union checked talents and activity that might have surpasses Wollstonecraft's. The widowhood is worthy and dull; there is no passion for Jane Hogg, no Beauclerk or Gatteschi, and the works are scanted. The success of her life was "the moral success of beauty of character."

Marshall denied Trelawny's charges of Mary Shelley's orthodoxy by defensive generalities. Concurrently, Matthew Arnold published Fanny Kemble Butler's story about Mary Shelley's wishing Percy "to think like everyone else," and that became the exemplary Mary Shelley quotation down to today.

In 1890 a critical biography, *Mrs. Shelley,* was published by Lucy Madox Rossetti, W. M. Rossetti's wife, for the Eminent Women series. She added some illuminating facts about the life, such as Godwin's supervision of Mary's education and the Gatteschi episode, but she deprecated the works, claiming, for instance, that Mary Shelley had "affectedly" and continually portraitized Shelley and Byron, who were "too subtle and complex to be unravelled by her."* The following year Garnett published Mary Shelley's *Keepsake* stories, to mixed reviews, *The Athenaeum* noting "some imaginative power and generous sympathy with all that is noble." Garnett, however, fixed the impression of her subsidiary importance in his essay for the definitive *Dictionary of National Biography*: "Nothing but an absolute magnetising of her brain by Shelley's can account for her having risen so far above her usual self as in *Frankenstein*."

Opinion about Mary Shelley continued to be polarized. For one turn-of-the-century follower of Marshall, Mary "broke over [Shelley's] head the precious vase of her heart's love, and wiped his feet with the hairs of her head."[12] Another defamed Shelley: "She was a lily, whom evil fate, in the garb of false philosophy, led to strike the roots of a pure and innocent nature into the shifting morass of a fickle heart . . ."[13] On the other side, William Graham, who claimed to have interviewed Claire Clairmont, wrote that Mary became "prim and proper," enjoying, as she supposedly did, respectable Sussex society, and had always had great respect for "Mrs. Grundy," while Mark Twain observed that she had set her "masculine grip" on Shelley.

Lady Shelley had her final say in 1897, in *Talks with Lady Shelley* by Maud Brooke Rollaston, daughter of a Fabian clergyman whose advocacy of socialism influenced Oscar Wilde.† Long ailing with kidney disease, Lady Shelley died on June 24, 1899, at Boscombe Manor and was buried in the common family grave at St. Peter's. But she extended her grasp on the Shelleys' papers. She had already given a third of her collection, mostly Shelley material, to the Bodleian Library with the proviso that it be filed away until 1922. Another third, Mary Shelley's journals, workbooks, unpublished papers, and much of her correspondence, she gave to her heir Baron Abinger, and the remaining, miscellaneous third to the Shelley-Rolls family, who succeeded to the Shelley baronetcy. The Abinger and Shelley-Rolls heirs restricted their materials until the 1940s.

In 1907 W. N. Rossetti published what by then seemed to be an obsolete tribute to Mary Shelley—actually written on the thirtieth anniversary of her death—as the daughter of radical parents and Shelley's chosen, immortal "heart-mate" in *Democratic Sonnets,* a volume whose sentiments had seemed so revolutionary that publication was delayed. Three years later her personal

---

*Lucy Rossetti had seen Trelawny's portrait of Mary Shelley by Amelia Curran, since lost, a stiff amateurish work depicting Mary Shelley with an oval face, high forehead, grey eyes tending to brown near the iris, and thin mouth.

†Lady Shelley gave university College, Oxford, a life-sized sculpture of the recumbent, drowned Shelley, which she commissioned from Onslow Ford, later a surrealist. The work has been unfairly said to have contributed to the Victorian legend of Shelley as a sexless angel, for the poet is pagan-stark naked.

repute suffered fresh Trelawnyan damage from which it has yet to recover when H. Buxton Forman published Trelawny's letters; a long succession to Claire Clairmont arraigned Mary Shelley, "a conventional slave," for loving society and for hypocritical piety. Forman took a more moderate position in his preface, stating that after talking with Florence Marshall he thought better of Mary Shelley, but that she was too vain and worldly to be a good wife. Subsequently, Roger Ingpen, a rising Shelley scholar who sympathetically presented the facts of her financial situation in widowhood in *Shelley in England,* commented that what she really loved was society.

What Stendhal would have termed a negative crystallization had formed. Mary Shelley's detractors sneered and accreted cause for so doing, an appetite that has fed upon itself. In 1918 Franklin B. Sanborn published *The Romance of Mary W. Shelley, John Howard Payne, and Washington Irving,* her and Payne's correspondence which was interpreted as her using Payne to try to marry Irving. (A 1930 embellishment declared that she "never embarked upon any emotional adventure without a return ticket in her pocket.")[14]

In the great disillusionment following World War I, modernist critics and political radicals alike deprecated Shelley; debunkers saw Mary Shelley as hypocritical. In 1920, a well-meaning bumbler wrote in a letter to the *Times Literary Supplement* that the relics in Boscombe Manor's sanctum had included pen and paper Shelley used just before his death, and that (possibly a Lady Shelleyism) Mary Shelley had put a glass cover over them and carried them from Italy to England on her knees (it was Percy she had on her knees, had she gone in for that sort of display).[15] "That's her final give-away for me," Katherine Mansfield wrote John Middleton Murry. "Did everybody know? Oh, *didn't* they just? I've done with her."[16] A. H. Kozul introduced Mary Shelley's poetic dramas "Proserpine" and "Midas" in 1922 by remarking at once on her "feminine" nimble invention and on *Frankenstein* as "that most unwomanly of all feminine romances."

Even so, Mary Shelley retained respect. Murry himself, and the *Times Literary Supplement,* reviewed her poems favorably, the latter observing that besides her acknowledged intellectual power, she had a tender, emotional side. Murry also lauded her "measured" commentary of Shelley's poems. In an introduction to a small edition of her letters and in an essay, Henry H. Harper praised her gifts. Walter Edwin Peck used and in some instances misused passages from her fiction to vivify *Shelley: His Life and Works,* as finding the-persons-in-the-fiction had become a major rationale for reading her work. Richard Church published *Mary Shelley* for the Representative Women series in 1928—a slender but exceptionally perceptive biography, though Church devoted only nine pages to her life after Shelley's death.

Frankenstein, moreover, had launched on the cinematic career that has imprinted Mary Shelley's story on mass imagination throughout the world. The first American film adaptation of 1910 was followed by Italian, Mexican,

Spanish, and additional English-speaking versions. In 1931 Boris Karloff became the monster for millions, and the rest is history. As for the original author, relatively few people have ever known more than Mary Shelley's name, if that, while her authorship, instead of clarifying her image for the cognoscenti, has mystified many and changed few minds. Thus the Shelley scholar Ellsworth Barnard, in 1936: "It ought to be obvious to the student of Shelley's life that Mary Shelley, for all her merits, was quite incapable, both morally and intellectually, of understanding her husband's opinions, much less of sharing them."[17]

Such gross misbelief is excusable insofar as all scholars must rely upon secondary sources and in restating them may overstate. All the same, the very romanticization for which they berate Lady Shelley has led some to make Shelley into a sort of Christ militant, with Mary Shelley as mythic foil, a lachrymose, dense, bourgeois Judas, and Claire Clairmont his Magdalen.* Besides, one's own superiority is enhanced by having an object to look down on. And finally, if new research is not exhaustive, it can ratify an established image.

Until the mid-twentieth century, Mary Shelley was of interest mainly to Shelleyans. What has remained a standard life, *Mary Shelley,* was published in 1938 by Rosalie Glynn Grylls (later Lady Mander). Alone of any biographer until the late 1940s, Grylls was given access to the Abinger and Shelley-Rolls collections for lives of Godwin, Mary Shelley, Claire Clairmont, and Trelawny. While she included new correspondence and a dozen new selections from the journals, she did not thoroughly investigate Mary Shelley's years after Shelley's death. Grylls saw her as the only one of his loves worthy to have been his wife, yet as a morbid moper, basically anti-Bohemian, conflicted between the feminine and the artist, between trying to be "like everybody else" and being unable to be so. If she did not become quite Trelawny's conventional slave, Grylls concluded in *Claire Clairmont,* she could not be recognized as Wollstonecraft's daughter.

Newman Ivey White's monumental critical biography, *Shelley,* published in 1940 when the intelligentsia embraced progressive heroes, reestablished the centrality of Shelley's sociopolitical ideas. He did Mary Shelley considerable justice during her union with Shelley, but believed that later she minimalized his radicalism, yearned for respectability, and, furthermore, manipulated her editions of his poems in order to conceal her supposed revulsion from him after her children's deaths. (White similarly assumed that Sir Percy intended to run for Parliament as a conservative rather than as a radical.)

---

*See Max Beerbohm's irreverent "but for Missolonghi" observation that our images of Shelley and Byron would be different if they had lived into middle and old age: Byron probably fat, balding, bewhiskered, grumpy; Shelley producing masses of dull poetry. It is equally possible that Shelley might have led about the same quotidian life as Sir Percy's at Boscombe Manor.

In 1944 Frederick L. Jones published seven hundred and five of Mary Shelley's letters as a resource for Shelley scholars. He stated that while some gaps remained (notably her letters to Hogg, which were published shortly thereafter), his edition gave an adequate picture of her. But many came from imperfect copies that left out amusing or colorful passages; other letters he did not know about, and he was not permitted to see the letters in two important collections: that of Lord Abinger and that of the American private collector Carl H. Pforzheimer. Jones declared that she was a remarkable woman in her own right, praised *Valperga,* and accused a succession of malicious and unsound scholars of injuring "the name of a good and noble woman." Yet he himself claimed that she was possessive, doleful, dependent, "insatiably" eager to associate with talented people. In 1947 Jones published her journals, perforce comprised of what had already been published, which he believed to be nearly perfect.

The reaction of one Shelley scholar, Carl Grabo, bespoke the now traditional outlook. He declared that Mary Shelley's letters after Shelley's death showed that she had little sympathy with liberal ideas, was preoccupied with society and trivial material things, and wrote mostly hack work, rarely showing "a gleam of intellectual curiosity." Then, Robert Metcalf Smith in *The Shelley Legend* claimed to expose a long sequence of "fraudulent and mistaken" efforts from their originator, Mary Shelley, down to White, by which Shelley had been made into a "Victorian angel" and Claire Clairmont deprived of her place as his lover. He also accused Mary Shelley of forging the letter in which Shelley charged Harriet Shelley with several love affairs. White and Jones exploded the forgery charge, and Jones denied the beautification, but the stain adhered.

With the centenary of Mary Shelley's death, interest in her revived, and has steadily grown. Muriel Spark led off in 1951 with *Child of Light: A Reassessment of Mary Wollstonecraft Shelley,* a short, sympathetic, and yet misleading, biography based on then available printed sources, with a critical study and an abridgement of the almost forgotten *The Last Man.* Spark published a retouched version, *Mary Shelley: A Biography,* in 1987. In 1953 Elizabeth Nitchie published *Mary Shelley,* the first critical biography to utilize the Shelley-Rolls and Abinger collections, which had been opened to scholars. Her assessment of the works was mixed and superficial. Not having investigated Mary Shelley's private life afresh, Nitchie felt that she would have been better and nobler had she not "compromised with conventional society." She cited works, however, demonstrating that Mary had remained a liberal— supposedly up until the last several years of her life. In 1959, Nitchie also published *Mathilda* (*Matilda*), Mary Shelley's previously unknown novella of father-daughter incest.

Among ground-breaking books since have been Jean de Palacio's *Mary Shelley dans son oeuvre* (1968), the most exhaustive critical study yet of her works, her place in literature, her thought and psychology; another critical study by William Waling (1972); W. H. Lyles's annotated bibliography (1975); Charles E. Robinson's edition of *Mary Shelley: Collected Tales and Stories* (1976); and *The Endurance of Frankenstein* (1979), a collection of essays edited by George Levine and U. C. Knoepflmacher. Many editions of *Frankenstein,* one of *The Last Man,* numerous scholarly articles, graduate studies, and several popularized books and biographies have also been published. At last count, *Frankenstein* has been translated into eighteen languages, its film and stage adaptations seem inexhaustible, and television is its latest media outlet.

The woman's movement has had revolutionary impact on social history and literary studies. Beginning with the late Ellen Moers's *Literary Women* (1976), followed by Sandra M. Gilbert and Susan Gubar in *The Madwoman in the Attic: The Woman Writer and the Nineteenth-Century Literary Imagination* (1979), many feminist scholars see Mary Shelley as an impressive contributor to a female literary tradition.

Despite all of this, however, Mary Shelley's reputation remains unsettled, even poor, largely owing to traditional misconceptions that cling in the absence of complete information about her. Whatever some contemporary academics may say about works being all and lives nothing, the urge to integrate lives and works goes irresistibly on, while interpretation of works can be affected by perception of lives. So, as *Frankenstein* seems to be an aberration, some scholars used it in the 1970s to illuminate Shelley's or Godwin's or even Byron's thought; James Rieger declared that Shelley was her "co-author with final authority for the text." Shelley's poems have been studied on a new level of scholarship, educing books and articles on Mary's editorship. But instead of creating the consensus of appreciation of her extraordinary achievement that might be expected from Shelley's admirers, these publications range from highly laudatory, to mixed, to picayune, to condemnatory, the last often attributing her editorial "flaws" to her presumed sentimentality, gentility, or even "vulgarity."

By the 1980s some influential Romantic scholars were reevaluating Mary Shelley's oeuvre with new respect, which, however, did not necessarily include her life, and character, while elsewhere the worst case against her is still being made.

That case was presented by Sylva Norman, witty author of *Flight of the Skylark: The Development of Shelley's Reputation,* and a 1970 essay in *Shelley and His Circle,* in other respects a model of modern scholarship. In sum, her girlhood education was irregular; Shelley awoke her vigor and independence. She had insufficient sympathy for him, developed conventionality during their union, and withdrew from him after her children's deaths. As a widow she was dazzled by lords, frequented fashionable parties, otherwise had "homely" friends like the Hares. Glad that Percy thought like everyone else, she "insisted" on exiling herself to Harrow. She deluded herself about her past happiness, prettified Shelley, and "simulated" ardor for democracy. In 1979, Trelawny's mendacity in regard to his own career was exposed by his biographer William

St. Clair, and yet not applied to Trelawny's criticisms of Mary Shelley, who is said to have "gone over to the enemy." A *New York Times* review of Ken Russell's 1987 film *Gothic* refers to her "renowned prudery." The feminist Mary Poovey reads her as passively submitting to the feminine ideal of her times except for the "defiance" of authorship.

This biographer is in no position to be indignant about Mary Shelley's negative repute, however she may regret it. Rather, I am testimony to its potency. It took two years of research, from 1975 to 1977, before I realized how dubious that repute was, and then it was necessary to start afresh in order to study her with an open mind. In 1980, 1983, and 1988, meanwhile, Betty T. Bennett has published three volumes of the first complete edition of Mary Shelley's letters, with important notes and introductions. In a review of Bennett's first volume, Richard Holmes, who had belittled Mary in his *Shelley: The Pursuit,* declared that he had never realized the breadth of independence of Mary Shelley's thought, her unconventional years following Shelley's death, or her restless spirit. Mary Shelley's complete *Journals* (1987), edited by Paula R. Feldman and Diana Scott-Kilvert, provides an additional invaluable resource.

Current studies of Mary Shelley, including this biography, will not be the final word, but they can be based on data that approach the complete, and without which human beings cannot be comprehended as they deserve, in all their complexity, in the context of their times as well as their significance to our own. As Mary Shelley quoted Edmund Burke in her last journal entry: "The first thing is justice."

Mary Shelley was an important Romantic who survived into the Victorian age. Her private life, career, and works are a rich resource for that historical evolution, a broader mine than those of her great associates, Shelley and Byron, whom kind death saved from erosion. Far from being subjected to romantic turbulence, she chose it. Aspiration, enthusiasm, challenge, active mind and spirit, and optimism were among her cardinal qualities, contrary to the impression that she was temperamentally cool, quiet and pessimistic, and it was her incapacity for resignation to cold reality that eventually wore her down.

She should be recognized as indeed her mother's daughter, heir to Wollstonecraft's Romantic feminism and to a fuller measure of punishment for it. From *Frankenstein* to *Rambles,* her heroes and heroines are those who confront custom, power, and unjust authority. Moreover, her creative and scholarly works establish her as a major literary figure of the first half of the nineteenth century. She belongs among the great editors for her editions of Shelley's works, even among the great disciples, given the veneration she also won for his character and ideas.

Perhaps she will be best remembered for her perception in *Frankenstein* and *The Last Man,* that the Promethean drive is at the heart of human progress and yet a bringer of new ills if not focused on ethical means and ends; and even so, if Nature shrugs we perish. In that ambiguity she may be said to have heralded the consciousness that distinguished the Post-Modern from the Modern Age.

Notes

1. Montague Guest and William B. Boulton, *The Royal Yacht Squadron* (London: John Murray, 1930), passim.

2. Una Taylor, *Guests and Memories: Annals of a Seaside Villa* (London, New York: Humphrey Milford, Oxford University Press, 1924), 336.

3. Irving Massey, "Some Letters of Shelley Interest," *Keats-Shelley Memorial Bulletin* 19 (1968): 16.

4. Henry Crabb Robinson, *On Books and Their Writers,* Edith J. Morley, ed., 3 vols. (London: J. M. Dent & Sons, 1938), II:791.

5. Abinger MSS [papers of Mary Shelley and her family, on deposit at the Bodleian Library, Oxford].

6. Hunt, "Shelly," 198–199 Thornton Hunt, "Shelley: By One Who Knew Him," *Atlantic Monthly II* (February 1863).

7. EJT, *Records of Shelley, Byron and the Author,* 2 vols. (London: Basil Montague Pickering, 1878), Appendix, II:255.

8. Richard Garnett, "Shelley's Last Days," *Fortnightly Review,* n.s. 23 [29] (June 1878): 854–856.

9. *Letters about Shelley from the Richard Garnett Papers,* William Richard Thurman, Jr., ed. (University of Texas, Ph.D. dissertation, August 1972), 130.

10. Robert Louis Stevenson to Lady Shelley, Jan. 15, 1890, Rosalie Glynn Grylls, *Mary Shelley: A Biography* (London: Oxford University Press, 1938), 293.

11. Marshall, *Mary Shelley,* I:3. [Mrs. Julian Marshall (Florence J.), *The Life and Letters of Mary Wollstonecraft Shelley,* 2 vols. (London: Richard Bentley & Son, 1889).]

12. Elbert Hubbard, *Little Journeys to the Homes of Famous Women* (New York: G. P. Putnam's Sons, 1897), 399.

13. I[sobel] S[tuart], *The London Star,* Mar. 5, 1894.

14. Muriel Norris, "Mary Shelley and John Howard Payne," *London Mercury* 22 (October 1930): 450.

15. J. E. Panton, *Times Literary Supplement* 983 (Nov. 18, 1920): 759.

16. Katherine Mansfield to John Middleton Murry, December 1920, *The Letters of Katherine Mansfield to John Middleton Murry,* 2 vols. (London: Constable & Co., 1928), II:83.

17. Epigraph to Part I, Robert Metcalf Smith, *The Shelley Legend* (New York: Charles Scribner's Sons, 1945), 1; from Ellsworth Barnard, *Shelley's Religion* (Minneapolis: University of Minnesota Press, 1936).

Index

♦

The Volume Editor

Mary Lowe-Evans, professor of English at the University of West Florida in Pensacola, was educated at Saint Mary's Dominican College in New Orleans, the University of Mississippi, and the University of Miami. She has authored two books, *Crimes against Fecundity: Joyce and Population Control* (1989) and *Frankenstein: Mary Shelley's Wedding Guest* (1993), as well as numerous articles and reviews, including contributions to the Modern Language Association's volume *Approaches to Teaching Joyce's* Ulysses, *"Frankenstein": A Case Study in Contemporary Criticism,* and *The Handbook of American Women's History.* She is a member of the International James Joyce Foundation, the American Conference on Irish Studies, the American Association of University Women, the National Council of Teachers of English, the Modern Language Association, the West Florida Literary Federation, and the Honor Society of Phi Kappa Phi, for which she currently serves as chapter president at the University of West Florida. She has also served as associate dean, College of Arts and Social Sciences, director of Women's Studies, and director of the University Honors Program at the University of West Florida.

The General Editor

Zack Bowen is professor of English at the University of Miami. He holds degrees from the University of Pennsylvania (B.A.), Temple University (M.A.), and the State University of New York at Buffalo (Ph.D.). In addition to being general editor of this G. K. Hall series, he is editor of the James Joyce series for the University of Florida Press and the *James Joyce Literary Supplement*. He is author of six books and editor of three others, all on modern British, Irish, and American literature. He has also published more than one hundred monographs, essays, scholarly reviews, and recordings related to literature. He is past president of the James Joyce Society (1977–86), former chair of the Modern Language Association Lowell Prize Committee, and currently president of the International James Joyce Foundation.